MARY MARY & JFK

Mary Mary & JFK

Presidential Mistress Mary Pinchot-Meyer

Michael Pinchot

Library of Congress Control Number:		2013914930
ISBN:	Hardcover	978-1-4836-8647-9
	Softcover	978-1-4836-8646-2
	Ebook	978-1-4836-8648-6

This book was printed in the United States of America.

Rev. date: 09/12/2013

To order additional copies of this book, contact:
Xlibris LLC
1-888-795-4274
www.Xlibris.com
Orders@Xlibris.com
139729

CONTENTS

PART III: FICTION

CHAPTERS 1-10

PART IV

To my Grandchildren:

Dustin Michael R.I.P.
7-18-1988 ~ 10-16-2010

Dustin redefined my understanding
of the word 'courage'

Paige Diana
Richlie Sarah
Evan Nathanial
Jacob Patrick

"Writing a book is an adventure. To begin with, it is a toy and an amusement; then it becomes a mistress, and then it becomes a master, and then a tyrant. The last phase is that just as you are about to reconcile to your servitude, you kill the monster and fling him out to the public."

Winston Churchill

I am far closer to Mary than I am to Eve,
And the apple never falls far from its tree . . . .

FOREWORD

They were born three years and four months of one another, Jack on May 29, 1917 in Boston, Massachusetts, and Mary on October 14, 1920 on the Eastern Shore of Maryland. Both families were a part of the deep rooted social elite of the north-eastern United States.

Being a part of the north-eastern social, economic, and political inner circle, along with Jack's and Mary's good looks, sexual free spirit, and of course fate, set the course for an eventual sexual affair that endured for a period of twenty-two months within the White House, up to the very time of the tragic assassination.

Mary Pinchot-Meyer was the only one of Jack's other women that Jackie, on record, insisted that he "get rid of my *friend* Mary". With Mary and Jackie being old friends, Jackie was only asking that Jack rid himself of Mary as a lover, for she, and others, could see there was far more to Jack and Mary's relationship than that of a usual Kennedy sexual fling.

As hard as it may be to imagine it today, Washington was actually a sexier town during the years of the cold war. Flirtation was an art. Marriage was respected and divorce rates were low, in spite of the 1950s and early 1960s being the dawn of a new era in male-female relations, with traditional relationships being tested almost in mass. Lines were crossed, and hearts were broken. However, the women of Mary Pinchot-Meyer's generation and class always operated with propriety. If they conducted themselves like characters from a romance novel, it was all but forbidden for a journalist of *that era* to report, let alone to investigate.

Although sex was the one reason that the CIA feared and destroyed Mary's diary, her life was no more about sex than anyone else's.

As a writer, I have tried to give Mary as much dignity and respect as I would grant that of a philandering man of importance of the same era. The recorded life stories of women throughout history are, more often than not, domestic histories of men, with this being no less true of the women of Mary's generation and class. While women typically figure in domestic aspects of lives of famous men, they are rarely portrayed as collaborators in their public sphere. Traditionally, historians are interested in mistresses for what they reveal about the lives of the men with whom they consorted, however, I will attempt to reveal what the men and the times had *on Mary*.

Mary's style was questing. She was an experimental, doubting woman, with a strong will of her own, and those qualities made her unusual, especially in the convention-worshiping 1950s . . . even more so among her female peers in Washington, D.C. Although she was clearly not ordinary in terms of looks and means, her life was one that ordinary women will recognize.[1]

PART 1

CHAPTER 1

Introduction

"To be absent from the body, is to be present with the Lord . . . ."
2 Corinthians, 5:8

"Hello, my name is Mary Pinchot . . . . the late Mary Pinchot-Meyer. Everyone knows Jack; however, before we begin our journey, allow me to reveal a little of myself and my family."

"My family is inherently political; I can nostalgically remember terms such as *candidate, party, caucus, election* being a part of my life before that of the indelible event of my first day of kindergarten. The older I became the more I was expected to contribute to the daily dinner time debate on current political events . . . locally, nationally, and foreign. Debate and discussion was the format, with arguing and fighting considered a weakness. Opinions from all ages were considered around the dinner table, and heaven forbid if one's opinion was without factual basis; empirical evidence was the format, with Party talking points rhetoric forbidden and scoffed upon. Further, being unable to intellectually contribute to any given subject was scorned upon.

"Ours being a north-eastern rooted family of means, the Kennedy family of Massachusetts was a household social-political name often part of our dinner time family discussions, as was the Pinchot name within the Kennedy household. Only in retrospect do I realize that during the late eighteen hundreds and early nineteen hundreds, the Pinchot family was more politically active than the Kennedy clan. Since then, our family has faded from the political scene, for reasons to be divulged along this journey.

17

"The patriarchal genealogical seed into America for the Pinchot and Kennedy families were uniquely different, aside from both *seeds*, as immigrants, being young single males traveling alone.

"Jack's great-great grandfather, Patrick Kennedy, was born in 1823 into a poor farming family in Dunganstown, Ireland. With the family farm raising barley and beef, young Patrick was not driven away by the potato famine, but rather by the desire to immigrate to America and make his fortune. His 1849 arrival into America, at the age of twenty-six, was fairly typical of the era; he was unskilled, except in farming, with a mid-grammar school education, with his possessions being essentially the clothes on his back. He soon found employment as a cooper, making yokes and staves for wagons destined for the burgeoning western gold rush.[2]

"My family's immigration story was quite different, being three generations deep as Americans at the time of my 1920 birth. My great-great grandfather, Cyrille Désiré Constantin Pinchot was born into French middle class in 1797. As an officer in the French military, Cyrille was involved in a plot to free Napoleon from the island of St. Helena. When the attempt failed, he escaped on a merchant ship to England where he returned to France long enough to retrieve his accumulated monetary spoils of war before moving to America in 1826. Shortly after his arrival into the *promised-land*, he bought four hundred acres in the area of Milford, Pennsylvania, which already had a significant French population, and soon thereafter became the county tax collector.[3]

"The Pinchot family had done well financially in America without drawing great attention to their wealth, while making remarkable achievements in the era of industrial robber barons.

"After making millions in the wallpaper business, my grandfather, James Pinchot, retired at age forty-four and turned to philanthropy, travel, and conservation. He and my grandmother Mary Jane Eno-Pinchot had three children: Gifford, Antoinette, and finally my father Amos, born in Paris in 1873. In New York they lived in Gramercy Park, where their wealthy neighbors included the Hewitts (furniture), Coopers (iron/steel), and Minturns (shipping). Theirs was the New York of author Edith Wharton: squalid, run by corrupt political bosses, pestilent along the waterfront, and yet at the upper reaches a very formal society of afternoon visits in carriages with footmen in red-topped boots and side-whiskers.

"Growing up in our idyllic country estate, Grey Towers, in Milford, Pennsylvania and a Park Avenue New York apartment, I was exposed throughout my youth to upper class mores and manners . . . . as well as radical American politics. Although our country estate was frequented by some of our country's most famous men, my family was able to pay respect to social convention while never being lavishly social. With such exposure, my place in society was so secure that decades later it was easy for me to become a member, to the chagrin of many others, of the President Kennedy in-crowd without the strain and failure of most Washington climbers.[4]

"The general lifestyle within our remotely private Grey Tower estate was Bohemian-like and we Pinchot women were, from childhood, practicing nudists, often wandering the expansive grounds, the stream and waterfall, the pool, as well as horseback riding, much to the delight of the many servants.[5] Over the years many a male or female guest were slightly shocked or charmed, depending on their degree of convention, when I casually stripped and dove into the pool above the natural waterfall located within the estate grounds. Being healthy, fit, very athletic, and uninhibited, I was proud, not ashamed, of my nudity."

Mary paused momentarily, chuckled, and continued with a wry look.

"At twelve, I was enrolled at the Brearley School, a private girls' pre-school in the upper eastside of New York, a short walk from our Park Avenue apartment. Although considered a finishing school, it was known for academic rigor as well as exclusivity. I wore a uniform of white blouse and dark skirt and took English, math, geography, history, science, and languages, including classic Greek and Latin, German and French. I was also involved in music, drama, art . . . and anything sport." She laughed. "And, for what it's worth, the school medic was Dr. Benjamin Spock. The faculty was mainly graduates of Columbia, Oberlin, and a number of the exclusive 'Seven Sisters' schools."[6]

Mary grinned.

"The centerpiece of the school's social life was the basketball team; my teammates simply cheered, "Pinchot", as I played a wickedly aggressive game as forward and playmaker. I was also on the tennis team and brought several championship trophies to the school. My popularity revolved around sports, for the school was dedicated to their teams. According to the coaches, I was blessed with the body, balance, and coordination of an athlete, along with natural aggression and passion.[7]

"On the heels of the sports topic, it's short of sacrilegious to bring up the subject of smoking."

She shrugged her shoulders, and shifted position in her high-back, throne-like chair.

"Anyway, at Brearley, my friends and I whiled away our lunch hours learning how to smoke cigarettes at a local sandwich and soda shop. In fact, smoking was so pervasive that Brearley provided us seniors with our own smoking room, a sunny space on the seventh floor overlooking the East River. Thank God (she dropped her voice and looked around as she spoke the word

God) I never became a heavy smoker, however, I did smoke socially throughout my life . . . . in fact I had a cigarette going at the time of my passing."[8]

Mary paused, looked right, and shrugged her bare shapely shoulders.

"My current state of being allows me to say that, according to my teachers and peers, I shone at Brearley."

She grinned.

"There, I said it." She laughed. "Further, I was smart, fit, amusing, not too intense, and, yes, popular. The consensus was that I was the model Brearley girl. In fact, my classmates selected me as Miss Brearley of 1938, with an announcement accolade that '*Pinchot looked cute at all times*'. One of my best friends, who walked to school with me from our Park Avenue apartments, jokingly claimed that I had lots of beaus."

She fanned her face with her hand.

"Enough said about that." Pause. "Many weekends we Brearley girls were invited to dances at the boys' schools, Groton, Choate, and Saint Paul's. On those weekends, the girls traveled to the New England campuses and the boys vacated their dorm rooms and slept in the gym, leaving little notes behind on their pillows for their dates. On one such weekend, William Attwood was my date to a dance held at Choate. Attwood, of course, grew up to become President Kennedy's U.N. ambassador, and later publisher of New York *Newsday*." She smiled warmly, "Well, it was on one such snowy night that I first met a skinny, funny boy named John F. Kennedy, who was a few years my senior." Mary half smiles and rolled her eyes. "I vividly remember that, although Bill told me that I was the best and prettiest girl at the dance, it was Jack that kept cutting in on the dance floor.[9]

"By the time we were fourteen, chaperones were no longer trailing us, so us Brearley girls explored New York on our own. My Park Avenue was still an uncongested, safe and friendly place, with the balance of New York our playground and a mere extension of our elite world on Park Avenue. Our favorite store was Saks Fifth Avenue, and we toured museums and explored and enjoyed the parks."[10]

She gave an abbreviated giggle, "And there were *so* many boys and young men that our formal coming out had, from our perspective, little glamour.[11]

"By my mid-teens, I was finding society interesting to the point that I was spending less and less time with my family at our Grey Towers country estate and more time with my classmates in the Hamptons, closer to New York. Sadly, during those years, the distance between me and my younger sister grew. And, of course, Tony being my four year junior, I had graduated by the time she entered Brearley.[12]

"As a teenager I was in great demand as a houseguest, with the four social seasons ruling our society; even though we made fun of them, we followed the rituals.[13] Spring was for horse racing, summer for the Hamptons, or other cool climes, fall was for riding hounds, with winter reserved for debutante balls, and deep winter for Palm Beach or sport fishing in the Keys."[14]

She shifted in her seat, and cleared her throat.

"That period was a whirlwind of debutante balls at the Ritz-Carlton and Waldorf-Astoria, followed by dates at the Cotton Club, Stork Club, and the Waldorf's Sert Room, where we drank and danced the night away.[15] In short, I was irresistibly attracted to the party life . . . . and I was literally invited to everything. My life revolved around lipstick, ball gowns, and silk stockings. In fact, I met my future husband, Cord Meyer, at one of the many debutante balls during those years.[16]

"As the war loomed, the pace of New York pre-war socializing increased." Mary paused in reflection. "We lived at a near frantic rate, not knowing just how long any of us would be alive.[17] In fact, my coming out year, 1938, was the year the New York debutante scene seemed most glamorous to the rest of America. The national press lapped up the glamour and fed it back to a public weary of grim times and receptive to fantasy."[18]

She smiled faintly.

"Many of my classmates made their debuts on an obscenely grand scale, but I did not. My father, recovering from the depression, refused to pay for a huge coming-out ball. But he didn't dispense with the custom entirely. I was presented at an exquisite Park Avenue home afternoon tea, with photographer David Middleton as my escort. Being well aware of the inanity of the endless round of debutante balls, I was all but indifferent with the downsized affair, as in having had enough of that."[19]

Mary's countenance changed as she shifted in her seat and squared her shoulders.

"Of course, when thinking about this period of time, my thoughts return to that of my half sister, Rosamund, who was the product of my father's nineteen-year first marriage to Gertrude Minturn. Well, it would be an understatement to say that Rosamund was beautiful. When I was a small child, she was a drop-dead gorgeous teenager, and a model of sophistication and glamour." Mary raises her chin and proudly continues. "My father adored Rosamund, who was a teenager as I was still a mere child. At sixteen she was long legged, curvaceous, and five-nine, with blond hair, deep set blue eyes and strong chin. In spite of being overshadowed by her, I was at awe of my adventurous and beautiful half-sister.

"At seventeen, Rosamund was *discovered* by producer Max Reinhardt". Mary brackets the word discovered with her fingers. "The Viennese film maker had spotted her on the deck of a luxury transatlantic ocean liner in route to stage a New York production, *The Miracle*. My sister was returning home from an extensive European tour. Reinhardt chose her to play the part of the nun, and," she grinned, "not to brag, she was an overnight sensation ... the socialite-turned-actress. Gosh .... her photograph appeared frequently in stylish magazines, and for a few years she was a budding starlet."

Mary smiled and rolled her eyes.

"I was always at awe of my half-sister's celebrity. She signed a contract with Metro-Goldwyn-Mayer and moved to Hollywood." She shrugged her shoulders. "On a modest level, I had my own share of photographic attention. As a teenager, I modeled clothes and hairstyles for *Vogue*. One *Vogue* shot, my personal favorite, in my late teens, was that of a glamorous profile, with upswept hair and diamond earrings," she chuckled, "an ice princess with full lips and a distant gaze."[20]

The thought made her chuckle.

"Anyway, after graduating from Brearley, I followed my mother to Vassar, located in Poughkeepsie, New York, between Sunset and Vassar lakes, a stone's throw from Marist College and up the road from West Point. I found the school's long tradition in women's education to be intimidating at first; however, by second semester I found my rhythm and, in turn, my comfort zone. I lived in the North Tower dorm, considered the most glamorous campus residence, and there, I met women who became lifelong friends." She chuckled in reflection. "While during the week we wore bobby socks and saddle shoes, during the weekends we dressed to the nines and daubed on Chanel No. 5. Of course, Tommy Dorsey was *thee* swing band, although we had to settle for Glen Miller live at our junior prom." As if in afterthought, "And, it goes without saying, we at Vassar were devoted to Yale. The Yale motto, "For God, country, and Yale", was displayed prominently on Vassar campus.[21]

"Many of us Vassar girls arranged our schedules to have no classes on Friday, or no more than two morning classes, in order to catch an early train to New Haven." She giggled, "We would go under any pretext, and once arrived we would always be taken care of. The men were more than willing to put us up in a hotel, feed us, and provide plenty of drinking and dancing." She paused to reflect. "And, as I recall, we were all virgins. Well not all of us. I can remember a handful of us waiting for one girl to return from a weekend when she proclaimed, prior to setting out for her weekend, she was going to go the whole way .... just to see what it was like." [22]

CHAPTER 2

Grey Towers and Park Avenue Era

Born on the Eastern Shore of Maryland, 14 October, 1920, Mary Eno Pinchot, was named after her paternal grandmother. Mary's father Amos had divorced his wife of nineteen years to wed Mary's mother Ruth Pickering, thirteen years his younger.

Born in New York in 1893, Ruth attended Vassar College and graduated from Columbia University, before becoming a journalist in New York, and working mostly for left-wing publications. An ardent, self styled feminist who wrote for the *Masses* the *New Republic*, and the *Nation*, she became the associated editor of *Arts and Decoration*. Ruth, too, came from a family of courageous thinkers. Her paternal grandfather, whom she referred to as Grandfather Haynes, lost his life in the underground railway while freeing slaves.[23]

When Amos met Ruth, she was a Greenwich Village writer and daughter of a middle-class businessman. Ruth's childhood was one of a continuously rebellious tomboy who grew up to be more of a pragmatist than feminist. As a girl, she befriended her poor and uneducated neighbors against the advice of her powerful Grandma Hayes, whose approval was doled out stingily. Ruth rebelled against the matriarch in spirit and letter. She sought out the toughest companions of the neighborhood, playing with boys summer and winter, whose bravado, being normal, seemed of a far less glorious nature than her own. [24]

In 1924 Ruth gave birth to her second daughter, Antoinette, called Tony. From childhood, little Tony was the more reserved and shy of the two sisters. She had more childhood illnesses, and many of Ruth and Amos's worries in the 1920s concerned Tony's bouts with mumps, scarlet fever, and even appendicitis. One summer, the family trooped to Fire Island because Tony was underweight and peaky and seemed to need salt air.[25]

Mary was closer to her father than Tony was. Amos wanted his daughters athletic, and of the two, Mary was far more inclined toward sports. Amos taught her to play aggressively, no matter what the sport. Decades later, her tennis playing friends in Washington were amazed when their beautiful, soft spoken, gentle friend suddenly turned ferocious on the tennis court, wielding a vicious serve, and mean back hand. [26]

Mary spent her formative years at the family estate, Grey Towers, located originally on 3600 acres overlooking the Delaware River in Milford Pennsylvania, where the family settled in 1818. The castle-like structure, with a mile-long tree lined driveway, was constructed by Mary's grandfather, James Pinchot in 1886, with architecture and material reflecting the family's French heritage. The main chateau was occupied by Mary's uncle Gifford, her father's elder brother, while Amos' family resided in the spacious guest house. Whereas the chateau had twelve workers, Mary's digs had a butler, cook, cleaner, and nurse.[27]

During the depression, while the lion's share of Americans worried over the source of their next meal, life for the Pinchots at Grey Towers, a mere one and a half hour train ride from their New York Park Avenue apartment, was that of serene and gracious living. While meals were prepared by skilled staff, the family enjoyed tennis courts, swimming pool, horses, and fishing, with the soothing sound of a natural water fall and stream trickling over stones through their own private forest.[28]

The family stocked their stream with trout and allowed neighbors limited access to fish and swim. But the locals had to follow strict rules, namely they could not use live bait or bring guests up from the village.[29]

The Pinchots had done well financially, going to great lengths to do little harm to others or to the environment, all the while drawing as little attention as possible to their wealth outside the grounds of the family estate; this was a remarkable achievement in the era of robber barons and conspicuous consumption.

Growing up at Grey Towers, Mary was exposed to upper class manners and mores, in addition to radical American politics. The silver spoon always contained a dose of skepticism. While the family paid respect to social conventions, it was never slavishly social. From these vaguely Bohemian beginnings, on an idyllic estate frequented by some of the country's most important men, Mary's place in society was so secure that decades later she became a member of the Kennedy in-crowd without the straining that marked most Washington climbers.[30]

While at Grey Towers, she learned by example, from her aunt, about female power in the world of men; Cornelia Elizabeth Bryce Pinchot, known in the family as Leila, was a thirty-three-year-old American aristocrat when she married Gifford. Her father, Lloyd Bryce, was a congressman, writer, and Teddy Roosevelt's ambassador to the Netherlands. Her mother was the granddaughter of iron magnate Peter Cooper, who founded the Cooper Institute (now Cooper Union). Cornelia was raised in Newport society but grew up to spurn the traditional role of well-bred wife. She marched in the suffrage parades and helped her husband get elected in 1922 by getting women voters in Pennsylvania organized for the first time since they had won the right to vote. In 1928, she ran for Congress herself on a platform similar to her husband's: support for Prohibition and opposition to utility monopolies. She was defeated but went on to work in women and organized labor, and in the 1940s she became the United States representative to the International Women's Conference. Cornelia was truly a 1920s superwoman, a supremely self-confident feminist who seemed able to have it all. She gloried in the kind of adventure available to rich young women.[31]

With two very strong willed individuals for parents, Mary was destined to respect people with strongly held views who marched to the beat of their own drummer.[32]

Mary's strong intellect came from her father and his brother, Gifford. The brothers were graduates of Yale, and members of the Skull and Bones society, with Gifford being president of the infamous society in his senior year. Upon graduation, Amos became a New York based lawyer, while Gifford, also a lawyer, completed his post-graduate work in Paris, mastering in Forest Conservation. Mary's fluent French came as natural as English, for she was spoken to in both tongues before she uttered her first word.[33]

The tall intense Gifford, close friend and advisor to Teddy Roosevelt, became the first head of U.S. Forestry, appointed by President Teddy Roosevelt to his newly formed Forestry Cabinet position. During Gifford's tenure, he angered conservationist John Muir by supporting San Francisco efforts to acquire a piece of Yosemite National Park for use of the infamous Hetch-Hetchy reservoir, eventually approved in 1913 under the Woodrow Wilson administration. Upon completing his service to Roosevelt, he went on to become two-time Governor of Pennsylvania.

Gifford's career with the federal government ended in 1910 when he accused President Taft's political appointee, Interior Secretary Richard Ballinger, of involvement in fraudulent claims to Alaska coal reserves. Taft sided with his cabinet members and fired Pinchot. A few years later, the Pinchot brothers led the fight to unseat Taft as president; when they failed, the Republicans re-nominated Taft and the Pinchots led the formation of the Bull Moose Party that nominated Teddy Roosevelt in 1912.

While Gifford was a gifted politician, Amos, named after his mother's father, aside fromr being an all but non-practicing lawyer, had the oratory skills of a politician but sorely lacked political charm and temperament. He was widely known as a champion of the underdog, a man who preferred lost causes to compromised ideals. His progressive views could be described with either admiration or disgust depending on one's political views, as dogmatic. He became treasurer of the defense committee for the magazine *"Masses"*, which had been banned from the U.S. mail for its anti-war position. Through his involvement with the magazine *"Masses"*, he became outraged at the attacks on civil liberties of the war protesters. That outrage led him, in 1917, to help found the National Civil Liberties Bureau, which eventually became the ACLU.[34]

In his youth, Amos had been considered a New York society *swell* who loved elegance and formalities of social life.[35] He belonged to a variety of social clubs, ranging from the Skull and Bones Society to Teddy Roosevelt's New York hunt club. A talented tennis player, Amos remained aggressive on the court even after sustaining a hip injury during the Spanish-American War in Puerto Rico.[36]

Living in New York or the Milford estate, life was always exciting for Mary, with a seemingly steady stream of visiting writers, artists, and men of politics and law. She grew up around family friends who included Max and Crystal Eastman, Louis Brandeis, Roosevelt's Secretary of the Interior Harold Ickes, and the flamboyant heiress Mabel Dodge. Mary's domestic world while cozy, it was also vicariously cosmopolitan. She received letters and presents from her aunt Antoinette, married to a British nobleman and always on the move between London and some exotic destination. Her uncle Gifford took a South Seas sailing trip in 1929 on the family yacht and brought back all manner of treasure. Amos took frequent fishing trips to the Florida Keys, often including Mary and Tony. Their half sister, Rosamund, was always steaming off to Europe or California.[37]

The winters of Mary's youth were primarily spent on Park Avenue, New York. Park Avenue became fashionable after World War I, when the trend toward apartment living among society people began. Most of the buildings were quite new. The structures were solid and square, a dozen or more floors rising into the New York sky. Park Avenue was divided by medians of fenced, well tended grass, flower-beds, and shrubbery. Only noncommercial traffic was allowed, no buses or trucks. The *WPA Guide to New York City*, written by Depression-era writers, claimed city planners described Park Avenue as "a super slum" because of the unappealing sameness of the design going into the greystone buildings. Still, the WPA writers disdainfully said the Avenue was all rather swish, with uniformed doormen tending top-hatted men and begowned women in their journey from foyer to car, and car to foyer.[38]

Late in 1929, Amos moved his family from their large apartment at 1125 Park Avenue, to a slightly smaller one at 1165 Park Avenue. Although the difference between the two apartments was insignificant, in the eyes of New York society, the Amos Pinchot family had dropped a rung on the societal ladder; this move also signaled that of old money.

The 1930s were relatively hard times for the Amos Pinchot family. Some renters in their New York real estate holdings, short of cash, had stopped paying rent, forcing the family to take second mortgages on some of their buildings. Being responsible for the family trust, Amos had taken on the role of family trustee when he realized that he liked to practice law only in connection with causes in which he believed. Amos began the decade with a protracted battle over the proceeds from the Eno family trust. Later, when that was settled, not to his satisfaction, the income from family holdings in New York real estate began to shrink.[39]

Amos suffered the darkness of the 1930s in his own way. He fretted and began to drink more . . . . a vice that eventually got out of hand. He took out his frustration and anger on his daughters. The tradition of public service in the family, and his own progressive politics, probably compounded the guilt and helplessness he felt strolling the streets of New York, passing once-employed people selling apples for five cents apiece.

Experiencing financial setbacks himself, he knew most other Americans were undergoing far worse; he tried to think about how to improve their lot. In 1931, in the darkest pre-New Deal days, he wrote a letter to his brother Gifford, then Pennsylvania Governor, to move forward with a proposal to provide work through road camps for the unemployed within Pennsylvania. "You could be the first American leader to lay down an act on the proposition that the government has an obligation to supply people with work, when they want and need it, and cannot get it elsewhere. This is going to be a milestone in American history."[40]

Until Franklin Delano Roosevelt's New Deal, America suffered and waited for the Depression to end. A great sense of betrayal and resentment filled the land. The 1920s had been the idolization of the dollar. When the gay party crashed to a halt and millions were thrown out of work, there was an outpouring of hatred toward the upper classes, toward the bosses and bankers and the system that had let so many down. Many American intellectuals regarded the Depression as an opportunity for rethinking of the entire American economic system.

Amos expected and predicted the worst. In one 1933 letter to his brother, he advised him to "keep and anchor to windward in case of a revolution."[41]

He was not alone in that view, "The Depression had many intellectuals believing that some sort of social and ideological apocalypse was at hand," wrote Robert McElvaine, a chronicler of the Depression years. In 1932, fifty-two prominent writers, critics, and professors signed an open letter calling for a Communist president. Among the signers were Sherwood Anderson, Theodore Dreiser, Malcolm Cowley, John Dos Passos, Langston Hughes, Edmund Wilson, and Lincoln Steffens.[42]

Between 1929 and 1933, unemployment rose until more than a quarter of the American workforce was out of a job. Hoover and the Republicans had followed a plan of inaction. The idea was to let the Depression run its course, that it was healthy for the market to drop and that it would improve by and by. One of Hoover's solutions was to launch an ad campaign to cheer up the unemployed and buy some time until the whole problem corrected itself. An ad that appeared in major periodicals displayed an unemployed worker with the following copy underneath: "We're not scared either. If you think the good old U.S.A. is in a bad way more than temporarily, just try to figure out some place you'd rather be . . . . I'll see it through . . . . if you will!"[43]

Amos was not amongst the boosters, his growing pessimism and anger were like nasty clouds over the houses Mary lived in as a girl. He never retreated in his attack on the monopolies. But, in the mid-1930s he started to display a passion for positions that were on the fringes of populism, that resentful no-man's-land where the *left* met the *right*. He advocated a social-credit system of banking, in which the monetary and credit power would go into the hands of nonpartisan authority. He carried on a correspondence with Ezra Pound, who was already flirting with fascism in Europe, about the evils of the monetary system. Pound's letters to him are a collage of insult, flattery, opinion, and economics. In one letter Pound wrote, "Yes, I am with you, power to coin money, is and of a right, should be vested in Congress." In 1936, Pound wrote: "I suspect the WHOLE of your generation in the U.S.A. was fed on second rate English slop . . . . You are an old man but you have not been a coward. On at least a number of occasions you have showed courage."[44]

By the time Mary was fifteen, her father was listening to and admiring Father Charles Coughlin, a right-wing Catholic priest and radio broadcaster whose vitriolic populism was a hit with disaffected, xenophobic Americans before World War II. The "Radio Priest", as he became known, started out attacking Communists; then he turned his attention to the bankers. Eventually he linked the two and railed against both capitalism and Marxism, claiming he supported a Christian democracy. He was behind FDR and his New Deal at first, but by 1936 he claimed the whole administration was "a government of the bankers, by the bankers, and for the bankers." By the late

1930s he was openly supporting fascists and calling for a corporate state based on the model Benito Mussolini had installed in Italy. When he began praising Adolf Hitler in 1940, he had all but lost his followers.[45]

In letters to his uncle William Eno—who was showing signs of anti-Semitism—Amos, in 1938, indicated some admiration for Coughlin. "I suppose you heard Coughlin yesterday. His delivery had greatly improved but he is getting himself into a death struggle with some very powerful foes." He further wrote, "The American Jews would be wise if they made themselves as inconspicuous as possible for the next few years. There is no doubt about the anti-Jewish wave of sentiment. It's a pity, but a fact, which must be reckoned with."[46]

William Eno, the father of motor vehicle traffic regulation, was not so circumspect. In a letter to Amos in 1938, he complained that most of FDR's advisors were Jews and wrote that the Jews were taking over most of business and media organizations in New York. "Think this over and you will see why we may wake up someday and follow Hitler," Eno wrote.[47]

Initially, Amos supported FDR and the New Deal, but he soon decided the new administration was usurping too many powers for the executive branch and heading toward dictatorship. He objected in radio speeches and in pamphlets to FDR's labor policies, his court-packing bill, and his reelection to a third term. He particularly feared the consequences of wage, price, and farm-production controls. In an April 1937 open letter to FDR published in the New York Times, Amos laid out his objections to both the judiciary bill, which he called "sinister," and the National Recovery Act, which, he wrote, would lead to a managed economy under "a personal government which places the fate of labor, industry, and agriculture in a bureaucracy controlled by one man . . . . I am forced to conclude that . . . . you desire the power of a dictator without the liability of the name."[48]

Amos felt some personal responsibility for the direction the country was taking, because he had so forcefully advocated public ownership of some monopolies. But the massive expansion of the federal bureaucracy under Roosevelt offended his fundamental beliefs that government should limit itself to furthering the interests of the individual. He did not believe the New Deal was helping the unemployed. He was convinced FDR was leading the country into a war, and, just as he had been two decades earlier, he was ardent in his opposition to getting involved in Europe's problems. He was one of the founders of the America First Committee, which was devoted to keeping the United States out of World War II; it disbanded immediately after Pearl Harbor was attacked.[49]

As late as mid 1941 Amos still held out hope that America could stay uninvolved. In a letter to William Eno that year he wrote: "I believe we will stay out of the war in spite of desperate efforts of the administration and the Jewish leaders . . . . it would be a monstrous folly . . . . to exhaust the country's resources and manpower in fighting and reforming half the uncivilized and part of the civilized world." [50]

Within the peaceful lilies and orchard environ of the sprawling Grey Towers estate, Mary and Tony were aware of their father's worries only as an ominous but distant storm. There was the night in the late 1930s when the adults gathered around the radio. The girls were old enough to understand the import of what was happening, although the impact it would have on their generation and their own lives was beyond their imagination. It was September 1, 1939, and Mary was almost nineteen. Hitler had just invaded Poland. France and Britain were declaring war on Germany. Fascism was rampant in Europe. Spain was in the last throes of a civil war General Franco would win. It looked as if a contest between good and evil was under way. "There was news that boded no good," recalled family friend Davis Middleton, who was with Mary that evening. "It was a continent away, and we were still just kids, but there was this sense of history and doom. It was a hot, late summer night. I remember it vividly. The moon was coming up and you could hear the crickets and the radio crackling, and we looked to the east and saw the first sign of dawn along the horizon." [51]

Chapter 3

School Days and Post Grad

Mary, at the age of twelve, was enrolled at Brearley School, a private preparatory school for girls, located a few short blocks from the family's Park Avenue apartment on the Upper East Side of New York. Noted for exclusivity and academic rigor, the school was founded in 1883 by Harvard educator Samuel A. Brearley. Over time, Brearley had a history of educating the daughters and granddaughters of Franklin D. Roosevelt, Eugene O'Neill, Katherine Graham, and eventually President John F. Kennedy's daughter Caroline. During Mary's era, Brearley catered to the New York white Anglo Saxon elite, and daughters of German Jewish immigrants who were not welcome at other private schools. Although the school did not exclude those not of upper class, there is no evidence that any of Mary's classmates were of lesser means than her.

Girls wore uniforms of white blouses and dark skirts. The curriculum was English, math, geography, history, science, and languages of Greek, Latin, French, and German, in addition to art, drama, and music, with Arthur Murray dancing classes conducted in the tenth floor gym. The faculty were mainly graduates of the Seven Sisters schools (Barnard College, Bryn Mawr College, Mount Holyoke College, Radcliffe College, Smith College, Vassar College, and Wellesley College), Columbia and Oberlin. The school doctor was Dr. Benjamin Spock, who became the sovereign-like advisor to mothers of Mary's generation.[52]

In spite of the state supervisor of schools criticizing the practice of awarding girls letters in sports because it made them too competitive, the center piece of Brearley's social life centered on their athletic teams. Mary starred in basketball and tennis. Teammate and chum, Francis Kilpatrick Field, recalled Mary as a natural athlete and star which made her popular because the Brearley girls were devoted to their teams.[53]

Mary and her classmates whiled away lunch hours learning to smoke cigarettes at a local sandwich and soda shop. Smoking was so pervasive that Brearley provided the seniors with their exclusive smoking room, a sunny space on the seventh floor overlooking the East River. Although Mary never became a chain-smoker, she smoked socially throughout her life. There were some constraints on their carefree existence; the Depression was one, and even Park Avenue girls were told to be aware of the value of a dollar. As the girls thought of college, some actually took on summer jobs and learned to budget their personal living expenses.[54]

Mary shone at Brearley. She was smart, fit, amusing, not too intense; in other words, the model Brearley girl. Her classmates selected her as "Miss Brearley" in her senior year, the girl closest to the school's ideal. "Pinchot looked cute at any time," was how her classmates described her in the 1938 yearbook. "She had lots of beaus," recalled Frances Field, who walked to school with Mary from their Park Avenue apartments. She was invited to weekend dances at the boys' schools, Groton, Choate, and St. Paul's, more often than her friends. On those weekends, the girls traveled to New England campuses and the boys vacated their dorm rooms and slept in the gym, leaving notes on their pillows for their dates.[55]

Choate's annual Winter Festivities Weekend was open to recent graduates.[56] Despite sickly Princeton freshman Jack Kennedy's health concerns, he wanted to attend his former alma mater's annual Winter Festivity dance.

The big question being, how far could a tomcat like young Jack Kennedy navigate the confines of a heavily chaperoned New England prep school dance? And what would a college boy, a freshman at Princeton no less, want with a parochial school function anyway? What drove Jack back to Choate that weekend remains a mystery. But he did return, unaccompanied, as a stag. Perhaps he thought the homecoming on familiar territory would be good for his self confidence, which had lagged since being forced to take a medical leave from his studies at Princeton. Whatever the force that drew him backward (or perhaps forward) isn't known, but something propelled him; for at the Choate Winter Festivity Dance of 1936, he would encounter Mary Pinchot for the very first time, etching into his being an unforgettable moment.

The Saturday night dance could have served as a backdrop for a Hollywood film portraying a bygone era: tuxedos and tails worn by the young gentlemen, couture dresses by the debutantes-to-be. It was a gala for

young people that would grow up to be dubbed "the greatest g
their service during World War II. Yet in February 1936, life
was an endless party. A full orchestra played the latest swing
danced.

Anyone could see that Mary Pinchot's beauty was alluring, and it
certainly wasn't lost on her date for the evening, young Bill Attwood. "God,
she's a smooth looking babe," Attwood scribbled in his diary. "I just hope
her success doesn't go to her head."[57]

As the dance progressed, Attwood unfortunately discovered he had a
rival for Mary's attention. Jack Kennedy tapped Bill's right shoulder and
asked to cut-in. It wasn't the only cut-in he had to contend with that
night, but it had to have been one of the more daunting—and it happened
repeatedly. The young Kennedy was entranced with Mary's beauty; he
kept coming back. To compound matters, Attwood wasn't feeling well
that weekend. "Frequent trips upstairs to flood my throat with Listerine,"
Attwood noted in his diary, meant leaving Mary unattended in a sea of
potential suitors, and none more aggressive than Jack. That evening, destiny
seemed to have made its first mark.[58]

Midway through their freshman year, Mary's class was no longer trailed
by chaperones and nannies outside school premises, allowing Mary and her
friends all but free-run of New York City. Mary's neighborhood was still a
relatively uncongested and friendly place to reside. New York itself was a
playground, an extension of their elite world on Park Avenue. And there
were so many boys, coming out had little glamour.

By her mid-teens, Mary had found society so interesting that she spent
less and less time with her family at Grey Towers in Milford and more time
with friends in the Hamptons, close to New York. [59] Mary was much in
demand as a houseguest.[60]

The whirls of lavishly extravagant debutante balls were held at the
Waldorf-Astoria and Ritz—Carlton followed by dates at clubs where
young people drank and danced to swing orchestras, and rumba bands. Cab
Calloway entertained at the Cotton Club. The girls and their escorts drank
and danced at the Stork Club or trooped over to the Rainbow Room. Mary
was irresistibly attracted to the party life. "She was invited to everything, she
was so popular," recalled Frances Field.[61]

Pre-war socializing in New York increased as the ever growing threat of
the United States entering the war loomed. Mary's Brearley chum, Barbara
Blagden Sisson, recalled: "We lived at a terrible pre-war pace; we didn't
know if we would be alive." [62]

Mary's coming out year was arguably the year the New York debutante
scene seemed most glamorous through the media. Not uncommon were

avish balls with seemingly no cost restraints, held at the most expensive hotels and with guest lists of three to four hundred. A few of the honored debutantes themselves had personal fortunes of over a million dollars. That winter, four hundred debutantes were introduced to New York society at teas, balls, and dinners. The national press lapped up the glamour and fed it back to the public weary of grim times and receptive to fantasy.[63]

Although many of Mary's closest friends made their debuts on a grand scale, she did not; Amos was against social flaunting of wealth publicly during the country's financially trying times. But he didn't dispense with the custom entirely. Mary was presented at her New York Park Avenue home at a small afternoon tea; well aware, first hand, of the inanity of the endless round of parties, she was relieved. One frequent escort, David Middleton, recalled Mary very much wanting to be seen at the places of the moment but never being fully satisfied. "Her attitude was, 'I've been to the debutante parties and I've had enough of that.' She was in that sense inquiring and exploring. There was also a little of 'What to do?' Ultimately she was trying to find out 'What do I do?' because she wasn't a person who would be content to be peripheral. You had this kind of paradox between 'socialite' and what she wanted to be."[64]

During the era, modern celebrity culture and mass media had altered the style and function of the debutante balls. Old New York society surrendered to commercial reality, and nearly had a publicist to shepherd photographers toward the prettiest or richest girls.[65] The debutante scene had, in fact, become crass and cruel. The *Park Avenue Social Review* of November 1938 offered a running commentary on the brutal social game, "No matter which way we turn these days the spotlight remains focused on the debutante of '38-'39. From now and to the beginning of the *petit saison* every function is arranged primarily for her benefit. This is her year to 'shine' if 'shine' she ever will, a year of constant vying and petty jealousies. It is entirely up to her whether she becomes one of the 'glamour' girls of the season or one of the 'duds.'"[66]

The glitter and glamour of the balls masked some unpleasant truths about high society. Brenda Frazier, the dark-haired *Life* cover deb of 1938, attempted suicide in 1961. She later wrote an article for the magazine headlined "My Debut—A Horror." She wrote that after years of psychoanalysis, when she looked at photographs of her coming-out party she saw "the mockery of the fixed smiles . . . and how many people there are in the world that were doomed like me by unfortunate childhoods to adult lives plagued by fears and inner emptiness."[67]

Those very fears plagued Amos when he watched his daughter on her gay rounds. The deprivations of the Depression had barely affected his daughter's lifestyle. While New York was grim with rumors of war, his daughter was frolicking from weekend to weekend, her mind only on the next dance or dinner date.

At home Amos sometimes, almost always while drinking, took out his bleak mood on his daughter, as their Park Avenue apartment echoed with his shout when he criticized her social life. His abuse of alcohol increased with age, the threat of the country going to war, and the negative affect the depression was having on the family fortune. But, it was the loss of his daughter Rosamond from which he would never recover.

The 1930s were a decade that saw the rise of movie-star celebrity; Depression America craved stardom and found as much of it in the society scene as it did in Hollywood. Mary was thrilled by the attention. Once David Middleton escorted her to "21" and gossip columnist Walter Winchell mentioned sighting the lovely debutante's appearance in a booth. Mary was beside herself at the item in the next morning's newspaper. "Rosamond, I think, was her role model," said Middleton. Mary was forever in awe of her half-sister's celebrity. Rosamond was always turning up in movie magazines and in 1934 had signed a six-month contract with Metro-Goldwyn-Mayer and moved to Hollywood. Mary enjoyed photographic attention as well. While a teenager, she modeled clothes and hairstyles for *Vogue*. Frances Field remembered that Mary earned a little extra money for clothes from the sessions. One *Vogue* shot by fashion photographer Horst shows Mary in her late teens in glamorous profile with upswept hair and diamond earrings, an ice princess with full lips and distant gaze.

Rosamond only landed one small role in Hollywood film, though she did appear eventually in some French films. But she was tall and voluptuous when the style for American female stars was still the thin-lipped wraith. She was also not much of an actress. On her return to New York, she announced she was retiring from acting, a development the New York newspapers covered with much interest. She and Amos bought some New York real estate together, including an old theater (possibly with the idea of giving her a venue). In 1935 and 1936, she returned to acting and performed in summer stock in New York and Massachusetts. She married a gadabout wealthy lawyer named William Gaston whose family owned textile mills in Gastonia, North Carolina. She had two children with him, but she soon fell in love with the Broadway producer Jed Harris, also a major Hollywood figure, whose bisexuality doomed the affair. Despondent over her failed marriage, movie career, and romance, in the spring of 1938, Rosamond rented a house on Long Island alone and killed herself inside a running car in a closed garage. She left two sons under the age of ten.

Rosamond took her own life during Mary's senior year at Brearley. Mary was whirling through the schedule of debutante parties and suicide was not mentioned among friends, much less in the press. The *New York Times* in those years did not publish the obituaries of suicides, so the death passed without publicity. But it would have deep and lasting affect on Mary, whose world until then had been unblemished by any sort of pain or tragedy.

Perhaps inspired by Rosamund's example, Mary became a committed diarist. Soon after her sister died, she would use the act of writing as a tool for self-realization and reflection, especially in times of emotional crises, and rely on it throughout her life. Most of her earlier diary is still in existence, but its contents are unknown outside the family. However, in 1940, on the second anniversary of her sister's suicide, the *New York Times* published Mary's poem "Requiem," a remarkable disclosure of verse that divulged a stirring dimension of Mary's own persona. According to author Bibi Gaston, "Requiem" had first been written in Mary's diary.

> I saw her lying there so calm and still,
> With one camellia placed beside her head.
> She looked the same, and yet, her soul and will
> Being gone she did not seem dead.
>
> I thought if one so loved and beautiful
> Should wish to leave, perhaps there was a voice
> That called her back—and she was dutiful.
> Somewhere the gods rejoice.
>
> In some far place, where all the lovely things
> Of earth are born, the gods no longer weep.
> She was returned to them. And what she brings
> We lose, but always keep.[68]

Rosamond's suicide broke Amos. She had been his favorite child, and after her death, Amos drank more and fell victim to a series of ailments that hospitalized him. Mary, who had been spending much time away from Milford, became a more frequent companion to him at Grey Towers. She loved her father and now was able to prove her worth to him. As Amos descended into clinical depression, Mary tried to cheer him up, though she continued to make the rounds of parties, and none of her friends knew about her private pain in her family. In letters Amos wrote during those years, he mentioned Mary more often than Ruth or Tony.[69]

In the fall of 1938, Mary followed her mother to Vassar. The campus in Poughkeepsie, with its ancient trees between two lakes, crisp country walks, streets of antique shops, dress stores, and inns, and its long tradition of women's education, was intimidating at first. Mary wrote home that she didn't much like it. But by her second semester she was used to the rhythm of women's college life. Weekdays were for classes, studying, and Gary Cooper movies. Weekends were for New Haven, Princeton, and football or basketball game dates. To Mary it was familiar ground, New York City society transplanted to upstate New York and Connecticut. Half the girls at Brearly went on to Vassar, so Mary was still among childhood friends. And the young men they visited on weekends were often the same boys who had been their escorts at the cotillions.[70]

Author Mary McCarthy graduated from Vassar several years before Mary Pinchot arrived. She described the freshman girl's sense of awe at first passing through Taylor Gate, where Yale men in roadsters were parked waiting for the upper-class women in their pale sweaters and pearls, "tall, dazzling . . . impeccable, with stately walks like goddesses." Entering Vassar was like entering "a Forest of Arden and Fifth Avenue department store combined." The college was founded in 1861by a self-made and self-educated Poughkeepsie brewer named Matthew Vassar, and by the 1930s the school had a reputation as the archetypal American women's college, "less intellectual than Radcliffe of Bryn Mawr, less social and weekendish than Smith, less athletic than Wellesley, less Bohemian than Bennington," McCarthy wrote. The very name of the college signified "a whiff of luxury and ineffable, plain thinking and high living."[71]

At Vassar, Mary met women who became her lifelong friends. She lived in a dorm known as the North Tower, considered the most glamorous campus residence. During the week, the women all wore bobby socks and saddle shoes, but for dates they daubed on Chanel No. Five, powdered their noses with Elizabeth Arden, and imitated Margaret Sullivan. Their favorite swing band was Tommy Dorsey, and they were deeply disappointed when he couldn't play for their junior prom and they had to settle for Glenn Miller, though they were pleasantly surprised at the outcome. Sophisticated girls, they voraciously read *The New Yorker* and the *New York Times*. Most of all they were devoted to Yale. They hung the Yale motto, "For God and Country and Yale," around the Vassar campus. "Doesn't it feel refreshingly feminine to wear stockings and a dress and to be on our way to purely non-intellectual doings?" asked the 1942 Vassarian editors above a photograph of a train packed with fur-clad young ladies headed to Princeton and New Haven. "We may have a test lurking somewhere in the near future, and come Sunday night and the 7:40, we will feel like *death*, but what else do we look forward to with such anticipation and what else is there to recall with equal glee?" In the 1941 yearbook, the same notation had been expressed: "We are forced to conclude that Yale and Princeton have more appeal for Vassar than

Vassar does for itself." The sense that men's endeavors were more appealing than women's, reflected in the way Mary and her contemporaries thought and acted in the decades to come.[72]

Many Vassar girls arranged their schedules so that they had no classes on Friday, the better to catch an early train to New Haven. They went on any pretext . . . a blind date was enough. Once they arrived, they expected to be taken care of. Sometimes the men put them up in hotels, and certainly they would pay for their dinners. "Going Dutch" was not done. In return the girls were good companions, but nothing more was expected. There was a great deal of drinking and dancing to swing bands and much heavy kissing, but also innocence amongst the Vassar girls. "We were all virgins, as I recall," said Mary Truesdale, who often took the train to New Haven with Mary. "Everybody was a virgin. I remember sitting in Main Hall waiting for somebody to come back who was going to go the whole way so I could see what it was like."[73]

In those years, finding a suitable husband was still a significant and quietly approved part of a Vassar girl's education. But there was a distinction at Vassar between the women who were seriously considering professions and those headed for early post-graduate marriage. There were those that felt Mary fell closer to the latter category. She was such a beauty that her classmates elected her to the Vassar Daisy Chain, an undergraduate honor that consisted of donning a white dress and parading around campus on Commencement Day with similarly clad nymphs linked by a chain of daisies. "She was someone you liked being around and was clearly pleasant to the eye," said classmate Frances Prindle Taft.[74] On the other hand, some of her more collegiate sisters, women striving for professional careers, found her, jealously, somewhat vapid. "Although very bright, she was not the type who took academia too seriously, but she wasn't snooty either. She was clearly decorative, as far as I was concerned," said one Vassar 1942 graduate.[75]

It is possible that the family tragedies of Rosamund's suicide, Amos' depression and alcohol abuse caused Mary to withdraw somewhat from college activities and shed the lively, highly involved personality she had projected at Brearley. Because the girls in her social class did not discuss private family matters such as suicide and alcoholism, it is impossible to know whether those were the reasons Mary was not, at Vassar, the widely admired and popular girl she had been at Brearley. But Vassar itself encouraged and rewarded a different kind of girl than the breezy prep school athlete.[76]

Vassar inspired its girls a reverence for, if not always the eventual practice of, a kind of independence of thought and spirit. The faculty was dominated by unmarried women, and students were expected to have ideas and express them with confidence. The young women were by and large the daughters of the upper and upper middle class who would soon marry Republican lawyers like their fathers, but the school urged its students to "do" something with their lives. It produced, Mary McCarthy wrote, women who were simultaneously two persons . . . . "the housewife or matron and the yearner and regretter." The Vassar girls would feel "she had let the college down by not becoming famous or 'interesting,'" McCarthy wrote. The most revered Vassar graduates were not the humdrum professionals, women who had become doctors or teachers, but those who had distinguished themselves in more dramatic ways, such as the poet Edna St. Vincent Millay (Vassar 1917), or the first woman to enlist in the Marines, Major Julia Hamblet (Vassar 1937). Vassar girls in Mary Pinchot's generation learned to admire daring. "An *arresting performance* in politics, fashion, or art is often taken by the Vassar mind to be synonymous with true accomplishment," McCarthy noted.[77]

Although encouraged by her counselor at Brearley as well as a professor at Vassar to strongly consider a career in medicine and become a doctor, Mary also had a creative side. The strong influence of her right-brain was more in keeping with the secret hope of Vassar girls of the time, to distinguish herself as different from other women, and a strong will quietly hidden under good manners and a pretty face. "She really did whatever she wanted to do," recalled Mary Truesdale. "She took any class she liked. She was there when she felt like it. She always walked with authority and held her head high. She looked like she knew where she was going and what she wanted to do. She was full of ideas and had her own way of looking at things." [78]

Her college friends saw a good-natured girl who kept to herself and was slightly offbeat. She didn't like to be on stage, and enjoyed the solitude of painting, and in prep school had already won awards for her artistic ability. She had a silly sense of humor. Frances Field, her Brearley and Vassar classmate, remembers an incident during their senior year when three girls and Mary were all studying for finals together in the same room. The tension was palpable and quiet as a vault. Suddenly, Mary stood up to go to the bathroom. As she was walking out the door she leaned over and took a bite of some tulips in a vase by the door, calmly chewing them as she walked out the door . . . never looking back. "She was very serene," Field recalled. "Never loud."[79]

In a short story called "Futility," which she wrote when she was an upper classman, and was published in the *Vassar Review and Little Magazine*, Mary described the boredom of party life and imagined a strange solution to it. In the story, a young woman named Ruth Selwyn sips a martini at a party in an apartment with a chartreuse sofa, a white fur rug, an aquarium inset above a mantelpiece, and "chicly cadaverous" guests who are "being too killing about Noel Coward's love life." Utterly bored, she fanaticizes about an imminent operation that will make every sensation "new and exciting and different and interesting." On her way home from the party, Ruth passes a florist shop where orchids are displayed in the window. "They look as though they had been grown in damp underground caves by demons. They're evil sickly flowers with no life of their own, living on borrowed strength."

The following day, Ruth Selwyn visits a Dr. Morrison, who performs an operation on her that connects her optic nerves to her auditory receptors and vice versa. In the voice of Dr. Morrison, Mary Pinchot mocks her own boredom. Explaining the operation to his nurse, the doctor says, "I wouldn't be trying it either, except that, well, she's been coaxing and phoning and trying to persuade me every day now over the past three weeks. She wants something new. You know the type. Bored with life, looking for excitement at any price . . . as though life weren't complicated enough as it is."

After the operation, Ruth walks outside and hears the clicking of her own heels on the pavement, which appear in the form of a troop of soldiers in plumed helmets marching alongside her. A green crossing light sounds like a bugle call. When she looks at a print of Van Gogh's sunflowers she hears Stravinsky's "Sacre du Printemps," and when she looks at peonies she hears the "purr of a dove." A church bell tolling sets off a series of colorful images, "with each ring a spectrum, starting with deep royal blue and ending with pale, pale blue." But soon the colors get jumbled up with the marching soldiers and some pigs after she hummed "The Three Little Pigs."

The little story ends badly for Ruth Selwyn. Exhausted by the clamor assailing her crossed senses, she returns to her apartment with the chartreuse couch and lies down upon it. As another evening of drinks and empty chatter begins, she closes her eyes. Like Sleeping Beauty, she goes into a permanent sleep, except there is no prince on the horizon. The last line is: "And because her eyes were closed, she heard nothing to disturb her, and slept forever on the chartreuse couch."[80]

The story essentially describes a condition known a synesthesia, a crossing of sensory experiences that poets have mined for metaphors for decades and that drug users discover to be one physical aspect of an LSD experience. It is unlikely that Mary was one of the estimated one in a hundred thousand people who experiences synesthesia naturally. Richard E. Sytowic, a psycho neurologist, has studied them and found that as a group, they are able to function normally. According to his studies, such people are often unusually artistic and drawn to creative fields. It is more probable that the idea of synesthesia was introduced to Mary in discussions on art or literature at Vassar. In fact, another later Vassar graduate Jacqueline Bouvier, indicated her own familiarity with the theory in a prize-winning essay for *Vogue* in which she analyzed how the French poet Baudelaire developed "the theory of synesthesia" in some of his works.[81]

Mary was very briefly involved in college politics in her junior year when she joined a club called the Polit Board, Vassar's major political entity. The group invited outside speakers and brought together left and right for heated discussions. Her interest was no doubt encouraged by Amos, by this time seething at FDR. Mary was trying to be somebody, and that somebody was her father. Her interest in politics, while in college, was tepid at best.[82] Amos had by then decided the president was being advised by "Marxian intellectuals, the most pestiferous and useless class that ever cumbered this sad world."[83] In November 1939, he wrote a letter to his brother Gifford that mentions Mary's political world. "Vassar seems to be very much interested in Communism. And a great deal of warm debating is going on among the students of Mary's class, which I think is an excellent thing. People of that age ought to be radical anyhow."[84]

With Mary off at college, Amos began to suffer from a variety of ailments and growing increasingly depressed. Mary stayed around him throughout her summer break of 1940, trying everything to cheer him up. After Amos attended the Republican convention in Philadelphia, which nominated Wendell Wilkie, he and Mary flew together to California for a vacation in the sun in an attempt to sooth his growing depression.

In the fall of 1940, FDR was elected to a third term, beating Amos's candidate, Wendell Wilkie. The world was at war and America was sidling toward conflict, with Amos firmly opposed. As Hitler rolled across Europe, began his reign of terror against the Jews, and signed a tripartite agreement with Japan and Italy, Amos still held onto the notion that America could stay out of the fray. [85]

At the start of Mary's senior year at Vassar, Amos wrote a long letter about Mary to his brother, Gifford. He lamented her failure to keep in shape for school tennis, but he approved her plan to study medicine. "A long hard road to hoe, but she really wants to do it. Good women doctors are rare and generally quite successful. My friends assure me there is a fine opportunity for women doctors in New York." Mary was just then a few weeks shy of her twenty-first birthday, when her substantial trust fund would come under her control. Amos wrote that she planned to keep it in trust, all but five-hundred dollars for clothing and other expenses.[86]

The winter of her senior year the war debate ended and Amos's protestations looked both wrong and unpatriotic, for on December 7, 1941, the Japanese bombed U.S. naval and air bases at Pearl Harbor, Hawaii,

Guam, the Philippines, and Wake Island. The nation was about to come face-to-face with what columnist Walter Lippmann called "ice cold evil."

For Mary and her generation, Pearl Harbor meant the dance was over.

Yale men went off to basic training, while many Vassar women joined the war effort themselves. The WAVES were created, and women also helped train troops in communications, joined the Red Cross, and worked in shorthanded stateside factories. The era of Rosie the Riveter, of spunky women in coveralls, or cinch-waisted business suits with broad shoulders commenced.

The war had a profound effect on Mary's social world. The national emergency dictated that there would be no Vassar prom in her senior year, 1942. Even the lights on Time Square were dimmed so as not to light the harbor for German U-boats. Mary also had more personal worries during her last year at Vassar. Her father was physically ill and unraveling mentally. The onset of war had compounded his medical and psychological problems. As an America Firster, he was badly proven wrong by the attack on Pearl Harbor. He began spending more and more time in seclusion at the Connecticut estate of his uncle William Enos.

At the Connecticut house on a hot summer afternoon in 1942, a few months after Mary's graduation from Vassar, Amos locked himself into a second story bathroom, climbed into the bathtub, and slit his wrists. The suicide attempt failed. Amos was found by his uncle and taken to the hospital in time to be revived with five blood transfusions. But the news of the attempt made the *New York Times*, and his mental instability was made public. His cherished dignity destroyed, he never recovered his physical or mental health and spent the remainder of his life in hospitals.

Her father's suicide attempt and deterioration transformed Mary's young life. Two of the most important people in her world—her father and her older half-sister—had decided that life was not worth the trouble. The Pinchot family tragedies remained deep but private wounds. Mary probably survived the anguish by separating herself from other people's unhappiness, an ability that would become pronounced in later years. Mary contained her feelings in the habit of her social class, which held it improper to grieve too long, especially over an event as socially reprehensible as suicide. Only those close to her ever detected the darkness underlying the light and easy facade.

After college, Mary's life was dominated by women. The streets of New York bristled with men in uniforms waiting to be shipped out. Inside the offices, women in suits took jobs vacated by the soldiers. Although all the Pinchot women had trusts, they went to work to aid the war effort as well as to earn extra money because the family fortune had been hard-hit by the depression. Ruth went so far as to take on boarders in their Park Avenue apartment, most of them friends of Mary and recent graduates of Vassar. While Ruth worked as publicity director at the YWCA, Tony worked a summer job at a women's magazine. Mary, her plans for medical school dashed by the war, went to work as a journalist.

One of the Pinchot Vassar boarders was Mary Brier Goodhue, a lawyer who went on to become a New York state senator. She later claimed that it was all the men going off to war that enabled her to gain employment in a New York law firm.

Mary took a position with United Press was as a feature writer, where she was an immediate success, gaining her own column.[87] Coworker and fellow Vassar classmate Barbara Gair Scheiber said, "Mary was very confident, and independent and that there was something very singular about her. In spite of her underlying problems, I felt that whatever Mary wanted to do, she would do." Mary inspired envy, as she flitted in and out of the office in stylish clothes, "There was an element of defiant fearlessness to her. She had this very throaty big laugh and a beautiful smile. There was this enjoyment, a twinkle and a laugh, but also a sort of steely coolness. There was some removal, like someone living in her own tower."[88]

In New York during the war years there were suddenly no powerful men in Mary's life to direct her. She was free to explore the world on her own. Socially she tried to distinguish herself from other college girls by associating with people from the movies and politics. She was seen around New York on the arm of Walter Pidgeon, who was old enough to be her father. That, of course, got the attention of gossip columnists. Her flirting with politics led her to join the American Labor Party; more than likely influenced by her father's leftist history. Woefully, her association with union leaders would later bring her under suspicion during the McCarthy-era witch-hunts that would ensnare her future husband. Although her friends scoffed at the idea of Mary being a political rebel, the FBI and its informers took her seriously.

Several of Mary's friends and associates were jealous of Mary; during the war, there was a shortage of men in New York, and Mary turned the heads of those that remained. Many in the journalism profession would frequent legendary Irish pub Tim Costello's on Forty-Third Street near Third Avenue. Until the war, Costello's had been a dark and smoky newsman's haunt that rarely saw female patrons, much less Vassar girls. With women having taken the spots vacated by men going off to war, they too bellied up to the bar. Tim Costello was very protective of the women, especially one fine boned girl who incongruously graced the bar with a Lucky Strike in one hand and a drink in the other.

Due to the call to war, there were very few young men to frequent the pub. One of them, Bob Schwartz from Ohio, wore a Navy uniform but was stationed state-side working for the military newspaper *Yank*. He was tall, dark, handsome, and very intellectual, with all of the girls working for United Press falling all over him; again a cause of some jealousy. Bob, seeing her alone at the bar, found her coolly perfect from afar, but witty and self assured up close, with a twinkle of mischief in her eyes. He found her wildly beautiful in a Grace Kelly sense.

Mary and Bob fell in love, he being Mary's first long-term lover. They stayed together for three years, much of the time living in his room at the Shelton Hotel, on Forty-Ninth Street and Lexington Avenue, where all the young men working for the *Yank* were housed on the same floor. It was a scandalous situation for young women of Mary's generation, if it hadn't been for the war. Not only did Mary not care, she took delight in blithely stepping out of a hotel every morning into a hallway filled with admiring young men. With her father ill and oblivious, she was, for the first time in her life, acting under her own authority.

Bob and Mary spent a lot of time at Grey Towers, where he became a pseudo family member, in spite of his Jewishness. He viewed the mother-daughter relationship as being respectful, and even deep, but hardly in a warm sort of way. Ruth was the kind of woman who commanded respect, and Mary was clearly proud of the fact that her mother had been one of the first suffragists. To Schwartz, Grey Towers was a dreamy, idyllic place where his girlfriend was free to swim nude and they could slide down a private waterfall with three levels of bubbling pools beneath the estate's whispering pines. She shared stories of her late glamorous sister who had acted in French films and ridden horses at full gallop around the grounds at midnight while her little sister could hear the pounding of horse hooves from her bed.

Schwartz saw his girlfriend as militantly wholesome, not wild like her half-sister she so admired. He found her to have a serious and questing nature. He saw her profound, a young women who was thinking about the higher questions, the meaning of love, life, and death. He found that there was no bull shit to her, she was definitely not light.

Mary was always more interested in relationships and ethics of human behavior than politics. While her mother, Ruth, was deeply involved in politics, Mary was less so. Mary was a devoted pacifist, and to say she was antiwar is to really not understand her; she was essentially an aesthetic.

Meanwhile, Mary's father was deteriorating, his lucidity gone after his suicide attempt and his physical strength had depleted. Mary spoke to him rarely, but with affection and sadness. In early 1944, Amos had so declined that his immediate family had to decide whether to act on a doctor's recommendation that he undergo a lobotomy. The family decided against it and Amos died in February 1944 and was buried in Milford, on a high hill. The affect of Mary's father's death, although not recorded, was probably a relief for her as well as the rest of the family, seeing that Amos was essentially gone from them already for two years.

As the war ground down and men began to return, displacing the women from the work force, in factories, newspapers, and on the Detroit auto assembly line. In Washington, journalist Marie Ridder, of *Philadelphia Evening Bulletin*, threw her typewriter at a young man when she realized that he had come to take her job. At the same time, Mary and Bob began to drift apart. He was heartbroken. "Our relationship was one of those phases in life; but I think we were meant to go on longer", he said decades later. Schwartz blamed himself. But in fact Mary was already on to someone else, a genuine movie-size war hero.

CHAPTER 4

The Knot

The wedding was a cumulative reflection of the bride having had her fill of debutante financial excesses to the extreme, the groom having fought and been disfigured in combat, and the austere atmosphere of war rationing. With mid-April 1945 spring in the air, the small gathering of family and friends at the mother of the bride's, Ruth Pinchot, spacious Park Avenue apartment, was cheerful and casually formal.

Mary, who would be beautiful in a sack-dress, looked gorgeous in her white-and-green printed crepe afternoon dress carrying a bouquet of white daisies and freesia. Her blond hair hung in a wave to her shoulders, pinned back at the temples. She wore a single strand of pearls on her neck. The groom, Cord Meyer, wore his Marine lieutenant's dress uniform and a wide, goofy smile on his wounded face.

Outside, spring tipped the tree limbs pale green on the Park Avenue meridian, WW II was entering its death throes as Hitler, a scared animal, was less than two weeks from committing suicide in a coward's underground bunker, and the world was a mere short season from the dropping of the atom bomb on clearly defeated, yet defiant, Japan.

Protestant theologian and author, an intellectual not a minister, Reinhold Niebuhr, a friend of Ruth's, presided over the ceremony. He stumbled a few times as he read from the Anglican *Book of Common Prayer*. At the appropriate times, the bride and groom responded in even and deliberate voices. The rings were exchanged and the vows sealed with a kiss, for which the new Mary Enos Pinchot-Meyer stood on her toes as Cord bent down. Mary had her handsome hero, a man of passion, experience, and ideas who showed great promise to succeed. His wound made his look more beguiling. He had pulled through a night of death and he believed in a higher calling. Behind the boyish grin and impeccable manners was a ferocious intensity.[89]

They were a happy couple but not giddy, two people who possessed a conviction about the rightness of what they were doing. The assembled shared that feeling. "Amos would have felt that Cord was right for Mary and she for him, I know," Ruth Pinchot wrote to Cornelia a few weeks later.[90]

All of New York's newspapers mentioned the wedding of the two socially prominent twenty-four-year-olds. The New York Times called Mary a writer and Cord a war hero, and both members of noted families. The night of their wedding the couple sped off to Washington for an abbreviated two-day honeymoon. Cord had been hired, a few days before the wedding, as an assistant to U.S. delegate Harold Stassen at the United Nations convention, so Cord had to take a train to San Francisco with the rest of the U.N. delegates. Mary followed him a few days later by plane, carrying her own press credentials for the event. The gossip columnists gilded the romance . . . . the dashing war hero heading off on a mission to solve world problems, scooping up a lovely princess on his way.

The tabloid's play of Cord's military heroism was both superficial and fairytale like. He was a decorated Marine lieutenant who Mary dated throughout the winter of 1944-45, after he emerged from a veteran's hospital where he was treated for shrapnel injuries and fitted with a glass eye. As part of his recuperation, he had been resting in New York, playing squash to become accustomed to his partial blindness. He and Mary, and any friends who were not away on wartime duties, prowled the New York clubs. They were trying to recapture the pre-war tempo, but much had changed.

Cord had an intensity that intrigued Mary. Mary, as a journalist, was taken by his literary talent whose writing had already been published in national magazines. He was a man of action who emerged from the war, deeply committed to peace. And there was something more: In many ways . . . . especially in his devotion to impossible ideals . . . . Cord was a lot like Amos.

The Pinchot family had its suicides, and the Cord family had skeletons of its own. Cord's great-uncle, Harry Thaw, was famous for murdering architect Stanford White (whose firm designed Amos Pinchot's relatively modest home on the Gray Tower estate grounds) in 1906 over a beauty named Evelyn Nesbit. When Cord was nine, his father had a breakdown and was briefly institutionalized.[91] Even when Cord was an adult, his father's mental troubles were evident in the anguished dreaming shouts that echoed through the New Hampshire summer home when Cord was home. But in the morning no one mentioned them.[92]

The Meyers were wealthy and socially connected, and like the Pinchots, they had spent the depression years in relative ease. Like Mary, Cord was a fourth-generation American descended from a successful European immigrant. His great-grandfather, Cord Meyer, emigrated from Germany in 1845 and began working as a grocer in Brooklyn. He soon owned a wholesale grocery business and a sugar refinery. Cord's father was a foreign-service officer in Washington D.C. when his first set of twin boys was born. Cord's mother, Katharine Thaw, belonged to the Pennsylvania Thaw family, which possessed a major coal fortune. Cord, and his twin Quintin, and their parents lived in diplomatic residences in Havana and Stockholm until their mother had a second set of twins and the family returned to America. Cord Senior then rejoined the family real estate business. The Cord Meyer Company was one of the prominent landholders in New York, responsible for developments in Long Island and Forest Hills. The Meyer real estate holdings had increased a fortune made in sugar refining by a company named Meyer and Dick that had operated in Cuba during the previous century.

Cord and Quentin (named for his father's friend, Quentin Roosevelt) attended private school in Switzerland and then St. Paul's School in New Hampshire, considered one of the most desirable private preparatory schools in the country. The school was academically rigorous and socially, almost monastic. Boys were required to attend chapel three times a day and were imbued with high Episcopalian formality. Both boys played hockey, but Cord was clearly less athletic than his twin.

St. Paul's headmaster concluded that Cord was an artist and poet; he edited the school newspaper, *Horae Scholastica*, and wrote poetry and articles for it. After graduating second in his class, he went on to Yale, where he continued his writing while editing the *Yale Literary Magazine*. His intellectual reputation grew. He won the Alpheus Snow Award, given to the student deemed to have contributed the most intellectually to Yale, and graduated summa cum laude.[93]

There were signs in the child of an argumentative man Cord would become. St. Paul's headmaster never forgot young Cord's tempestuousness. "As a boy, he had a fixed habit of going off the deep end; he blew like a half gale," said Gerald Chittenden in a 1940's interview. "He may have been a little absurd in those days but when he cooled down, as he sometimes did, he amused himself as much as he did the rest of us." The headmaster went on to describe a boy who was driven to fury by cynicism and who, on questions of morals and morale, "was always right." The boy exercised his will as a dormitory supervisor.[94]

On the Yale campus during Cord's years there, discussion about the war in Europe raged and young men bitterly argued question of isolationism and pacifism. Cord considered, for a time, becoming a conscientious objector should the United States enter the war. After Pearl Harbor was bombed, the question of objecting to the war suddenly became obsolete. He enlisted in the Marines in the fall of 1942.

Cord's father had been an Army airman in World War I, and military service was assumed of the four Meyer sons. Meyer's father told interviewers later that, of the boys, he felt that Cord would be the least able to take the stress of war. His mother believed he would be killed, since he was the most sensitive of the boys.[95]

David Challinor, Cord's roommate at St. Paul's, credited the school for promoting a desire for public service in its pupils. "I think boarding school instilled an idealized obligation into the extraordinarily privileged elite group of young men. It was less so for women, whose only option, then, was to get married. For the men there was a very subtle obligation. You owed something back for the unbelievable privileged life you led."[96]

Cord and his social peers had endured few deprivations in their young lives, and they could easily be accused of being soft. Aware of that possibility, schools such as St. Paul's, with their iron rules of honor, ethics, and manhood, drilled everything soft out of their pupils. Some historians have blamed upper-class machismo for a variety of military disasters engineered by men of Cord's generation, from the Bay of Pigs to the Vietnam War.

In July 1944, on Guam, Cord would make an awful contribution. While half asleep in his foxhole, a Japanese grenade rolled into his foxhole. It blew up in his face as he tried to fling it from his hole, killing his partner and severely wounding him. When the sun rose over Guam, Cord was still conscious but unable to move or speak. Marines surveying the damage discovered he was still alive only when someone took his pulse. A medic on the beach declared that Cord was on the verge of death, and he was hurriedly taken to a rescue station on a nearby coral reef, where he was revived with blood plasma. After a time in a hospital near Pearl Harbor, he was transferred to a naval hospital in New York. For his injuries, he received the Purple Heart and Bronze Star.

Cord and Jack both returned home from the war as heroes with tremendous. Cord had lost an eye, while Jack suffered the physical trauma of PT-109 and, early in the war the loss of his older brother, Joe. He was never pushed off this hard, sensible center of his being. Thus became the hardened character of both men who has looked up the asshole of death and survived war's slaughter.[97]

Although Cord was imbued with the sensibility of a poet, the province of genuine human intimacy often challenged and eluded him. Cord's deepest emotional expressions were all but confined to his near excessive compulsive journalizing. Cord's anesthetization to grief would eventually main his capacity for sustaining intimacy in relationships, and not just with Mary. On the other hand, Jack appeared content to avoid intimacy in human relationships entirely. Emotionally crippled in his relationship with women, he detested being embraced, and then compulsively showered, sometimes as often as five times a day, only to crave the most intimate merging of all . . . . sexual union.[98]

In the fall of 1944, he was home and resuming his acquaintance with Mary. She spent nearly every free waking moment with Cord most of that fall and winter. Years later, their mutual friend Mary Goodhue said, "I thought Mary and Cord were a good pair. They had broad interests, worldwide. They were not small, picayune people."[99]

Paul Moore, a St. Paul's and Yale chum of Cord, was also wounded in the Pacific and back in New York recuperating at the same time as Cord. He and Cord played therapeutic squash together and socialized; two veterans-about-town with their dates. Years later he would recall, "We were happy to be back, and we were doing a lot of drinking. Mary danced exquisitely, and was the kind of young woman who attracted attention when she walked into a club. She was an extremely bright and responsive conversationalist, up on current events. And Cord was bright and amusing"[100]

Although Cord's writing talents had been discovered and opportunities surfaced, the writing life alone did not satisfy the wounded man. He needed a platform and a point of authority from which to write. Union Theological Seminary tried to interest Cord in the seminary, but Cord was not interested in religion, either. There were no answers for him in the Bible, even though he possessed the moral certitude of a preacher. Fresh from the battle-field, Cord was serious about one thing, world peace, and he threw himself wholeheartedly into any efforts he believed could ultimately ensure it. The new United Nations looked, to him, as the place to start. He felt that the UN formative convention in San Francisco would be his start. The hope-filled event also constituted he and Mary's honeymoon. Mary attended as a journalist with press credentials from the *North American Newspaper Alliance*.[101]

Among the press representatives was a young man Mary remembered from a pre-school dance and Vassar weekend dates—John F. Kennedy. He was attending on *Hearst* newspaper credentials, and he and Mary got reacquainted as young peers among the hordes of older journalists and pundits. Kennedy's relationship with Cord was not as warm. Cord talked to the *New York Times*, but he turned down a request for an interview from Kennedy. Kennedy wrote his skeptical reaction to Cord's ideas into a notebook: "Admittedly, world organization with common obedience to law would be a solution. Not that easy. If there is not the feeling that war is the ultimate evil, a feeling strong enough to drive them together, then you can't work out this international plan. Mustn't expect too much . . . there is no cure-all.[102]

John Kennedy and Cord Meyer got off on the wrong foot at the United Nations convention, and Kennedy never got over his dislike for Cord.[103] The bad blood between the two men might have come from Cord's arrogant personality. Was it Kennedy's old friendship with Cord's new wife . . . . a woman whose questioning style of thinking and upper-class poise matched his own . . . . or simply a rivalry between two equals? The two men actually had much in common. They were from moneyed East Coast families, were well educated, and had war wounds and medals for heroism. And both already seemed headed for national prominence.

Seemingly on a collision course with ironic destiny, Jack and Cord were featured in a July 1947 issue of *Glamour* featured an article entitled "Wise American Leadership Is the Hope of World," by Vera Michaels Dean. Immediately following the article was a portrait gallery of ten men, entitled "Young Men Who Care," ranked in the order of importance. The first two, ironically pictured side by side, were none other than Cord Meyer Jr. and John F, Kennedy.[104]

Just before the convention ended in May, Cord received word that his twin brother, Quentin, had been killed in the American assault on Okinawa, in one of the final battles of the war. Cord initially held the unlikely hope that his brother was the subject of a false report, as he himself had been, but his death was soon confirmed. Quentin had been hit by a Japanese grenade while trying to retrieve a wounded soldier from the line of fire. After Cord heard the news, a passage from E.E. Cummings poem, "Buffalo Bill's," kept running through his mind: "and what I want to know is / how do you like your blue-eyed boy / Mister Death." For days he was despondent, unable to express himself, even to Mary. He wrote later, "My wife tried to comfort me. I could do nothing for a time but sit in my hotel room."[105]

Cord was permitted to leave the convention to mourn. He and Mary boarded a train to a ranch in Montana owned by the Meyer family. They spent a month having the vacation honeymoon they missed in San Francisco. Mary was already pregnant. Their first child, who they would name Quentin, would be born in January, just a few days shy of nine months after their wedding day. At the ranch, Cord began writing an article for the *Atlantic Monthly* about the UN convention. The piece was twice as long as it was supposed to be. Proofing the article, while on a train back home, Mary took out paragraphs and Cord promptly replaced them. They argued on intellectual ground, turf on which Cord would never give an inch. Cord responded to her criticism of his work with derision. The man who had shared his ideals with her and listened to her with what she thought were understanding and respect just a few short months ago had vanished. He was so vehement and cutting that at one point she burst into tears and disappeared into the ladies room.[106]

As they changed trains in Chicago, they froze in their tracks in shocked disbelief as they heard a young newsboy hawking the latest headline. A single atom bomb had demolished the entire Japanese city of Hiroshima. The newlywed's earlier arguments on the train suddenly seemed petty, as the implications of the new weapon hit them. Cord had decided that the UN convention was already obsolete, since the gathering had occurred without the delegation's knowledge of the new weapon of mass destruction.

In the fall of 1945 Cord and Mary, now six months pregnant, moved to Cambridge. There Mary took a job as an editor for the *Atlantic Monthly* and, at the suggestion of her editor, Cord began writing a book about the affect of the atom bomb on world affairs, to be called *Peace or Anarchy*. He continued to read and write poetry, study Shakespeare, and jot down ideas for novels, plays, and short stories. The Harvard Society of Fellows awarded him a three year grant to write. Through the fellowship, he was invited to dine weekly with prominent intellectuals and men of letters who came to the university, among them Alfred Whitehead, Vladimir Nabokov, and T.S. Eliot.

Cord and Mary spent the Thanksgiving holiday together with his parents; it was the first Meyer family holiday without Quentin, and death was never far from Cord's ever darkening thoughts. Mary saw his darkness and tried to cheer him up. It was a task that she was familiar with, having served her father in the same capacity. Although *they* were bringing a child into the world, it was already becoming her job to attend to practicalities and live in the present, because she had married a man who would not or could not do that.

At the dawn of the cold war, Cord's book, *Peace or Anarchy*, and his vocalizing that the UN play a major authoritative roll toward world peace, made him, in the eyes of many, an international visionary. In late 1945, Cord was invited to a conference, organized by Supreme Court Justice Owen J. Roberts and Wall Street lawyer Grenville Clark, on the affects of the atom bomb and the possibility of a world government. Clark continued to promote a world government into the 1960's, long after Cord had moved on to less idealistic pursuits.

Mary and Cord settled into a pattern of married life typical of post-war couples their age: They followed his career, and Mary committed herself to his dream and bore their children. Mary, determined not to be as distant as her own mother had been, did not turn her babies over to a nanny. In the fall of '47, Mary gave birth to a second child, Michael. Mary bore the brunt of the child care during the early years, because Cord was often traveling.

Mary still managed the occasional companionship of old friends from Vassar, who were also married and mothering babies. They would meet at playgrounds with their toddlers and exchange anecdotes of family life, yet there was little time or inclination for talk of higher questions or of art. Still, Mary managed to keep her hand in creative pursuits, taking morning classes at the Art Students League in midtown New York for one month sessions in 1948 and 1949. The students were encouraged to invent freely, by examining underlying organic structure, focusing on pure color, space, and volume.

In the spring of '47, Cord was elected president of the world Federalist movement. The five American world federalist organizations had coalesced into one, United World Federalists. Cord and Mary moved to New York so he could take charge. Under his leadership, the membership quickly doubled. The group attracted prominent citizens; among them were Cass Canfield, Norman Cousins, Justice William O. Douglas, Harris Wofford, who one day would be associate director of the Peace Corps, and future California Senator Alan Cranston. Albert Einstein allowed his name to be used on the organization's letterhead, and personally solicited funds for the association.

With their combined trusts and occasional money from Mary's mother, Ruth, the couple could afford to do without much of a salary. In addition, they lived rent free in Ruth's Park Avenue apartment. There, they had a minimum services housekeeper, with Mary, for the most part, cooking and caring for her children on her own. As time would afford, she would do volunteer work at Cord's headquarters.[107] As a result, her picture appeared next to him in the September issue of *Mademoiselle*, the couple posed on a staircase looking down at the camera over the ornate wooden banister. The article was titled "Steps to Peace", with the article saying, "Mary and Cord Meyer work together toward world peace through the United World Federation." The article noted that, "Mary, a Vassar graduate, was assistant fiction editor for the *Atlantic Monthly*. Now she writes for UWF and directs volunteer workers, having put aside, for the moment, her free-lance writing."[108]

Cord's radical pacifism was born of his war experience. Deep down, he knew federalism was a shout in the wind, but the memory of his wounding and dead comrades compelled him to carry on. No one besides Mary saw Cord's despair. His associates saw him a tireless worker, but no matter how heavy his schedule, Mary never intervened, and as his most ardent volunteer, she was as good with people as he was with ideas.

As the movement grew, so did Cord's stature and demand as a speaker. He was a natural public speaker who never used notes, and always spoke with a cigarette between his fingers. Amongst female college students, he became something of a sex symbol, since the *Glamour* article, titled "Ten Men Who Care".[109]

However, as his stature grew, Cord the idealist was beginning to crumble. A few short years earlier he had expressed himself on the war vividly and with great emotion. Now, in his writing on federalism and the atomic bomb, he became pedantic; writing for the sake of imparting knowledge. He had gone straight into the public fray with a message he was becoming unsure of himself. He had become weary and torn by doubts about whether world federalism could ever work. He began having internal dialogues about whether his life's true path lay in public service or in the private sector; he admitted that his peculiar temptation was not money but notoriety and fame.

He continued to write notes for essays that condemned both war and the American system. In considering a piece on the reasons for low morale of soldiers, he noted, "The answer lies in the complete degeneracy of our way of life. Profits and material comfort never were a cause worth dying for and never will be, and they knew it . . . . the troops have been lied to for far too long."[110]

The world federalist movement reached its apex in 1948, and by the end of the 40's Cord was disillusioned with the world government movement. The postwar world was not going to unite but was already disintegrating into two blocs, East and West, Communist and capitalist. The Soviet Union and East European allies established a Council for Mutual Economic Assistance, and NATO was being formed, as China became a Communist republic. With battle lines drawn, the nation's brightest men gravitated toward Washington in a chance to prove their mettle in this new undeclared "cold" war. Comparing himself to them, Cord suddenly felt left behind.

In an attempt to rediscover and redefine himself, Cord and Mary moved back to Cambridge late fall of 1949, where he resumed his Harvard fellowship. During his years on the road as a celebrity, his relationship with Mary and the kids had suffered greatly. Mary was seven-months pregnant with her third at this point, and he barely knew his first two children.

Back in Cambridge, Mary began to take art classes at the Cambridge School of Design, happy again cultivating her own passion. However, changing diapers and now minding three sons, the time she could spare for painting was always contingent upon the children's needs. Guilt was the monster at the door, as she would retreat into solitary with her art. Along with guilt was memory of her mother, remote, writing at her desk behind closed doors during Mary's childhood.[111]

Cord made a last ditch effort to get out of the public eye and find some quiet work in academia; also while contacting friends in government service. A job with the State Department would put him where the action was, however, he quickly found that his high profile with the world federalists made him too controversial for the State Department. By March of 1951 he turned down a teaching fellowship with the University of Chicago. He was already on to a more exciting job in Washington D.C.[112]

In the 1940's and 50's the American intelligence service was almost a graduate extension of the Yale secret societies. Its officers were socially, as well as professionally, connected to one another. Forty-two members of Cord's class of 1943 went into the Office of Strategic Services . . . . the World War II organization that preceded the CIA. Nine went on to the CIA.[113] It was a pair of Yale graduates that eventually "masterminded" the Bay of Pigs disaster.

In 1951, thanks to a meeting between his father and CIA director Allen Dulles on the Hamptons summer social circuit, Cord interviewed for a CIA position. Using his early postwar commitment to fighting Communism, he won over director Dulles, and was offered a job so classified Dulles could not discuss it with him in any detail until he was hired and sworn-in. He considered the position over the weekend, and decided to accept the intriguing offer. Later Cord cites as the deciding factor Allen Dulles's "cosmopolitan, sophisticated" manner, translating into the fact that Dulles belonged to all the private clubs Cord Meyer's family also called their own.[114]

The philosophy that accompanied Cord from world federalism into the CIA did not require any great alteration. The cold warriors truly believed *themselves* to represent the more rational and higher authority to which small sovereign countries in danger of falling into Communism would want to *submit* for their own good. Cord's politics were never really revolutionary, he had chaffed in the roll of outside agitator. He believed, as he had preached to college students in 1947, that civil rebellion against tyranny had been made obsolete by the atomic bomb. The era of military revolt was clearly over for him.[115]

Cold war policy architect George Kennan called the atom bomb the most serious danger in the history of mankind, and the most serious insult to God.[116] As the United States and Russia began to face off over the corpse of Germany, their differing visions of postwar Europe set the stage for the coming decades of brinkmanship. Nuclear tension set in almost before the ink was dry on agreements ending World War II. Just two months after Hiroshima, the American Joint Chiefs of Staff had drawn up a secret plan that outlined the destruction of twenty of the largest Soviet cities with atomic bombs.[117] In 1951, President Truman for the first time authorized the Defense Department to take control over the nuclear and nonnuclear components of nine "Fat Man" bombs. [118] The cold war had commenced.

In 1952, President Eisenhower accurately defined the national mood, "The problem of America today is to take that straight road down the middle."[119]

A war-tired people wanted normalcy, but an ominous array of weapons of mass destruction were being planned, built, and tested around the world. United States and Russia raced to design the best, fastest means possible to deliver their bombs. In addition, it was an era of mind control with publications such as best selling *The Manchurian Candidate*. Competing ideologies, capitalism and Communism, depended on the belief system of individuals; if beliefs could be altered, then there would be no need to use the new doomsday technologies.

At the start of a new decade Mary and Cord were thirty and married five years. Mary continued to be his occasional editor, which he needed, but in frustration he would criticize her attempts to write fiction. They began a dangerous little psychological game straight out of *Who's Afraid of Virginia Woolf?* She would read his private journal, and write her comments on his thoughts in the margins. In 1950, Cord wrote in his rambling style, "There is a special pleasure in the objectivity that one wins by imaginative creation of other characters to face the dilemma that one is tired of wrestling with in terms of personal decision and action." In the margin, in red ink, in her left leaning rounded script, Mary underlined the words "tired of wrestling" and wrote, "You are a romantic! We're in the same bed honey . . . . Pooped!" Left with the raising of three boys under the age of five while Cord was off all day with his books, she knew the literal meaning of "tired of wrestling." [120]

In Cambridge, Mary and Cord had settled into a pattern of behavior that increased her domestic responsibilities even further. Cord played the absentminded professor, and Mary the practical, efficient mother.

When they moved into their rented house, the landlord asked Mary whether her husband intended to put up any paintings and would need to hammer nails into the wall. Mary laughed hysterically, saying that her husband had no idea of how to use a hammer. On another occasion, the couple and their sons were driving in the Massachusetts countryside when they experienced a flat tire. As Cord told the story later, he got out of the car and wandered around a bit wondering what to do. When he turned around, Mary was on the ground replacing the tire . . . . to his masculine humiliation. [121]

As the pressure on Mary to be the practical one in the household grew, Cord's melancholy and self-absorption began to look self pitying and ridiculous to her. At one point he wrote of the growing Korean conflict, "I am without hope, and yet I live day-to-day as before." Mary, again, commented in the margins, "When you say you are without hope you imply that you thought humans were not that way . . . . humans." [122]

Their banter soon reached a bitter crescendo. In June 1951, Cord wrote a four-stanza poem entitled "Proper Tribute." The verse appeared as a thinly disguised expression of his feelings about Mary, and he surely meant her to take it as such when she discovered it.

Proper Tribute

Beauty, she wears carelessly like a bright gown,
Lent for a night by some indulgent guest
And is dismissed to find that no man loves
Only herself in that brief garment dressed.

She lacks the arrogance that lovely women
Habitually show. In genuine surprise
She smiles at praise that would-be lovers bring
As proper tribute to her transient eyes.

And in a way she's right. She never earned
With work or special talent her tall grace,
Her full breasts or her abundant hair.
By luck with genes she won her dreaming face.

But now that beauty's hers by nature's gift,
She must its burden bear and growing learn
What damage in poor hearts her passing wrecks.
And how for her desire sleepless burns.

Mary took the bait. She added a closing stanza of mocking self-criticism that was also a warning to be husband: If he considered her passive or dormant, she would prove him wrong.

She bites her fingernails,
Fails to shave under her arms,

Has no sense of humor,
And is totally a mundane soul.
But silence fires the imagination of the spiritually timid.[123]

Whatever marital dissatisfaction seethed between Cord and Mary, they had three children under the age of five and a life together. The postwar ethic was all about family and home, however, beneath that placid surface, nuclear inhalation was a submerged threat. The Soviets had tested their first atom bomb in 1949, and a year later the United States raised the ante with a hydrogen bomb. Scared families were building household bomb shelters, while the children practiced duck-and-cover drills at school. Air raid sirens wailed in weekly tests across the land. Mary Pinchot-Meyer and her husband, Cord, entered the new decade doing what those who could afford it did: They put the best possible face on it and moved to the suburbs. But McLean, Virginia, was not just any suburb. It was across the Potomac River from Washington, D.C., the strategic command center of the cold war. [124]

CHAPTER 5

CIA Wife

Their wives were oblivious to their business, other than knowing their husbands worked for the CIA. Each woman might be called a cleared wife . . . women the agency believed to be a safe repository for any secrets her husband might utter in his sleep. The CIA denies it had a formal clearing process for wives, but some of the wives believed there was background checks performed on them. [125] Two early CIA documents have been released mentioning Mary. One is completely redacted, with a single sentence at the end left visible: "There is no indication that Mary P-Meyer was ever a member of this organization." The other is a one-paragraph "summary" of her life statistics, titled "A Review of the Appropriate Office of Security Files Relating to Mary Pinchot Meyer." The two documents *seem* acknowledgements that, early on, Mary had been investigated and *perhaps* vetted by the CIA to some degree.

The Freedom of Information Act process is very slow and there is no reason to believe the CIA doesn't have more documents mentioning Mary Pinchot-Meyer. FOIA requests can take up to five years. Although President Clinton issued an executive order in 1995 declaring that records over twenty-five years old will be presumed to be declassified beginning in 2000, little has been accomplished in beginning the process at the CIA. [126]

Cleared or not, the men in the early years of the CIA didn't confide in their wives anyway, and the women learned early on not to ask questions.

Cord had signed up with the CIA to do psychological and intellectual battle with the Communists, a task that his involvement in the federalist movement had left him well qualified. It was the one-world utopians, pacifists, and left-leaning intellectuals that the CIA was most concerned. The goal was to control potential rebels, to co-opt the leadership, and to steer the left generally toward capitalistic ideals, not those of Communism. To achieve this, the CIA hired informants, channeled money into organizations, and eventually created its own front groups.

For Cord and his colleagues, the early battles were in labor and political organizations in European countries, especially France and Italy, where Communists seemed to be gaining political power. Before long, Cord was infiltrating groups ranging from those in South and Central America to organizations in Asia. Eventually funding was directed toward American student and labor groups in the domestic battle against Communism. [127]

Within the CIA, Cord soon came to be regarded as creative and inspired, with CIA officer Dick Bissell referring to him as "the creative genius behind covert operations". [128] He oversaw the secret funding of intellectual groups, most famously the National Student Association, but also the Congress for Cultural Freedom, which engaged some of the best minds in the Western world by providing forums for discussion throughout the 1950s and '60s. The CCF published a respected journal, *Encounter*, and involved such intellectuals as poet Stephen Splender and critic Frank Kermode, who for years were unaware of the source of their money. [129]

Cord's connections with liberal intellectuals and groups served him well, however, his infiltration of domestic groups was eventually exposed. In 1967, a student member of the National Student Association revealed in *Ramparts* that the association had been accepting funds from the CIA for years. The news prompted larger American newspapers to investigate and expose a vast picture of the CIA front groups, including dummy foundations set up to channel millions of dollars in federal money.

CIA money was also disseminated domestically to trade unions throughout the United States, including the Communications Workers of America, the American Newspaper Guild, and the National Education Association, which used it to fight Communism in their own ranks and abroad. [130]

The CIA grew exponentially from its small clubby beginnings in a pair of old and neglected buildings in downtown Washington, to their posh headquarters in Langley. They went from a relatively small budget to one astronomical in size, as they gained a clandestine foothold in back alleys from Saigon to Teheran. They had to stop Communism and the threat of global destruction at any and all costs, and the men who ran the CIA gained tremendous power but never faced election or many constitutional restrictions. Typical of men who take themselves far too seriously, the only graffiti on the headquarter restroom walls was, "$E=mc^2$",[131] and a biblical self righteous one of "And ye shall know the truth and the truth shall make you free".

The secrecy of the CIA was justified in the early years because the cold warriors believed the KGB could infiltrate their organization; an unease compounded by the McCarthy era being in full swing. The IOD, International Organization Division, where Cord worked, was regarded by some hawks as a nest of liberals who might be a little soft on the Reds. However, Cord was never as close to the left as he was accused of being in 1953.

In the second year with the agency, Cord was summoned to a meeting by his superior, Richard Helms. After offering Cord a cigarette, Helms said that he had a "rough one" to discuss with him. The FBI had been investigating Cord and came up with a list of charges that questioned his fitness for government service, based on his political associations. The charges were made by anonymous accusers, but had to be taken very seriously; Eisenhower had decreed that it was up to the accused government employee to offer a defense against such charges. Cord flew into a rage. His enemies would remain forever invisible. He would have to resign until cleared.

The charges were a hash of his youthful associations and acquaintances. He was accused of consorting with one of his Harvard professors, a man who, in fact, was a leftist. His world federalist past and his AVC work were suspect, even though he had been fighting the Communists. His association with publisher Cass Canfield and poet Richard Wilbur, both progressives, but neither of whom was known to be a Communist, were part of the charges. And the charges claimed that his wife, Mary Pinchot-Meyer, had once belonged to the American Labor Party . . . . a relic from her wartime days as a New York journalist. [132]

Mary was unable to take the charges seriously. The notion that her buttoned-down, ambitious husband with his craft antagonism toward the Reds was actually a leftist must have struck her as ludicrous. But the accusations seared him.

Three months after the ordeal began, a secret court of CIA executives, including Allen Dulles, convened to consider Cord's case. It ended abruptly on Thanksgiving Day when Dulles called Cord to tell him his employment had been found consistent with national security.

For beating a suspicious-association charge during the McCarthy era, Cord became a legendary figure within the CIA. He had faced down an attack from the provincial, isolationist right and remained standing. The fact that he survived made him a hero, not only of his generation but, of his class.

But the ordeal was the final stroke in the demolition of the one-world idealist. Cord's patriotism would never again be questioned. His devotion to the American system and to the CIA eventually went beyond the pale. As the years passed, he grew more and more vociferously anti-Communist. At dinners and cocktail parties he buttonholed people who disagreed with him, jabbing a finger into their chests and arguing with loudness and ferocity that even his friends found rude.[133]

When Cord and Mary moved to the Washington area, the city still had its small-town southern flavor. The Virginia suburbs, where the Meyer family lived, were just being carved out of red farmland, and the locals still spoke in thick backcountry accents. However, the capital city itself was two distinctly separate cities. Although the majority of DC capital, in the late 1950s, was black, the black and white communities were strictly segregated. In neighboring Georgetown, the wide green divide of Rock Creek Park separated the blacks from the white community; it would remain in that ugly state until the late 1960s. In the meantime, Washington race relations remained a silent problem. As the influx of unskilled black migrants increased, the fervor of urban renewal was destroying black ghettos causing a critical black housing crisis. Jobs were completely segregated. Even by the late fifties, not one Washington finance institution or bank employed a black teller, clerk, or secretary except the black-owned Industrial Bank of Washington. Most blacks worked as janitors, elevator operators, servants and day laborers. [134]

The political and social center of Washington was Georgetown and the internationalists who moved there to wage the cold war. The warriors had little interest in the urban affairs of the capital city; their sights were set on China, Russia, and beyond. In theory, they endorsed civil rights, but in practice the only contact those of Georgetown had with black people was with the domestics who traveled from the D.C. ghettos to work in their houses.

The friendships between Georgetown neighbors were, for the most part, men who ran the State Department, the intelligence service, and the national media. The men knew when and how to use the media and nurtured friendships in the journalism field. Of course, Cord nurtured his own stable of journalists: Walter Pincus of the *Washington Post*, W.C. Baggs of the *Miami News*, Charles Bartlett of the *Chattanooga Times*, and foreign affairs free-lance writer Herb Gold. Cord's ties to academia also served him when he needed favors from publishers and journalists. He and *Time* writer C.D Jackson, together, recruited Steinem. According to his journal, Cord dined in the Paris home of American novelist James Jones.[135]

Cord and Mary lived across the Potomac from Georgetown in a comfortable, sprawling eighteenth-century white wood house locally known as Langley Commons, with a wraparound porch and an acre of sloping lawn only a few miles from the site of what was to be the new CIA permanent headquarters at Langley.

Langley Commons had served as an inn and post office and later as a makeshift hospital that housed wounded Civil War soldiers. Redecorating her house, Mary discovered some writing beneath wallpaper on one of the bedroom walls; it turned out that in several rooms wounded soldiers had scrawled their names and other graffiti with lead bullets. The house and lawn were shaded by a towering oak reputedly five hundred years old, with the balance of the sprawling grounds being a garden showplace. The house, with its four bedrooms and two wings, had more than enough space for the entire family and occasional visiting guests. It was a functional house, and Cord would sometimes joke about its simplicity.

The Meyer family lived, as did most other upper-middle-class families, in Washington. Cord's concerns were global and his responsibilities vast. Mary's life was by contrast limited and domestic. She became a devoted gardener. She took art classes and painted in a two-story shed she had turned into a studio on the grounds of the house. While Cord lived in the world of James Bond and Hemingway, Mary admired the work of artist Helen Frankenthaler and had a casual artist's style of dress and manner. Women who knew Mary then recall that she "came alive" when discussing art and literature. One of her favorite quotes was from French writer Paul Claudel: "Order is the light of reason but disorder is the delight of reason."

As a couple, they were politically progressive. Cord disliked religious institutions, and none of their three sons were baptized, a fact that angered Cord's side of the family but wouldn't have bothered Ruth Pinchot. Being nonreligious was common among the cold warriors in the Meyers' set, for whom secular humanism and Freud had replaced the creeds of their parents. Years later, many of their children, including Mary's sons, turned toward both institutional and nontraditional religions as a source of comfort and security.

They had a black live-in maid who did housework and some cooking in order to give Mary time to work on her art. Mary's painting was important to Cord, and he encouraged it. When they entertained, Mary usually cooked. Cord's innate argumentativeness was tempered by Mary's presence. Cord would almost always start an argument after dinner, but Mary would always make a joke about it, and everyone around the table would end up laughing. Mary lightened Cord and had an agreeable effect on him, but sometimes even she could not divert him, embarrassing her by the scenes he created. Cord could easily disrupt any dinner party.[136]

The soft side of Cord was that he was genuinely interested in his wife, and she returned the affection. One could see that he loved her enormously. A family friend recalled meeting Cord and Mary together at a photo exhibit at the National Gallery, followed by dinner at a Georgetown restaurant. "The photographs were very artistic, and when we came out of the museum, Cord only cared about Mary's opinion. He kept asking which one she liked the best and why." [137]

But Mary's own creativity was tempered by the mundane of carpools and trips to the dentist. The questing girl had been largely replaced by the capable wife, breezy, efficient, and in command. Like many other Vassar graduates from the class of 1942, she channeled her education and craving for drama into solid, family-oriented work, became trustee of her sons' private day school, and ferried children to and from school and after-school recreation.

Mary was not representative of Georgetown appearance and dress code . . . . she was clearly different. She did not get her hair set every week and she wore loose, comfortable clothes. Her short blond hair was always windblown, and she wore little makeup. "She always looked as though she had just come from a tennis match or a walk in the woods," said Eleanor Peck. "She had the most extraordinary vivid coloring . . . . rosy cheeks and brilliant blue eyes," said Elizabeth Eisenstein. Other women hired gardeners and ordered up a hundred yellow daffodils when the mood struck them. Mary loved gardening herself, working the earth with hands and spade. She carried on the Pinchot women's Milford habit of nude sun bathing to McLean. She was comfortable with her body even as she grew older. On summer afternoons she casually doffed her clothes and found a sunny spot on the lawn upon which to read. One of the Meyer son's young friends, Peter Janney, never forgot stumbling upon her in a moment that vastly expanded his nine-year-old understanding of the opposite sex. Her reaction to discovery by the gaping little boy was nonchalant. Peter Janney was permanently altered. [138] "I saw her lying there naked on her stomach and she sort of turned, smiled, and greeted me. She never said anything to me. She put me very at ease, but I was so embarrassed and awestruck. She was like the softest human creature I had ever experienced. She was exquisitely soft." [139]

The most prominent Washington wives knew how to host dinner parties, their primary political function during the 1950s. At these dinners, the cold war was always present, and although things went on as usual at the parties, there was always a great undercurrent of tension. Often after dinner on warm nights, the male guests—spooks, diplomats, and American and British statesman—gathered in the garden and talked quietly of the cold war. The women deliberately stayed ignorant of the details, for fear of hearing something that they would inadvertently, or simply out of ignorance, repeat at a later date.

Mary went to these parties when she had to. Although polite, she never became close to hostesses such as Polly Wisner. "I found her utterly charming. She had every single grace you'd hope your daughter to have," Polly said. "She was—a very old fashioned expression—the epitome of a ladylike person. She had very good manners, a lovely voice, and great charm." Polly found Mary reserved and possessing "a great deal of dignity. She wasn't the type who would share her woes." [140]

Mary and Cord were closer friends with some of the younger couples in Washington, including Mary's Vassar classmates and their husbands. The Vassar women felt a tiny disdain for the Washington hostesses, whose avocation seemed to them rather frivolous. Among the Vassar women was Mary's sister, Tony, then married to lawyer Steuart Pittman, who became assistant secretary of defense under Kennedy. Journalists were also part of the clique, including James Truitt, Bill Bradlee, and Phil Graham.

Even amongst the cliquish Vassar women, Mary's social distance was unusual. She was simply not interested in the social whirl. Save her sister Tony, many of her old friends were put off by her Washington persona, so much more remote than theirs. "She was aloof and not interested in keeping the friendships nurtured," Eleanor Lanahan said, looking back. "She made my mother feel a bit too social. Unlike my mother who was very gregarious, Mary had a grip on herself. She was poised." [141]

CIA wife Joan Bross recalled that Mary always recoiled at the prospect of making appearances at official dinner parties. "She always asked me how many people were going to be there. She was a serious thinker and hated small talk. She always preferred big question such as, 'Why are we here?'" [142]

Mary did not really embrace the Washington social scene until she became a frequent guest at the Kennedy White House. Rather than make small talk with diplomats, the younger families spent a great deal of leisure time together. There were evening get-togethers, and weekend camping trips. On Saturday mornings in the fall, the adults got together and played touch football in the park north of Georgetown, while the children biked around the sidelines. Mary, still athletic, was always enthusiastically involved in these games. On hot summer nights, pool parties were loud, drunken affairs, filled with laughter, dancing, the sound of ice cubes in glasses, and people being pushed into the pool. Mary loved to dance. Her favorite tune at the time was "Chantilly Lace," a snappy tune about a girl with "a pretty face, ponytail hanging down, a giggle in her talk, and a wiggle in her walk." One admirer recalled that "the song suited her fine and she knew it."

The boisterous partying of their parents left strong, sometimes bitter memories with the children. Peter Janney became a psychologist outside Boston. His memories of the 1950s Georgetown remained infused with his childhood emotional reactions to the conflicting habits of heavy drinking and cool denial among adults. "It was a circus," he recalled. "They used to drink so much." He blamed his father's premature death to the abuse of alcohol and nicotine. [143]

Heavy drinking was an occupational hazard for CIA men during the cold war. The capacity to hold one's liquor was deemed important because the Soviets were such notorious big drinkers and American agents in direct contact with them were forced to try to keep up. "Everybody had a drinking problem," CIA psychologist John Gittinger said. "It wasn't regarded as a problem because most of them felt they could handle it. There was much more concern about tooth work or operations because they had the feeling that being under anesthetic would cause you to betray secrets." [144]

Cord's boss, Jim Angleton, was one of the heavy drinkers. Jim's problems with alcohol and his penchant for imagining elaborate Communist plots were balanced by his charm, intellect and a deep familiarity with the arts, and his habit of quoting Homer and Ezra Pound. His intellect and his interest in literature and art, as well as his penchant for drinking, were matched by Cord who became his fast friend.

The revelation that Jim's British friend Kim Philby worked undercover for Moscow would escalate his suspicions of the Soviets to a level that some within the CIA have compared to clinical paranoia. "That defection was a shattering experience for Angleton," Gittinger recalled. "From that period on he was the most suspicious man in the agency. My own feeling is the emotional wreckage of that close friendship made him mistrust everybody and changed his life from that point on." [145]

Angleton's paranoia driven "monster plot" theory was that the Russian intelligence service had already successfully invaded the Western intelligence agencies with moles. Russian ex-spy Oleg Kalugin wrote a book about his thirty years in the KGB in which he said that Angleton was considered by the KGB to be a sort of unintentional mole because of his extreme paranoia. But Angleton was a favorite of CIA chief Allen Dulles, in part because of the gossip about Washington he was able to share. Angleton was known to have bugged a dinner party given by a Treasury Departments official's wife simply to amuse Dulles with captured conversation.[146] In years to come, Angleton would boast that he had placed a wiretap on Mary's phone and bugs throughout her house, but it is unclear why he would have done it or whether he shared the information gleaned with anyone at the CIA.

As chief of counterintelligence, Angleton was both "scholarly and cold-blooded." He authorized the writing of a handbook on interrogation that endorsed torture by various psychological and physical means, including chemical, electric, and medical procedures. The CIA was fully aware that the detentions and methods were illegal, and the handbook instructed its users to notify headquarters when it was being employed. The torture handbook remained in use until 1985.[147] Of course, since then, the G.W. Bush administration reinstated the still illegal torturing, including water-boarding, into their interrogation repertoire.

Mary's sons and nephews idolized Angleton. "He had more depth than any man I'd ever met," said one of Tony Bradlee's children. "He has extraordinary sensitivity and an interest in people." He was so nurturing of his friends that one of his nicknames was "mother". [148]

The Truitts were another socially prominent and artistically inclined Washington couple. Like Mary, Anne was a thoughtful, cultivated young mother and artist. She had been born into a Maryland family that lived on inherited wealth, and the family fortune had been devastated by the Depression. Also, like Mary's father, Anne's father had had problems with depression and alcohol. Trained in psychology at Bryn Mawr, she painted and sculptured and showed her work in exhibitions in Washington.

Anne's husband, Truitt, was a journalist with *Newsweek* and later the *Washington Post*. He had a reputation as a serious intellectual and writer—and as a big drinker. People who knew him had differing recollections. "Truitt was incredibly smart and incredibly well read," David Middleton recalled.[149] Kary Fischer found him porcine and boorish. Serious Washington artists respected him, for he had a sophisticated and broad taste in art. He was eccentric and experimental; keeping an alligator in his bathtub of his Georgetown house for a time. He eventually came to regard Mary as his spiritual sister, probably because her experimental nature was so like his own. He often indulged his alcohol habit with his friend and colleague Phil Graham, the publisher of the *Washington Post*. Like Ben Bradlee, Truitt was a blue blood who also had the Rat Pack style down. Charming and genteel, cigarette always in hand, he gave the impression of a man of street savviness.

Anne was more severe in her presentation. She dressed in the style of Georgia O'Keeffe and favored southwestern attire, shawls, and large silver rings. Her relationship with Mary was complicated. She adored and admired her, but she was eventually hurt by her husband's attention to her friend. She was in her thirties when she and James had two daughters, Alexandra, and Mary (named after Mary Meyer), and a son, Sam. Years later, Anne wrote with revulsion of her role in the fifties-style marriage: "I had actually *eaten food earned by someone else.* I tasted something slimy and rotten in my mouth and felt kind of servitude utterly familiar. With the force of a blow to my solar plexus, I felt clearly the position I had placed myself in: I had been beholden to James for the food in my mouth; I had been frightened that he would not put it there or in the mouths of my children; I had felt as if I owed him something because he kept me and the children—and that's the truth, I had awed him." [150]

The Angletons, Truitts, and Meyers grew very close, and they were especially bound together by their mutual interest in art and culture. They were deeply involved in Washington's relatively limited cultural life. One journalist who was assigned to cover the cultural scene in the late 1950s, derisively called the whole city "a cultural backwater".

Mary was amongst a small group of Washington artists working in abstract expressionist style through art classes at the American University. "Artists felt that they were on the brink of something new then and it was very exciting," recalled Ben Summerford, an instructor at the American University who taught and befriended Mary. [151] The preeminent art critic of the decade, the man whom Mary and her friends in the Washington art world looked for notice and approbation, was Clement Greenberg. These Washington artists in the early part of the decade would have paid dearly for Greenberg's attention. Before long, some of them did get it.

At home in Langley Commons, Mary worked on canvas in her studio shed, experimenting in abstract style, when she had time, but art clearly came second to children. Although Cord traveled and worked late hours, when the family was together they were "gregarious", recalled one relative. The Meyers spent a lot of time in Milford during summers. Mary fished for trout with the boys in the private stream at Grey Towers.

The three boys, all blond and blue eyed, were growing up with distinctly different personalities. The eldest, Quentin, was smart, adventurous, and, more than the other boys, argumentative like his father. Michael, the middle child, was not as intellectually quick as his two brothers, but he was an extremely popular boy, the kind of kid who drew other children to him. "Everybody wanted to be on Michael's team," recalled Peter Janney, who used to belong to what the kids called "the Mike Meyer gang." Physically and emotionally, Michael took after his mother far more than his father. The baby, Mark, was shy, soft spoken, and more lyrical and artistic than the other two. He was so shy when he was little that he often wouldn't speak for himself when in a group of people: he would whisper in Mary's ear, and she would speak for him. "We called Mary Mark's spokesman," said one relative.

It was rare for Mary and other CIA wives to know what their men were doing by day. A man who just attended a meeting plotting the assassination of Castro came home at the end of the day, mixed a drink, ate dinner, and tried to interact with the family. There was little give-and-take conversation in the households. Husbands opened their souls to their martinis instead of their wives.

The cold war years were trying times for CIA wives, but also thrilling because of the women's proximity to power. Husbands did sometimes bring their wives along on trips abroad, which set them apart from other housewives of the fifties. But the strains were enormous, often destroying family life. They were loyal women, who got the short end of the stick. The men were decent enough, but their nerves were shot; lives depended on them. It was more than just a career.[152]

Another source of stress relief was sex. In Mary's set, extramarital affairs were under way in the 1950s. Her friend Anne Truitt was having an affair with a married artist. Even Cord would be accused of being "incurably promiscuous." [153] He was among those who earned a reputation as a married man on the make. Several women who first met Mary and Cord at their McLean home in the early fifties, were hit upon by Cord within days of their meeting. One woman, who became close friends of Mary, never forgot her first impression of the couple. "When I first met Mary and Cord, she was literally a golden girl. She had on these clothes that looked like wheat, and her hair was gold. Cord called me at my hotel the next day, and asked to come see me. I was shocked. She was so beautiful, and it was disgusting. He thought he was such an operator. I can't imagine she didn't care."[154] But if Mary was bothered, she didn't let it show. In any case, when Cord began attending parties and Georgetown dinners without Mary, it quickly became clear to their friends that there were problems in the Meyer marriage.

During the busy summer of 1954, the family's golden retriever was hit and killed by a car on the curve of highway in front of their house. The dog's death worried Cord, and he mentioned to his colleagues at the CIA he was afraid the same thing might happen to one of his children, and he repeatedly warned the boys to stay off the road. He even considered moving the family, but the house was comfortable and it suited them.

In the summer of 1954 Mary and Tony, feeling left behind by their husbands and a little dissatisfied, set off on a European adventure. Their mother, still holding out for female individuality and independence in the midst of the baby boom, urged her daughters to cut loose. Ruth gave each of them a round-trip ticket on a ship to Europe and a thousand dollars in pocket money—a large sum in 1954. "Ruth felt her daughters were being buried under their bourgeois marriages, and she wanted to give them a break," said one relative. [155]

The sisters went first to France, then to Rome, where their blond hair and American breeziness attracted the attention of Italian men. Mary was delighted.

Every sense was enlivened by the smells and sounds of Europe, the aroma of coffee, pipe tobacco and fish, the gurgling of fountains, the old women in black with their rosaries and baskets, the food and wine. They wrapped their hair in scarves, donned slacks, and drove, top down, to the Mediterranean. Children, husbands, responsibilities, and past fell away in the breeze.

In Positana they came across an Italian gadabout who spent his summer days on a yacht with his dog, and had an affinity for attractive American women. He had a wealthy wife, a good Catholic woman who indulged her husband and stayed home in Florence with his children. He also painted; Mary was enchanted. The record of the man's name has been conveniently lost, but various descriptions of who he was survived. James Truitt told journalists he was an Italian count. [156]

For the first time in ten years Mary was away from Cord and the children. Her half-sister, Rosamund, had committed suicide, when she was the same age as Mary was now, thirty-four. Perhaps it was this fact, or perhaps it would have happened in Washington anyway. But she left Tony and joined the Italian on his yacht, where, for several days, they sunbathed and swam nude. The Italian was a carefree uninhibited man in his late thirties, prematurely gray and a little on the paunchy side. His soft spoken, non-aggressive gentleness differed greatly from the possessiveness and cold indifference of Cord. There was certainly no serious talk of love or commitment. Much later, she would tell Cord the brief affair of that summer as being sexually satisfying, but nothing more. [157]

After Italy and a lusty *arrivederci* to the Italian, Mary moved on to Paris with Tony. There they connected with the American expatriate crowd, a party going group of journalists, diplomats, and spooks who loved nothing more than wild women and all night parties. Journalist Blair Clark, who met the sisters in Paris, later referred to their Paris adventure as "the husband dumping trip." In Paris, Mary ran into an old Vassar chum, Anne Chamberlin, who was working for *Life* magazine; while Tony fell head over heels in love with Ben Bradlee. He knew the sisters from Washington, and invited them out one Saturday afternoon to a rented nineteenth century estate, the Château Boissy St. Leger. The shabby and romantic château had sixty-seven bedrooms, and a ballroom where Bradlee and other Americans routinely hosted three-day parties for British, French, and American friends.

Blair Clark remembers that particular party as a "Fitzgerald-ish sort of affair" attended by Americans and Europeans with lots of leisure time on their hands. In the ballroom, a couple of dozen people drank, jitterbugged, and danced the mambo—the latest American dance craze.

After the party, Mary returned to Paris while Tony spent the night talking to Ben Bradlee in a café. The following day, Ben and Tony realized they were in love, but Tony would not consummate the affair until after she consulted with her sister. That done, the couple spent the next day and night in *bel endroit*, "exploring", as Ben Bradlee put it in his memoir, "hungers that weren't there just days before, and satisfying them with gentle passion, new to me." [158]

Back in Washington, Tony's life changed almost immediately, as she confessed to her husband, Steuart Pittman, Assistant Secretary of Defense under Kennedy, that she had fallen in love with another man. She moved into the basement of the massive house on Rhode Island Avenue owned by her aunt Cornelia Pinchot, now a widowed Washington hostess active in women's politics and atomic disarmament. Throughout the late forties and early fifties, her two nieces and their husbands had been frequent visitors to the grand old brick mansion.

After the summer of 1954, Cord and Mary maintained their marriage on unstable ground. When Mary had returned from Europe, Cord felt his wife had changed. She had probably recovered some of her old way of looking at life, and she was beginning to feel a sense of creative possibilities. Her independent spirit was buttressed by her time away, and she delved more seriously into modern art.

As they had in their younger days, Cord and Mary continued to shadow-box in and through their writing. Mary wrote a short story about a married woman rejuvenated after a brief love affair. Cord criticized it as "sophomoric in emotion and badly written," although he suspected it was autobiographical and so attacked it even more mercilessly. Mary began her practice of confiding in her friends, the Truitts. She told them about the affair with the Italian, and thought her secret was safe with them. In fact, James Truitt was keeping copious notes on Mary, a woman whom he found both desirable and fascinating.

In February of 1955, Cord traveled alone to Europe. In Lisbon, he became filled with self—pity for the direction his life had taken, and regret over his growing estrangement from his wife. "I'm changing not necessarily for the better," he wrote in his journal. ". . . I thought of how through rude indifference and selfish carelessness I had so alienated Mary, and of how all my days would be as lonely and melancholy as this one, if she left me."[159]

Later that same year, the Meyers got new next-door neighbors. The young senator from Massachusetts, John F. Kennedy, and his wife, Jackie, bought Hickory Hill, the estate down the road from Langley Commons. It was close enough that the family dogs wandered over and had to be returned. Soon, Mary befriended the senator's dark-haired wife, ten years younger than she. One of the things that the two women had in common was that Jackie Kennedy and her sister Lee Radziwell, had also taken parent-financed, sisters-only trip to Europe together, theirs in 1951, and had written about it.[160]

Having an intensely ambitious husband, angling for a national nomination in 1956, Jackie was often left alone. He was also incorrigible in his skirt-chasing. He and a congressional pal had rented an apartment in downtown Washington, where they partied with groups of secretaries.[161] John still had no use for Cord Meyer, and Cord would not support him politically, even though both men were Democrats. But the men's wives shared an appreciation of the outdoors, and frequently went for walks together. Like Mary, Jackie had attended Vassar and had an interest in the arts.

The summer of 1955, Tony married Ben Bradlee in Paris. The Meyers attended the wedding, and then traveled to Italy. In Positana, the Italian was still anchored in the harbor, living on his yacht with an American college girl. Mary lithely introduced Cord to her Italian friend, and then arranged for them all to move onto the boat and sail together to Capri and Naples. Cord, unaware of his wife's relationship with the man, agreed. Later, Cord remembered only that the man whom he called "the Italian" "painted casually, and not very well", and had a dog who kept him company on the boat along with a "sequence of women he successively entertained." [162]

After Cord returned home, Mary stayed in Italy on the pretext that she was going to remain with Tony in Paris. In fact, as Tony and Ben Bradlee both knew, Mary was actually staying in Italy to return to her lover. She sailed with him alone for ten days, living as the recently departed American girl had, in a bikini on the azure water. While the first summer with the Italian had been a mere sexual fling, this time was different. Mary was smitten with him as he with her.[163]

As they floated together, they spun out a dream future, with the Italian immigrating to Canada, where he could divorce his wife.[164] Then they would fling their pasts, like gloves or champagne glasses, take her three children, and move to a farm in Idaho, Montana, Colorado, or California, where they would paint together and experience the freedom of their fondest imaginings. Filled with the romance of these possibilities, and inspired by her younger sister's daring change in her life, Mary returned to McLean with her heart set on changing her own course.

A year passed, and Mary did nothing but plan and paint and quietly try to figure out an appropriate time and place to tell Cord of her secret desire. Her new neighbor at Hickory Hill made a failed bid for the vice presidential nomination at the 1956 convention. Many Democrats thought the handsome young senator was the real winner at the convention, not Adlai Stevenson. Back in McLean, after the convention, Jackie gave birth by cesarean section to a still-born child, and was so ill a priest was called to give last rites. During the ordeal, Kennedy was away in France, recovering his confidence by sailing the Mediterranean with one of his congressional friends, Florida senator George Smathers, and a boatload of young female beauties. One of the blondes always referred to herself in the third person as "pooh". Kennedy had to be persuaded to return to his wife three days after the stillbirth. [165]

The night of her thirty-sixth birthday, October 14, 1956, Mary and Cord went out to a cocktail party for drinks and then to dinner with their friends, Anne and James Truitt. The Truitts were aware of Mary's plans with the Italian, and they had encouraged her to talk to Cord instead of merely treating him coolly, and leaving him to wonder what was wrong. That night after they returned home, she confronted him with the truth, and laid out her plans to move to a western farm with the children and her lover. She loved the Italian and planned to make a life with him, she said.

Cord had suspected something was up. He was not about to accede to her wishes. The idea that an Italian gigolo would give his sons a good home on a western farm was preposterous. "My only hope is to allow time to dull her feelings and to permit reality to show through her presently grand illusion," he wrote in his journal, adding bitterly: "one cannot argue with someone who is in love with love."[166]

That fall, Cord waited for her to get over the Italian and Mary waited for her husband to concede that their life together was finished. With the boys all in school, Mary painted at home as the garden slowly lost its color, the oak leaves turned yellow, and the walnuts in their green skins fell to the earth. The first frost came. Cord and Mary kept up the appearance for the boys. But Cord no longer went to art openings with Mary, and his CIA friends ceased inviting her to come to the parties and dinners for visiting dignitaries, since she was clearly no longer interested. Mary wrote long letters to the Italian and spent hours in her studio, mixing paint with daydreams and swathing it all on canvas. Her awakening was beginning.[167]

Television had become part of most American homes, and was about to utterly change politics. In the fall of 1956, the young Senator Kennedy traveled to twenty-six states campaigning for the Stevenson ticket, all the while garnering adulation for himself. Female college students crowded Kennedy's car and screamed for him. "We love you on TV," they shouted. "You're better than Elvis Presley."[168]

In spite of the television rage, the Cord Meyer family was not yet among the households with one of the new devices. The Meyers boys, like their peers, loved television, and when they were visiting friends, they preferred sitting in front of the tube to playing outside. The Cords were visiting the Janney family on their patio one warm summer night, when shy little Mark suddenly blurted out: "Goddamn, let's go inside and watch TV!" The two families doubled over in laughter at the profane outburst from the normally silent child.[169]

In the fall of 1956, Mary's two oldest boys, Quintin, now eleven, and Michael, nine, had gotten in the habit of going to a neighbor's house after school to watch the westerns that were on TV in the afternoons. They were so captivated by the glowing box, that they began coming home later and later each afternoon. Mary had recently laid down the law: if they didn't stop arriving home late for dinner every day, there would be no more television at the neighbors' for them.[170]

She might have been in her little shed painting on the late afternoon of December 18, when tragedy struck. Or she might have been putting dinner on the table, for she never left all of the cooking and table setting to the maid, especially this time of the year. The holidays had arrived, and the festive air had infected her boys with the usual excitement of Christmas. A decorated tree was up in the living room, and the presents were hidden away in closets. The children were bursting with anticipation for the big day. The family always made much of Christmas, and Cord and Mary and the two grandmothers usually showered the three boys with a mountain of presents.

The light faded early that time of year. Across the curving road at the neighbors' house, Michael and Quintin reluctantly tore themselves away from the television at the last minute and ran for home, trying to make it back to dinner on time in compliance with their mother's recent order. The two boys crossed the road at a point on the asphalt curve near where their golden retriever had been killed a few years before. The road was not lit and there was no shoulder. No driver could see the Meyer house, high on a hill behind trees, much less anticipate that a nine year-old boy would suddenly run into the headlight beams. The man who hit Michael stopped and began screaming helplessly; this sound and Quintin's horrified cries called Mary to the roadside. She ran the twenty some yards downhill to the road, and long before she arrived at Michael's side, she could see her son, a crumpled heap on the side of the road. When the ambulance arrived, Michael was already dead and Mary, no doubt in shock herself, was consoling the hysterical man who had been driving.

No one can be sure what went through her mind in those minutes, but parents who have lost children say that the deep grief sets in only later, when the shock has worn off and the reality of the child's forever empty bed settles in. Waiting for the ambulance to come for her lifeless son, Mary might have retreated into the reflexes honed by her upbringing, and the challenges she had faced in her life. She was there to be leaned on, even in her life's worst hour.

In the next few days, when family friends came to visit, she hugged their children to her, offered them comfort, and sent them up to her dead son's bedroom to select one of his toys to remember him by. She and Cord distributed Michael's Christmas toys to his friend in the Mike Meyer gang. Little Mark, only six and deeply shy, did not fully understand what had happened to his older brother. People who visited Mary in those days saw a woman in deep grief, still trying to behave with her youngest boy as though the world were safe and his little life would continue undisturbed. In the years to come, Mary would grow even closer to and more protective of Mark.

They buried Michael in Milford, just before Christmas in 1956, under the stars and the trees near Amos, the grandfather he never met. Cord traveled alone with the coffin on the train for five hours from Washington to Milford. Mary traveled with Mark. Quintin, so like his father in intensity, could not attend.

A relic of Michael's short life remains on the shelves at Grey Towers in the form of a favorite book, *My Secret Garden*. Inside it he had written his name, Michael Pinchot Meyer, in a childish hand. Later, the surviving sons asked if they could divide up the rest of his toys.

It would take a few months for Cord to realize the boy's death was not going to bring his wife back to him. Mary, tumbling into a depression, might have found refuge in thinking about the Italian and their dream farm out west. But there was now a great weight pulling her away from all that folly, and that frolic.[171]

CHAPTER 6

Experimentation

"It took about a half hour to hit. And it came suddenly and irresistibly. Tumbling and spinning soft fibrous avenues of light that were emitted from some central point. Merged with its pulsing ray I could look out and see the entire cosmic drama. Past and future, all forms, all structures, all organisms, all events were television productions pulsing out from the central eye."

Timothy Leary,

Describing his first LSD experience in spring, 1962

Alone in the gallery, in October 1957, Mary felt at home in the small Jefferson Place Gallery, amongst the paintings of fellow art students, personal friends, and her own, as well as other art professors-instructors. The gallery served as both a sanctuary and a connection to other people while she weathered the worst of her grief.

At the end of the 1950s, depression was a plague in Mary's group. Three of her, male friends would kill themselves by the same means, with guns to the head. Others from her group, men and women, would be hospitalized for breakdowns. Alcohol and a stiff upper lip were the most common self treatment. With a family history of emotional instability, the tragedies of her son's death, and the disintegration of her marriage, Mary was not immune to despair and depression, which was little discussed and rarely diagnosed.[172] She had begun regular psychoanalysis with Washington's premier analyst, a man who was also seeing many other prominent Georgetowners.[173] But no amount of analysis could have erased the sense of powerlessness emanating from that one instant on the roadside in McLean, and nothing she did could have shut off, for long, the running cinema of her son's death. In her worst moments, the preceding summers in Italy must have seemed brief flickers of light in a personal history of recurrent darkness: Cord's pessimism, her father's decision that death was preferable to life, Rosamund's suicide. "She was lost, and she needed something to be attached to, and the gallery and art gave her that," said artist Kenneth Noland, who eventually became a lover.[174]

In the silence of the gallery, Mary began her fight to regain and keep possession of herself. It was a struggle, her close friends observed in her, for the remainder of her life. Art and eventually her self-discipline became antidotes for despair. In those early years, she sat near the gallery door on weekdays and waited for the occasional visitor. She was "helping out," recalled gallery director Alice Denney.[175] When visitors came to the gallery they found a woman eager to assist in a quiet, well-mannered way, but with red-rimmed eyes and a fragility that made them cautious and tender around her. In a small town that was Washington, D.C., everyone knew what had happened and no one knew quite what to say. They all agreed it would take time: and perhaps no one ever got over the loss of a child, not really.

During the long hours when there were no visitors inside the gallery, Mary would simply absorb the silence. Surrounded by abstract art that made language irrelevant, she was in retreat. The past had snapped free like a cable in a high wind. Cord was gone, Michael was gone, and the Italian was gone. She was cut loose and starting over.

The previous spring, with bad memories in every room, Cord and Mary sold Langley Commons and purchased together a townhouse on Thirty-Fourth Street, in the heart of Georgetown. The townhouse was actually a house, maisonette, and garage, all connected, with four bedrooms, one for each boy and Mary, plus a guest room. It is unclear whether Cord intended to live there with Mary; he never did.

For a time after Michael's death, Cord hoped his marriage might be renewed by the shared sorrow. But he soon realized Mary would never come around. He felt that she needed a weak and needy man to lean on her, and he simply had grown too strong.[176] "This Italian, who has sworn to change his old ways and seek a new simplicity on a western farm, is a challenge to her protective instinct; she knows he needs her," he wrote.[177]

But that proved to be wrong. Late that summer the Italian broke it off, to Mary's great humiliation. By then the Meyer marriage was beyond repair, reconciliation with Cord was impossible. That fall, less than a year after their son's death, Cord agreed to leave the family house and begin the separation required for a divorce. The night he left, he admitted to himself that his manipulative behavior might have been improper. "The worst thing was my own tendency to take perverse pleasure in exercising my power over Mary, and it's better for me and everybody around me to have done with that."[178] He moved into an apartment in Georgetown where, on his first night alone, he tried to believe his solitude would resurrect his old writing talents.

The summer of 1958, Mary went to Nevada for a stay at Gus Bundy's divorce ranch. She filed for divorce in June in Washoe County, Nevada, and spent a few months in the Nevada desert waiting for it to become official. The Truitts, on their way to Jim's posting to the San Francisco Newsweek bureau, stopped in Nevada and the three of them sunned together by the pool. Anne was already pregnant with her middle daughter, whom she would name after Mary.

In her divorce petition, her lawyers alleged "extreme cruelty, mental in nature, which seriously injured her health, destroyed her happiness, rendered further cohabitation unendurable, and compelled the parties to separate."[179] Cord was furious with the legal description, since he believed himself to be in the right and perhaps the injured party. But he agreed in principle to the divorce, and someone had to be at fault in order to proceed. Cord borrowed Tony's ex-husband Steuart Pittman's domestic separation agreement to design his own.[180] These men had an emotional bond; if they had just kept their wives home that summer in 1954, their families might still be intact.

Cord's Nevada attorney accepted the decision of the divorce judge, but specifically denied any guilt of mental cruelty. At Mary's request, the divorce records were sealed.[181] Any evidence of the "perverse pleasure" Cord admitted he had taken in "exercising my power" over her would never be made public.

Mary's friends had always surmised that she had a "terribly rough" time with Cord.[182] The divorce was acrimonious and the children were used as weapons. "Cord was bitter. He said that Mary was an unfit mother and compared her to the whore of Babylon," recalled one friend of both.[183] Mary would be able to survive on her own on Pinchot money from her mother, but the children would tie her to Cord forever. Cord gave her physical custody of Quintin and Mark, now twelve and eight, but demanded and won the right to control their education. Mary never spoke ill of Cord, but there were acrimonious fights in private.

Cord quickly took advantage of his control over the boys' schooling and moved them from Georgetown Day School, with its racial integration and relatively liberal principles, to the more staid and exclusive St. Albans

School, an Episcopal institution more like Cord's own prep school. In spite of complaints from both boys, they were eventually sent to boarding school.[184]

The couple's post-divorce relationships with other people were fodder for future battles between Cord and Mary over the possible affect on their sons. Cord's ongoing relationship with Kennedy White House young aide, Jill Cowen, was singled out by Mary in the margin of Cord's personal journal that she somehow managed to have access to.[185]

It was while volunteering at the gallery that Mary embarked on a romance with Ken Noland. He was a boyish, sandy haired southerner with a passion for abstract art, jazz, women, and baseball, not always in that order. Shortly after his eighteenth birthday he had enlisted, and spent four years, in the air force. He trained as a glider pilot but never got close to combat. With the aid of the GI Bill, he attended Black Mountain College, a tiny mecca for American artists in the middle of the North Carolina mountains. Many of the people in Noland's hometown of Asheville, just twenty miles from the college, thought of the school as a "behavioral sink of communism and free love."[186] The college never had more than ninety students and sometime as few as twelve, but it was extremely influential. A number of seminal American artists taught there, including musician John Cage, painters William de Kooning and Franz Kline, and dancer Merce Cunningham. Noland studied under European émigré Ilya Bolotowsky, an abstract artist.

With his southern accent and deliberate "hick" persona, Noland could not have been more different than Cord, at least on the surface. Part of his charm was that he did not naturally fit into Mary's more refined circle. Through her relationship with him, she learned a new style of abstract painting and observed his deeply serious attitude toward it. He was also financially insecure. When he started seeing Mary, he was in the middle of a divorce involving three children, and drove a cab to supplement his income. Beneath the surface, Noland was another deeply ambitious man. He was working with single-minded determination to carve out his own style in the competitive art world.

Outside the Georgetown group of artistic wives and powerful husbands, to which Mary belonged, the American government was hardly supportive of modern art, nor was the Washington community any more appreciative than the rest of America. The state department, in 1946, cancelled a European exhibition of works by seventy-nine modern American artists after members of Congress complained that it was "Communistic." President Truman pronounced that "so-called modern art is merely the vaporings of half-baked, lazy people."[187] But by the late 1950s, modern art was not regarded as subversive; rather it was just silly, or at best baffling. This general sentiment only drew the Washington abstract artists closer together. The art scene was so tight that at gallery openings "you'd know nine out of ten people at every one", said artist Ed Kelley, a former student of Noland.[188]

Artists congregated around two poles; one was American University and Robert Gates, the other was Catholic University and Kenneth Noland. The artists formed a little Bohemian subculture, and Mary could enter it whenever she felt inclined, always able to return to Georgetown. The artists went to parties at each other's houses, visited each other's studios, and drank beer together at the Bayou in Georgetown, the Showboat Lounge or the Bohemian caverns, legendary Washington jazz clubs on the black side of town that attracted such jazz greats as Thelonious Monk and Miles Davis.

When Mary threw herself wholly into the art scene after her separation from Cord, Ken Noland was already the leader of the group of Washington artists working in the color field style, one in which the importance of color superseded form; this group became known as the Washington Color School. Eventually Noland became a success, followed later by lesser-known artists who had studied with him, including Mary and her friend Anne Truitt.

The Color School artists worked in the capital of the cold war in a style that elevated cool and rejected sentimentality. Like the spies among them, they communicated in a secret language comprehensible to others in their group but cryptic to outsiders. Their work could be seen as metaphors for American cold-war society, cool and serene on the surface, in turmoil below. The United States was booming economically, and efficient gadgets kept the burgeoning suburbs running smoothly. General Eisenhower was in charge, cleaving to the middle road. Yet there were bomb shelters, duck-and-cover exercises, and experimental aircraft being mistaken for UFOs, all referring to a mortal danger that never really showed itself. The secret signs of menace were visible only to men such as Cord Meyer, the cold warriors who believed they were all that stood between the United States and the dread disasters of Communist takeover and nuclear war. To them, the surface was never all it seemed.

At the height of their romance in the late 1950s, Noland often spent the night with Mary at her house in Georgetown, where she had a canopy over her bed and Spode china tucked away in the closet. Mary tended her garden religiously, and before long it was a profusion of flowers, which she proudly showed visitors. She also grew her own salad greens. In those years Mary became close to Noland's young daughter, Lynn, a blue-eyed child with silky long blond hair. Even after the relationship with Noland ended, Mary sometimes went to the fence near little Lynn's school and watched her from afar at recess.[189] Lynn Noland regarded Mary as a woman "in command of herself and always in charge," in contrast to some of the other adults in her life.[190] For two years Noland and his three children summered at the Gray Towers estate in Milford with Mary and her boys. This raised eyebrows in Georgetown and enraged Cord, who only referred to Noland as the young painter, because he was four years younger than Mary.

Mary's sons adapted differently to the new arrangement. Her youngest son, Mark, was easier going and accepting, and remained close to Noland for years. Quentin was more hostile toward Noland's presence and troubled by his parents' divorce.

Mary was a very involved but not overbearing mother. She encouraged and supported her sons in team sports. Still athletic herself, she played a powerful game of tennis with Quentin, passing on to him what Amos had taught her. With Cord in charge of their schooling, they were sent to camp in the summer, and went away to boarding school in New England as soon as they reached their teens.

Noland thought Mary tended to be a distracted, perfunctory mother, but women saw a devoted, almost over protective woman.[191] "Children were a big part of her life," said Barbara Higgins, a poet and longtime friend. "She was very, very motherly, but she didn't come on as 'Mom'." After Michael's death, Mary grew closer to Mark and was very watchful about him. Noland remembers that Mary was frustrated with Quentin's unhappiness, for she didn't like brooding people. She disciplined him in her own way. Once when he stole money from a friend, she drove him back to the friend's house and made him personally hand the money back and apologize.

She took pride in the fact that she had sent her sons to the integrated, progressive Georgetown Day School before Cord moved them to St. Albans. She had a flowering peach tree planted at the Day School in Michael's memory. "She was very concerned that they have black friends," recalled friend Helen Husted, who lived at Mary's Georgetown house briefly in the early 1960s, after Helen's hospitalization for depression.[192] One of Mark's best friends was, in fact, a black schoolmate from Georgetown Day, Brent Oldham, who recalls many afternoons at play inside Mary's Georgetown home. Yet such was her fear for the boys' physical safety that, when Quentin wanted to go down to the Mall in August of 1963 to witness Martin Luther King Jr.'s march on Washington, Mary forbade him.

During her Georgetown years, Mary supported herself on a combination of Cord's alimony, income from her trust fund, and her mother's money. "Her mother really held the purse strings," Noland recalled.[193] If Mary ever had cash flow troubles, no one saw the signs. She did not have to work for a living, although she was never lavish in her lifestyle, either. She had a housekeeper two days a week, and on those days she'd say she liked to live rich. She liked a breakfast of eggs and bacon brought to her in bed, and a salad waiting for her when she came home in the afternoon.

Personally, Mary was better off; she was no longer married to Cord and immersed in a daily battle of wills with him. But Noland was as self-absorbed and dismissive in his way as her ex-husband had been. He was so much so, he acted as if Mary's painting was of no importance . . . . it was clearly all about him.

Indeed, the work of women in Noland's contemporary-art milieu was all but invisible. The women who got noticed owed such attention to their painter husbands or other significant male in their lives. The Washington artists trying to become noticed in New York were all working in an extremely defined style, and there was not room for them all to succeed. Noland recognized the competition, and some of his contemporaries have suggested he might have felt threatened by Mary showing ever increasing ability. If so, she still had a long way to go.[194] Mary "had an instinct" for her art but had begun following it too late in her life, said curator Alice Denney.[195] But Mary was a dedicated novice with a very strong will and she knew the right people and moved in their circles. Mary's friends believed that she was on the right track. She was disciplined about her work, and seemed to idolize the lifestyle of artists she admired. "There was nothing phony about Mary. She didn't pose as an artist," said one Georgetown friend, who grew close to Mary in the early 1960s. "She was earnestly engaged in art. I thought she went overboard sometimes because I personally don't think artists are all that fascinating. But for her, like so many others, they were romantic figures."[196]

To Kary Fischer, Mary's art was part of her effort to overcome emotional turbulence. Self discipline was her balm. She tried to work on her painting a certain number of hours a day, and she took long daily walks on the towpath to force herself into a routine. "She was not at peace," Fischer recalled. "There was a lot of turmoil beneath the calm surface. She tried hard to keep possession of herself, and although she didn't acknowledge it, art was sort of a therapy for her. She saw art as a way into herself."[197]

The discipline paid off, and Mary's art eventually was noticed, with several of her paintings were selected to be part of a Pan American Union show that toured Central and South America. Artist Sam Gilliam, whose work was also in the exhibit, met Mary at the opening. "Her language was the same as every other strong abstract artist. There was a sense of concentration on the idea of painting and what was new. She pointed out to me that she was unable to recognize whether my painting was oil or acrylic. I said I had a way of flattening oil so it looked acrylic and she said, 'You should be given credit for that.' "[198]

In 1954, Clement Greenberg chose a Noland painting and a Morris Louis painting for an exhibition, and by 1959 he was showing Noland's work regularly. The two men had a close personal and working relationship. Noland occasionally brought Mary with him when he visited Greenberg in New York. The Greenbergs visited Ken at Mary's Georgetown house, and spent weekends at Gray Towers. In both places the Greenbergs were impressed by Mary's style, her country ease, and the "tattiness" of her house, which Greenberg's wife, Jenny, thought seemed "just perfect." Jenny, herself not an artist, never thought of Mary as a painter. She was the very attractive woman on Ken's arm, tweedy and casual. Jenny was so impressed with a beige wide-wale corduroy trench coat Mary wore, that she went out and bought one for herself and wore it for years. She remembered Mary as vibrant but, in the manner of the times, very deferential toward men. "She was all there, but like many of the women of her day, she would pay more attention toward men. I think she wanted to learn from my husband. If a man and a woman were talking, she'd listen to the man."[199]

Noland was impressed by Mary's spirit and body, not her art. To him she was lissome, graceful, and feminine. "She was refined, very soft-appearing and soft voice, and delicate and mannered in the way privileged women sometimes are." Noland said. "That was kind of the style in Washington at the time, Ivy League, a certain kind of humor, lots of catch phrases and things." She also had, Noland discovered, a strong will. "She did whatever she wanted to do," he recalled.[200] She was dedicated to adventure, and was searching for something or someone to set her right again after the death of Michael, and the divorce, and she was more than willing to try something new. When he suggested they both go to see a Reichian therapist in Philadelphia, she agreed.

Their romance was very passionate, at least in the beginning. "Noland was absolutely crazy about Mary," Jenny Greenberg remembered.[201] "They really were attached," recalled Elizabeth Eisenstein. "That was quite an intense affair."[202] Noland was physically and emotionally captivated. Mary occasionally talked about her son's death, and her sadness had a magnetic affect on him. "There was attraction, empathy and sympathy," he said. "It's natural to feel that in people, whether you know the nature of the wound or not. You could sense it in her, the deep sadness."[203]

But she was not an easy woman for Noland . . . . or many of the men of her generation . . . . to be with. He thought she did what she wanted to do, at a time when men were accustomed to women doing what men wanted to do. Noland's daughter remembered Mary as always "being in charge," not a very popular feminine trait then. For her part, she found Noland attractive. She also enjoyed the access he had to the New York art world.

Although Anne Truitt and Mary were profoundly different, it is possible to gauge Mary's artistic direction by looking at the life and art of her friend. Anne Truitt's art was intricately connected to her relationship with Mary and Ken. Her husband, James, was one of the first journalists to write about the Color School; some artists believed he had coined the name. Anne's personality differed greatly from Mary's. Where Mary was expansive, Anne was obsessively introspective, and where Mary could be reckless, Truitt was fastidious and took herself very seriously. But the two women's artistic lives were entwined. In one of the three books she had published about her work as an artist, Truitt dates her art epiphany, as it were, to a weekend in New York with Mary in November 1961, during which they visited an exhibit of work by Barnett Newman and Al Reinhardt at the Guggenheim Museum; the exhibit changed her view of art. "For once in my life, enough space and color," she wrote. "That night we slept at Mary's mother's Park Avenue apartment, where I was too stimulated to sleep, and at some point during the wee hours I decided exactly what *I* wanted to make. The tip of balance from the physical to the conceptual in art had set me to thinking about my life in a whole new way. What did I know? What did I love?"[204]

That epiphany led her to carve out a place for herself through the 1970s and 80s as a minor artist whose work was exhibited occasionally and purchased by a few regional museums.

Anne and James Truitt were divorced in 1971. In one journal, Anne lamented the effect of World War II on the men of her generation and, by extension, on women such as herself. She wrote of the "subtle sorrow" experienced by these women and especially the loneliness felt in their relationships with the men who had fought in the war. "Confronted by the probability of their own deaths, it seemed to me that many of the most percipient men of my generation killed off those parts of themselves that were most vulnerable to pain, and thus lost forever a delicacy of feeling on which intimacy depends. To a less tragic extent, we women also had to harden ourselves with them."[205]

Unlike Anne Truitt, after her own divorce, Mary did not abandon hope of finding happiness with a man of her generation. On the contrary, she was sometimes irresponsible in her relationships with them. An unnamed source, a close friend, simply said of her behavior with men that "she was bad", and consequently hurt people. Some of her wildness may have been a reaction against Cord's infidelities. And perhaps, having been hurt deeply herself by her own failed marriage and the death of her son, she rebelled by inflicting emotional pain. The full extent of her affairs with men, married or single, was simply unofficial Washington gossip most likely exaggerated.

She told Noland that after her divorce, and before her long affair with him, she had dated a teacher at her son's school and a television journalist. Several friends said that she had an affair with Jim Truitt, her best friend's husband, and that Anne learned of the relationship only after Mary's death. Jim Truitt was openly entranced by Mary and came to think of her as his spiritual twin, someone he believed he could communicate with even after death.

Men adored Mary but did not know what to make of her. One anonymous ex-lover rather ungratefully called her a "star-fucker." To some, she was that classic female type, the "collector" of men, a woman who attached herself to men who were rising in politics or the arts in order to gain power herself. But her friends regarded her affairs as something she did for her own fulfillment, not to gain any political or social cachet.[206] "We thought of her as an independent, free spirit in a way, having left Cord and then shacking up with Noland," said one Georgetown friend. "She was not a feminist. She was much too seductive and fond of men. She was very fond of men. I don't think gender entered into her consciousness at all. She didn't have a cause in mind at all."[207]

No feminist. She was no gold-digger, either. Mary was an American aristocrat with Pinchot family funds, money from her mother's family, and alimony from her ex-husband. Firmly ensconced in Georgetown society, she did not need men for social ascension or financial support. But men were her teachers, and they brought her into places women didn't enter on their own, from jazz clubs of black Washington to the Oval Office of the White House. She also genuinely enjoyed their company and attention. She studied them in a way a scientist or a connoisseur would, and became known to her friends as an astute and humorous observer of the meaning behind peculiar male behavior.[208] Anne Truitt described Mary as "an acute judge of masculine character."[209]

One man that assumed the role of teacher and admirer was LSD guru Timothy Leary. In a spring afternoon in 1962, Leary was working in his office at Harvard's psychology department, where for several years he had been conducting tests of hallucinogenic mushrooms on himself and his graduate students. He had just taken his first dose of LSD. He was about to be relieved of his duties by skeptical department heads who thought Leary's experiments were out of control. "I looked up to see a woman leaning against the door jamb, hip tilted provocatively, studying me with a bold stare," Leary wrote in his autobiography. "Flamboyant eyebrows, piercing green-blue eyes, blond hair, and fine boned face. Amused, arrogant, and aristocratic, 'Dr Leary,' she said coolly, 'I've got to talk to you.' She introduced herself as Mary Pinchot.[210]

In retrospect, it was no surprise that Mary introduced herself to Leary using her maiden name. Mary was no doubt aware that he and Cord had had a number of combative encounters when Leary was part of the American Veterans Committee during his graduate days at Cal Berkeley.[211]

By the time Mary had made this first appearance at Leary's Harvard office, her influence in Jack Kennedy's life was already well established. Not simply a visitor to the White House residence when Jackie was away, Mary was seen in the Oval Office regularly. She attended any number of policy meetings at which the president discussed sensitive national security business and sought out her counsel.[212] Mary's close friend Anne Truitt described the importance of their relationship: "He saw she was trustworthy. He could talk to her with pleasure, without having to watch his words."[213]

Leary was a collector of beautiful women. Adventurous models, dancers, heiresses were flocking to the good doctor to offer themselves as subjects for his fabled tests. Often the intimacy of the drug experience led them into emotional and sexual experiments as well. Leary took Mary home with him that first afternoon, where his girlfriend at the time, a Moroccan model who went by the name Malaca, and British LSD guru, Michael Hollingshead, were waiting. The foursome took a low dose of hallucinatory mushrooms. In the middle of the experience, Leary said, Mary gave a lecture on the CIA's interest in using such drugs for brainwashing and interrogation. Leary wrote that even though the four had a "pleasant, conspiratorial feeling of those who are sharing a psychedelic session," he was uneasy with Mary Pinchot: "There was something calculated about Mary, that tough hit you get from people who live in the hard political world."

He further portrayed Mary as a woman in possession of considerable feminine power, someone who had undergone her own personal transformation. Leary wrote that she said that she wanted to learn how to "run an LSD session." She told him that she had already tried LSD herself, but wanted to learn how to administer it properly to "this friend who's a very important man." Leary said that she told him that she and a group of women were planning to get their men high. According to Leary, she said: "Washington is run by men. These men conspiring for power can only be changed by women."[214]

Mary's relationship with Leary continued for the next two years. He said that she periodically dropped in without warning, sometimes called him from a hotel in Boston, and had him up to her room where they shared champagne and discussed the fantastic possibilities offered by what he called "utopiates." She seemed to him the ultimate female insider, a kind of Mata Hari of drugs. At one meeting in a hotel room at the Ritz in Boston, Leary said she told him the CIA had actually started the American Veterans Committee, of which he, like Cord, had been a member. She also told him the CIA had created radical student organizations, and was running them "with deep-cover agents." The latter was eventually revealed to be true. He claimed she then asked him for drugs to take back to Washington, and at that point, Leary decided Mary was wilder than he. "I want to learn to brainwash," he claimed she said, to which he responded, "That doesn't sound very ladylike."[215]

Leary sent her information on how to run an LSD "session" (and presumably drugs, although he never admitted to it). According to him, Mary seemed to know things about the government's tacit approval of his drug testing. "I told you they would let you do anything, if you kept it quiet," she said at one meeting after he was fired from Harvard. Seeing her again in 1963, Leary wrote that he was "struck again by the brittleness this aristocratic woman had picked up from those stern-eyed, business-suited WASPs working for Wild Bill Donovan in Zurich, for Allen Dulles in Washington, for Henry Luce as bureau chiefs." He also said she told about failing to create an LSD factory in Mexico (one of Leary's many schemes), because more drugs were sure to arrive soon. Mary told him, Leary wrote, "I can give you a contact in England. They'll sell you everything you need. And if things go the way I hope, we'll be seeing lots of good drugs produced here at home."[216] If she gave him such a contact, Leary never wrote of it later, and did not recall it in several interviews shortly before his death in 1996.[217]

It is not known how Mary came to experiment with drugs. She might have discovered drugs through the art world, for many expressionists tried to unlock their creativity through LSD, marijuana, and forms of psychological therapy. Another, perhaps more likely avenue for Mary's initiation into drug experimentation was her friend Jim Truitt. Truitt was an eclectic intellectual, a man whose interest in Eastern art might have led him to experiment with the more holistic Eastern religions. In the minds of drug pioneers such as Leary, the tenets and occasional practice of Oriental religions were quite enmeshed with LSD use. In later years, Truitt became interested in the practice of Huichol Indian religion, which involved the use of hallucinogens, and built an alter decorated with psychedelic colors and symbols in his retirement house in Mexico. He also grew peyote on the rooftop of the same house.[218]

As to the other part of Leary's story, as Cord Meyer's wife, Mary could have learned about CIA infiltration of various academic and other organizations. No public documents link Cord to the CIA's extensive drug experiments, but at his level in the hierarchy he would have had access to such information. The CIA's search for mind-control drugs started in the very early part of the cold-war with zombie-like confessions of Soviet dissidents at the purge trials in Eastern Europe. The confessions provoked fear at the CIA and the Pentagon that the Russians had developed some kind of mind-control drug or procedure. A search was begun for drugs that could probe minds for secrets, change personalities, or make agents invulnerable. The cold warriors were influenced by Aldous Huxley's *The Doors of Perception,* about LSD. "He made something totally impossible seem possible," CIA psychologist John Gittinger recalled. The experiments involved academics and researchers in universities across the country.[219]

Over the years, the agency funded thousands of experiments involving drugs, including LSD that promoted sleep, illogical thinking, and hallucinations. The agency also experiments with unconsciousness, hypnosis, paralysis, amnesia, and shock treatments. As early as 1950, a CIA memorandum from the Interrogation Research Section addressed the "problems involved in finding a psychiatrist" who might work on a mind-controlled project. One potential worry was that "his ethics might be such that he might not care to cooperate in certain more revolutionary phases of our project."[220]

The CIA was fascinated by the possibilities inherent in LSD, especially because such a small amount was so powerful. One CIA man told writer John Marks the agency was obsessed with the fact that "a two-suiter suitcase could hold enough LSD to turn on every man, women and child in the United States." Public water supplies were vulnerable, they believed.[221] CIA psychologist John Gittinger recalled that the army was at one point very worried about the drug being administered through air-conditioning systems, and so the CIA researched the possibility of delivering LSD to large groups unwittingly. "You got entirely different reactions when it was administered unwittingly than you did when you knew you were taking it," Gittinger said. "I was engaged in a very foolish project trying to make it an aerosol spray, but we were never able to achieve it."[222] At one point in the early fifties, rumor passed to the CIA that the Swiss company, Sandoz, which then had a monopoly on production of the drug, was about to put twenty-two pounds of it on the open market. Allen Dulles personally authorized the purchase of the entire stock with a quarter of a million dollars delivered by agents in a black bag. It turned out the rumor was not true, but Sandoz agreed to take the money and send weekly shipments of the drug. The CIA funded research into LSD, disguising the source of the funds through false foundations. One of them was based in Georgetown University Hospital. The hundreds of experiments conducted by the CIA used witting and unwitting subjects, and some were conducted under clearly unethical conditions. In one CIA funded experiment, seven men in a Kentucky prison were kept on LSD for seventy-seven days straight. After another experiment, an army officer, who had been unwittingly administered LSD, committed suicide.[223]

Not all the subjects had bad trips, however. In addition to the CIA research, some of the nation's top universities, including Harvard and Stanford, were conducting independent research of their own. Graduate students were some of the first Americans exposed to the drugs. One of them was Ken Kesey, a student in a Stanford writing program. The experience led him to become the original Merry Prankster and preceded his novel *One Flew over the Cuckoo's Nest.* Kesey and many other test subjects later promoted LSD use when the drug became widely available through the black market. Thus the CIA's tests were a catalyst for the acid scene in the 1960s. "No one could enter the world of psychedelics without first passing, unawares, through doors opened by the Agency," John Marks concluded. "It would become a supreme irony that the CIA's enormous search for weapons among drugs—fueled by the fear that spies could, like Dr. Frankenstein, control life with genius and machines—would wind up helping to create the wandering, uncontrolled minds of the counterculture."[224]

In the early sixties, when Mary used it, the people trying LSD still wore suits and ties and got regular haircuts. The drug itself was legal and something of a fad among the intellectual elite. Henry and Clare Booth Luce, publisher and ambassador, were among the establishment types who tried the drug. LSD was also being used as a tool by some psychoanalysts. One patient, who reportedly underwent LSD treatment, was Ethyl Kennedy.[225]

Some CIA officers who officially tested the drug later spoke reverentially of it. But if some CIA officers and friends had formed a 'cell" in Washington to use the drug privately, none have admitted it. And there is no one who has come forward to say that Mary was involved in any organized effort to turn on powerful men.

Mary could very well have arrived at the idea herself, however. She was already a bit contemptuous of Washington, and once she had the LSD experience, she might have decided it could change the world. While other avid LSD users could only daydream about getting it into the water supply of a large city, Mary was connected enough—by 1960, she was an intimate of the president elect of the United States—to promote or disseminate the drug at very high levels.[226]

At this point, Mary was no longer a suburban housewife. She had a circle of Georgetown friends with whom she could sit up with late into the night and discuss art, books and, of course, politics. She was working hard at being a disciplined artist. She was attracted to the new and unconventional, and was thirsty for experience and fame. She had traded in her Plymouth station wagon for a sporty, sleek, Studebaker coup. She wore peasant blouses and blue tights. Although her style was casual, she was a meticulous dresser with a distinctive look. "She could walk into a secondhand dress shop and immediately pick the one perfect dress on the racks," one friend recalled.[227] She liked bright colors and would wear a huge hot-pink flower in the buttonhole of a mango-colored knit suit; she was offbeat.

Mary was attracted to glamour and to dramatic types. She made a point of meeting movie and theatre people who came to town. When Otto Preminger came to Washington to film *Advise and Consent* inside an abandoned mansion north of Georgetown, she met Preminger and managed to get a walk-on part, and persuaded Kary Fischer to come along as an extra.[228]

She paid attention to her emotional health and, through those years, regularly saw a therapist and really worked on herself. But the earlier Reichian therapy left a lasting impression of having to pay attention to what she *felt*. As a result, she was drawn to the kind of physical and emotional experience not commonly available or even desired among Georgetown wives. Pleasure became, if not a mantra, an important objective in her daily life.[229]

When a Georgetown hardware store caught fire, Mary called a friend and begged her to accompany her to watch the fire. The friend reluctantly agreed. When they arrived, the three-story building was in full blaze, and sparks and smoke were flying onto the sidewalk. Mary wanted to get as close as possible to the blaze, but her friend was afraid the building was going to collapse. Mary seemed literally turned on by the sight, the woman recalled. "She kept saying, 'Oooh, I wish it would just explode, don't you?'" Fearing that would in fact happen, the other woman left, leaving an ecstatic Mary laughing with glee as the flames devoured the building. "Mary tended to be courageous and foolhardy. If she wanted to do something crazy, she would just do it," said the friend.[230]

She was intensely interested in danger; perhaps the writer-journalist in her was curious. When a couple she knew were robbed at gunpoint inside their Georgetown home, Mary demanded a minute-by-minute account of what happened. She was fascinated by the idea of experiencing and surviving such an ordeal. Mary's quest for intense experience, and her new interest in pleasure, might have been related to her son's death and her divorce. She did not wear pain on her sleeve, but her sadness was a palpable part of her. Noland attributed her extremes of behavior—her reeling between artistic self-discipline and emotional heedlessness—to the tragedy. He felt that death had "unbalanced" her.[231] Her boy's death "was the point where she broke loose," said her longtime friend David Middleton. "I think she wanted to build another world for herself, which she had been trying to do back in New York in the forties, mixing the social world with the theater, the glamour. She really wanted to be something of her own, rather than being an ornament or spectator."[232]

Women were inspired by her independent spirit. Eleanor McPeck lived in a house across the street from Mary on Thirty-Fourth Street, and they had drinks in Eleanor's garden occasionally. Mary laughed a great deal, McPeck recalled. Although Mary was near her forties then and McPeck in her twenties, McPeck felt that they were about the same age. "Feminism was rarely discussed, but I always thought of her as an independent spirit," McPeck said. "She was quite ahead of her time." McPeck also liked her because, unlike most of the Washington crowd, she didn't seem so embroiled in the politics of the era.[233]

Mary took pride in standing outside the crowd, knowing that she could always slip back in at will. Jackie Kennedy visited her in the afternoons, sometimes bringing her daughter Caroline. She was a favorite at Washington's political and social doyenne Alice Roosevelt Longworth's house, and also a friend and visitor of Joseph Alsop. She attended parties at Bobby Kennedy's, when that family moved into Hickory Hill after JFK and Jackie moved out. Noland recalled leaving one of the Hickory Hill parties in a rage one night, while Mary was urging everyone to strip and jump into the pool.

"She had this sense of *la vie en bohème* and the *outré* and the way out," said her friend, Elizabeth Eisenstein. "She wanted to be on the cutting edge of what was happening." Mary persuaded Eisenstein, a rather conservative university professor, to see the cult film *Mondo Cane*. The film intersperses footage from anthropological documentaries of head-hunting tribes with scenes from Chinese restaurants that serve very fresh dog and scientific film of radiation-sickened animals on Bikini Atoll, all to make a point about human beastliness. Eisenstein recalls being disgusted within the first five minutes and wanting very much to walk out of the theatre. "We came out and I said, 'God, that was repulsive,' and she said, 'That's what it is meant to be,'" Eisenstein recalled. "She was astounded at my reaction. I had given her what she felt was a philistine response."[234]

Otakar 'Kary' Fischer, who married writer Jane O'Reilly in Mary's garden in 1962, nursed a secret love for Mary. Although she spent many hours talking to him at Martin's, a favorite bar in Georgetown, and inside her home, a romance never developed. Fischer was one of the friends who knew Mary, in Georgetown, as a woman who would stay up into the wee hours after black-tie dinners, sipping bourbon and water and talking about art and philosophy. She liked doing the same thing at home. She gave casual dinner parties, serving fried chicken and mashed potatoes, prepared by her maid. She herself always prepared an onion tart appetizer for the gatherings. She was an avid reader of fiction and poetry, and books covered nearly every available wall. Kary Fischer became her older Bob Schwartz, an educated man who adored her, and with whom she could talk about the higher questions. Unlike Noland, Fischer took her seriously. He saw the same side of her personality that Schwartz had. "Politics rather bored her. She was not political, she was aesthetic," Fischer recalled, echoing a man he had never met.[235]

"I think Mary was a serious person," said Marian Schlesinger. "She had philosophical turn of mind, and she was really quite different from most of the women on the scene. I found her most sympathetic and at the same time, elusive and very private, on the periphery and observing the passing show. She was an experimentalist, as shown in her paintings. Nothing she did would surprise me."[236] Kary Fischer called her a "doubting" person, one who questioned everything and would not settle for conventional wisdom. "She was ready to try almost anything," he thought.

After the divorce, Mary and Cord occasionally ran into one another at cultural events. But otherwise, their lives only intersected through their sons. Cord wanted to date other women, but he was having a difficult time. He squired many young Georgetown women but didn't seem to connect with any of them. His dates thought he was too quick to pounce. He drank heavily and began to show the argumentative, confrontational side for which he became known during the Vietnam War; said Marian Schlesinger: "If you were to meet Cord at a cocktail party, you would always find him drunk." One woman who dated him then remembers that he seemed well read but "he loved to hear himself talk."[237]

Mary and Cord and the boys continued to spend Christmases together as a family. The two parents communicated about tuition, about sporting events, and sending the boys to summer camp, to Milford, to Cord's family farm in New Hampshire, and to their prep schools for the winter. Of course they continued to squabble over which parent caused the divorce. Cord's mother had never much liked Mary, who was far too independent for her taste. When Cord told her they were getting divorced, she replied, "I divorced Mary a long time ago."[238] During these years, Jim Angleton came to play a greater role in the Meyer family affairs. He took it upon himself to be a second father to the boys, taking them fishing and checking in on them periodically. Eventually he was overseeing their trusts and intervening for them at their colleges.[239]

Mary's love affair with Ken Noland was fading by 1959. He was moving to New York, and she had her life in Washington with her children and friends. They eventually agreed to see other people; it was an amicable ending.

Mary remained a member in good standing of a social world to which Noland belonged. Her sister, Tony, was married to one of Georgetown's most powerful men. Although the two sisters were very different—Mary's madcap, single lifestyle was the polar opposite of Tony's married life with Ben Bradlee and six children—Mary was close enough to the Bradlees to drop in on them occasionally. With her fresh views and attractive face and figure, she was a welcome addition at the Bradlees' and at other Georgetown social venues. The men in the world of power politics were happy to have a newly single woman in their midst, especially one who might be called a swinger, a woman who could do the Twist, drink and smoke, keep up with the action, and, above all, get the joke.

One evening in the spring of 1959, before their breakup, Mary and Ken dropped in on the Bradlees' for drinks. Ben's friend and Georgetown neighbor, John Kennedy, was also there. The very suave senator from Massachusetts was about to announce he was going to run for president in 1960. Mary and Kennedy greeted each other with familiarity. To Kennedy, Mary was a trusted member of his crowd, someone who got the wink and nod.[240] A few years before, Mary had housed one of his young girlfriends, Pam Turnure, at her house on Thirty-Fourth Street, at Kennedy's request, after the girl had been kicked out of a rooming house for associating with a married man.[241] And as the four of them sat there, drinks in hand, Noland noticed what he called "a stirring" between Mary and Kennedy. She was coming alive in a way Noland remembered from the early days of their affair.

Later that same year, Noland rented a house on Long Island for a few weeks in the summer with his children. Mary drove up north to Provincetown alone, and rented a one-room shack out on the end of a pier and stayed there by herself for two weeks before coming down to join Noland at his rented place. In later years, Noland attached some significance to the fact that Mary's little cottage in Provincetown was within a few nautical miles of Hyannisport. [242] According to a confidential source who spoke to author Leo Damore, they did.

"Jack was distraught over his marriage to Jackie," that source told Damore. "He was miserable. He wanted out in the worst way but he knew it would be political suicide. He visited with Mary because he knew he could talk with her. He trusted her. She was one of the few women he really respected, maybe the only one. Her independence always impressed him—she didn't need or want anything from him.[243]

CHAPTER 7

Mary and Jack

Just as Washington had reluctantly come to accept abstract art, 1963 signaled the advent of pop-art. While abstract art was incomprehensible and therefore not politically offensive, pop-art was clearly ruffling feathers in the nation's capital. Artist Tom Wesselmann featured his "Great American Nude" series at the Washington Gallery of Modern Art "Popular Image" show.[244]

In 1963, long before Andres Serrano's *Piss Christ,* people took offense at a painting, within the Wesselmann "Great American Nude" series, that paired the president of the United States with the silhouetted nude body of a movie star. The stir brought close scrutiny by the museum board who questioned the propriety of the collage. Katharine Graham, Marie Harriman, and other museum trustees called for a personal meeting with gallery curator Alice Denny. They demanded that she remove Tom Wesselmann's *Great American Nude No. 44* from the show.[245] "The board was very conservative, and were simply not prepared for it."[246]

Alice Denny objected, but the board members were the gallery's financial lifeline. Reluctantly, the curator prepared to remove the Wesselmann. But behind the scenes, the matter had come to presidential attention. Mary Pinchot, by then one of the president's occasional lovers and a confidant, told him about the brewing art imbroglio. She described the Wesselmann collage with the Monroe nude with his official portrait. She told him about the ladies of the gallery board, all in a dither. The image of the grande dames, such as Marie Harriman, scrambling to protect his reputation was too funny. The president laughed at the story, and told Mary to tell the little Gallery of Modern Art that he wanted the Wesselmann to hang. The controversial collage stayed in the show.[247]

President John F. Kennedy represented the changing of the guard from the old generals of World War II to the young company officers. He could laugh at the image of the prudish gallery board aghast at the pairing of his image with that of a nude actress. If they only knew. A decorated World War II veteran, Kennedy approached government as he has approached war: as a macho, high stakes game, relieved as often as possible by the sinful delights of shore leave. His image floated along on good looks and a sharp wit. His election elevated a new generation of federal government employees: expensively educated, well-bred, and schooled in the subtle art of cold-war relations. These men kept him and his image on course. They coined a notion of a "New Frontier," which was more than just a political slogan. Kennedy and his administration were going to conquer space, Communists, the jet age, nuclear power. All of the modern culture lay before them, a vast twinkling newness to be explored, staked out, and named for America.[248]

As the first television-age president, Kennedy deftly manipulated the new medium. He institutionalized the televised press conference. Americans were dazzled by this telegenic, witty man, a president who looked like a movie star and who had real guts. The Kennedy style was everything middle America longed for: moneyed but causul, nautical, all salt air, wind, and ease, clad in Ray-Bans and khakis, apparently bounding with good health and wholesomeness. He could express all of that on camera. Author Norman Mailer was awed at the way Kennedy, who looked his full age in person, seemed to drop ten years in front of the camera and microphones and metamorphose into "a movie star, his coloring vivid, his manner rich, his gestures strong and quick." Mailer thought Kennedy "had a dozen faces."[249] Behind the wit and grin, his war record and his vitality had been embellished by some of the best political strategists in the nation, and his intellect was bolstered by the work of his speechwriter Ted Sorensen.

Author Truman Capote, frequent guest at White House dinner parties, recalled of Jackie, "She was sweet, eager, intelligent not quite sure of herself, and hurt—hurt because she knew Jack was banging all those other broads."[250]

The antecedents of Jack's long-standing problem of intimacy with women had a more dynamic dimension than just the imprinting of his childhood. Author Nigel Hamilton's analysis of Jack's mother Rose Kennedy as "a cold, un motherly, and distant woman whose main contribution to Jack's character was his strangely split psyche, leaving him emotionally crippled in his relations with women," was only a part of the equation.[251] Unlike Mary Pinchot, Jack seemed to have had little interest in any sober self-examination, reflection, or understanding. No doubt his experience of abandonment as a child, sustained by the lack of little direct maternal care, aroused a projected vengeful disposition toward the opposite sex: Women were to be used, and then discarded at his whim. Failing any deeper internal investigation, conquering his emptiness—and keeping it at bay—required an infusion of one sexual triumph after another, however momentary the relief. He *had* to have known he had a problem.[252]

Yet whatever infirmities Jack battled, however fragmented and impaired his capacity for genuine intimacy, something kept driving him toward Mary.[253] Many say that social historian Ralph Martin got it right, "One of the women who loved Jack for himself was Mary Pinchot."[254]

Between Kennedy being elected and his being sworn in, his ship of state appeared to be navigated with a steady hand on calm waters. However, by the time he took the oath of office in January 1961, Fidel Castro had signed an economic agreement with the Russians, and the U.S. assets in Cuba had been appropriated by the Communists. Gary Powers, a U2 pilot shot down over the Soviet Union and captured, to the great embarrassment of the U.S. government, was serving a seventy-five year prison sentence in a dank Moscow prison.[255]

Early in his presidential run, Kennedy staked his political future in the missile gap with the Soviet Union. "We are facing a gap on which we are gambling with our survival," he had said for months during campaign stump speeches.[256] Over time, he had implied into the American consciousness that the Russians might actually win an all-out nuclear war or, short of that, threaten America into submission. During the campaign, Eisenhower and Nixon looked weak by comparison. It did not matter that Kennedy was aware, thanks to his privy to classified information, that the missile gap might not in fact exist.[257]He was further assured of American might, when he met with Eisenhower on the eve of his inauguration. He told him that the United States had the edge, in addition to having the invaluable asset in the Polaris nuclear sub patrolling the Soviet coast.[258]

The following morning, poet Robert Frost set the tone for the coming thousand days of international tension in his inaugural poem:

"For John F. Kennedy"

Of a power leading from its strength and pride
O young ambition eager to be tried
Firm in our beliefs without dismay
In any games the nations want to play.

In 1961, any nations that didn't want to play East versus West were in the game anyway. The CIA believed that it was on the top of its game; but Kennedy's more hands-on style and the disastrous Bay of Pigs episode, which he had inherited from Eisenhower, signaled the agency's decline. Attorney General Robert Kennedy saw Cuba as the gateway to Communism in Latin America and became involved early on in discussions with the CIA about what to do. In March of 1961, the CIA continued its attempts to assassinate Castro, a process begun under Eisenhower. Poison intended for Castro was handed off to mobster Johnny Roselli.[259] In April, the Bay of Pigs was launched and failed, with Cuban exiles left waiting for U.S. backup fighter jets that never materialized. The jets never came and the exiles were captured by Castro forces. It was not the first time that the CIA had encouraged a deadly rebellion against Communism only to fail to backup the rebels. In Hungary, thirty-two thousand people had died in 1956 in an anti-Communist uprising encouraged by the CIA in radio broadcasts.[260]

The CIA was not discouraged. On May 30, 1961, Dominican Republic president Rafael Trujillo was assassinated with CIA assistance. He was killed by so called Dominican dissidents supplied with U.S. weapons. All of this transpired as the Kennedys were in route to Paris, via Air Force One, for a summit with Khrushchev in Vienna. As Trujillo lay dead, Kennedy and Charles de Gaulle rode in a convertible limousine up the Champs Élyées to the Tomb of the Unknown Soldier under the Arc de Triomphe.[261] Kennedy's talks with Khrushchev resolved nothing. Worse than the impasse was the fact that Kennedy was proclaimed the loser. In the long plane ride home, Kennedy wanted answered, how many Americans would die in an all-out nuclear exchange with Russia. The Pentagon's answer was about seventy million people.[262] The president spent the remainder of the summer of 1961 dealing with the Berlin crisis and watching the Berlin Wall go up.

*   *   *

It was surely no accident that at the very first White House dinner dance on March 15, 1961, just two months into the Kennedy presidency, Mary was seated next to Jack at the president's table: but the price of admission was that her sister Tony would be seated on Jack's other side, "making the Beautiful People from New York seethe with disbelief," according to Tony's husband Ben Bradlee.[263]

Although Mary had been amongst invited guests to many White House functions, it was in October 1961, just six weeks after the Berlin Wall was erected, that Mary Pinchot-Meyer's name appeared solo for the first time on the White House Secret Service gate log, signed in to see the president in the evening. Jackie, of course, was away with the children in Newport. The handwritten logs kept by the Secret Service recorded the names of all visitors entering the White House, and the person they meant to see.

That night, October 3, at 7:30 P.M., according to the gate log, "Mary Pinchot-Meyers" had an appointment with Evelyn Lincoln, the president's personal secretary, and was authorized by Lincoln to enter the White House.[264]

The world Mary entered into that evening was the slippery but star-dusted deck of the cruise ship Kennedy had been piloting since his election. With the end of the eight-year Eisenhower administration, the Midwesterners had been pitched overboard, along with their isolationist leanings and provincial morality. In their place entered men and women who were sophisticated about world travel, art, politics, and sex. Smoking and heavy drinking were the norm, and a certain kind of sophisticated sin was synonymous with life in the capital. Jean Friendly, one of the socially prominent women of the time, recalls the sheer naughtiness of their crowd, crowned by the outrageous infidelities engaged in by the president himself. In those days, few cared. "There was no horror to it," recalled Friendly in 1995, a white-haired grandmother who was still receiving visitors into the setting of the same Georgetown house that had seen so many wild parties then. "It was a little game. There wasn't the kind of desperation to the city that there is now."[265]

Women who wanted to be "in" with the Kennedy set understood the ground rules. A quick act of love shared between a willing man and a willing woman, whether married or not, one prone of the small pleasures of life well lived. It was accepted that one code of behavior applied to the peasants and middle class, another to the sophisticates, who were better equipped to handle certain emotional ambiguities.

Kennedy had spent the better part of thirteen years in Georgetown before his election, and he tried to retain his connection to the casual, intimate lifestyle of the community. Early on, it became a strain to maintain, so Kennedy simply began having Georgetown into the White House. The old mansion had yet to be redecorated, and Mamie Eisenhower's vomit green and rose pink color scheme hung in the air like old stale air, having escaped from a time capsule. However, there were clear signs of better times ahead. Suddenly this inbred new-style society, that was utterly foreign to the rest of the country, was on stage. The new Washington society was on stage and visible to the entire world. They were young people who liked a good time. They were very self-satisfied, but also idealistic. That formed a new Washington.

With the Kennedy Georgetown social life having transplanted into the White House, Ben and Tony Bradlee, and Mary Pinchot became frequent guests. But there was a difference between the parties to which the Bradlees were invited, and those Mary attended.

Kennedy's sexual escapades were legendary in Georgetown. To the rest of America, he was a family man with a beautiful wife, a man of caution, wit, and strategy. In private, he was dazzlingly reckless. There was an aura of Hollywood around Kennedy, even though he was not of it himself, and the women around him appeared as nameless starlets, even though they were secretaries from within the "beltway". Some of his most infamous sexual liaisons were with actresses from the West Coast, women procured with the help of his brother-in-law Peter Lawford. Lawford ran with Frank Sinatra, and Dean Martin, who converged with Kennedy and various actresses and prostitutes for wild parties at the Lawford beach home in Santa Monica.[266] Dean Martin's first wife, Jeanne, would later say, "The things that went on in that beach house were just mind-boggling."[267] Among the actresses Kennedy was linked with before and during his marriage were Marilyn Monroe, Angie Dickinson, and Gene Tierney.

Kennedy was a jet-setter long before he entered politics. His cares had never been those of an ordinary man. His father had endowed each of his children with ten million dollars in trust, ensuring they would never have to work. [268]

In his rarefied world, he had developed certain habits few common men could match. One was an obstinate, often foolish risk-taking, a need—like Mary Pinchot's—to establish himself as an individual outside the expectations and confines of the sheltered, upper-class world into which he was born.

Throughout Kennedy's youth, his father, Joseph Kennedy, had been a flagrant philanderer, even going so far as to install actress Gloria Swanson on a cruise ship along with his wife, Rose. The Kennedy boys expected wives no less long-suffering than their mother.

The females that were officially part of their lives, their wives, and staff, were on the sidelines. They came around sometimes with the children, but they were by and large decorative elements. Cecil Stoughton's White House photographs of the Bradlees sporting with the Kennedys are even more telling than Bradlee's frat-boy prose. On the skeet shooting range, Kennedy took aim while Jackie Kennedy and Tony Bradlee sat demurely on a bench watching, legs crossed at the knees, sweaters on shoulders. On the golf course, the women sat primly on a golf cart, while Ben and Jack walk the greens, swinging clubs. The men rolled with the children on the grass while the women sat nearby, always watching, never acting. Although Jackie was a great rider and athlete in her own right, when Kennedy was with his male friends, Jackie was not involved in their games. Politics was a man's game, too, and she grew to dislike it over time.[269] At an early campaign event, Bradlee recalled, his own wife, Tony, and Jackie "stayed in a stairwell, totally ignored" throughout the speeches.[270]

Kennedy first encountered Mary Pinchot as the date of his future U.N. Ambassador, Bill Attwood, during Kennedy's senior year at Choate. Attwood later recalled, Mary was "the best and prettiest girl at the dance, and that Kennedy kept cutting in on him."[271] Their paths crossed again while Mary was at Vassar, and Kennedy dated some of her classmates, and again at the U.N. organizing convention in San Francisco in 1945. Their backgrounds were similar in terms of wealth and politics. Kennedy's father Joe, like Amos Pinchot, had been notoriously opposed to U.S. involvement in World War II.

Mary and Kennedy met yet again in Washington, while he was still a senator. Her nonchalance, an unusual quality in protocol-conscious Washington, was one they truly had in common. Light irony was her style, and she got his sense of humor. She was his kind of woman. Besides agreeing to house Pam Turnure for a brief period in 1958, Mary saw Kennedy socially in Georgetown with Ben Bradlee and Tony when Kennedy was still a senator.[272] After Joe Alsop's impromptu inaugural party, Kennedy's first attendance at a Georgetown supper as president, came on January 31, 1961, at Ben and Tony Bradlee's. According to Kennedy secretary Evelyn Lincoln's personal records, Mary was at that supper party, along with Bradlee's parents and Helen and Walter Lippmann, although Bradlee did not mention Mary in his account of the dinner party in his 1976 book about Kennedy.[273]

The White House relationship between Mary and President Kennedy was first revealed by journalist James Truitt in 1976, and later corroborated by Ben Bradlee's eyewitness description of Mary's diary, and by Tony Bradlee's comments to journalists. Mary apparently told the Truitts about her meetings with the president while they were happening, and Truitt kept notes with dates, times, and details.[274] It is unclear whether Mary knew or approved of Truitt's note taking, although she did tell a female friend during this period that she regarded her trysts with Kennedy as interesting history.[275]

Following Truitt's revelation, the seminal 1976 article "The Curious Aftermath of JFK's Best and Brightest Affair," Ron Rosenbaum and Phillip Nobile were the first to pay homage to the relatively obscure women who had made more than a considerable impression in the life of John F. Kennedy. How influential her impact may have been was unknown; but the authors, at the conclusion of their investigation, refer to her as "the secret Lady Ottoline of Camelot."[276] They relied on an unidentified source who, the authors claimed, was "in a unique position to comment authoritatively [about Mary Pinchot-Meyer's relationship with JFK]" and who, until 1976, had "never before spoken to the press about it." The unidentified source had "agreed to entertain a limited number of questions about the affair."

> "How could a woman so admired for her ingegrity as Mary Pinchot-Meyer traduce her friendship with Jackie Kennedy?"
>
> "They weren't real friends," he [the unidentified source] said curtly.
>
> "Did JFK actually *love* Mary?"
>
> "I think so."
>
> "Then why would he carry on an affair simultaneously with Judy Exner?"
>
> "My friend, there is a difference between sex and love."
>
> "But why Mary over all other women?"
>
> "He was an unusual man. He wanted the best."[277]

No matter how Mary and Jack Kennedy became intimately involved during the last few years of their lives, both seemed to be deeply affected by their union, sometimes taking enormous risks, in part for the sake of a better, hopefully more peaceful world in the future. How their paths intriguingly—and repeatedly-crossed, suggests some mysterious force at work: perhaps a trail of destiny, a shared fate, or the engagement of a force of redemption entwined in love.[278]

Secret Service gate logs and White House social lists document many of Mary's evening visits to the *private residence* of the White House, and they corroborate Truitt's accounts, although Truitt was unaware of the first evening visit in October, 1961. White House gate logs show Mary signed in to see the president at or around 7:30 P.M. on fifteen occasions between October 1961 and August 1963, always when Jackie is known to have been away from Washington, with one exception, when Jackie's whereabouts are not verifiable by White House records or news reports. Truitt claimed there were at least thirty White House meetings. The gate logs do not tell the entire story of who was in the White House, because there were other entrances and many occasions when people have said they were inside the White House without being signed in. Frequently, a Kennedy retainer such as David F. Powers would sign in at seven-thirty with only the notation "Powers plus one." The fact that Mary's name is so often entered means she was not hidden and was probably there more often than logs indicate.[279]

Jim Truitt said the pair also met outside the White House, at houses in Georgetown. He told all to the *National Enquirer*, which published the revelation in 1976. Tony Bradlee then confirmed the liaison to the *Enquirer* but insisted it be called a "fling." [280] In Truitt's account, Mary's sexual relationship with Kennedy began in early 1962. Gate records and White House social logs indicate Mary was at a White House dance in the late fall of 1961. There, according to Truitt, Kennedy first propositioned her, and she refused.

Kennedy aides, while still clinging to the fiction that Kennedy was always true to his wife, admit Mary was one of his favorite women, and it was never a surprise to find her in the private residence after a workday. White House counsel Myer Feldman recalled that Mary was almost part of the furniture around Kennedy. Unlike with some other women—and men—in the White House, the president did not ask her to leave the room when he discussed business. So frequent was her proximity to the president, and so obvious Kennedy's admiration for her, that Feldman felt that Mary might make a good conduit to the president's ear, if and when Kennedy was unavailable to discuss matters of state with him. Feldman played tennis with her occasionally, and remembers that she expressed an interest in his special area, Israel, and in other foreign issues. Although he had never seen any indication that they were lovers, Feldman said, "I'd walk in and out of the office all the time, and I would see her in the Oval Office or over in the residence. Around eight-thirty, when the day was over, often I'd walk over to the residence, and she'd be sitting there. There wasn't any attempt to hide her in the way there was with most of the other women." [281]

Other Kennedy aides were also aware of Mary's relative status in the president's life, and soon found that the mere mention of her name was considered helpful for job seekers. Longtime Kennedy aide Dave Powers recalled that "Jack loved to talk to Mary, and felt free to discuss just about anything with her." Powers recalled that their relationship was "extremely warm" but would not, in his *professional* opinion, go so far as to call it a romantic relationship. "He trusted her and he didn't feel he had to restrict himself around her." [282]

While Kennedy aides have publicly insisted that Kennedy was always true to his wife but, on the other hand, they were sometimes complicit in delivering women to him. Mary was usually escorted to White House dinner parties with the president by Kennedy friends and retainers who served as *beards*. Mary was usually escorted by Bill Walton, a former tough-guy war correspondent, who headed the Fine Arts Commission. Walton loved power, art, and society. He was a favorite of Jackie Kennedy, and frequently advised her on White House décor. After the president was assassinated, he combed history books to find out how the White House had been draped in mourning after Lincoln was shot, and proceeded to array the mansion accordingly. [283]

The president's flings and liaisons, including his romance with Mary, while carefully hidden from the public eye, were no secret to various government institutions. J. Edger Hoover collected information on Kennedy and his girlfriends. This information on Kennedy and many others in high places, without question, helped Hoover keep his job over the decades.

The CIA was also interested in Kennedy's indiscretions, since the potential for blackmail was always a threat to national security. Information such as Hoover had on Kennedy's sex life was probably collected by James Angleton, as head of the counterintelligence office. No evidence exists that he taped Kennedy and Mary, but Angleton boasted of it, and had already shown his capacity for making surreptitious tapes of unwitting Georgetowners at play.[284] More dangerously, the Mafia and the Teamsters were also collecting tapes and information about Kennedy's extramarital sex life, as a defensive weapon against the administration's crackdown on crime. [285]

In this climate, a less reckless man might have curtailed his urges. But Kennedy was not going to be hemmed in. Early in his administration, he began devising ways to elude his Secret Service guards. His appetite for women and fun reached a peak in the summer of 1962, the period when Mary was logged into the White House most frequently for private visits with him.

While Hoover, Angleton, and a variety of other Kennedy-watchers had been aware of Mary and other women, after Truitt's story about Mary was published in the *National Enquirer* in 1976, the Kennedy entourage was quick to deny it.

Mary's friendship with Kennedy was no secret to Jackie Kennedy. The two women were friends themselves. They shared some life experiences, not the least being the death of a child. They had been neighbors in McLean in 1956, when Jackie experienced the stillbirth of her first child, while Kennedy was away on a yacht in the Mediterranean. Both had attended Vassar—Jackie five years after Mary—and both women had complicated relationships with their fathers; Jackie's father, "Black Jack" Bouvier, had been an alcoholic roustabout who doted on his daughter, but was rarely available to her. They both were molded into women of impeccable speech and manners by cotillions and girls' prep schools. And both had married World War II heros who were ambitious, powerful players on the national scene.

There, however, the resemblance ended. Mary was private and casual in her personal relationships, and relaxed and unassuming in public. Jackie had been thrust onto the public stage by her husband's political career, a situation she both accepted and rejected. She belonged to the world of fashion designers and hunt club members. She enjoyed lavish parties and antique furniture, which she collected to restore the White House. In a famous incident, she completely ignored the presence of Martin Luther King Jr. next to her in a White House elevator, so excited was she at the discovery of an antique chair in the basement.

Both women were aesthetes, but from vastly different schools. Jackie's taste ran to prerevolutionary France. Mary was thoroughly modern. Rather than become an artist herself, Jackie was the grandest art patron of them all, bringing the nation's musicians, poets, and artists to Washington and fêting them at White House balls. Many of her friends were people who took pride in their knowledge of art, without actually practicing it. Jackie also painted, but unlike Mary, who was actually trying to paint with the painters and understand the reasons behind the new style, Jackie Kennedy's paintings were old fashioned albeit witty illustrations. She had a special committee for White House Paintings help her select paintings to purchase for the White House; they bought Americana and some French impressionists. Her interest in the arts and in White House events, such as the dinner for Nobel Prize winners, gave the Kennedy administration an aura of high culture, but the president himself was uncomfortable around intellectuals and knew little about art. It is possible Mary talked to him of her work in the Color School, though.[286]When Jackie showed the president a red, yellow, and blue finger painting by Caroline, and pretended it was an abstract painting by William Walton, Kennedy responded with, "Pretty good color." [287]

Kennedy had married a woman who was above him in class and taste, and he liked that about her. "There was an awful lot of the Irish mick in him about his attitude toward women," journalist Laura Bergquist said. "In marrying Jackie he, in a sense, knew that he was outclassed, that he was married above his station." [288] He thought that important in a woman, in that who wants to come home at night and talk to another version of himself?

Mary had no equivalent sense of personal grandeur. She had a curiosity about life and the world, and she had never been exposed to the kind of pressure Jackie had. "Mary was not in the boiler room, and she didn't have to react against politics the way Jackie did," said Marie Ridder, a friend of both women.[289] She also had a personal simplicity. "She had the style of an artist," Recalled Helen Husted. "Everything was beautiful, but simple and clean and airy."[290] Her short, natural blond, windblown hair was never covered with a pillbox hat. Mary was not immune to the thrill of her nearness to power, but, unlike most within the beltway, she did not live her life with a consuming need for it, either. She did not have the financial means to live Jackie's jet-set lifestyle, and because of her artistic wardrobe, she was known to borrow a dress from a friend for a formal White House occasion.

Mary and other women in Kennedy's stable of girlfriends were never sure exactly how much his wife knew. It was part of Jackie's mystique to seem unconcerned about such matters. "There was some question about why we did this, knowing Jackie," said one woman who was an occasional lover of the president's. "But there was a kind of sense that Jackie felt it was okay. She knew he had this *problem*."[291] The same woman recalled a particular White House ball in 1962 at which guests were seated at round tables for ten. Jackie had seated this woman on one side of Kennedy and Mary on the other, at a time when both were having occasional romps with him. "I always wondered what that meant, and I'm sure Mary did, too," the woman said.

On another occasion, the March 1961 dinner for eighty, Mary was seated on one side of the president and her sister, Tony Bradlee, on the other, at the same table with Helen Husted, recently divorced from a Russian prince, and the journalist Rowland Evans and his wife, Kay, a close friend of Mary's from Vassar days. The women filled the role once held by dancing girls in the courts of sultans. They were there to amuse the president visually, conversationally, and in some cases in bed. Usually both the women and the men on the guest list were selected and seated by no one other than Jackie. Mary, much older than the retinue of regular party girls at the White House, clearly matched Kennedy's taste.

Mary's involvement in the arts might have given Kennedy a more realistic appreciation of American art than his wife's position as a patron did. By 1961, Mary was a working artist. She had to scrape paint off her skin and from under her fingernails before going to the White House. With the grand opening of the Washington Gallery of Modern Art in 1962, she and other artists finally had a venue for the kind of work they most admired. The gallery was dedicated to the new, and it had attracted the financial backing of some of Georgetown's biggest names.

The modern artists appreciated the fact that the Kennedy White House was art-friendly, but the avant-garde scene was hardly democratic. One either belonged to the aristocracy of consciousness or one did not. Mary belonged. She could also cross the line and be one of the few female White House insiders.

Mary had avoided Washington society throughout her years in McLean. Now, through her relationship with Kennedy, she was at the top of Washington's A-list. Besides seeing the president privately, Mary was invited to many of the big White House dances and smaller dinners organized by Jackie Kennedy. The dance of the moment was the Twist, danced to the tune by Chubby Checker. The Twist represented youth and the end of the dreary 1950s.[292] Mary "knew exactly how to do it, and Jack just adored it," said Helen Husted. "Mary had this sense of perfect taste, and she dared to do things other people wouldn't."[293]

As one of the president's favorites, Mary was both discreet and nonchalant. She had drinks in the Oval Office, danced in the Green Room as a guest of the President and Mrs. Kennedy, dined in the private residence, and even left her slip behind, only to have it sealed in a White House envelope and returned to her. But very few people understood how close she was to Kennedy. She told Kary Fischer about her frequent dinners with the president, and observed to him that she didn't believe all of the woman who said they had flings with Kennedy. "She seemed to think that more often than not, he had these women over to talk, to test out his ideas on them," Fischer said. "She felt that his relations with women were exaggerated." [294]

However, Mary also believed Kennedy, and not the First Lady, was responsible for her many invitations to White House events. "She rather liked it, being put on display by the president of the United States," Fischer said. Mary told Kary her relationship with Jackie was not warm, and that Jackie did not particularly enjoy the fact that her husband was so fond of both Mary and her sister, Tony. "Although good friends, she never felt Jackie had any *real* feelings for her," Fischer said." Mary liked to have some kind of conversation with people, in the metaphorical sense, and she did not have that with Jackie. Jackie was impenetrable."[295]

All of Washington was dying to be part of the new crowd, and she was there. She was far more inside than most men, including her ex-husband, who would never find his name on a White House guest list, even though he was at the pinnacle of the intelligence community. When Kennedy was elected, Cord Meyer had hoped that his long wait in bureaucratic obscurity during the Eisenhower years would end with the advent of a Democratic administration. But that was not to be. The bad blood between him and Kennedy, dating back to the 1945 U.N. conference in San Francisco, precluded that, as did the president's apparent fascination with his ex-wife.[296]

On a raw fall night of November 11, 1961, the Kennedys hosted a dinner dance for more than eighty in honor of Mrs. Kennedy's sister, Princess Lee Radziwell. It was at this party that, according to Truitt, Mary refused Kennedy's initial advance. Ten weeks later, on January 22, 1962, with Jackie away at Glen Ora, the refurbished Virginia estate where she escaped from Washington, Kennedy's phone offer to send a White House limousine to Mary's townhouse proved irresistible. Kennedy had attended Sunday morning Mass in Washington, helicoptered to Glen Ora, and then choppered back from Virginia the next day, leaving his wife and children at the estate.[297] Monday night, "Mrs. Meyer" was signed into the White House by Evelyn Lincoln to see the president at 7:30 P.M.[298]

In February 1962, the Kennedys hosted another White House dinner dance to which Mary, her sister Tony and husband Ben Bradlee were invited. Jackie prepared the initial guest list, and then scrutinized by her husband, dropping and adding people, and suggesting other names. Bradlee, like the rest of Washington, was awed by the scene, which he described as "a dazzling mixture of 'beautiful people' from New York, jet-setters from Europe, politicians, reporters who are friends, and Kennedy relatives. Unlike the Eisenhower era, the crowd is always young. The women are always gorgeous, and you have to pinch yourself."[299] During that dance, Kennedy fed Mary's brother-in-law, Bradlee, the story of the return to America of U2 pilot Gary Powers. Bradlee called it in from the White House to his *Washington Post* for the morning's paper, a major scoop.

During the summer and fall of 1962, Mary was logged into the White House frequently—in one case, several times in one week—while Jackie was away on a three month vacation that included Virginia, Newport, Cape Cod, and Rome. The routine at the White House was always the same. Mary arrived around 7:30 P.M., often delivered by a White House driver, after having been phoned by the president earlier in the day. She was ushered into a private dinner with the president. Sometimes the dinners included other guests, usually Kennedy's close male buddies. When the buddies were of Irish descent, Kennedy cut loose and sang Irish songs with them, with Mary joining in.[300] After dinner, the men would retire, leaving Mary alone with the president.[301] Frequently, she would call his private phone line the day after the dinner, and they would talk.[302]

The Kennedy aides were correct that Mary was not a surreptitious guest at the White House. She was never hidden, as most of Kennedy's other girlfriends, whose names were not even entered in the official logs.[303] But discretion was always observed when Mary visited the White House. The true nature of her relationship with the president was not obvious to the other dinner guests. Those who were not in on the secret could be confused by the refined woman so incongruously present among the ribald Kennedy retainers.

The private evening visits were random, sometimes they coincided with historic events or statements; other times, Mary was merely a pleasant diversion after a long day of mundane ceremonial events. Sometimes the visits were preceded by private telephone calls, also logged by Kennedy's secretary. On March 13, 1962, Mary called the White House and was transferred to the president. On March 15, 1962, with Jackie away on her famous visit to India, Mary signed in for an evening with the president. That afternoon, Kennedy gave a press conference and answered one of the first questions about shipping arms to Laos. That night he called the Secret Service at 11:50 P.M. for a car to pick up "Mrs. Meyer" at the South Gate.[304]

On the evening of July 16, 1962, "Mrs. Meyer" was signed in for an appointment with the president at 7:30 P.M.[305] Kennedy had returned that day after spending the weekend on Cape Cod, where Jackie and the children were to remain throughout July.[306] That morning, the head of the Business and Professional Women's Federation had again blasted the president in the press for failing to appoint women to his cabinet. Color television pictures were beamed across the Atlantic via satellite for the first time that night.[307] That evening, according to Truitt, Kennedy and Mary smoked marijuana together.

The White House was due to hold a conference on narcotics in a few weeks, and the irony was not lost on Kennedy, who mentioned it to Mary. Truitt claimed that he himself provided Mary with the pot. The president smoked three of the six joints Mary brought to him. At first he felt no effects. Then he closed his eyes and refused a fourth joint. "Suppose the Russians did something now," he said.[308] Kennedy then told Mary the pot "isn't like cocaine," and told her he would get her some of that.[309] White House phone logs for the next day indicate Mary Meyer was the first caller on the morning log to the president, at 6:43 A.M., followed by two calls from Mrs. Kennedy.[310]

The pot smoking story received much ink after the *Enquirer* published Truitt's account in 1976. But pot, as every anti-drug message would warn Americans for years to come, was only the top of a very slippery slope; Mary's visits to Timothy Leary during the time she was also Kennedy's lover suggests that Kennedy knew far more about hallucinogenic drugs than the CIA might have been telling him. No one has ever confirmed that Kennedy tried LSD with Mary. But the timing of her visits to Timothy Leary do coincide with the dates of her known private meetings with the president. Angleton later said Mary took one low dose of LSD with Kennedy after which, Angleton said, "they made love." Angleton said he got this information out of Mary's diary.[311]

No one has ever corroborated Truitt's account of the drug use. If Kennedy did experiment with drugs, his *protective* aides had *no* idea about it.

The private evenings continued through the summer of 1962, while Jackie remained away from Washington. On July 30, Mary arrived at the Southwest gate of the White House, with Kennedy friend Bill Thompson, for seven-thirty dinner with the president. A week later, on August 6, she was with Kennedy the night after Marilyn Monroe killed herself in Los Angeles.[312] The suicide by pills intimately involved the Kennedys. Marilyn had been close to their brother-in-law, Peter Lawford, and Lawford had introduced her to the Kennedy brothers and arranged their meetings. Published reports have linked both the president and his brother Bobby with the blond actress.

The star's suicide was one of those private crises that made all the other craziness of Kennedy's life stand out in bold relief. At the White House on August 6, with Marilyn Monroe's death the banner headline in all the papers, telephone records indicate mob moll Judith Campbell called for the president from Los Angeles mid-afternoon, and was told no by Evelyn Lincoln, indicating Kennedy was not taking her calls. "Mrs. Mary Meyer" called a little later and left a number. Judith Campbell called again that evening, shortly before Mary was logged in, and phone records indicate Mrs. Lincoln again put her off, telling her the president was in conference. That evening, while Mary was with Kennedy at the White House, Mrs. Kennedy called from New York at 7:50, and was told the president was out. At quarter to nine, Peter Lawford, in the thick of the *suicide* story by virtually having spoken with Marilyn just before she died (reports claim he was talking to her when she passed out), called Kennedy from Beverly Hills and got through. At 11:28, Kennedy called for a car to be sent to the South Gate, presumably to take Mary home.[313]

Marilyn's sultry "Happy Birthday Mr. President" appearance three months earlier at a combined fund-raiser birthday party for Jack in New York had already become an iconic American moment. Surely Mary knew that Jack had been involved with Marilyn. But had she known how the relationship had disintegrated, or how his brother Bobby had recently "taken his turn" with the world's most famous sex goddess—who had been unwilling "to go away quietly"? That Bobby Kennedy and Peter Lawford were at Marilyn's house the day she died was suspicious enough; that Bobby returned a second time that evening, according to two witnesses, immediately prior to her alleged suicide was a bit unsavory.[314]The situation, according to people who knew Marilyn closely, had become critical. Should she have proceeded with her intention to publically reveal the affairs, the Kennedy political machine might have been dealt a severe blow. The events immediately following her death created more questions than answers.[315] Marilyn's alleged crusade "to expose the Kennedy's for what they are" has had enormous reverberations, including the close guarding of fifty-four crates of Robert Kennedy's records at the John F. Kennedy Presidential Library and Museum that are so confidential even the library's director is prohibited from knowing what's in them.[316] Such have been the extensive efforts of the Kennedy image machine to keep the full disclosure of truth from the American people.

Interestingly, to date, of all the 'who done it' conspiracy theories over the suicide vs. death of Marilyn Monroe, it seems as though no one has considered the scenario of Ethyl and Jackie as *persons of interest*.

As the summer passed, the situation with the Soviets reached a critical level. Threats and counter threats had made Cuba the crisis point. All the while, Mary's visits to the White House, both private and at dinner parties, continued at a steady pace. One such visit that summer coincided with a memorable crisis.

Domestically, race tension and violence were rampant in the American South, as civil rights workers clashed with white racists all summer long. On September 30, 1962, the situation exploded. That day, an attempt to integrate the University of Mississippi by bringing James Meredith to register, resulted in a six hour riot that killed two and wounded scores of others. That night, Kennedy went on television and spoke about the race violence for nine minutes, asking for order. He addressed white Mississippians directly, appealing to their sense of honor.[317]

The following evening, October 1, Mary was logged in for dinner with Kennedy.[318] While she was at the White House, Mississippi's segregationist governor, Ross Barnett, who had been urging Mississippians via TV and radio broadcasts not to "surrender," spoke on national television to accuse the federal government of inciting violence. "The responsibility for this unwarranted breach of the peace and violence in Mississippi rests directly with the President," Barnett said.[319]

The fall of 1962 closed an era of reckless fun for the president. The final sobering event came in October, when Kennedy learned that the Russians had delivered missiles to Cuba. Kennedy's response brought the world closer to nuclear war than it had ever been. By then, Jackie had returned to the White House.[320]

Mary remained on the First Lady's A-list. On October 10, 1962, one day after Jackie returned from her three-month holiday, the First Lady threw a small dinner party for eight at the White House. Anne and James Truitt were two of the invited guests, along with Kennedy's friend Bill Walton and Mary.[321]

On the night of October 22, 1962, Mrs. Kennedy hosted a small dinner party that included Mary, Bill Walton, and Mrs. Kennedy's favorite designer, Oleg Cassini, among others.[322] An hour before joining the guests, Kennedy went on national television to announce that the United States planned to blockade Russian ships heading toward Cuba, unless the missiles were removed. The statement was taken as a declaration of war, and for several days the world was on the brink of annihilation. Millions watched on October 24 as American television cameras showed Russian ships steaming toward a line of demarcation in the ocean, beyond which Kennedy had promised to stop them. A television announcer's voice choked with emotion as he counted down the miles and waited for U.S. ships to open fire. They did not. The Russian ships did not approach the line.[323]

Behind the scenes, a series of tense meetings between the Soviet ambassador and Robert Kennedy had been under way during the middle of the night, invisible to newsmen and other diplomats.[324] Through the back channel, Kennedy was able to *secretly* agree to remove U.S. missiles from Turkish bases, in exchange for the *public* Russian removal of missiles from Cuba. The missiles were removed with much relief on all sides, ending an episode that made Kennedy look tough and uncompromising with the Soviets.

Jack regarded Mary as completely trustworthy; increasingly, he sought out her counsel. Having had a life with Cord, Mary was already well acquainted with CIA skullduggery. Likely, she even knew a few things that Jack didn't. Throughout his most critical moments during his presidency, Mary invariably found her way to his side, and *always* by invitation. No moment, however, was more critical than the thirteen day Cuban missile crises.[325]

That fall and winter, the glowing White House balls and dinners continued, and Mary remained on the guest list. One week in November she was at the White House two nights in a row, once for an informal dinner whose guests included Isaiah Berlin and Joe Alsop.[326]

In January 1963, an event occurred that surely alarmed Mary, and worried the president. *Washington Post* publisher Phil Graham, suffering from alcoholism and manic-depression, had broken an unwritten code of Washington journalists, and mentioned Mary's affair with the president at a convention of American Newspaper Editors in Phoenix. Graham had attended the convention without being invited to speak. In the middle of the proceedings, he stumbled to the podium, grabbed the microphone, and began a rambling tirade that included a story about the president's "new favorite", Mary Pinchot-Meyer. It is a testament to the discretion of the newspaper editors in those days, and their unquestioning reverence for the highest office in the land, that not one newspaper carried a whisper of Graham's revelation. Perhaps the fact that Graham was also taking off his clothes onstage affected his credibility with the editors. In any case, the outburst by the consummate Washington insider was deemed so astonishing and such a threat to the status quo, that the White House itself provided a government jet to get Graham's doctor to him quickly. Back in Washington, Graham was committed to the care of a private mental institution.[327] Later that year, he shot himself to death. It is possible that the Graham outburst prompted Mary and Kennedy to all but break off their relationship.

Blair Clark, then vice president of CBS news, was Mary's escort to a White House dance on a snowy night in the last winter of Kennedy's presidency. Clark had met Mary in Paris on her husband dumping tour, and was pleased to be asked to escort her. He had no clue that the woman he was squiring to the ball was actually the president's favorite mistress. Clark noticed nothing out of the ordinary at the dance, other than she had disappeared in the middle of the evening for well over an hour. "I finally caught up with her and found the bottom of her formal dress was sort of wet, and she looked a little odd. I said, 'Mary where have you been?' I can still see the bedraggled bottom of her dress. She said, 'I've been out walking around the White House'. I said, 'In the snow?' I can remember thinking she must have been upset, although I have no memory of her not being in control of herself." The party lasted until past three in the morning, and Clark and Mary and the Bradlees were among the last to leave. Kennedy and Jackie saw them off on the front portico of the White House, everyone teetering a bit from the effects of endless bottles of champagne. Clark speculated, "That night he may have told her they were through." [328]

Without Mary's diary, it's impossible to know for certain if the sexual part of their relationship ended that night, or if ever. In 1963, Kennedy and Mary kept a lower profile; they stayed in touch, sometimes by lengthy phone conversations, and occasionally seeing one another in the White House residence, when Jackie was out of town. Mary was one of a small number of guests invited to a birthday party Jackie threw for the president in May aboard a yacht floating in the Potomac. Mary was the first person Kennedy wanted to see after being away on a ten-day European trip. He returned very early on the morning of July 3, 1963, and they dined privately that evening. She also spent two private evenings with Kennedy in June of 1963: on June 12, the day civil rights leader Medgar Evers was shot, and again two days later. That weekend, she and Marian Schlesinger played tennis on the White House courts. She dined privately with Kennedy in August 1963, two days after *Post* president and mutual friend Phil Graham shot himself.[329]

As his presidency wore on, Kennedy retired from most of his congressional romping ways. But unlike the actresses and secretaries, Mary made the transition from a plaything to a close family friend. She kept up a cordial relationship with Jackie Kennedy. When Mrs. Kennedy's last pregnancy ended with her son Patrick dying several days after a premature birth, Mary sent off a handwritten letter of sympathy on stationery with her mother's New York address. "Dear Jackie," she wrote in her rounded, left leaning handwriting, "Anything that I write seems too little—but nothing that I feel seems too much. I am so so so very sorry."[330]

Bill Walton, the closest to Jack, Bobby, and Jackie, uncharacteristically let it slip to author Ralph Martin: "You know, in the end, Jackie knew everything. Every girl. She knew her rating, her accomplishments."[331] But Mary wasn't just another dalliance for Jack, and Jackie knew it. By 1963, Mary had become a fixture in the president's life, as close a confidant as he was capable of having.[332]

In the fall of 1963, Kennedy took a trip to Milford, Pennsylvania, and Grey Towers, where he accepted the old stone château and hundreds of acres of the grounds as a gift from the Pinchot family to the U.S. Forest Service. The official donor was Mary's cousin, Gifford Bryce Pinchot. Kennedy insisted that the Pinchot sisters fly from Washington to Milford with him. They landed at a military base near Newburgh, New York, and helicoptered into Milford. Film of the event captured the two Pinchot sisters standing on a bunting-draped dais among other dignitaries. As the president walked past them and the crowd began to roar at the sight of him, Mary appeared to be laughing and cast a sidelong look at her sister Tony, who primly stared straight ahead, unwilling to share the private joke.[333]

In his remarks, Kennedy referred to the late Amos Pinchot, Mary's father, several times, even though the late Gifford Pinchot, former Governor of Pennsylvania, renowned as a conservationist and father of the U.S. Forestry Service while serving under Teddy Roosevelt's administartion, was the main subject of the speech. He dedicated the grounds to "the greater knowledge of land and its uses" and christened Grey Towers and the donated grounds the Pinchot Institute for Conservation Studies. After the speech, Kennedy insisted on visiting the smaller house on the premises where the Pinchot sisters had spent so many summers. Ruth Pickering Pinchot was by then a rabid conservative and Goldwater supporter, but she welcomed him cordially. A photographer snapped Kennedy standing with the elderly Mrs. Pinchot, Tony, and Mary at the steps of the smaller house. Mary, in her dark glasses and yellow coat with a scarf knotted at her neck, was still grinning broadly. Afterward, the president looked at baby pictures of Tony and Mary with their mother.[334]

In the following week, Kennedy traveled with the press corps to the western states, where the scheduled main topic was conservation. But at a stop in Montana, Kennedy was surprised at the fervent crowd reaction he received when he mentioned the passage of the nuclear test ban treaty. Realizing he had struck a popular note with the bomb-fearing American populace, he spent the rest of his trip extolling the virtues of disarmament.[335] The western trip concluded with a wild party in Las Vegas organized by Frank Sinatra and Peter Lawford.[336]

Over the next few weeks, with Kennedy and Mary's calendars all but fully booked, they only managed two private dinners in the White House, during Jackie's absence. However, they conversed on the phone on a regular basis. She was very excited during her November 20 phone conversation with Kennedy, when he promised a special evening together after returning from a short trip to Dallas. She wished him all the best on his early election fundraising trip. "Have a safe trip, Jack." Pause. "I'm really anxious for your return."

Mary's Father
AMOS RICHARDS ENO PINCHOT
(12-6-1873 Paris, France ~ 2-18-1944 New York)

Yale graduate, member Skull & Bones Society, Lawyer. He never held public office but managed to exert considerable influence in reformist circles and did much to keep the progressive ideas alive throughout the 1920s. He was a charter signature in the founding of what is today's ACLU.

Mary's Mother
RUTH PICKERING PINCHOT
(6-20-1893 New York ~ 12-24-1984 New York)

Daughter of wealthy businessman, Vassar Graduate, journalist of *The Masses, The Nation, New Republic,* and very active in the labor movement and women's suffrage.

Daughters of Mr. and Mrs. Amos Pinchot
of Park Avenue, New York

Mary and Antoinette Pinchot

Healthy....happy — and guarded
by this simple care

SISTERS MARY (r) and ANTOINETTE "TONY" (l) PINCHOT

Socialite daughters of Amos and Ruth Pinchot were 1929 advocates of Cream of Wheat.

Mary's Uncle GIFFORD PINCHOT

Yale graduate, member and senior year president of the Skull & Bones Society. Two time governor of Pennsylvania, 1923-27 and 1931-35. 4th Chief of Forestry, 1898-1905, under William McKinley, and Theodore Roosevelt, and 1st Chief of the United States Forest Service (founder), 1905-10, under Theodore Roosevelt, and Howard Taft.

GREY TOWERS, The Pinchot Estate

The Pinchot family mansion, located on 102 acres of rolling countryside immediately east of Milford Pennsylvania, was designed in 1884 and completed in 1886. The L-shaped mansion is anchored on three corners by towers that give the mansion its name. The 19,000+ square foot French chateau style mansion was designed by famed architect Richard Morris Hunt. With 44 rooms and 23 fireplaces, the house originally was built as a summer home. The cost was approximately $19,000 with an additional $24,000 for furnishings.

September 24, 2013 marks the 50th Anniversary donation of Grey Towers to the American public. President Kennedy, along with Mary Pickering Pinchot and daughters Mary Pinchot-Meyers, and Antoinette Pinchot-Bradlee were there to transfer the gift of Grey Towers to the American public and to dedicate the Pinchot Institute for Conservation Studies. Dr. Gifford Bryce Pinchot donated the mansion and its entire acreage to the US Forest Service to carry forward the conservation legacy of his father, Gifford Pinchot.

"Every great work is in the shadow of a man, and I don't think many Americans can point to such a distinguished record as can Gifford Pinchot," the President told the enthusiastic crowd. *"He was more than a forester,"* the President remarked. *"He was the father of American conservation."*

www.fs.fed.us/gt/

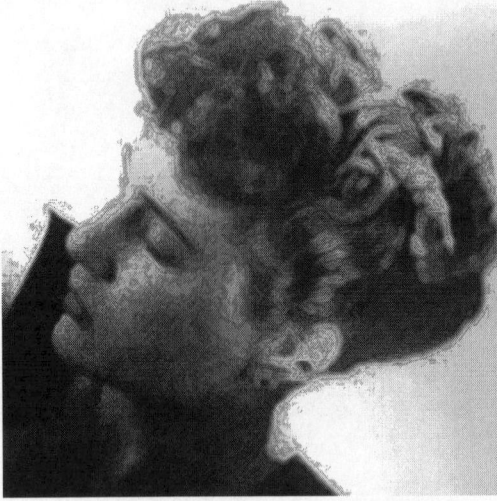

MODEL, MARY PINCHOT
With *"Vogue"*

As a glamorous New York debutante, in 1938

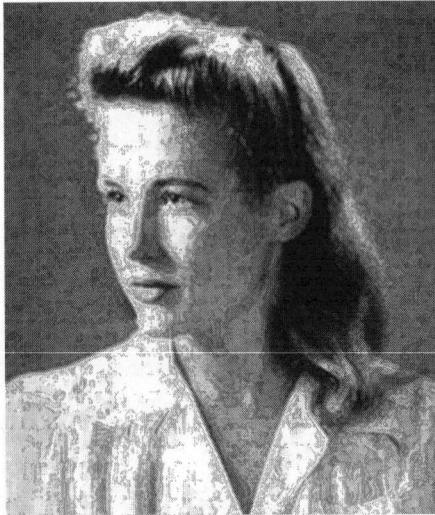

MARY ENO PINCHOT
Vassar Class of 1942

In her 1998 biography on Mary, *"A Very Private Women"*, Nina Burleigh wrote, "Mary Pinchot-Meyer was an enigmatic woman in life, and in death her real personality lurks just out of view."

JOURNALIST, MARY PINCHOT
In 1944 with *"Mademoiselle"*

WEDDING BELLS

April 19, 1945, at the Pinchot Park Avenue, New York, apartment; Mary Pinchot and Cord Meyer, Jr. were twenty-four and seemed perfect for each other.

119

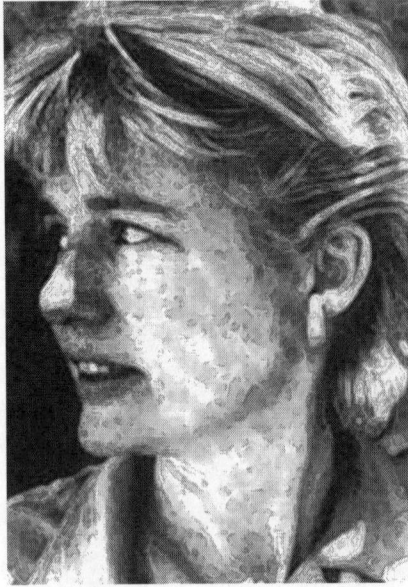

MARY PINCHOT-MEYER
As CIA wife and mother

KENNETH NOLAND
(4-10-1925, Asheville, NC ~ 1-5-1910, Port Clyde, Maine)

Abstract artist, and fellow member with Mary in the Washington School of Color. He was Mary's post-divorce boyfriend for several months.

NORMA JEANE MORTENSON
(AKA, MARILYN MONROE)
(6-1-1926, Los Angeles, CA ~ 8-5-1962, Brentwood, CA)

Alleged suicide by Barbiturate overdose. John and Robert Kennedy have been at the center of one of several conspiracy *theories* surrounding her death.

MARY PINCHOT-MEYER

Mary Pinchot-Meyer at President Kennedy's 46th birthday party on May 19, 1963, aboard the presidential yacht *Sequoia*

FOUR!

Undated photo of Jackie Kennedy and Mary Pinchot-Meyer while in the midst of a golf game.

AT GREY TOWERS

Jack Kennedy and Mary Pinchot-Meyer attend the September 24, 1963 presidential ceremony donating the Grey Towers Pinchot family estate to the US Government.

AT GREY TOWERS

Ben and Tony Bradlee, Ruth Pickering Pinchot (mother of Mary & Tony), Jack Kennedy and Mary Pinchot-Meyer attend the September 24, 1963 presidential ceremony donating the Grey Towers Pinchot family estate to the US Government.

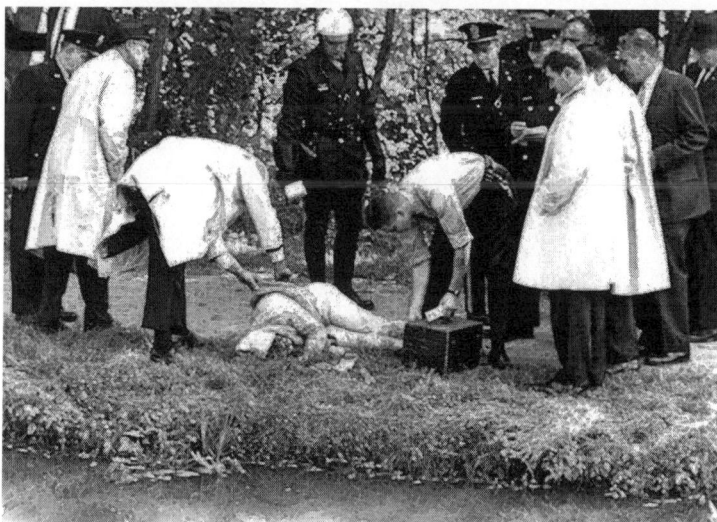

MURDER IN GEORGETOWN

The crime scene on the C&O Canal towpath within thirty minutes after the murder of Mary Pinchot-Meyer on October, 12, 1964.

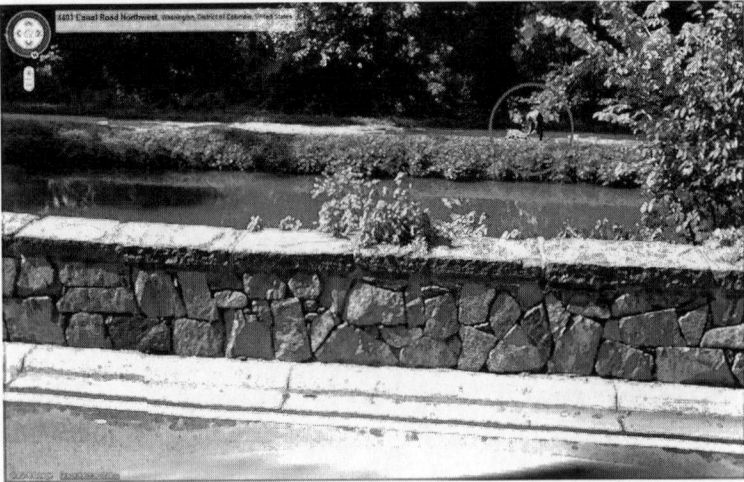

VIEW OF CRIME SCENE

View of the C&O Canal towpath that the witnesses to Mary's murder had from 4401 Canal Road, where the mysterious disappearing Nash Rambler was stalled.

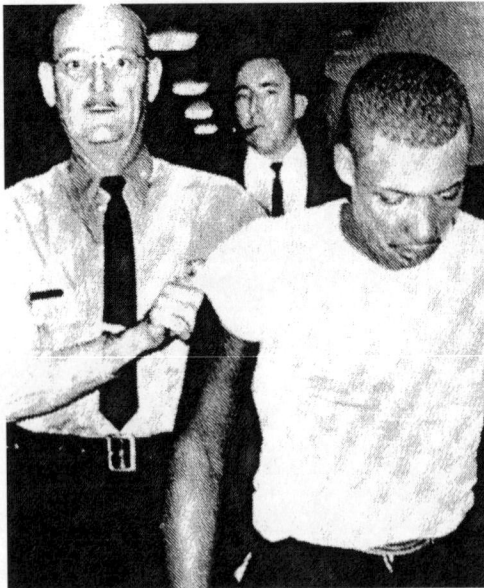

ALLEGED MURDERER

Washington DC resident Ray Crump, the alleged murderer of Mary Pinchot-Meyer.

FOR THE DEFENSE

Dovey J. Roundtree, Esq., defense attorney for Ray Crump, alleged murderer of Mary Pinchot-Meyer.

MARY'S GEORGETOWN HOME

Mary Pinchot-Meyer's Georgetown home from which the CIA illegally broke and entered to confiscate her tell-all personal journal / diary . . . . while she lay murdered on the towpath.

James Jesus Angleton
(12-9-1917, Boise ID ~ 5-12-1987 Washington, DC)

CIA Counter Intelligence Chief, James Angleton, led the illegal entry into Mary's home to confiscate her tell-all diary.

Benjamin Crowninshield Bradlee
(8-26-1921, Boston, MS ~)

Husband of Mary's sister Tony, and Editor of the *"Washington Post"* during the publication of the Pentagon Papers, and the Watergate Scandal with cub reporters Bob Woodward and Carl Bernstein.

CORD MEYER, JR.
(11-10-1920, NY ~ 3-13-2001, NY)

Ex-husband of Mary Pinchot, and CIA Chief Operative. Late in life when asked "Who killed your ex-wife, Mary Pinchot?" He replied, "The same son-of-a-bitches that killed JFK."

Mr. & Mrs. Aristotle Onassis
Wedding Bells
November-11-1968

Ari and Jackie were married on his private Greek island of Scorpios; the newlyweds are shown seated at the reception held aboard his private yacht Christina O immediately following the wedding. Arguably, her marriage to Aristotle was the biggest mistakes in her life.

Michael Pinchot

"CHRISTINA O"

Anchored in port at Aristotle Onassis' private Greek island of Scorpios is his 325 foot yacht *Christina O*.

A STRUGGLING PRESIDENT

A rare photo exposing President John F. Kennedy's back problems caused by his WWII PT-109 heroism and life-long health issues in general.

128

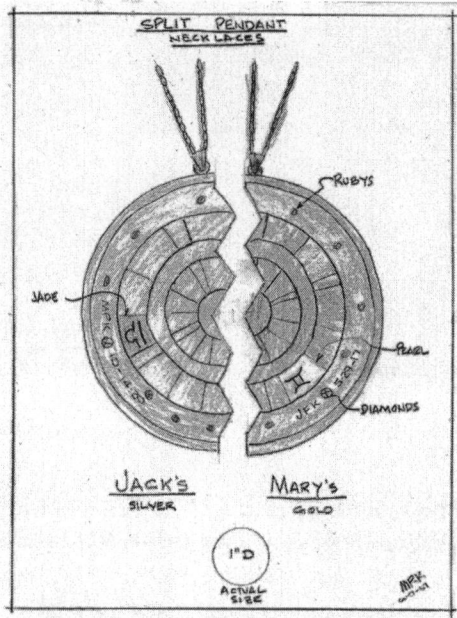

MARY & JACK'S SPLIT PENDANTS

Mary's design sketch of her and Jack's split pendant necklaces. An Italian jeweler crafted the pendants from this sketch, which she initialed MP-K.

MARY & JACK AT SEA

Mary's final painting . . . of her and Jack sailing off the Italian vacation port city of Positana, which she initialed MP-K. Note the wedding bans and split pendant necklaces.

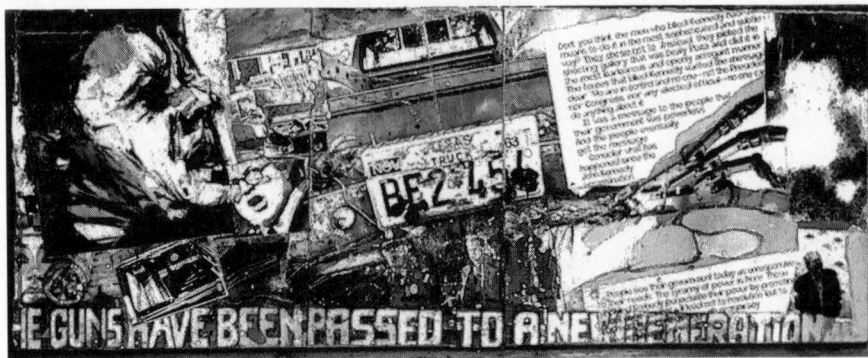

JOHN F. KENNEDY
ABSTRACT-CARICATURE PAINTING

Abstract-caricature assassination painting of President John F. Kennedy by artist Johanna Vogelsang (6-18-1929 ~ 12-1-1911).

MARY PINCHOT-MEYER
ABSTRACT-CARICATURE PAINTING

Abstract-caricature painting of Mary Pinchot-Meyer by artist Johanna Vogelsang (6-18-1929 ~ 12-1-1911).

www.vogelsangartwork.com/

ROSAMOND PINCHOT
(10-26-1904 ~ 1-24-1938)

Rosamond Pinchot was Mary Pinchot's half sister by her father's first marriage to Gertrude Minturn Pinchot; she was a socialite, stage and screen actress. Rosamond took her own life by carbon monoxide poisoning.

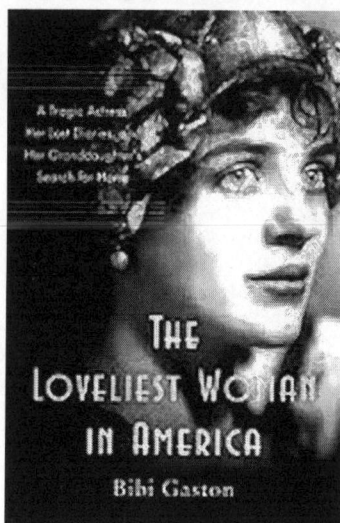

"THE LOVELIEST WOMEN IN AMERICA"
ROSAMOND PINCHOT

The Loveliest Woman in America: A Tragic Actress, Her Lost Diaries, and Her Granddaughter's Search for Home", by Bibi Gaston (2009), HarperCollins.

131

MICHAEL PINCHOT MEYER

Michael's gravestone at the Pinchot family plot in the Milford, Pennsylvania, Cemetery; he lies next to his mother Mary Pinchot Meyer.

MARY PINCHOT MEYER

Mary's gravestone at the Pinchot family plot in the Milford, Pennsylvania, Cemetery; she lies next to her son Michael Pinchot Meyer.

PART II

POETRY

CHAPTER 1

In spite of Kennedy and Johnson having barely won Texas in 1960, and, in fact, having lost Dallas, throngs of Lone Star citizens lined the 35 to 40 minute route from Dallas Love Field airport through downtown Dealey Plaza to the Dallas Business and Trade Mart.

The roar of the crowd intensified as the first glimpse of the motorcade appeared at Dealey Plaza, turned right off Main Street onto Houston Street and nosed its way toward the Houston Book Depository building tucked in the corner of Houston and Elm Streets.

The lead car was an unmarked late model white Ford four-door containing Dallas police chief, Dallas county sheriff, and two secret service agents.

Of course, all eyes focused on the second vehicle, a 1961 Black Lincoln Continental, code named *SS-100-X*. Waving and smiling from the rear right seat of the open convertible was President John F. Kennedy, with First Lady Jacqueline Kennedy on his left wearing a fashionable pink suit and matching pill-box hat. Texas Governor John Connally occupied the right middle seat, with his wife Nellie Connally seated to his left. Secret Service agents drove and occupied the front passenger seats.

Following Kennedy's limousine was the presidential follow-up car, code named *"Halfback"*, containing four secret service agents and two presidential aides, with a pair of agents on each side of the convertible's custom running boards.

Next in line was the vice presidential limousine, with Vice President Lyndon Baines Johnson, his wife Lady Bird Johnson, Senator Ralph Yarborough, a single agent, and driven by a Houston police officer.

Next in line was, of course, the Vice Presidential follow-up car, with three agents, one vice-presidential aide, driven by a State police officer.

The last cars in the motorcade, numbers six and seven, contained the traveling press core. As the last car turned right onto Houston Street, the lead car was passing the Texas Book Depository as it turned left onto ill-fated Elm Street. As the presidential limo turned onto Elm Street a sniper placed Kennedy's head into the crosshairs of his scope, knowing his first shot must be his best over the hurried shots that were to follow.

As the last two cars began their turn past the Book Depository, the sniper took a slow deep breath, paused and squeezed off his first round. With the frenzy driven noise echoing about Dealey Plaza, few heard the non distinguished muffled pops, until those closest to the presidential limousine clearly associated the pops with what was being indelibly etched into their minds. One moment the president was smiling and waving. Then, suddenly his mouth opened widely in shocked expression and his hands momentarily clenched into fists, before he raised his hands upward towards his head as he turned leftward towards his wife. As the president recoiled back into his seat the spatter of blood droplets boldly appeared on Jackie's pink pill-box hat and the padded shoulders of her matching jacket.

With amazing speed and agility, secret service agent Clint Hill jumped from his running board perch and onto the trunk of the accelerating presidential limo as the volley of shots played out; one of the final shots blew away part of the president's skull. The crowd instantly transformed from one of jubilance to that of horror, as they watched the gore spattered limousine speed up with multiple police sirens echoing throughout the plaza.

Several of the spectators standing on the grassy knoll to the right of the presidential caravan turned their attention to a block wall located on the top of the knoll, and behind the John Neely Bryan (founder of the city of Dallas) concrete pergola. One gentleman screamed, "There, he's behind the wall with a gun." The gunman had not fled more than fifty-yards before a pair of Dallas foot patrol police officers took pursuit as the president's limo sped across town to Parkland Memorial Hospital, all the while sirens continued to echo about the plaza.

As the two officers gained ground on the flight-footed gunman, he cut down an alley and shed ballast by discarding a rifle in an open dumpster. At that point he accelerated and opened some distance between he and the officers who were loaded down with gun, club, and cuffs, all within a bulky equipment belt.

At the same time, two people near the book depository building signaled a nearby police officer and pointed upward to an open window on the seventh floor of the depository. Within moments the lone officer entered the building, secured the lobby and called for back-up. Within moments a half dozen officers arrived and began to clear the upper floors, while two officers concentrated on the first floor and its cafeteria. In the cafeteria they found a pair of canteen workers and a dozen or so Depository employees, including Lee Harvey Oswald, who was identified by the building manager as a Depository employee. Although Oswald, just moments earlier, had allegedly partook in the assassination of the President of the United States, had stashed his weapon, and scrambled down five flights of stairs (due to the elevator needing repair), to the officers he appeared calm, unruffled, breathing normal, and showing no signs of perspiration.

As the officers moved up toward the fourth floor, Oswald casually strolled from the building, walked two blocks to a bus stop, and within moments was aboard a Dallas City Bus heading toward his boarding house.

Within a couple of long minutes from the last of the undefined number of shots being fired, the president arrived at Parkland Hospital. As the president's gurney was quickly wheeled into emergency surgery, several units of B+ blood were ushered in before the door could be closed. All faces within the surgery, including two stone faced secret service agents, reflected the gray, ashen, blood spattered face of their president . . . . grim.

The chief surgeon, a retired naval officer, mumbled through his mask, "By the grace of God, we'll do whatever it takes to save our commander-and-chief." A quick assessment revealed a severely shattered right shoulder, a disfigured right ear, and, most frightening, a missing portion of skull above the right ear; miraculously, the skull had been violently blown away, and yet, as if by divine intervention, appeared to be skillfully peeled off up to the final membrane that contained and protected the brain. The membrane, being translucent, provided a window view of the president's brain. The surgeon glanced at the two stone faced feds, "I hope that you mannequins are not above prayer."

*   *   *

The two officers, in pursuit of the grassy knoll shooter, being familiar with the area, split up as the suspect turned down an alleyway. The alleged shooter paused, for the briefest of moments, and glanced over his shoulder, as he discovered the alley was a dead end. The athletic suspect then exploded forward, accelerating to full speed as he approached a brick wall at the end of the alley. The loaded-down pursuing officer realized he was no match for the suspect, who attacked the seven foot wall with the grace and agility of a trained gymnast. "Halt or I'll shoot!" As the suspect crested the top of the wall, the officer fired his weapon in the air. The suspect, unfazed, disappeared over the wall, only to encounter the second officer within fifty feet of him. The olive complexioned suspect raised his handgun toward the officer who got off three quick shots; one shot shattered the man's right knee cap, the second tore through his left thigh, with the third hitting low on the brick wall. The impact of the 45's dropped him, causing him to twist ninety-degrees away from the officer, as he landed in a heap. The officer yelled from a crouched position with his weapon at the ready, "Toss your gun aside, now!" No sooner has the command left his lips, a final shot rang out . . . . self inflicted to the roof of his mouth.

* * *

In her studio, brush and palette in hand, humming along with Dave Brubeck's *Take Five*, Mary paused and grumbled at a sudden new bulletin, cutting off Paul Desmond's alto-sax solo.

"We've just received word that the President of the United States has been shot in Dallas . . . ." Mary's mind went numb; she gasped, and dropped her brush and pallet to the floor.

"Oh . . . . my . . . . God . . . . no . . . . no . . . no!"

Weak kneed and faint headed, she staggered across the studio through a maze of blank, completed, and partially filled canvases, and flicked on her small black and white television.

* * *

Chaos prevailed throughout Parkland Hospital, with focused medical professionalism working at its best within the emergency trauma surgical room, in spite of the desperateness of the situation . . . . with an undercurrent of reality that the life of the President of the United States of America was in their hands.

* * *

As the surgical team struggled, a police radio reported that the first alleged assassination suspect had been spotted, by Dallas officer J. D. Tippit, walking down the sidewalk in the residential area of Oak Cliff, about three miles from Dealey Plaza. As Tippit stepped from his car to question the suspect, he was immediately shot four times and killed. While officers convened on the area, another report came in that the suspect was seen ducking into a movie theater in the same neighborhood.

While officers responded to both reports, a team of Dallas Crime Scene officers busied themselves at the site where the second shooting suspect lay dead, while a second team searched the trash dumpster where the dead man reportedly discarded his rifle during the pursuit. To the investigating officer's dismay, the rifle had been removed from the dumpster; a key piece of evidence was now missing, without a witness to be found.

* * *

Mary starred at the television through tear drenched eyes and sobbed while trying in vain to reach her insider contacts by phone. "No, Lord, I beg of you . . . . I cannot lose one more person that I love . . . ."

* * *

As the world waited in stunned disbelief in front of televisions and radios for news of the president's condition, a team of Dallas officers entered a local movie theater with extreme caution. In the dim light of the theater, they spotted their suspect in the middle of an empty row of the sparsely occupied low class theater. When approached from both directions, the suspect was successfully apprehended following a brief scuffle in which he attempted to shoot the officer that first caught his attention. In the light of day they determined, through carried identification, that their suspect was one Lee Harvey Oswald. Within moments of the arrest, the suspect was in route to Dallas police headquarters where the feds were already asserting their authority over the locals.

The Dallas police chief slammed the phone down and pounded his fist of his desk. "We lost the fucking discarded weapon, and the son of a bitchn' dead shooter has no identification . . . . surprise, fucking surprise." He slammed the palm of his hand on his desk and barked at his assistant. "Lift a set of prints off the dead bastard and run em' through the system . . . national and global."

Before he could catch his breath, he grabbed his phone mid ring. "Yea . . . well, tell me some good news." He half smiled. "You found the weapon? Great, where?" He furrowed his brow, as he reached for a half empty soft-pack of non-filtered Camels. "You're shitn' me . . . . at the Book Depository? Surprise, surprise." He flicked his Zippo and took a heavy drag on his cigarette, exhaling as he talked. "The eighth floor . . . . between boxes of books". He stood and turned toward the window overlooking Dallas. "Good work, you know the drill." He dropped the receiver into its cradle, and turned toward stern faced Federal agent Forrest Sorrels dressed in all black. "Well, that half makes up for the rifle missing from the dumpster."

The Fed spoke, as he looked the chief squarely in the eyes, "You're wrong there, my friend, that's precisely why you boys have to step aside."

The red face chief exhaled a thick Camel cloud toward the clean cut Fed as he jabbed his finger at him across his desk. "You fuckn' city boys had better never under estimate us cowboys."

The Fed answered in calm, slow, normal tone. "Yee, hah!"

The phone cut off the chief's defensive reply; he dropped his voice as he turned ninety degrees toward the window. "Great! Quick book him, and I'll meet you in 2B for a little chat." The chief slowly placed the receiver down and turned back toward the Fed., trying hard to hide a wry smile, "Now then," as he stepped toward the door. "If you'll excuse me I have a department to run."

The stoned face Fed responded amiably, as he tapped his discrete ear piece with his index finger. "I understand, I too have business to attend to: the booking of Lee Harvey Oswald and his initial interrogation in IR 2B."

The chief froze in his tracks and exploded, finger jabbing just short of the Fed's stone face. "You ass holes had better tread lightly on *my fucking turf.*"

The Fed stepped calmly between the chief and the exit, and placed his hand on the door knob. "When the president of the United States is assassinated on your *turf*, you surrender said *turf* to the Feds." The Fed cut off the chief's attempted response. "In the future, us Feds, in all due respect, are anus orifices."

*   *   *

With one wet, red eye on the television, Mary mumbled as she desperately continued to try and make contact with at least one of her insiders . . . . all of which, no doubt, were tied up in the Dallas fiasco. "Please, please, Lord . . . . please no."

*   *   *

As the Chief and Fed approached the interrogation room, he took the chief's arm and slowed to a stop, as he pointed to his ear piece. "The weapon from the Book Depository just arrived and is in route to the Federal lab."

The chief forced a red faced smile and spoke through gritted teeth, "I appreciate being in the fucking loop."

The Fed paused with his hand on the interrogation room door knob. "Let the government do all the talking . . . . me and the two waiting inside."

Sarcastically, "I wouldn't dream of opening my mouth in my own house."

"You learn quickly, it's no wonder you're the chief."

They stepped into the interrogation room and quietly shut the door. The large two-way mirror on the far wall enlarged the relatively small pale green room, which contained a small rectangular metal table with four cushion free metal chairs. Two of the four corners contained matching chairs. The grey speckled asphalt tile floor was well worn, and the white acoustic drop ceiling and recessed fluorescent fixture were yellowed with nicotine. The Fed, with the chief at his elbow, was handed a manila folder by one of his two colleagues already present in the room. He quickly perused the file in the stone silence of the room, save for the shuffling of feet and the sound of circulating cool air. The suspect sat still, solemn, and quiet, staring blankly at the center of the green paint chipped table. The chief gave the appearance of wanting to speak but wisely remained silent, as the Fed casually placed the folder on the table and spoke clear and soft.

"Lee . . . . Harvey . . . . Oswald."

Oswald looked up, and the Fed continued as he paced slowly with his hands behind his back.

"Now then, what shall we call you?"

Oswald's crooked smile, caused by being on the wrong end of a struggle with police in the Texas Theater, seemed forced and swollen.

"Just call me Lee . . . . Mr. Lee."

The Fed replied slowly and with no emotion.

"Well, Lee, you appear to have placed yourself squarely in a world of deep poop today."

He choked off a smile. "If you say so."

"Well, Lee, it's not so much what I say, as much as what your own actions of today, that have spoken loud and clear."

Silence, as the Fed continued his slow pace.

More silence.

Finally Oswald shifted in his seat and cleared his throat. "Which were what, besides carrying a concealed weapon into a movie theater?"

Agent Forrest answered Oswald without missing a beat. "For the record, the concealed weapon being a loaded gun, which you used, less than a half-hour earlier, to kill Dallas police officer Tippit. Of course, that's after having shot and killed the president of the United States an hour earlier."

Oswald stiffened upright in his chair, wincing at the discomfort of his arms being tightly manacled behind his back. "Whoa, hold it right there, you guys are fucking crazy . . . . I did no such things." Seemingly bewildered, he continued. "Listen here, guys, I have rights, and you are clearly violating them."

More silence, with no reaction from the Feds.

"I want to call my attorney, a Mr. Abt in New York City. He is a staunch defender of civil liberties."

Forrest raised his hand in a halting fashion, as he adjusted and listened intently to his ear piece for nearly a minute before speaking. OK, let's hold it for no more than another minute." He looked at the chief, "Join me in the hallway."

They stepped into the hallway and closed the door. "What's up?

"Just got word that our dead second shooter's finger prints are not in the global system."

The chief rubbed his chin, "Shit, we're flying blind with a John Doe."

"At your request, you're now in a very exclusive loop, so do not, I repeat, do not leak this information to anyone . . . . especially the press. We need to keep our cards close to our chest for a while."

* * *

Parkland Hospital's chief surgeon, stepped and turned away from the operating table, pulled his mask down around his neck, shook his head, mopped his forehead, let go with an exacerbating sigh, and spoke to the two stone face agents.

"You can do what you wish with this information; it appears that our president is out of the woods . . . . he has a rough road to recovery, but I'm quite sure he'll make it."

One of the agents smiled, "Praise God!"

CHAPTER 2

Agent Forrest and the chief stepped back into the interrogation room. "Now then, Lee, let's take it from the top; starting again with your name, and we'll simply listen."

Oswald shifted painfully in his seat. "Before I start, could you please loosen the pressure on the cuffs, and perhaps shift my arms to the front?"

Within moments he was re-cuffed, he leaned back in his chair, with a fresh smile on his black and blue, swollen face. "Ahh, that's much better."

He gathered his thoughts, Now then, let's see . . . . oh, yeah." He glanced around the room, making momentary eye contact with all present. He paused and cleared his throat. "Like I said, my name is Lee Harvey Oswald.' Pause. "I work at the Texas School Book Depository building." He smiled, "I lived for a time in Russia, both Minsk and Moscow. I worked in a factory and liked everything over there except for the weather." He paused and shifted in his seat. "I have a Russian wife, and two children. My current residence is twelve-o-six North Beckly, here in Dallas.' Pause, "Although I have never been in Mexico City, I have been in Tijuana." He cleared his throat, and paused for a long time.

Agent Forrest prompted him. "Go ahead, we're all ears."

"I observed a rifle in the Book Depository on November twentieth. Mr Roy Truly, my supervisor, displayed the rifle to individuals in his first-floor office. I never owned a rifle myself." He scanned the room, as if in hoping someone would respond to his statement. With no takers, he continued . . . . to ramble

"I resided in the Soviet Union for three years, where I now have several friends and relatives through marriage. I was secretary of the Fair Play for Cuba Committee in New Orleans a few months ago." Again, stone faces.

"While in the Marines, I received an award for marksmanship." He panned the room, "While living on Beckly Street, I used the name O. H. Lee. I was present in the Book Depository during the chaos outside. I have been employed at the Depository since this October fifteenth, as a temporary contract laborer and have access to the entire building." More long silence, whereupon he shrugged his shoulder and continued.

"My usual place of work is on the first floor. However, I frequently use the fourth through seventh floor to gather books for prescribed orders; I was on all of those floors throughout this morning." He pause looking for a sign of support, seeing none, he continued.

"Because of all of the chaos and confusion, I figured that there would be no work performed the remainder of the day, so I decided to go home. When I got home I decided to go to the movie, so I changed clothes and left." He shifted in his seat. "I carried a pistol with me to the movie because the days are short and, without wheels, I'd be on the street in the dark. Besides, it's not news to anyone in this room, hello it's Texas where a large percentage of folks carried concealed weapons." He grinned because there was no arguing about Texas and guns. "So, being guilty of nothing, I instinctively, as in reflex, resisted the police who snuck up behind me in the dark while I was preoccupied with the movie." He raised his cuffed hands and touched his face. "Of course, me being seated, and a hand full of cops pounding on me, my face received the short end of the apprehension stick." He cleared his throat. "Now, as for shooting a cop and the president, I have no idea what the hell you boys are talking about."

Long silence.

Agent Forrest moved as close as possible to Oswald, forcing him to look up. "So then, what about the handful of extra bullets in your jacket pocket? Do you feel that the Dallas streets are that dangerous after dark?" He locked into Oswald's eyes, and within moments Oswald broke contact.

"I'm through with this. I want to contact my lawyer."

Agent Forrest, very casually, "As I was about to say, we're through for now, we'll pick it up again later today." He raised his hand to silence Oswald, "As for your legal rights, you'll be able to contact your attorney today. If you don't have his phone number, we'll assist you in any way . . . . simply ask."

The wind taken out of his sail, Oswald responds meekly. 'OK, thanks."

"In the mean time we have Dallas' best Public Defender on his way."

On their way up to the chief's office, agent Forrest, paused mid-hallway to listen intently to his ear peace. As they continued down the hall the chief queried, "Anything you'd care to share with the Dallas chief of police?"

"Oh that . . . . it was just procedural crap." While in fact he had been given the highly confidential news of the president's high survival prognosis. The Feds decided to hold that information back for a few more hours for political and investigative reasons. Forrest was instructed to keep the information to himself, and that the less Oswald new, for the time being, the better.

As they stepped into the chief's office, a news alert was flashed on his office television. NBC newsman Bill Ryan announced that the president remained in extreme critical condition with his survival hanging by a thread. Agent Forrest thought to himself. *"I guess that's the official party line."*

The commentator went on to say that a Lee Harvey Oswald was in custody as a prime suspect, and was currently being held at Dallas Police Headquarters. Not a word was spoken about the grassy-knoll 'second shooter', let alone his fate.

* * *

Torn between relief and agony, Mary sobbed at the news on television of the president's precarious survival. "Please, please, dear Lord, don't take Jack from me. "She choked and caught her breath; I can't and won't make it without him."

* * *

By late afternoon Oswald was protesting aloud while being escorted into a lineup conducted for two witnesses in the shooting death of officer Tippit. "It isn't right to toss me into a lineup with my face being battered and dressed shabbily compared to the others." Ignored, he protested further when he saw the lineup of what appeared to be teenagers, all wearing nice Eisenhower style jackets. "Hell, you guys know exactly what you're doing; I'm beat up and wearing a dirty bloodied tee shirt. You're railroading me . . . . again, I want my attorney . . . . hell, any attorney . . . . I've got my rights."

From the line up, of which he was told nothing of its outcome, he was marched directly to a Dallas Police Captain Fritz's office for a second interrogation, grumbling along the way. "It doesn't take a genius to figure out the outcome of that kangaroo lineup . . . . and I suppose you're not sharing the results."

Silence.

Oswald was taken aback when he stepped into Fritz's office and recognized FBI agent, James Hosty. He froze in his tracks and spoke angrily. "I know you, Hosty." Oswald turned and glared at Fritz. "I wrote a letter to his boss because he and one of his sidekicks interviewed my wife when she was home alone. You were rude and threatening to my wife, telling her that the FBI was going to deport her back to Russia."

Agent Hosty sat stone faced and perfectly still, raising Oswald's anger level as the escorting officer set him in a straight back chair with his hands cuffed behind his back. Oswald looked at Captain Fritz. "Again . . . . I say, again . . . . I want my attorney."

"And your attorney is?"

"You know Fritz, you must be the only player in this circle jerk that doesn't know the name of my attorney."

Fritz shrugged his shoulders and opened a manila folder lying on his desk, as Oswald continued.

"Not being allowed access to a telephone is pure bullshit."

Silence.

My New York City attorney is a Mr. Abt . . . . I don't know him personally, but I'm very familiar with a case he had a few years ago, where he represented the people who had violated the Smith Act . . . . which makes it illegal to teach or advocate the violent overthrow of the U.S. government.' He paused and glanced around the room. "Like I said, I don't know him personally, but that's the attorney I want."

More silence.

As he had done in the previous interrogation, he began to ramble.

"I went to school in New York and Fort Worth, Texas . . . . but it was while I was in the Marines that I completed my high school education." He paused. "I support the Castro revolution. My landlady didn't understand my name correctly, so it was her idea to call me O. H. Lee."

With more silence, as he shifted in his chair.

"The only package I brought to work today was my lunch. I never had a card to the Communist Party . . . . I am a Marxist, but not a Leninist Marxist." He cleared his throat. "I bought a pistol in Fort Worth several months ago . . . . I refuse to tell you where I purchased the pistol . . . . I never ordered anything through the mail . . . . I'm not a malcontent . . . . nothing irritated me about our president."

More silence, then Fritz spoke. "Do you believe in the Deity?"

Oswald tried to hide his being taken aback, and paused for several moments. "I don't care to discus that." Pause. "How can I afford to buy a rifle on my Book Depository salary of a buck twenty-five an hour?' Pause. "John Kennedy had a nice family."

The chief and Forrest looked at one another at the same moment when Oswald spoke in past tense of the president and his family. In his own mind, the president was dead.

Captain Fritz leaned forward and placed his forearms on his desk. "Cut the crap, Oswald; you know and we know that you shot the president and officer Tippit."

Oswald's face turned momentarily blank, "Again .... I want to make my one lousy phone call to my attorney .... I know my rights."

Pause.

Fritz continues, as if nothing had been said, "Sheriff Roger Craig witnessed you getting into a white station wagon approximately fifteen minutes after the assassination ...."

Before Fritz could continue, they received the first knee jerk reaction from Oswald. "That station wagon belongs to Mrs. Ruth Paine; don't try to tie her to this. She had nothing to do with this. I told you I did ...."

Pause.

"Please .... my attorney. It's been nearly five hours since my booking, and I have yet to be given the chance to have legal counsel .... pinch me, am I back in Moscow?"

Captain Fritz answered his phone mid first ring. "You bet, he's on his way."

Within moments Oswald was ushered through multiple hallways to a second line up before three additional witnesses in the Tippit shooting. In the vicinity, was a trio of court reporters. By the time Oswald realized who they were, he was forced to yell over his shoulder. "I didn't shoot anyone. I'm being refused my constitutional right to counsel .... I killed no one."

Within moments of finishing the lineup, he was pushed back into his cell, only to be removed again within a handful of minutes.

"Get moving, Oswald, it's arraignment time."

"For what?"

"For killing one of my fellow officers, asshole; they'll fry you for that alone."

Before his brief, cut and dry arraignment, Oswald took advantage of two reporters taking notes that were warned ahead of time by the judge to only report, with questions and comments disallowed.

"Please report that I'm being denied my constitutional right to legal counsel. I may as well be in Moscow." Not being silenced, he continued. "Also, I've been a victim of two kangaroo lineups earlier today."

Straight from his hearing, where he was formally charged with the shooting murder of Dallas police officer Tippit, he grumbled all the way back to Captain Fritz's office.

"Well, that was neat and tidy; I'm as good as convicted of murder without legal counsel .... for doing nothing more that caring a concealed weapon and resisting my false arrest."

* * *

Mary, in deep pain, couldn't sleep, eat, focus or make contact with any of her inside White House contacts. She was in the process of leaving her studio to take a brisk autumn night walk, thinking that it would clear her head and bring on a sense of hunger, when the phone froze her half out the door. She grabbed the phone on the third ring, he heart racing with anticipation.

"Hello."

"Mary, it's Evelyn Lincoln, are you alone?"

Her heart sunk trying to figure out the meaning behind the question.

"Yes." She tried to swallow but failed. "Good news, Evelyn, please, please."

"Yes, I have good news Mary."

The words released a flood of emotions and sobs. "Mary, please, I need you to be clear headed in order to make me a promise."

In spite of her emotional state she was able to grasp the seriousness of the words spoken by her friend, the personal secretary of the president. "Trust me, Evelyn, my word is my bond."

Evelyn dropped her voice, even though she was speaking alone in her own living room. "First and foremost, Jack is going to make it; he has a long rough road to recovery, but the doctors are reasonably certain that he will survive."

"Oh, praise God, Evelyn, praise God."

"Now then, Mary, the catch." She paused to let the words sink in. "Like I said, I need an iron clad promise from you, Mary, that you will share this information with no one; I've been told it's a matter of national security for the public to think otherwise for a few more hours."

"Yes, yes, Evelyn, of course, my lips are sealed."

"In that I can believe." Pause, "Mary, I know I can trust you; Jack told me a long time ago that your word is rock solid."

"Thank you, Evelyn."

"Mary, the reason I'm putting my neck on the line is because I know full well that Jack would want you to know."

* * *

Re-settled in Captain Fritz's office, Oswald states matter-of-factly. "I think I've said enough; until I have an attorney, I have nothing further to say." After several minutes of silence, with his eyes closed and head bowed, Oswald was unceremoniously escorted back to his cell.

Around eleven p.m. Oswald was awakened, without explanation, and escorted to an office that he had yet to visit. Awaiting him was a police officer who stood when Oswald entered the room. Seated at the table was a sober looking man dressed in all black.

The officer dismissed Oswald's escort and spoke. "I'm Dallas police detective, Captain John Adamcik, and this is FBI agent M. Clements."

Oswald snickered, "M . . . . what the hell kind of first name is M . . . . you sound more like a fiction writer . . . . with a Roman numeral for a first name."

The agent showed no emotion as the police officer spoke. "We're sorry to get you out of bed, however, we have a few question."

Oswald grinned, "Sorry boys, I'm all out of answers until I have legal counsel." With that he clammed up, closed his eyes and put his head down in a snoozing position.

Several minute passed before the phone broke the silence. "Yeah, sure, it appears that we're through in here."

"You're off the hook Oswald, the chief wants your face at a press conference; they've been demanding one ever since we brought you in."

As the door was closing behind him "M" barked, "Nice talking with you, asshole."

Officer Adamcik chuckled and poked a little fun at the Fed. "So, he did get to you."

"Yeah, right."

He used his fingers as quotation marks, to rub it in further. "You have a right to remain silent . . . ."

Oswald stepped into the room and was immediately blinded by the press conference lighting. He squinted as he was led to a chair on a stage and was pushed down, the cuffs behind him pinching his wrists. To Osawld's left, the chief stood at a podium with a cluster of network logoed microphones. Behind the chief stood a half dozen of what Oswald guessed as male hanger-ons. In the audience were about a dozen folks from the press, forced to sit behind two empty front rows as a buffer. They were pre-instructed to not speak unless spoken to by the chief. To make it even more restrictive, they were told to place their name in a bowl from which the chief would draw three names for the strict limit of a total of three questions. In the row behind the press was a scattering of about a dozen lookie-loos that clearly had connections that placed them there. Amongst the dozen, standing apart from the others and wearing a fedora hat, was one Jack Ruby.

The chief stepped closer to the podium and spoke. "This press conference will last about ten minutes, or could end abruptly depending on the behavior of the press and/or our suspect. To protect both the suspect and our ongoing case . . . . ," He motioned behind him, and a well dressed, distinguished looking man stepped forward. ". . . our District Attorney, reserves the right to cut off any question."

With that the chief motioned toward Oswald, "This is our shooting suspect, Mr. Lee Harvey Oswald; I emphasize the word suspect . . . . that's Oswald with an 's'."

Oswald spoke, ignoring the first question. "If the chief and District Attorney are soooo concerned about the legal process, ask them why I have yet been allowed my right to legal counsel."

All hell broke loose amongst the journalists and the small group of guests, save for Jack Ruby, who remained silent and apart from the group.

The chief raised both hands and loudly called for order into the cluster of microphones. "A public defender is on his way as we speak, and we left a message, with Oswald's lawyer of choice for him to call me on my personal number. In my message phone message I stated very clearly and specifically who was requesting his services, and by now Oswald is a household word."

In spite of the first journalist having been shortchanged, the chief pulled a second journalist's name out of a bowl.

"Yes sir, Mr. Oswald, I have two quick questions. 'What's with the bruised and swollen face, and tell us about your earlier arraignment."

"I was hit by a Dallas cop." He left it there and moved on quickly. "I was arraigned for the shooting death of police officer Tippit, of which I had no part of. I protested to the judge for not having been provided counsel; he simply said, it was routine and for me to plead not-guilty."

The third and final question, "Did you shoot the president of the United States?"

"No, and I have not been charged with that crime." He cleared his throat. "In fact, the first I heard about the assassination of our President, was after my Tippit arraignment; I was shocked of the news, to say the least." He shifted in his folding chair, "So the short answer is that I did not shoot anyone; time will prove that to be true."

*　　*　　*

With the news that Jack survived hours of intense surgery, and was being monitored around the clock by the best of the best in all aspects of the medical profession, Mary literally collapsed like a rag doll in her favorite studio chair, falling into a coma like sleep mid-sentence. "Thank, you Lord, there is no way I could have survive without Jack in my . . . ."

*　　*　　*

At daybreak Oswald was rudely awaken and given a cold breakfast with weak, lukewarm coffee, without cream or sugar. Up and at 'em, Mr. Asshole, you have a busy day ahead of you."

He grumbled as they left his cell, "Again? Oh boy." He sneezed.

The guard laughed, "There is no way God can bless you, man . . . . so don't keep your sneezing to yourself."

"Another big day . . . . starting with what?"

"An arraignment."

"I was arraigned yesterday."

"True, but this is the big one."

"The big one?"

"Yeah, for killing the president; they don't come any bigger than that."

"I didn't kill anyone . . . . when am I getting some legal console."

"Save it for the judge, ass hole."

"Anus orifice, please."

Within moments, Oswald stood before the same judge who presided over his earlier arraignment; unlike before, this arraignment had the highest of security . . . . no bailiff officer, no stenographer, no press; the judge himself was making dated, timed, signed, and later to be notarized, longhand notes.

"You, sir, stand before this court in the State of Texas verses you, Lee Harvey Oswald, for the attempted murders of the President of the United States, John Fitzgerald Kennedy, and the Governor of the State of Texas, John Connally."

Upon hearing the word "attempted", Oswald choked off a gasp as he felt a sudden rush of blood to his head along with a numbing surreal feeling of being removed from the here and now. He mumbled in near hushed agony. *"Oh noooo . . . . I failed . . . . we failed . . . . I'm finished . . . . I'm as good as dead."*

With words bouncing around in a deep echo chamber of his brain, Oswald gradually came around. "Mr. Oswald . . . . Mr. Oswald . . . . Mr. Oswald . . . . are you all right? What are you trying to tell us? Speak up please."

In a daze, "Yeah . . . . yeah . . . . I'm alright . . . . I wasn't saying anything . . . . just mumbling." He clears his throat. "I think this whole ordeal has left me with a sugar shortage . . . . or something. A sip of water should begin to set me straight."

He gulped several swallows of water. "Of course, my lack of legal counsel is a big factor as well."

"Mr. Oswald, as before, this is a formality, so plead not-guilty."

"Not guilty, of course.

"Mr. Oswald, you have been arraigned by the State of Texas, for the attempted murders of John Fitzgerald Kennedy, and John Connally. You will hereby remain in custody, without bail, until trial."

"So, when will I be allowed counsel?"

The judge ignored him, "Court is hereby dismissed."

No sooner had he returned to his cell and picked over the balance of his cold breakfast, he was again dragged from his cell. "Where the hell to this time?"

"Another chat with Captain Fritz and the FBI."

He grumbled as he was seated across the desk from Fritz and agent Forrest. "Well, it's going on twenty-four hours since my arrest. I've been beat up, arrested, booked, printed, arraigned two time, for crimes I did not commit, been through two lineups, a half dozen interrogations, and a press conference; all without legal counsel." He laughed aloud, "As far as I know, Texas is part of the United States . . . . hell, you could have fooled me."

Silence.

"Well, how about it?"

Fritz spoke in soft monotone, "The State has a lawyer on the way." He cut off Oswald's attempt to speak. "Now then, your rifle?"

"I never owned a rifle . . . . next question."

With no sign of emotion Fritz continued. "And, an automobile?"

"I don't own a car either. Mr. Paine owns a car, and his wife, Ruth, owns two cars."

"Tell us about your brother."

"My older brother, Robert, lives in Fort Worth. He and the Paines are close friends." Oswald shifted in his seat. "Of course you know, agent Forrest, that the FBI has thoroughly interrogated me on various occasions in the past. They've used both the hard and soft approach on me . . . . as well as their buddy system technique. I'm familiar with all types of questioning and have no intention of making any incriminating statements." Revealing a sudden air of confidence, "You are also aware, agent Forrest, that in the past three weeks the FBI has talked to my wife; they were abusive and impolite. They frightened my wife, and I consider their activities to be obnoxious." (When arrested, Oswald had FBI agent James Hosty's name, office phone and license numbers in his possession.)

They both reserved comment, as Captain Fritz jumped in. "And, your recent arrest?"

"In new Orleans?"

"Yeah, unless there's one more recent that that."

"I was arrested for disturbing the peace, for demonstrating for the Fair Play for Cuba Committee. I had a fight with some anti Castro refugees. As the system goes, they provoked the scuffle, so I was fined and, of course, they were simply released."

Silence, save for the shuffling of paper.

152

"So you'll know, I refuse to take a polygraph test." Pause. "Believe me, I did not shoot Kennedy, and I had no idea Connally had been shot until it was said during my arraignment." Pause. "Like I said, I don't own a rifle."

Long silence.

"I owned a shotgun while living in Russia; there you are not supposed to own a rifle. I speak Russian and I correspond with friends there; I also receive Russian newspapers."

Agent Forrest queries, "And your Communist party affiliation?"

"I am not a member of the Communist Party; I do belong to the American Civil Liberties Union."

Captain Fritz, "And the package you were seen carrying into the Book Depository on the morning in question?"

"I did, I carried my lunch, a sandwich and an apple."

Agent Forrest, "And you had no gripe with President Kennedy?"

"None really . . . . in fact I laud him for his failure of the Bay of Pigs."

*   *   *

Mary held her breath while watching the press conference held within a Parkland Hospital conference room, as thunder showers pummeled the Dallas region.

"The president remains heavily sedated in a medically induced coma, in the comfort of his own private intensive care suite. His vitals are stable, which is a very positive sign when you consider the trauma he has been through."

The chief surgeon paused for effect and scanned the dense crowd of journalists, cameramen, hospital employees between shifts or on break, a handful of White House officials, and local dignitaries. "The president had two major injuries. His entire right shoulder and socket were shattered as a result of a high powered rifle bullet passing directly through, shattering everything in its path. At this time, we only performed pre-orthopedic surgical clean up and prep for a complete shoulder rebuilding within the next few days. Arguably, we have the best orthopedic surgeon in the world who is currently studying the many pre and post preparatory surgery x rays. He is extremely confident that the president will recover nicely over time."

He paused for a sip of water, "The second trauma is amazing; amazing in that the bullet that violently tore through his skill did not kill him on impact. It was by the grace of God that our president is still with us, and without question it was divine intervention that guided our surgical moves to complete the initial miracle." He paused and slowly panned the audience,

"The bullet tore away a section of his skull, above his right ear, down to the very last fine and translucent membrane that protects the brain. The brain itself was not touched; however, the impact and violence alone sent a concessional shock wave throughout his entire brain cavity. To illustrate that point, the whites of both of his eyes are solid red, and the complete area around the right eye is literally black and blue."

Mary's knees weakened, she felt sick to her stomach and light headed, causing her to literally collapse on the sofa in a cold and clammy sweat. "Oh, my poor Jack. Thank you, Lord, thank you; your divine finger prints are all over this."

Questions were not allowed, and the press conference ended abruptly.

For the select few who were privy to the President's complete life-long poor medical history, they strongly felt that the President's health history could possibly lead to serious near future problems.

* * *

Oswald, in between being hungry and not caring to eat, forced himself to ingest every scrap of carbohydrates on his plate to aid him in the seemingly non-stop frenzy he was caught up in. He pushed away his half empty plate, as he chewed the last of pasta, bread, and butter, washing it down with putrid weak black coffee.

No sooner did he attempt to lay down for a quick snooze than, the guard yelled before reaching his cell. "You've got visitors, Oswald . . . . on your feet."

Groan, "Plural?"

"Yeah, two."

"Two who?"

"That's not in my job description . . . let's go."

Cuffed with his arms behind him, no sooner had he stuck his face into the visitor's room, "Lee, honey, you look awful."

"Ah, Mom, you look great as well."

Next to his mother, Marguerite Oswald, sat his Russian wife, Maria Oswald, whose face and eyes gave strong evidence of lengthy bouts of crying. She gasped, "Oh, Lee, they've beaten you."

"Don't you worry, honey, this is not a gulag. I scuffled with the police during my false-arrest in the movie theater."

"But . . . ."

"But nothing, honey," He whispered, "they've actually been treating me nice."

His Mother spoke with concern, "Honey, we're here to see what we can do, and were sorry it took so long, but nobody seemed to care about us wanting to see you."

Assuredly, "No, there is nothing for you to do. Everything is fine. I know my rights, and I will have an attorney. Don't you two worry about a thing."

He turned to his wife, "Don't cry, honey, it's all a mistake. I'm guilty of nothing except resisting a false arrest." Pause, "Please Maria, don't cry. There is nothing to cry about. Like I said, it's all a mistake. There are people who will help me. There is a lawyer I know in New York, on whom I'm counting on for help."

Silence, save for Maria trying to choke off her crying. ""Please, Maria, don't cry. You'll soon find out that there is nothing to cry about."

Pause.

"Now then, if they ask you anything, you have a right in America to say nothing; just simply remain silent. Do you understand? This is not Russia." Silence. "Do you understand?"

Irritated by the double questioning, "Yes, yes, Lee, I *do* understand."

Lee glanced at his mother before returning to Maria. "You are not to worry, you have friends; they'll help you."

"Yes, but we also have a brand new baby."

"If it comes to that you can ask the Red Cross for help. Above all, you must not worry about me."

She slowly nodded her head as she dabbed her red, wet, swollen eyes with a pale blue hanky.

The guard signaled that their visiting time was up. Lee leaned across the table, straining with his hands cuffed behind his back, and gave them both a peck on the lips, before being led toward the door. He looked over his shoulder in afterthought. "Be sure and kiss Junie and Rachel for me."

"Of course, Lee, we both will."

Half way through the door, "Don't forget to buy Junie those new shoes I promised her."

Maria began to cry as the door closed behind her pathetic husband, *"Shoes? Right, when I don't have two Rubles to rub together."*

The guard spoke through the side of his mouth as they continued down the hallway. "From here you go to a line-up."

Irritated, "What the hell is going on; this will be my third line-up?"

"Yeah, two more witnesses; Bills a pair, Scroggins and Whaley . . . . they claim to have seen you shoot officer Tippit to death."

As he stepped into the line-up room he froze in his tracks. "Whoa, not so fast. I'm about to get railroaded one more time. Look at these guys, they're dressed up in nice street close and wearing jackets . . . . looking presentable."

"Look at me, my face looks like a punching bag, I'm un-shaven, and been wearing the same jeans and tee shirt for the past two days."

An official took Oswald by the elbow and led him to his mark at the end of the line-up. "Stop your whining, asshole. You know the drill, stand straight and still on your mark, and look straight forward without a smile or frown."

"What a bunch of crap . . . . and all without an attorney."

* * *

With the televised reports on the president growing more optimistic, Mary, emotionally drained and sleep deprived, finally collapsed on her studio sofa in a fetal position . . . . with the main source of light in the drape-closed studio being the black and white glow of Walter Cronkite from the television.

* * *

Oswald and his escort were intercepted by another officer while leaving the line-up room. "He has a visitor."

Oswald lit up, "Oh boy, my lawyer."

"Sorry Oswald, but rumor has it one is on the way."

"Shit, shit, and shit."

"For what it's worth, it's your brother."

Unlike the visit with his wife and mother, his visit with his brother was at the normal visitor facility, over the phone separated by glass. He was ushered to a chair with his six year older brother, Robert, waiting on the free side of the glass. Lee gave his brother a crooked smile as Robert stared back quizzically. Lee picked up his receiver. He immediately cut his brother off. "Be very careful of what you say; it's safe to assume that the phones are tapped."

Robert gave him a silent thumb up. "Holy shit, Lee, you look a mess; what the hell have they been doing to you?"

He dropped his voice, "Actually, Robert, I got all the black and blue from my false arrest at the movie theater. Don't worry they're treating me fine," Again, he cut off his brother. "Other than the fact that I have yet to be provided legal counsel."

"Holly shit, Lee, it's been well over twenty-four hours."

"Yeah, I'm beginning to think that I'm back in Russia." Chuckle. "Hey, on the brighter side, what do you think of our new baby."

"She's gorgeous, bro."

"Yeah, no thanks to me."

They both laughed. "Of course, already having Junie, I was hoping for a boy, but we know how that goes."

Silence. "Well, Lee, it looks like you really stepped in it this time."

"Seriously, Richard, I have no idea what's going on; hell, I didn't kill anybody."

Silence, as Robert stared deep into his troubled brother's eyes for a clue.

Knowing that his older brother was searching, he broke the silence in a sober tone. "You won't find anything there, Bob."

With a face full of sorrow, Robert slowly shook his head in silence.

Lee broke the long silence. "Anyway, Bob, my friends will take care of Maria and the children."

Knowing the Paines well, Robert shook his head and said that he didn't believe that the Paines were friends of Lee.

Lee acted astonished, "Yeah, sure . . . . yes they are, Bob."

Bob's face saddened; his little brother seemed mechanical and detached . . . . not the brother he knew.

The guard placed his hand on Lee's shoulder, signaling the visit had come to an end.

"Oh, one last thing Robert."

Robert stared blankly at his troubled brother.

"Junie needs a new pair of shoes."

"Yeah sure." He placed his receiver down, turned and walked away, rolling his eyes, knowing that this was the beginning of a painful life-long journey.

As early darkness fell over Dallas, Oswald was, again, rousted from his cell bed. "Get your ass up and moving, Oswald."

"What the hell is it this time?"

"You can finally stop your belly aching, an attorney is here to see you."

Oswald froze midway through his cell door. "Are you shitn' me?"

"I'd like to think that it could make a difference. However, as far as I'm concerned you're a dead man walking."

"Thank God you're not on my jury."

"Anyway, I don't know how you rate."

"Rate . . . . what the hell do you mean by that?"

"He's *the* president of the Dallas Bar Association."

"Yeah, but he's not *my* choice."

He was escorted to the same visitor's room used by his wife and mother. No sooner had he entered the room a tall, heavy, red faced, middle aged man, in a western cut suit and string tie, stood and extended his beefy hand. "Louis Nichols, Attorney; how may I assist you?"

"The name's, Lee Harvey Oswald, let's chat."

At the end of the hand shake, the police guard, turned and paused at the door and addressed the attorney. "I'll be right outside the door, just give me a yell."

They both sat down and Oswald got right to the point. "Well, I don't know what this is all about. I was booked a day and a half ago, interrogated several times, participated in a press conference, and been through three line-ups, and two indictments .... all without legal counsel." Oswald cut off the lawyers attempt to speak. "Do you know a New York City attorney by the name of John Abt? I would like to have him represent me."

Nichols, all business, rubbed his chin, "No, I can't say that I do."

"Well, Abt is my first choice, If not him, I want an attorney who is a member of the ACLU .... of which I am a member."

"I am not a member. However, being the president of the Dallas Bar Association, I will check our database and make a few phone calls. Don't worry, Mr. Oswald, we'll find a good match for you."

"Good, in the mean time I'll try to connect with John Abt ...."

"I'll be back first thing Sunday morning with a name, in case your Mr. Abt doesn't materialize. I've spoken to the powers that be within the Dallas P.D., and the Feds, so don't worry about having legal coverage." With that, Nichols called for the guard, shook Oswald's hand and left.

The guard then escorted Oswald from the visitor's room, "Ok, Ozzie, Captain Fritz wants to have another chat."

Feeling empowered by his visitor, "Without counsel, can I simply refuse to go."

"Listen Oswald, as much as I hate to say it, we're both ex Marines, so we both will understand taking orders."

"Understand."

"After I deposit you in Fritz's office, you're free to discuss the issue with him."

Captain Fritz greeted him with disrespect, "Sit your ass down, Oswald."

Oswald looked around the office, "Oh, I see tweedle-dee is missing today."

"So now we have an assassin who thinks he's a comic."

Oswald grinned.

Fritz opened a manila folder sitting to his right, and slipped a photo in front of Oswald. "The cover of *Life* magazine, February of this year; what are your thoughts?"

Oswald stared at the photo of him holding a rifle, with a grin on his face. "In time, I'll be able to prove that this is not my picture." Pause, "But I don't have to answer any more questions." Pause, "I will not discuss this photograph without the advice of my attorney."

Long silence,

Oswald finally spoke, "There were other rifles in the Depository Building." Long pause. "I've seen them, Warren Caster has two rifles, a 30.06 for himself and a 22 for his son."

More silence.

"The magazine photo is not me, but the face is mine; my face has been skillfully superimposed. The remaining part of the body is clearly not me." Pause. "I've never seen this photograph." Silence. "Like I said, over time I'll be able to prove that the photo is not of me."

Oswald shifted in his chair and went on the offense. "Now then, Mr. Fritz, let me ask you of your thoughts on the photograph, seeing that it was the Dallas Police who cooked up the photo . . . as you're well aware."

Captain Fritz spoke as he placed the photo back into the manila folder. "I appreciate your thoughts, Mr. Oswald, now then back to the rifle."

Long silence.

"Mr. Oswald?"

Silence.

"I never kept a rifle at Mrs. Paine's house, in Irving, Texas." He sneezed, then paused. "Thank you for the blessing."

"It would have been disingenuous of me."

He slowly shook his head in disgust. "For the record, I had no visitors at my digs on North Beckley."

Silence.

"I have no receipt for purchase of any gun, and I have never ordered any guns. I do not own a rifle, never possessed a rifle."

Long silence.

"Tell me about your Selective Service card."

Oswald hesitated and shifted in his chair. "I will not say who wrote A. J. Hidell on my Selective Service card." (It was confirmed later that Maria Oswald wrote in the name Hidell). "Further, I will not tell you the purpose of carrying the card, or the use I made of it."

More pause.

"In the address book I carried, you will find names of Russian immigrants I've visited while in Dallas."

Fritz took a phone call which brought an end to the interrogation.

Just before mandatory lights-out, Oswald was granted an earlier request to call his wife at Mrs. Paine's home, only to be told that his wife and kids had moved to a new location not shared with Mrs. Paine. The news left Lee both angry and worried. Oh, how he missed his girls. Again, he worried about Junie's need for new shoes. He was angered further when his police escort had flippantly commented. "Hell, Oswald, can you blame them? Look at you."

After a night of worry and fitful dreams, he finally dozed off just before daybreak, only to be rudely awakened. "Up and at 'em, Oswald, rise and shine, it's chow time." Oswald groaned and buried his head beneath his pillow. "It's Sunday . . . . the Lord's day."

He reluctantly climbed out of bed to a cold floor and colder breakfast, and news of further interrogations and the possibility of being transferred from city to county jail. He yelled over his shoulder at the retreating guard. "Please, as a personal favor, have the authorities locate my wife and kids." Without a response, he grumbled and turned to his cold breakfast, with weak, lukewarm coffee. *Oh for a good strong, hot, black cup of Russian coffee.*

Within moments the guard returned, "It's official, butt head, you're being transferred to county jail today around mid-day."

"Yippee, I'll finally get out of these filthy clothes and into a clean Orange jump-suit."

"Yeah, Oswald, I guess you've finally arrived."

*   *   *

With the muffled sound of his girly bar, Jack Ruby sat in his private backroom office savoring a double 30 year-old Glenfiddich-rocks when the phone rang once, stopped, then rang twice and stopped. Jack grunted and mumbled, "Fuck me dead . . . . coming mother." He stood, grabbed his trademark Fedora hat, and downed the last of his private scotch. He called the barkeeper with the in-house intercom, "Hey, Peter."

"Yeah, boss."

"I'm stepping out the back for no more than fifteen."

"Gotcha covered."

He walked down the short end of the alley, hung a left for two blocks, and crossed the street to a bank of four phone booths outside a super market. Careful to select the phone booth of order, he dialed a number committed to memory. On the first ring a male with a deep voice simply stated, "Mama Mia's Pizza."

Ruby looked over his shoulder, "Can't be, I dialed the Orpheum Theater."

"Sorry buddy, wrong number."

"OK, thank you kindly."

Pause. "Listen our *lord and savior* has spoken, it's now *Plan B*. Do you understand?"

"Yes, *Plan B* is a go . . . . or me and my sibling will be called home."

"Amen."

The phone went dead.

He shook his head, stuffed his cold hands in his coat pockets, and began a slow walk back, in the late November chill, to his awaiting half-full bottle of Glenfiddich . . . . which he could finish tonight, or not at all.

He mumbled, "You can't claim to not know the rules. When the second part of the *trinity* speaks, it's a done deal. Even though we're both one of *them*, I have no choice but to toss you under the buss, Lee . . . . and you know it."

CHAPTER 3

Sunday, at 9:30 AM sharp, Oswald was escorted into Captain Fritz office, for a last minute one-on-one session. As he was seated, "Please, tell me that you've located my wife and children."

"No, not yet, but we're working on it."

"Good, when you locate them, I'll talk."

Fritz took a sip of coffee, "Yeah, right."

Fritz swiveled in his chair forty-five degrees to his right and stared out the window. "Now then, Oswald, let's go back to the Book Depository, and talk about what you witnessed from within the building after the president was shot."

Oswald looked up at the ceiling, "Let's see . . . . immediately following the assassination, which of course at that point we were still not aware that a shooting had occurred. The first inkling we had was the chaos within the building, starting with the single policeman running into our lobby yelling, 'where is your telephone'. At that point he began to waive his credential in the air for all to see, so I showed him the phone."

Pause.

"I refuse to discuss the shooting of the president or officer Tippit, because I know nothing about either shooting. As far as I'm concerned, I'm here because I popped a policeman in the nose while defending myself during a false-arrest. As far as carrying a loaded weapon, half the guys in Texas carry guns and you know that; you know, this is not exactly California."

Pause.

"It was cheap for me to visit Mexico; of course, all I had was food and one night's lodging. I went to the Mexican embassy to get permission to go to Russia by the way of Cuba. I filled out the papers and was told to return in thirty days."

Long silence. "The Fair Play for Cuba Committee, New Orleans chapter, was loosely organized, and we had no officers. You could probably call me the secretary or treasurer, because I did collect money." (The Warren Report stated that Oswald was the only member in New Orleans).

Fritz turned his chair and looked directly at Oswald. "What other major city has a Fair Play for Cuba chapter?"

"I know that New York has a large, well organized chapter, as does Miami. And I had no intention to organize a chapter in Dallas. Besides, I was too damn busy trying to find a job."

"And your New Orleans P.O. Box?"

Subdued surprise, "First of all it is not my P.O. Box, it belongs to the Fair Play for Cuba Committee."

"With who having access?"

"Just I .... and I had my wife pick up mail there occasionally." Pause. "Let's be clear, I never ordered any form of firearm through the P.O. Box." Pause. "Nor did I permit anyone else to order a rifle, or anything else, to be received through the box."

"And your map of Dallas covered with X's?"

"Oh, that map, you found in my room. Each X is the location where I had an interview for employment. The X at Houston and Elm Streets is my current place of employment, the Texas Book Depository." Pause. "That's all the map amounts to .... other than for general use."

Lengthy pause.

"Tell me, Oswald, what religion do you subscribe to?"

Taken aback, "Religion?" Pause. "What the hell does that have to do with anything?" Pause. "I have no faith .... I suppose you mean in the Bible. I've read the entire Bible. It's fair reading, but really not that interesting." Pause. "As a matter of fact, I am a student of philosophy, and I don't consider the Bible as even a reasonable, or intelligent, philosophy. I don't think of it ...." His unintelligible words simply trailed off and stopped.

"Let's talk about target practicing, and the zeroing in of your rifle."

Angered, "How damn many times must I tell you that I *do not* own a rifle." Pause. "Holy shit, man." Pause. "And as far as firing a weapon, hell, I haven't fired a rifle since leaving the Marines." Pause. "Maybe a .22, but absolutely nothing larger."

"Tell me about the package you received through your Dallas P.O. Box."

"I never received a package through that P.O. Box, under my name or any other name" Pause. "Now, that's not to say that my wife could have ordered something through the box; you'll have to ask her."

Long silence.

"I'm through talking without an attorney."

"Get off it, Oswald, we offered you an attorney, and you turned your nose up at him."

Indignant, "You're wrong sir, Mr. Nichols, the president of the Dallas Bar Association, only offered to help find an attorney for me."

Captain Fritz dismissed Oswald with a wave of a hand, "Same thing."

"No it's not." He shifted in his chair, "Nichols said that he would contact me today, or no later than Monday, with the name of an attorney, in case I'm unable to contact my attorney, Mr. Abt."

Silence.

"Tell me about Marxism."

Oswald perked up, "I've been a student of Marxism since the age of fourteen." Pause. "I know that it's a bitter pill for you to swallow, but the American people will soon forget that their president was shot. But, man, I didn't shoot him."

Oswald continued, "You know, all of us, you and me, are extremely dispensable and can easily be replaced. That applies to Kennedy; he could be replaced as if nothing happened, and his replacement's views on Cuba would really be no different than Kennedy's."

Long silence.

"Again, I did not kill the president or officer Tippit. If you want me to cop a plea for hitting a police officer during a false arrest, then you've got it. But, that's as far as I'll go."

Officer Fritz glanced at his watch as the phone rang. "Yeah, sure, he's on his way." He hung up the phone and stared at the contents in the folder, as if to avoid eye contact. "Well, Oswald, you're being transferred to County Jail, where we'll continue this interrogation."

"Gee, I'm so looking forward to it."

"So you'll know, Oswald, you will not be well received by other County Jail inmates."

Oswald shrugged his shoulders, "How and when will I receive information on the whereabouts of my family?"

Fritz gave a dismissive wave with his nose still buried in the manila folder, "That information will find its way to you in due time."

At 11:15 AM Oswald, with hands cuffed in front of him, was escorted from his cell at Dallas City jail in his first leg of being transferred to County Jail. A bogus later transfer time was released to the media in hopes of avoiding a circus. However, as mysterious as the missing sock in the clothes dryer, the information on the real transfer time had been leaked, with police crowd control in progress within the underground portion of the City Jail parking structure.

As Oswald was preparing for transfer, a crowd of thirty to forty news media and public lookie-loos were jockeying for position under the loose control of a half dozen rookie police officers, and one officer paying more attention to the door from which Oswald was scheduled to exit than to the details of crowd control.

The shuffling for camera position remained dynamic within the confines of the egress route from the door, to the police department basement, and the short walk through a small portion of the garage area, to an awaiting secured vehicle. The odd man out among the clamoring journalists and rookie cops was a local small time gangster and Dallas nightclub owner Jack Ruby.

Within seemingly arms reach of Ruby, stood two men who would soon join Ruby in a shared place of infamy. Cameraman George Phenix of Dallas CBS affiliate KRLD-TV and photographer Jack Beers of the *Dallas Morning News*.

Suddenly, an unnamed officer stepped forward to the inside edge of the roped off area, raised his arms and shouted. "Quite, please! Again, absolutely no questions will be allowed from the media or anyone else present. Everyone keep their mouth shut . . . under the threat of arrest. Also, starting immediately, I repeat, immediately, everyone remain in place and flat footed."

With that, the door to the garage opened and Oswald emerged handcuffed to two plain clothes man, one on each wrist. Wearing a white western cut suite with matching brimmed hat was Jim Leavelle, cuffed to Oswald's right arm. Cuffed to Oswald's left arm was L.C. Graves wearing a dark western cut suite and dark grey wide brimmed western hat.

In spite of the attempt to secretly transfer Oswald earlier, they were now faced with a crowd of their own, in addition to an estimated live television audience of sixty million. The black and white television coverage was being handled as a news flash or bulletin that Sunday, November 24, at 11.21 AM, Central Standard Time. The viewers observed a sober enveloping crowd in the unlikely, soon to be, killing ground.

Of all the media present, it was cameraman George Phenix who dutifully shot what was supposed to be the simple transfer of the purported assassin to an awaiting car that would carry the accused a mere single mile to the County Jail. Phenix, as fate, or luck, would have it, was ideally positioned, just a few feet behind Jack Ruby, as the cuffed trio emerged from the doorway and stepped clear of the crowd.

As experts later would conclude, for a brief moment Oswald turned and made eye contact with Ruby, facially expressing ever so slightly, *"What are you doing here Jack?"* The following instant Oswald turned away from Ruby to the same straight ahead position of his two manacled escorts.

The very next moment, Ruby lunged forward jabbing his .38 caliber Colt Cobra revolver point blank into the left side of Oswald's sternum, and fired a single shot that stunned Oswald, his escorts, and the entire world.

At that precise moment, photographer Jack Beers shot a still black and white photo, forever sealing the moment for history.

Oswald winced in pain and fell like a rag doll to the brush finished concrete garage floor, bringing his two cuffed escorts to one knee.

The escorts removed the cuffs as Oswald lay between life and death. He had already taken on the same shade of grey as the concrete floor.

The police officers quickly moved the crowd back a good ten yards from Oswald, who lay silently in shock, clearly wincing in spasmodic intense pain. He looked around with a blank, thousand-yard stare. Attempts were made to comfort him without medical attention, as the sound of sirens rose above the clamor of the crowd.

Within fifteen minutes of Oswald having emerged into the garage, the crowd had dispersed, leaving the cigarette littered crime scene empty and eerily quiet.

Ironically, Oswald was taken to the same Parkland Hospital, still occupied by the very man he allegedly attempted to murder. Within twenty minutes of Oswald's arrival to the emergency room, he was declared dead.

Those of us that witnessed, on live television, Jack Ruby shoot Oswald, knew that something was terribly wrong and that Oswald was *clearly* being silenced.

CHAPTER 4

With the alleged *lone* assailant dead, a second gunman also dead but unannounced, and the president on the mend, the American public stirred with mixed emotions. Initially, the masses rejoiced as they viewed the countless full and slow motion replay of the murder of Oswald. However, no sooner had Oswald been laid to rest at Rose Hill Memorial Park in Fort Worth Texas, the public was beginning to feel cheated in never being able to witness the public spectacle of a show-trial.

Mary was amongst the minority who took comfort in the juxtaposition of quick good-versus-evil closure. As she skillfully applied oil to canvas in the comfort of her studio, she uttered a near silent prayer of thanksgiving. "Thank you, thank you, Lord, for watching over Jack, and please have mercy on Oswald's pathetic soul." She hummed as she returned to her palette in an attempt to step-blend the colors of a beautiful sunrise within her canvas seascape. "Oh, Jack, I'm soooo anxious to see you."

The daily progress reports on the president remained optimistic, in spite of him remaining in a medically induced coma. The plan being to leave him in the coma through his extensive shoulder orthopedic rebuilding surgery scheduled the Monday following Thanksgiving. And, of course, partisan politics was alive and well. Paramount in the GOP talking points was a solemn toned question of JFK's ability to lead, as well as a sympathetically veiled call for him to reject the idea of a second term. All of this solemnly prefaced with *"In all due respect, we must consider what is best for the country"*. Which any simpleton translated into *'what is best for our party'*.

Although the Democrats were dismissive of the GOP's *'can he continue to lead'* campaign, the Kennedy clan was conferring, behind the scenes, with the president's long-time personal physician. Central to their concern was Jack's dismal life-long record of poor and failing health, which in detail was not a matter of public record.

The public, informed by 1976 era communication and record technology, knew as much about the president's life-long health record as the Kennedy White House chose, which was next to nothing, including details of his military related bad back glamorized in the book and movie *"PT-109"* (Kennedy was in fact wearing a rigid back brace at the time of his assassination). Additionally, a miniscule number of history and news buff fanatics were aware of the president's near lifelong struggle with debilitating Addison Disease. In reality, from a medical standpoint, Kennedy was a mess.

His personal medical records indicate that he had been hospitalized more than three dozen times throughout his life, and that he had been administered the Catholic Last-Rights on three occasions. In total he had suffered up to forty injuries, childhood illnesses, and diseases from his earliest infancy, his war injuries, and nagging health issues throughout his presidency.

Many of Kennedy's disorders had genetic roots. Some speculate that being his mother was the product of a consanguineous union between second cousins; it may have been a factor. This clearly did not affect *her* longevity, for she lived to 104 years of age.

Those closest to Kennedy were amazed at how he carried on at such a high level with his constant pain, medication, and level of medical susceptibility.

Understandably, all of this impacted his temperament. He had an inner hardness, often volatile anger, beneath an outwardly amiable, thoughtful, carefully controlled demeanor. Kennedy described himself as "always on the edge of irritability".

On the QT, Kennedy's secretary, Evelyn Lincoln, made after hours personal calls from home to Mary, bringing her up to date on the president's progress . . . . often times prior to media release, and without spin. Mary was assured that her love and best wishes for a speedy recovery would be personally relayed to Jack through unconventional channels.

Mary had risen from the depth of despair to that of upbeat joy, clearly evident by the work in her studio.

Being a long-time Washington insider, Vice President Johnson performed his 'acting' presidential duties near seamlessly, in spite of GOP making subtle behind the scenes political hay of *their* president's health dilemma. The Republicans softly and respectfully were leaking out doubt as to weather the president would be able to return to duty, and, if so, would be incapable of the day to day rigor of his office.

The day after Oswald had been laid to rest, Kennedy's medical team decided it was best to perform the reconstructive surgery of his entire right shoulder while in Dallas, with the president remaining in his medically induced coma.

While the president lay in a coma, no stone was being left unturned by the FBI and CIA, all while the political wheels turned slowly in forming what would eventually become the CIA controlled and rigged Warren Commission.

CHAPTER 5

The day following the president's successful shoulder reconstruction surgery, the medical team agreed that their patient was ready to be phased out of his medically induced coma. The First Lady was informed when to be present at her husband's bedside for the big event.

While Jackie, the medical team, the closest of presidential aides, and one lone Secret Service agent were seated comfortably within the spacious private suite, they waited in hushed conversation. As their badly wounded Commander In Chief began to stir ever so slightly, for the first time since entering Parkland Hospital emergency care, the group held their collective breath as they inched as close as allowed.

Mary was skillfully applying oil to canvas, using a mini-spatula, managed to grab the phone mid second ring.

From her desk right outside the Oval Office, Kennedy's secretary spoke in a hushed tone with an edge of excitement "Mary, it's me, Evelyn, with a flash bulletin long before given to the media."

"Hurry, Evelyn, you're killing me."

"Jack, as we speak, is in the process of regaining consciousness."

Mary gasped and placed her open palm on her breast, transferring oil paint to her work smock, as her blond hair fell across her free cheek. "Thank you, thank you, Lord . . . . millions of prayers, global wide, have been answered."

Evelyn grinned with satisfaction. "I certain that Jack would want you to know ahead of the media."

"Thank you soooo much, Evelyn, I owe you big time."

"Don't you worry, girl, you owe me nothing" She chuckled softly, "However, for the record, I am keeping score."

"Oh God, Evelyn, I love you."

"Me to you, Mare." Pause, "I'll continue to keep you in the loop . . . . again, that's what Jack would want."

"Thanks again, Ev."

"You bet, gotta run, another line is beckoning."

*　　*　　*

Tears welled in Jackie's eyes as her husband's eyes slowly fluttered open for the first time in nine days. He slowly shut his eyes for half-dozen seconds then reopened them with a sign of confusion on his face. To prevent him from having to turn his head, Jackie stood and positioned herself directly above him. As the eyes of the medical team darted between the multiple monitors, their president, and First Lady, they jotted notes into medical records as necessary.

Jack parted his lips and struggled to speak. Jackie placed her forefinger across his lips, "Shhhh, take your time honey, there's no hurry. You've had an accident, you're in the hospital, and you are going to be just fine."

The sight of Jackie erased the confusion from his face, and he gave a slight nod of his head.

With his head remaining still, his eyes darted around the room fixing on nothing. His eyes met Jackie's with a scared, puzzling look, before struggling with his first words.

"My God . . . . wh . . . wh . . . what . . . ha . . . . happened?"

Jackie looked at the chief surgeon with a quizzical stare. He responded with a clear nod.

"Jack, honey . . . . you've been shot."

The words seem to hang in the air, as the president blinked, then gave a *thousand yard stare* beyond the ceiling. He struggled and finally locked eyes with the First Lady with a quizzical look. Jackie gently squeezed his limp hand as he closed his eyes. Within moments, with eyes closed, a lone tear rolled slowly down his pale right cheek.

With that, the chief surgeon gave a head-nod toward the door, signaling the presidential visit was over.

Within an hour of the president being medically roused to consciousness, the chief surgeon conducted a press conference atop the entrance steps of Parkland Hospital.

"We are delighted and relieved that the president of the United States has regained consciousness, with all medical signs pointing toward a steady and full recovery. He and the First lady exchanged a few simple sentences, including the president asking what had happened."

An aggressively anxious journalist loudly interrupted, "Doctor, can you tell us how the First lady answered the president's question?"

Calmly, and without missing a beat, "I cannot speak for the First Lady. But I'm sure that in due time she will speak to the press."

An even less sensitive reporter shouted, although from the second row from the front, "Can you tell us of his ability to lead?"

"As I said, *but you failed to hear*, all signs point to a full recovery."

The same reporter drowned out a fellow journalist standing within arms length. "Is your silence suggesting that the president is not fit to complete his current term?"

'No, sir, it is you that are making that suggestion." The reported began to retort, but was cut off by the surgeon raising his hand in a silencing gesture as he continued. "I suggest that you direct questions of that nature to the White House."

The surgeon turned toward the opposite edge of the crowd and spoke quickly. "You, mam?"

"Sir, can you share with us when the president will be fit to leave Dallas?"

"Yes mam; we, the medical staff, are looking at within the next couple of days. As we speak, a team is being assembled at the other end to accommodate the president's every need."

She managed to slip in an additional question, "And, sir, the other end being where?"

The surgeon raised both hands as the woman spoke, "That's all for now, thank you for coming."

With that, he turned and re-entered the hospital to the shout of collective inaudible questions.

Mary mounted the outside stairs to her second story art studio, located above a detached garage behind the spacious Georgetown home of her sister Tony and brother-in-law Ben Bradlee. She was feeling clear-headed after a brisk routine walk along the Chesapeake and Ohio Canal towpath. She switched on the television and stood back critiquing her morning's work. She turned toward the TV news bulletin in time to see the live newscast from the front steps of Parkland Hospital. She pumped her fist, "Yes, yes . . . . what's breaking news for some is a mere replay for others." Upbeat, she chuckled aloud, "Play it again, Sam."

Her eyes were brimmed with tears as the chief surgeon ended the press conference and turned to enter the hospital,

"Thank you, again, Lord. Thank you."

Acting president Lyndon Johnson leaned back in Kennedy's chair and placed his cowboy boots on the Oval Office desk as he spoke to his press secretary.

"Well, partner, I'd be less than honest if I didn't say that I'm beginning to feel right at home in this here ob-round office." They laughed as Lyndon raised his Commander In Chief gold monogrammed navy blue coffee mug.

"Now then, the press conference." Johnson raised his hands in a sign of frustration. "Acting president . . . . with an emphasis on the word *acting*." He removed his boots from atop the desk and leaned forward on his forearms. "The Kennedy clan is alive and well as I speak." Johnson frowned and handed his press secretary the talking points for his press conference. "Here you go, straight from the Kennedy clan . . . . and we had better dare not be *creative*."

The press secretary shook his head before perusing the outline. "What chance do we mere cowboys have against the Irish mafia?" He shook his head as he worked his way down the single space type written page. "Man, these folks are clearly unwilling to give a mere fraction of an inch." He returned the paper to Johnson, "Hell, it's as if their *godfather* simply stubbed his tow."

Johnson placed the paper on the expansive desk. "Yeah, and all the while the GOP continues to fan the flames." He shifted in his seat and picked up his coffee, "With the election a short ten-plus months off, the GOP's latest insistence is that Jack resigns, I assume the presidency, and Speaker John McCormack moves into the role of Vice President."

"Yeah, in hopes of, in their opinion, weakening the presidential ticket and placing McCormack's seat up for grabs . . . . clearly, huge chunks of red meat for their base."

Johnson laughed as he again placed his boots on the presidential desk, "You've got that right, partner. Except, the Constitution clearly states that in a case such as ours, the Vice Presidency shall remain vacant throughout the remainder of the term . . . . playing right into *my* own plans."

The press secretary stood to leave. "Heaven forbid that the GOP let facts stand in the way of their rhetoric."

CHAPTER 6

White House press secretary Pierre Salinger called the press conference to order.

"My duty this morning is a singular introduction." He paused to grab everyone's attention. "Ladies and gentlemen, the Vice President of the United States."

Lyndon Johnson appeared and stepped to the podium.

"Good morning," He smiled and paused, "Or is it afternoon?"

The press corps laughed as they looked at their watches; it was, depending on one's time piece, one or the other.

"I'm privileged to be the one to inform you, and all of America, that earlier today our president had fully successful orthopedic reconstructive surgery to his shattered right shoulder. The entire process took place as he remained in his medically induced coma."

He slowly scanned the room. "Although the recovery process will be long and physical therapy driven, our president will resume his duties, albeit initially at a temporary combination hospital room and office being set up, as I speak, at the Hyannis Port Kennedy family compound."

He paused long enough to have to raise his hand in a silencing gesture. "Throughout the president's brief stay, at what we'll henceforth refer to as the Hyannis White House, I will be back and forth and he and I will be all but in constant phone contact with one another."

He took off his glasses, "Now then, I have time for no more than a half dozen questions."

The room suddenly came alive with clamor. "Yes, the gentleman from CBS." Typically Johnson, whose deliberate avoidance of names, kept the press at arm's length.

"When can we expect the president to be back in the Oval Office, and fully functional at every aspect of his job?"

"The president's medical team assures me that the president is recovering nicely and will return to the White House as soon as possible."

Johnson quickly turned to the opposite side of the room. "Now then, the lady from NBC."

"We keep hearing the word *normal* being used in regards to the president's recovery. When one examines his life-long health record, the last word that comes to mind is *normal*. Having said that, what can the American people really expect in terms of recovery?"

Johnson shifted his position at the podium, and chuckled. "Well, I'm not a doctor, nor can I speak as one. I suggest that you address questions of this nature to the president's medical team during their next press conference."

Johnson again turned away, "Now then, you, sir, from the *Washington Post*."

The *Washington Post* guy was cut off before he started by the gal from NBC, "Sir, if I may, one final statement germane to my unanswered question." She did not wait for permission. "Sir, I directed that very question to the head of the president's medical team earlier today." She paused and hoped the Vice President would take the bait, and within seconds he grabbed the lure and ran.

"And, young lady, would you mind sharing the answer you were given by the chief surgeon?"

"Yes sir, I was told to redirect the question to the White House; and your answer is?"

He smiled in spite of being angry at himself for being led into a trap by the young journalist. "Well, then, young lady, I guess it falls back on the White House, and all I can say, in all honesty, is that we'll have to get back with you."

She smiles and pointed at the television camera, "Thank you, sir, but get back to the American public, they have an interest and a right to know."

"Right you are, young lady" He returned to the man from the Washington Post, "Now, again, sir, you were starting to ask."

"Thank you, Mr. Vice President. My question is when the White House does get back to the people regarding the previous question; you can be assured that they would like to know at least three more things. When will the president be out of bed, when will he be on his feet and mobile, and how will all of this affect the rigors of his run for a second term?" He paused. "The extreme rigor of a presidential campaign is enough to kill the healthiest of us."

Johnson smiled, "The points of your question are well taken, sir. I can assure you that all of the public's concerns will be addressed in a follow-up news conference within the next day or two."

He raised his hands and spoke above the press corps clamor, "That concludes this press conference. Thank you all for coming." With that he turned and abruptly left the room.

President Kennedy closed his eyes and turned away from the television and spoke slow chopped words, with a tone of disgust. "I've . . . . seen . . . enough . . . . turn . . . it . . . off."

His aid turned off the television and whispered in his ear. "Mary has repeatedly, immediately following your incident, tried to get in touch with you."

The president opened his eyes wide with a trace of a smile on his face that still had a grey hew. "Please . . . . tell . . . her . . . . that . . . I . . . will . . . . call . . . from . . . Hy . . . annis . . . . Port."

"Yes sir, Mr. President, right away."

"Hello Mary, Evelyn Lincoln here."

A rush of adrenalin drove Mary to her feet. "Oh, Evelyn, thank God."

"The president has a message for you, through an aid."

"Thank you, Lord."

"He said that he will call you as soon as he's transferred to Hyannis Port."

"Oh, Evelyn, I can't begin to thank you enough. I've been worried sick over Jack . . . . the president."

"I can well imagine, Mary."

"Do we know when he'll transfer to Hyannis Port?"

She paused as if distracted, before dropping her voice.

"Well, as always, Mary, the move is on the QT. All I can tell you is that the move will be over before the press is in the loop."

Mary sat down, "Oh, I see. Trust me Evelyn, my lips are sealed."

"Mary, it's not only me, but it's also the president who thinks that your word is your bond." She dropped her voice to whisper and covered her mouth and the phone with the hand, "He'll be leaving Dallas this evening, as soon as darkness sets in."

"Oh, Evelyn, how can I ever thank you?"

"With your presence."

"My presence?"

"Still at a whisper, "Yes, with your presence; you are such a breath of fresh air around here." She took a deep breath. "Again, I speak for the President as well as myself."

"Why thank you Evelyn, you just made my day . . . . again."

"Got to go . . . but one more thing."

"Yes, what."

"You're such a positive influence on the president, he'll need you around as much as possible during his recovery . . . . please."

"Of course, Evelyn, of course," She cleared her throat. "However, we both know that Jackie is the key to that."

"Got to go, another call beckons."

Mary danced around the studio and reached for her painting smock . . . . feeling so alive.

CHAPTER 7

Mary smiled as she watched the 10 PM news, feeling privileged and a wee bit smug. The *big hair* blond Dallas newsreader stood on the steps of Parkland Hospital and spoke of her 'exclusive' to breaking news. "Moments ago a hospital administrator informed KNBC Dallas that president Kennedy secretly left the hospital under cover of darkness, and that he is currently resting comfortably in the Kennedy family Hyannis Port compound." She looked at the camera full of pride, prompting Mary to chuckle.

"Kind of late aren't we dahlin."

Big hair continued, "We've been told that a four room second story suite within the Kennedy compound has been set up as a combination hospital physical therapy room and remote Oval Office." She smiled. "We've also been informed that upon arrival the president was transferred into the compound on a gurney, and that he was wide awake and alert to the point where he saluted the pilot of Helicopter One." As the station logo and call letters scrolled across the bottom of the screen she signed off. "We will keep you informed as more news unfolds."

* * *

On the early morning news, the GOP was already spinning the president as 'stealing away under darkness' with their perception of what they thought as a cover-up of the president health recovery going poorly; all for political gain on the cusp of an election year.

The following evening the White House checked and dismissed the spin with a well choreographed closed press conference from Kennedy's bedside.

Jackie, with all of her charm, began the lead-in as if accepting a personal guest at the front entrance of the Hyannis Port compound. 'Welcome,

178

America, to the temporary beach-front White House." She stepped aside as if allowing an imaginary guest to enter. She stepped from the expansive entry foyer into a wide hallway and continued. "The president has been expecting you." She paused. "I want the American people to know how happy I am with the president's progress, and the courageous spirit that he's been exhibiting." She paused in the hallway, "He wants all of you to know that he is fighting for himself as well as each and every one of you." She turned and entered a wide, deep carpeted stair case and continued to speak to her imaginary guest. "Also, here to welcome you this evening is Vice President Johnson and, perhaps, a representative of the president's medical team." She stopped, placed her hand on the knob of a closed door and lowered her voice to just above a whisper. She smiled and turned on her famous charm. "Just like any hospital, the visiting hours are short, and no more than several million American guests being allowed at any one time." With that, Jackie allowed the American public to enter the room ahead of her.

The camera man (aka the American public) paused inside the doorway as if waiting to be invited further into the spacious, carpeted 'hospital room'. Jackie paused mid-room and turned toward the cameraman, "Please do come in, the president is expecting you."

To the 'visitor's' right was a medical bed with a view of Centerville Harbor through a large window with heavy drawn curtains. The bed was adjusted to a forty-five degree angle, with the president, reading glasses on the end of his nose, studying an opened manila folder held in his frail hands. Standing at the president's elbow was Vice President Johnson, leaning while pointing at a document in the folder. They concluded their hushed dialogue and the president handed the closed folder to Johnson who stepped across the room. With that, Jackie stepped toward her husband as he turned and greeted her with a smile.

"Honey, Mr. President, the American public came to visit you."

Although the president's color had improved, he clearly looked convalesced with his trademark thick head of hair covered, except at the temples, with a gauze wrapping, which gave his face a different look.

Vice President Johnson suddenly reappeared and whispered in the president's ear. As he and the president shared Johnson's pocket watch, an aid appeared and whispered in Johnson's ear. At that Johnson and Kennedy had a brief hushed conversation before Johnson, again, disappeared, and a nurse's aid appeared, answering the president's buzz. They spoke in hushed tone before the nurse turned his bed thirty-degrees toward the cameraman.

Jackie reclaimed her bedside position and took her husband's hand before giving him a short peck on the lips. He smiled . . . . and spoke to the invisible audience, "Ahh, just what the doctor ordered."

Jackie turned toward the camera and gave an abbreviated wink, as Jack began to speak.

He shifted a bit in his elevated bed, "Good afternoon, America, I've been anxiously expecting you; I apologize for the distraction, but my duty to all of you calls." He paused for a breath. "Please do come in." The cameraman inched closer. Although his speech had improved dramatically, his words had a trace of measurement.

"I would like to thank all of you for coming, and for keeping me and my family in your thoughts and prayers." He cleared his throat and took a sip of water through a flex-straw. "With all of you seeing me for the first time since my ordeal, you cannot begin to appreciate the amazing progress I've made." He looked at his wife, "Right, Jackie?"

"Oh my, yes; his progress has been unbelievably dramatic, praise God." She turned and looked directly at the camera, "I want all of America to know and appreciate what an absolute *PT-109* of a warrior they have for a president."

* * *

Tears rolled down Mary's face as she stared at Jack on television, with a touch of sky blue oil paint on her right cheek. "Oh, Lord, I cannot begin to thank you enough." She smiled, "You're looking good, Jacko."

* * *

In spite of the president's bravado, he exhausted quickly, with 'America's' visit lasting no more than ten minutes. Of course, with the opposition all being much tougher than the president, they would make political hay with the brevity of the televised visit.

The president's rate of recovery from his gun shot was without question remarkable, especially when you consider his life-long health record. The White House plan was to maintain focus on the president's positive recovery of his assassination wounds to the point of creating a diversion to his general health, which his medical team was secretly beginning to shift its focus toward.

* * *

Mid morning following 'America's visit' the phone rang in her studio, pushing Mary's anger button in the middle of trying to mix a desired color on her palette. *"Crap . . . why can't it ring while I'm on my butt?"* She glanced at the clock as she set aside her palette and stepped to the phone. *"Wrong time for the kids . . . . I hope to hell it isn't Cord."* She grabbed the phone as she brushed her hair aside.

"Hello . . . hello . . ." She was about to hang up when she heard a chuckle. "Gee, I had hoped you would be happy to hear from me, Mary, Mary."

Mary gasped, put her free open hand across her breast as she sat down.

"Oh . . . my . . . God." She gasped. "It's really you . . . . Oh, Jacko, the sound of your voice is as if a pair of shock-paddles brought me back to life . . . . praise God."

"It must be contagious, Mary, because I too suddenly feel so alive."

They both laughed aloud. "Thanks, Mare, I needed that."

"Oh, Jack, we both came soooo close to dying."

"Yeah . . . . but at least I was in a coma through the lion share of the ordeal."

"Jack, I really enjoyed visiting you with the American masses."

"Our PR folks have been getting nothing but rave reviews . . . . except for the opposition, of course."

"Yeah, as if we care."

"Listen, I'm in a bit of a hurry. I just got off the phone with Mrs. Lincoln, and she'll be expecting your call. We have a twice-a-day air shuttle between the White House and Hyannis Port. I've just got to see you, Mare. So, call Evelyn and let her know what flight works for you."

"Oh, Jack, thank you, thank you, thank you."

"You bet, Mare." Pause. "I'm really hoping that you'll be able to leave your return open-ended."

"Yes, Jack, yes . . . . open ended."

He chuckled, "For the record, you've volunteered to come down and help in any way possible."

"I like the sound of *any way possible.*"

"Me too."

She dropped her voice, "And Jackie?"

"Oh, she's totally on board, and is anxious to see you; she needs to get away for three or four days with the kids, so you'll be a big help for her personally."

"Gee, I hope so."

"Well, Mare, I've got to run, presidential duties are beckoning."

"Thanks again, Jack."

"Thank you, Mare."

CHAPTER 8

White House press secretary, Pierre Salinger, smiled and maintained his composure as he stepped from the podium and exited the White House press corps room. With the corps room door closed behind him, he abruptly dropped his façade with his aid walking beside him. "Son of a bitch, it's become so predictable; the heat from the press corps is inversely proportional to the recovery rate of the president."

The aid chuckled, "So you've noticed, eh Pierre?"

Pierre laughed, "I would hope so."

"Yeah, and the GOP is controlling the *gas valve*."

"Like sharks and blood, for god sake."

Pierre stopped halfway down the hall and dropped his voice to a near whisper. "I can't imagine how the opposition will react when they get wind of the president's real underlying health problem."

The aid shook his head as they continued down lush carpeted hall. "Yeah, a campaign manager's worst nightmare."

"Can't begin to imagine what the campaign year will bring."

*   *   *

The distant sound of an approaching helicopter drew the president toward the window in his wheel chair, after just having received a call from Mrs. Lincoln confirming Mary was on the flight. He scanned the skies above the blue expansive harbor and smiled as his heart quickened. "Yes indeed, I am alive . . . . praise God."

In spite of the helicopter approaching from offshore in an attempt at noise reduction, the local community had grown noise weary early in the Kennedy presidency.

First off of Air Force Two was a pair of aides, each carrying a banker box of documents for the day's official business. Next, followed Pierre Salinger carrying a leather attaché case. The final passenger, escorted down the stairs by the co-pilot, was Mary, bringing a breath of fresh air to the bleak north-eastern winter day. The co-pilot set Mary's carry-on down and extended the handles, and bowed to Mary as he bid the natural beauty farewell.

The president took a deep breath, smiled and turned his wheel chair away from the window. As pre-arranged, the work party stopped in the kitchen for a coffee break while Jackie embraced Mary, a friend of nearly two decades, and arm-in-arm they went off to visit the president.

"Mary, it's so nice to see you; I can only imagine how difficult it is to pull an artist from their work."

"Oh, Jackie, I can't begin to tell you how sorry I am for all that Jack, you, and your entire family have been going through .... to me, it's unimaginable."

They paused mid-way to the president's room with Kleenex in hand. "Thank you, Mary, you're right, it's been an absolute nightmare. The trauma has left an indelible scar on my persona, while Jack, thank God, remembers nothing."

"Tell me, Jackie, what's the last thing that Jack remembers."

"Up through yesterday afternoon, the last thing he recalls is waving to the crowd, but he has no idea where that is along the parade route." She dabbed her eyes with Kleenex, "And God only knows what more, if anything, he'll recall over time."

"It's in God's hands."

"Let's dry our eyes and move on .... we can't let Jack know we've been crying."

Jackie looped her arm through Mary's, "Jacks anxious to see you, Mary."

"I've been soooo looking forward to this, Jackie." She half blushed. "And, gosh, I'm flattered that Jack feels that way."

Jackie paused a few steps short of the president's door. "You have no idea; all morning long it's been nothing but Mary this, and Mary that."

Mary felt a bit awkward as Jackie stepped to the door and paused with her hand on the knob. "As always, the president has a busy schedule, so we're allowed no more than fifteen minutes." She smiled. "Not to worry, though, we'll have him all to ourselves tonight over dinner."

Mary was pleased to hear that she would be having dinner with the president and First Lady.

Jackie opened the door a couple of inches. "Mr. President, there's a pair of wayward women to see you, may they come in."

"Ahh, yes, my favorite kind . . . . and a pair, to boot." He laughed, "Keep a kicker and draw two."

Jack, with his wheel chair backed to the window, struggled to his feet and made a point to stand erect and proud in his navy blue silk presidential bath robe. He grinned, "Ahh, just what the doctor ordered, a pair of gorgeous women."

With that he opened his arms, "Oh, Mary, Mary, come give me a big hug." Mary hesitated until Jackie softly nudged her forward. "Please, Mary."

Mary was surprised and thrilled by the strength in Jack's arms. She had told herself ahead of time to be strong, but the smell of Jack, and wrapped in his arms, she began to sob like a baby with the face buried against the gold presidential seal on his robe. She turned her face upward and met Jack's eyes. "Oh, Jack, it's so good to see you . . . . I was worried sick over you."

Through tear welled eyes, Jackie looked on in silent envy as she saw a tear roll down his cheek . . . . the first time since the death of their newborn son, Patrick.

CHAPTER 9

Two months to the day of the attempted assassination, the White House issued an early morning press release stating that the president would be returning to the White House that afternoon.

The president, through Mrs. Lincoln, called for a White House limo to pick up Mary; Jack and Jackie both agreed to make Mary part of his official return home to the White House.

The late January weather in the entire north-east region was made to order for an outdoor staged triumphant return, which would surely be a journalistic feeding frenzy at both ends of the event; Hyannis Port and Washington D.C.

The medical staff, along with the entire domestic staff of the Kennedy Hyannis Port compound, was the first to emerge through the front door. Although the movement was cleanly un-choreographed, their standing positions were clearly assigned. At that point the chattering press corps became silent in anticipation, with commentators speaking in hushed tones into their microphones and to their domestic and worldwide audience.

As a light false-spring breeze wafted through the assembly, a marine color guard appeared from the blind side of the compound and positioned itself at parade rest adjacent to the awaiting Air Force Two helicopter, with the stars and stripes billowing lazily in the soft breeze.

Suddenly, the sound system began *"Hail To The Chief"*. A dozen beats into the hail, the front double door of the compound slowly opened wide, and the president emerged in a wheel chair pushed by a uniformed nurse's aide, with the First Lady at the right side of the wheel chair.

The president, his head wrapped in gauze, waved to the crowd as he approached the bank of network microphones adjusted to his level. As the wheel chair reached the microphones, "Hail To The Chief" trailed off.

The president smiled, "Good morning America." He paused, raised his arms upwards, and looked into the heavens. "It's indescribably wonderful to be blessed with yet another day . . . . praise God,"

The crowd erupted in applause.

"I'll keep this brief because of the international live coverage of my White House Rose Garden welcome-home reception."

He paused for effect, "As I prepare to depart a place that so many Kennedys refer to as home, I would like to thank my wonderful medical team and dedicated domestic staff that have made a tremendous contribution toward my recuperation by their warm, loving, professional care. I would also like to thank the Vice President and his White House staff, and my personal presidential aides who worked tirelessly to make the impact of my tragedy as seamless as possible for the American people, who I serve."

Mary smiled and looked toward the heavens as she stepped with the White House staff and top presidential and vice presidential aides. Once in position, she closed her eyes ant thought as she dabbed a rolling tear from her right cheek. *"Again, Lord, I thank you from the bottom of my heart."*

Exhausted, the president dozed as Air Force Two reached its cruising altitude and straightened its course toward the Capital. Later, the copilot turned toward his Commander and Chief and verified that he was awake. "Sir, we're two minutes from touchdown." The president smiled and nodded as the co-pilot continued. "I understand you have a heck of a welcoming committee awaiting you." He nodded toward the ground.

The president peered out the window and gasped. "Oh . . . my . . . God. The streets are total gridlock at least a half mile deep from the White House." He shook his head and smiled. "And there appears to be no breathing room around the White House fence."

Again, Mary dabbed a tear as it lost its struggle against gravity and began to roll down her cheek.

The president, fully charged with adrenalin, orders the helicopter pilot, an Air Force Coronel, "Security procedures be damned, I'm ordering you to circle the periphery of the White House grounds twice as a thank you to the masses of well wishers."

At the Commander and Chief's request, "Yes, sir, Mr. President."

The national televised networks immediately picked up on the meaning of the gesture, and transmitted it to the roaring crowd as well as to every corner of the globe.

The president took a deep breath and exited the helicopter standing with the assistance of a physical therapist. Jackie followed immediately and joined her husband at the bottom of the helicopter exit stairs; she then helped assist her husband into his wheel chair. Within moments he was in car shot of the standing ovation from the awaiting press corps, special aides, and the closest of family and friends, including Mary, awaiting him in the Rose Garden awash in a beautiful false spring day.

Hail To The Chief wound down and the president slowly stood, proud, straight and erect, before stepping slowly behind the podium. The president took a deep breath and welcomed the safety of the podium as he gripped it tightly with both hands. The president felt a rush of adrenalin as he thought to himself *"Well, Jack, here you are . . . back . . . . praise God."*

With the demeanor and confidence of someone truly in charge, the president spoke in his oh so welcome Bostonian accent.

"Do not rub your eyes . . . . Do not adjust your television sets . . . . Standing before you is not an illusion . . . . Nor is it a figment of your imagination." He paused, panned the audience, and smiled. "Your president, your humble servant, through the grace of God, is back and standing before you."

With that, the crowd erupted into a roaring applause as he and his First Lady joined hands and raised them triumphantly into the air . . . . as the president gripped the podium tightly with his free hand.

Jackie, sensing his need for both hands released her hold. As Jack secured his dual grip on the podium in an attempt to simply hang-on through his brief speech, he flashed back to his August 2, 1943 PT-109 experience:

Having suffered a back injury in the sinking of PT-109 in the Solomon Island region, boat Commander, Lieutenant Kennedy and his crew, using timbers from a gun mount for support, swam three and a half miles to a postage stamp sized island. Kennedy, a member of the Harvard swim team, towed his badly burned crew-mate, Patrick McMahon, using a strap from a life vest clenched between his teeth.

As he did way back then, he had no choice but to simply hold on.

Gripping the podium with beads of sweat forming beneath his gauze head-wrap, the president continued. "I would like to thank all of those present and the American masses, for sharing in my return to duty."

Again the crowd erupted in cheer.

"I cannot possibly find the words worthy of expressing my eternal gratitude to the emergency and critical care staff of Dallas Parkside Hospital, as well as my medical staff in Hyannis Port for their care and service up to this stage of my recovery."

More cheers.

The president spoke for another four plus minutes before taking a predetermined number of questions from the press corps.

"Mr. President, how much of the assassination attempt do you remember?"

"The amount I remember may or may not increase over time, however, at this point, I remember absolutely nothing. The last thing I recall was waving to the crowd from within the limousine; I have no idea where within the parade route." He shifted his feet and grip on the podium. "The next thing I recall is coming out of my medically induced coma in the Dallas hospital." He shrugged his shoulders and smiled, "All I know is that it'll take more than a social outcast with a high powered rifle to take out this Irish Mick."

With that there was a roar of approval and the raising of pints of Guinness within every pub in Ireland . . . . and throughout the globe.

As the Irish within the White House crowd settled down, the president fielded the second question from the press."

"Mr. President, what is your current progress status."

He took a deep breath, gripped the podium, and tactfully spun an answer. He said how pleased his medical team was of his progress and that they expect a full recovery of both his shoulder and head injuries, in spite of minor follow-up surgeries over the next six to eight weeks. What the president did not share were issues lying below the surface related to his general heath history. His *personal* medical team had secretly informed him that the main underlying issue was debilitating in nature that would lead to permanent crippling and premature death.

As the president was about to address his final question, he reposition his feet and grip on the podium while reminding himself of his teeth clenching the strap tethered to his badly injured PT-109 shipmate.

"Mr. President, in all due respect, there are those who are not only questioning your ability to perform the extreme rigorous duties as president for the remaining months of your current term, but even more so for a possible second term. Sir, would you care to respond to the growing number of those posing those questions?"

A soft undercurrent of groans, from the left, swept through the press corps.

"I'd be more than happy to respond, but first I need to clear the air by saying that the lion share, if not all, of those raising those question are of the opposition and therefore clearly politically driven."

There was a soft applause from half the crowd.

"My progress has been such that my medical team feels that I'll be back up to speed within a few short weeks and will be able to not only perform in the Oval Office, but also on the campaign trail."

At that point one half of the American viewing audience cheered while the other half jeered. Although the president had skillfully, and disingenuously, spun an answer to the politically driven question, he took solace in the fact that democracy would ultimately have the final word.

"With that, Mr. and Mrs. America, I thank you all for my tremendous welcome home, and now I must get to work for all of you."

As the crowd cheered he released his death grip on the podium and Jackie helped him to his wheel chair.

After a short intimate welcome home coffee with his personal staff, Jackie and Mary, the president pulled Mary aside. "Mary I am so grateful for all that you did for me in Hyannis Port over the past several days. Believe me, Mare, your presence made a huge difference in my recovery."

"Thank you as well, Jack. Being with you after your brush with death was indescribably therapeutic for my own recovery." Jack attempted to speak, "Shh . . . one last thing, Jack; I, too, experienced a brush with death, and now I have a reason to live."

They simply stared into one another's eyes, experiencing a new high in their connectivity.

"Mary, I realize your need to go home and get re-settled, so I'll have Mrs. Lincoln call for a house limo."

She took his hands, "Thank you, Jack, you're too kind."

He winked, "And there's more to come."

"Oh, Jack, you make me feel so alive."

"Likewise," He smiled, "Miss Contraire."

They both chuckled softly and slowly released their hands.

"One last thing, before you go." He glanced across the room and dropped his voice. "Jackie and the kids are leaving, in a couple of hours, for three days. I'd like you to come for dinner tonight . . . . just the two of us." He smiled. "There are a couple of things that I'd like your opinion on."

"Jack, I would love to."

"Good, I'll arrange for a limo to pick you up at seven-thirty."

"Again, Jack, thank you."

CHAPTER 10

Out of respect Mary never kept the White House limo driver waiting, nor was the driver ever late.

The black limo crept to a stop in front of her Georgetown home, and she immediately emerged and stepped to the awaiting open door. Per Mary's style, she kept things casual and knew all the drivers by name.

"Good evening, Miss Mary."

Cheerfully, "Good evening, Steward."

He slipped behind the wheel, "You're in a bubbly mood this evening."

"Stew, I'm still on cloud nine over our president's recovery."

Steward smiled at her in the rear view mirror, for Mary always insisted that the privacy window be down in her presence. "Amen, for the grace of God goes we."

A sudden force overwhelmed her. "Yes Steward . . . . yes indeed."

It was that simple, yet profound, spiritual reply from Steward that gave her a fleeting thought on how she had, for the first time in her life, been calling for help from a higher being. Unbeknownst to Mary, her subconscious began to explore that very issue as the limo slowed to a stop at the White House gate.

As with the limo driver, she was with West Gate security. "Good evening, Robert."

He slid the sign-in clipboard toward her, "Good evening, Mary."

She signed in on the *Expected Guest* form, 'Mary Pinchot' and under 'appointment with' she simply wrote 'president', and under 'location' she wrote 'private quarters'.

The guard verified her information with that on his guest list. "As always, Mary, you're good to go. The president is expecting you."

She was immediately ushered to the presidential private quarters, where the aide knocked softly on the door. The president responded, "Yes, who is it?"

"Mary Pinchot is here to see you, sir."

No sooner was the door closed behind her; she was greeted with open arms by the most powerful man on planet earth, who stood proud and erect from his wheelchair. They kissed softly on the lips, and then he rocked her slowly. "Oh Mary, you have no idea how I've longed for this moment. I missed you terribly."

They pressed their bodies together, "Oh, Jack, there is no way I could have gone on without you."

He kissed her sensuously on the lips, "Now then, young lady, dinner is served."

He shuffled to the table, pressed the service button, and pulled out her chair, "With your great, great grandfather Cyrille Désiré Constantine Pinchot having served as an officer under Napoleon; we will open with escargot, and a nice red Domaine Serene Pinot Noir."

When they settled into dinner, Jack shifted the conversation to a more serious tone. "Mary, because I trust and respect you as much as my staff and advisors, with top security clearences, I want to bounce something off you. It's something that Bobby and I have discussed at great length earlier today, as well as this evening before your arrival."

"Of course, Jack, I'm honored to say the least."

"Mary, besides trusting you, I value your insight and opinion."

She blushed, and Jack continued before she could respond. "Mary, I've been disingenuous with the American people. On one hand my progress with the assassination injuries has truly been remarkable, and I could not be happier."

"And Jack, I thank God every day."

"I as well, Mary." He paused, took a deep breath and leaned forward. "Now then, on the other hand, I've been less than honest with those who have placed me in the White House as their servant."

Mary's brow furrowed, "Oh, and how's that, Jack?"

"It's not so much that I lied, Mary, as it is I withheld information."

Mary chuckled, "Sounds to me like politics as usual . . . . except to a point . . . ."

He cut her off, "See, that's what I mean about respecting you; your about to give me, the president, the what for." He raised his hand in a silencing gesture. "And we're at the point in time, with the election a mere eight months off, where ethics overrides or trumps politics."

Finished with dinner, Jack placed his napkin on the table, "I'd like to continue this conversation over brandy, sitting next to you on the sofa."

Before settling down on the sofa, Jack was informed that Bobby was on the phone. "This should take but a minute, I'm sure it's an afterthought on our earlier conversation. You mind pouring the brandy while I'm gone?"

No sooner had Mary poured the brandy and sat down, she was joined by Jack. "It was just that, an afterthought." He raised his brandy snifter, "Here's to an enduring friendship; one that means more than I dare say."

They touched glasses and kissed softly on the lips. "And to your health, Jack."

With that they savored a sip of Courvoisier L'Espirit. Jack placed his arm around Mary and she snuggled closer."

Jack took on a serious tone, "Speaking of my health, that's precisely what I need to discuss with you, Mary."

Mary turned toward him with a sudden look of concern. "Your health, but you're doing so well, Jack."

"That's exactly what I was talking about; that's only the truth on one side of the coin."

Mary took the president's hand and held it tightly, "Jack this doesn't sound good, so just give it to me straight and we'll deal with it."

Jack squeezed her hand, "That's one of the things I love about you, Mary, your willingness to be part of the solution."

She kissed him on the cheek, "Oh, Jacko, I love you."

"Me too you, Mare."

They savored more brandy.

"Now then, Bobby's afterthought was about what we are going to discuss."

She squeezed his hand as he continued. "The situation with my health is such that not only do I have to come clean, but we've got to have a viable game plan when I do."

"Jack, you're scaring me; what's up?"

"Mary, we've been using my remarkable assassination recovery as a diversion from my underlying debilitating condition."

Mary winced, "Debilitating? What's the problem, Jack?"

"Mary, I don't know how aware you are of my life-long health history."

"Aware enough to know that in spite of being a walking miracle, you've gone on to become the most powerful man on planet earth."

He lightened up, "Well, money and name recognition do help."

She chuckled, "Yeah, you and FDR."

"Exactly."

"Well, speaking of FDR, like him I'll soon be confined to a wheel chair."

"Oh no, Jack!"

"Oh yes, Mary." He squeezed her hand. "Debilitating to the point where I must come clean with the American public."

Silence.

"Clean, how clean?"

He looked Mary squarely in the eyes. "I can't run for a second term."

She wrapped her arms around him, Oh no, Jack, no." and began to cry.

Jack was taken aback, "Mary, Mary, that's ok." He squeezed her as tight as he could with his shoulder injury in mind. "We'll be alright."

"But Jack, your long range plans and dreams for the American public that mean so much to you."

He squeezed her again before looking her squarely in the eyes. "It's not my legacy, Mare, it's the Kennedy legacy, and I'm handing the torch to Bobby."

They separated, "Oh, now I see the afterthought and all with Bobby."

She dabbed her eyes as he continued, 'Yes, he and I, alone, have been formulating a plan driven by necessity . . . . a plan that he and I want your input."

"I'm flattered, of course, Jack. But, first tell me more of your health situation." She smiled and kissed him softly; you're not getting off that easy, Jacko."

They were interrupted, "Sorry, sir, but the First Lady is on the phone."

Seemingly out of nowhere Jack pulled a single sheet of paper. "Here, this is a summary of my life-long medical record. The assassination injuries triggered issues lying dormant beneath the surface for years, just waiting for something to set them off."

He struggled to stand from the comfortable sofa, "Be back in a minute," He looked over his injured shoulder as he stepped from the room. "You can freshen up our brandies while I'm gone."

As the door closed Mary downed her brandy, *I think I'm going to need this.*"

She was aghast as she studied the medical summary. "My word, Jack, the only thing you haven't had or experienced is death itself. Never mind you've twice have had the Catholic Sacrament of the Last Rights; once before starting school and again as a pre-teen."

Jack stepped back into the room, "Jackie sends her regards."

"That's nice . . . . does she . . . ."

"Know about the plan? Not so much the details, but she knows I'm unable to run for a second term. She knows that Bobby and I are formulating a plan, and she knows why you're here . . . . and she approves."

He chuckled and raised his brandy in a toasting gesture, "Let's be clear in that she approves of half the reason for you being here, the other half she willingly turns a blind eye." He sensually squeezed her thigh. "Here's cheers."

"Now then, the plan is for Bobby to run as my replacement, which in itself will be a bomb. However, things will politically intensify when it becomes apparent that vice president Johnson will not be his VP, but will be his opposition. With no love lost between Bobby and Lyndon, you can well imagine what an all out war it will launch within the Beltway."

Mary's enthusiasm climbs, "That's true, Jack, but at the end of the day Bobby will be left standing because of his and Lyndon's diametrically opposed personalities." She paused in thought. "Not to mention the public . . . . or I should say the Democrats and the lion share of the Independents . . . . will be clamoring for a Kennedy legacy."

Jack smiled, "I humbly have to agree with you, Mare."

They sipped their brandy, as Jack continued, "The key to the plan is timing. On one hand, for the good of the party, we have to allow ample time for the nomination process; while on the other hand, also for the good of the party, we do not want to turn the entire remainder of my term into that of a lame duck."

Mary, snuggled closer to the president, "Realistically, it's a bad news good news situation; the bad news, of course, being your health, with the good news being a twelve year Kennedy run on the white house."

Jack laughed aloud, "Again, just like FDR . . . ."

CHAPTER 11

It wasn't long before Jack spent a good deal of his waking hours wheelchair free. Although the White House advertised and played on the president's recovery, it was becoming obvious that his vice-president maintained the president's role as world traveler, well beyond his normal second-in-command duties.

However, it wasn't long that those closest to the president began to notice the debilitation slowly creep into his motor skills; Jack found himself beginning to lean against tables, desks, door jambs, and chair backs. He also spent more time sitting out of necessity. His aides watched him closely, anticipating when to launch the well crafted political plan; they were ready.

It was two days into spring when it happened, while fundraising on the campaign trail. The president had just left a high-dollar per plate luncheon in Newport Beach, California. He was fielding questions from the press outside the beach front hotel when one of the journalists unknowingly set the *plan* into motion. The observant young journalist, from the local Orange County Register, noticed the president deliberately take four steps away from the news media to lean on his awaiting open limousine door. The young USC journalist seized the opportunity and spoke aggressively above the senior journalists. "Mr. President, sir, while covering your current campaign swing through southern California, I've noticed that more and more you are leaning on various objects for support; is it just me, or is it in fact you?"

The president looked admiringly at the lone journalist in the group without graying temples. Anticipating this moment, the President was well scripted. "Sir, I give you high marks for keen observation." He paused, gave a charming smile which drew the press corps closer in anticipation. "The gentleman is both observant and correct." The president patted the top of the limo door for effect. "The answer is yes, I do seem to be experiencing a bit of a motor skill problem."

The press clamored a bit before the president raised his hands in a halting gesture. "The doctors are checking into it; but they seem to think it's a medication problem. I can assure you, if it's to the contrary, the American public will be informed post-haste."

Mary, while painting, saw the clip on the late afternoon news. She turned toward the television and froze with brush and palette in hand. She mumbled as she set aside her painting. "I'm sure that this is the *trigger* they were anticipating."

No sooner had she cleaned up for the day and began to think of dinner, the phone rang. "Hello, is this Mare contraire?"

Mary giggled, "Can I ask whose calling?"

"Yes you may. Tell her it's her beau from seventeen-hundred Pennsylvania Avenue."

"Ahh . . . . let's see, seventeen . . . . it rings a bell . . . . Oh, yeah, the White House." Giggle. "Hold on while I see if she'll take your call."

She returned with a different voice, "Hello, beau."

Chuckle, "Yeah . . . . as in boyfriend . . . . not *dandy*."

"Yeah, sure . . . . but you're a *dandy* of a boyfriend."

They both laughed. "Seriously, Mare, the *trigger* event happened today." 'I know, I happened to catch it on the news."

Hurried, "Listen, Mare, I've got a call. I'd like you to come to my quarters this evening to an impromptu dinner and kick-off discussion; can I send a driver to pick you up at seven?"

"Sure, Jack, I'm honored."

Rushed, "You bet, I'll see yah."

The White House limo picked up Mary at her Georgetown home and within minutes deposited her at the West Gate, where she signed in as *Mary Pinchot, guest of the president.*

She was both surprised and pleased when she heard the playful sounds of Carolyn and John as she approached the door to the president's private quarters. Within moments, she had a squealing child at each of her legs competing for attention. As the clambering died down, she was greeted from behind by Jackie, "Mary, it's so good to see you."

They embraced warmly, "It's good to see you as well, Jackie." Mary dropped her voice, "I feel so honored to be a part of this."

"Jack insisted and, of course, I agreed."

With that Bobby arrived, and the kids deserted her for their favorite uncle; Bobby, more often than not, becoming the third child.

After several moments the children calmed down and Jackie became the mother. "All right, it's bed time, off we go." Well disciplined, not a word was said by either child as they dutifully disappeared with their mother.

Mary and Bobby took the opportunity to greet one another with a warm hug and kiss, as Jack's publically known campaign manager, Stephen Smith, arrived. In addition, Steve was Jack's brother-in-law through his sister Joan. On Steve's tail was Bobby's highly secret campaign manager, Kenneth O'Donnell.

Dry gin martinis were served all around and within a few minutes the mood was lighthearted, with dinner being announced the moment Jackie returned. The intimate group seated themselves at designated spaces, with a clockwise order of Jack, Jackie, Bobby, Ken, Steve, placing Mary to the right of the president. As the martini glasses were removed, wine was poured and Jack raised his glass. "To the *plan.*" With that, he nodded to LBJ's current campaign manager. "Go ahead, Steve."

"Thank you, Mr. President."

"Please, it's Jack tonight." (It's called protocol permission).

They all raised their glasses in silent acknowledgement.

"Jack will officially launch the *plan* first thing tomorrow morning during his bi-weekly coffee with Lyndon. Jack will inform him that his medical team strongly advised him against a second term, and that Lyndon is released to launch his own campaign for the presidency, if he so chooses."

Jack chuckled, "What do you mean, if he so chooses? Hell, he'd just as soon kill me for the job. He's always resented being second in command to a *young political upstart.*"

While Jackie showed a trace of a frown, Mary smiled and gave Jack a soft undetectable elbow.

Jack adds, "Of course, immediately after informing Lyndon, I'll call for a press conference where I'll inform the public that I am being medically forced to suspend my campaign for a second term."

Smith continued, "And with no love lost between Lyndon and Bobby, there is no way he could bring himself to ask Bobby to share his ticket."

Bobby groans aloud, "Oh God, the mere thought of he and I as running mates makes me ill."

Laughter all around before Smith continues, "So, it's a sure bet he'll quickly announce his candidacy with no mention of a running mate, which will clear the way for Bobby to run before Lyndon is pushed for a VP short list."

With that, Jack raised his wine glass, "To Bobby and the Kennedy legacy."

They all touched glasses and seconded the president. Smith then nodded to Kenneth O'Donnell, "At this point I'll hand things over to Kenny."

Kenny downed the last of his wine, "Bobby and I are set, and ready to go. While Lyndon remains totally unaware, Bobby is in his starting block, and like a coiled spring, ready to explode. While Lyndon is still in the thought stage, Bobby will be halfway around the track, fueled by a campaign chest full of money."

Brother Jack queries, "At what point will you announce?"

Ken shifted in his seat, "Within twenty-four hours of you announcing your inability to run for a second term, or as close as possible after Lyndon announces his run."

Mary looked at Jack, "May I?"

"You bet Mare, that's why you're here."

She nodded, "In all due respect, in order to establish some up-front credibility for our plan, I think it would be best to forget the twenty-four hour option and announce first thing in the morning following Johnson's announcement."

Jackie chimed in, "I agree with Mary, Jack."

He raised his glass, "I agree."

Bobby and Ken nodded at one another and Bobby responded. "Fine with me, as well."

Jack queried, "One last thing, Bobby, Ken, are you any closer to finding a running mate."

Bobby nodded to Ken to field the question, "We've gone as far as we can in vetting our short-list, but have been severely restricted in order to maintain our plan's secrecy."

Jack chuckled, "Of course, when we let the cat out of the bag it'll be no holds barred."

Bobby adds, "When we finally drop the puck on the ice, the entire campaign process will be fast and furious."

CHAPTER 12

Vice President Johnson suspected nothing as he arrived at the White House at seven in the morning for his regularly scheduled private Wednesday morning coffee with the president.

As always, he paused, after stepping across the threshold of the Oval Office, greeted the president, closed the door, stepped forward and shook hands with his superior, his arm extending across the expansive desk. "Jack, how are you this fine spring morning?"

"Just fine, Lyn, and you?"

"Fit as a fiddle, praise God."

As part of their weekly informal private coffee ritual, Jack stood and poured the coffee from its sterling silver pot. The president took his place behind his desk, and they both had their first sip of coffee. The president then got down to business.

"Lyn, I'll get right to the point this morning, and not mince my words."

Lyndon took a second sip of coffee, "Whoa . . . . good morning to you as well."

The president did not blink or flinch as he looked his vice president squarely in the eyes. "My medical team has advised me that I should not consider running for a second term."

Astonished, "What the hell are you saying . . . . that you're taking their advice?"

Without hesitation, "Yes, Lyndon," He paused for effect, "I will not run."

"My God, Jack, how bad is it?"

"The assassination trauma has triggered life-long medical issues that will debilitate me at such a rate that a second term is out of the question."

He took a sip of coffee, "I'll spare you the details; let's just move on."

Jack selected a sweat roll utilizing a pair of tongs, and Lyndon, who was literally speechless, followed suit. The vice-president washed down his first bite of roll with a healthy gulp of coffee, cleared his throat, and broke his silence. "So when are you going public?"

"While you were driving across town this morning, I made arrangements for some air time, for one o'clock this afternoon; it'll be a private news announcement from the Oval Office."

"And the press?"

"None, we'll have a follow up full blown news conference, perhaps tomorrow, here in the press corps room. It'll be more effective if we let the press sleep on my announcement."

The VP shifted in his seat searching for words. The president, sensing the awkwardness, continued. "I realize that this is sudden, but we need to have a chat in preparation for my announcement." Johnson nodded and Jack continued, "I hate to rush you but we both know the clock is rapidly ticking down on the amount of remaining campaign time; so what can I tell the American public about your campaign plans . . . . I'm assuming you'll run . . . . will you not?"

Silence as Johnson shifted in his chair and took a sip of coffee. "It's funny, Jack, one would think that I'd have a knee-jerk 'yes' to that question, but instead, I'm simply taken aback."

Silence.

"Lyndon, I can appreciate your reaction."

Silence,

Jack continued, "So then, do you simply want me to say that you'll have a press conference of your own, where you'll address the question of your running?"

Lyndon washed the last of his sweet roll down with coffee. "Jack, I think that's a good idea to break major historic news such as this into two sessions, so as not to overwhelm the general public."

Jack rocked back in his high-back executive chair, "Ok then, I'll not tip your hand one way or the other. I'll simply say you'll address your personal decision in your own press conference."

Long silence.

"Jack, do you mind telling me who is aware of your decision not to run . . . . as we speak?"

Anticipating that very fact-finding question, Jack does not hesitate, "Of course not Lyndon; I've told Jackie, Bobby, and Teddy . . . . that's it."

Silence, as they both finished the dregs of their coffee.

"Ok, Jack, here's what I'd like you to say about my plans in your press conference. Tell them that I was taken aback and saddened by the sudden unexpected news, and that I'll be making an announcement tomorrow at my own news conference; all, of course, being true."

"And your announcement will be . . . . or do you know?"

Somewhat surprised, "Well, of course I'll run . . . . It's the suddenness that's overwhelming; there is just so much to do."

"I'm glad to hear you're running. Unless you tell me otherwise, I'll say nothing."

Lyndon closed the Oval Office door behind him, and Jack picked up the phone. "Bobby, it's a go; Lyndon just left my office; he's going to run."

"That's fine; we have that in our plan."

"Mum's the word until after his press conference tomorrow afternoon."

"Good . . . . gotta go."

The global news media was abuzz in anticipation and speculation about the White House news release of an announcement from the Oval Office.

Although the press corps felt slighted and dismissed from not being a part of the unknown big announcement, it didn't prevent them from speculating between one another, or from contacting reliable candid inside sources. The only thing they were able to uncover was that there were no leaks to be found. However, the consensus amongst the tight-knit news corps was near unanimous in that the subject of the announcement had to be related to the president and his second term.

With the start of the sixty-second countdown, the president took his place in his executive style chair behind the Oval Office desk. He looked both great and presidential. The gauze head-wrap was gone, his hair had grown out and his color had returned. On the desk in front of him was a short stack of index cards, a clear glass half full of water, and a fresh cup of black coffee in a navy blue cup with a gold presidential seal.

The press tech yelled, "Silence, we're in final . . . . ten . . . nine . . . eight . . . ."

Mary had taken a break from her painting long enough to tune in her television to local network news and make a fresh cup of black coffee. No sooner had the news begun, they switched over to the White House. There, in black and white, looking his old self, was the man she had been with the previous evening. She was amazed and impressed with how very presidential he appeared. Other than a slight loss of facial weight, he looked like his old self; truly a rock-star president. As he spoke, it was so hard for her to believe what was going on with his health. She dabbed her eyes with Kleenex, *"I love you, Jacko."*

Unlike the rest of the world-wide viewers, Mary was fully aware of what was about to go down. She smiled and relaxed during the preamble of Jack's speech, then instinctively stiffened as he launched into the central purpose of his speech.

"So then, my fellow Americans, although my progress relating to the injuries of the assassination attempt continue to improve exponentially toward a full recovery, there are serious issues related to those injuries. Those very injuries have triggered a life-long history of medical issues into a progressive debilitating situation."

He paused for effect, "What this means is I'll soon return to the very wheel chair I was freed from a short time ago. The doctors have diagnosed that not only will I never leave the wheel chair, but I'll continue to debilitate to the point of premature death."

Again he paused, "Because of this, I must, with deep regret and a broken heart, announce that I can no longer consider running for a second term." He took a noticeably deep breath, "Therefore, as of today I am suspending my campaign for a second term as president of the United States."

He smiled, "Now then, it begs the question; if not me who? Although I cannot speak for my vice president, I can tell you he will be holding a press conference of his own tomorrow at a time yet to be announced."

"If vice president Johnson does announce his candidacy, I'm sure you'll give him all the respect and consideration he has earned."

"As far as the few remaining months of my current term, my medical team assures me that my projected condition is such that they liken the remainder of my term to be no less of a handicap than that of our late-great president, Franklin Delano Roosevelt."

"I will hold a follow-up fully open press conference within the next couple of days."

He smiled, "Again, I would like to thank you, the American public, for all of your thoughts, prayers, words of encouragement, and outright support in general since my near-fatal day in Dallas."

"May God continue to bless the United States of America."

Mary dabbed her eyes, "Well done, Jack, but oh how my heart aches for you." She stood and turned off the television. "America is truly losing a great man." She poured a second cup of coffee. "What is also sad is the countless people who profess to be Christians that openly profess to *hate* you . . . . and will to their grave." She chuckled, "Not to worry, because God will sort those folks out and deal with them."

CHAPTER 13

Vice President Johnson, wanting to create a "position-of-strength" image, chose the White House press corps room for his press conference, with a full complement of news media. The room was abuzz until press secretary Pierre Salinger brought silence by his entrance. He immediately went to work.

"Ladies and gentlemen, as a follow-up to the president's announcement that he is unable to run for a second term due to medical issues, I bring you the Vice President of the United States, Lyndon Baines Johnson."

Johnson stepped through the press room door and moved directly to the podium wearing his usual warm disarming smile. "Good morning," He paused as the press corps murmured their response.

"Following yesterday's unexpected announcement from our president that he is unable to run for a second term, I come before you with a heavy heart." He paused and slowly panned the room full of journalists. "To enable democracy to run its course, I, as vice president, need to either take the torch and run for the highest office in the land, or clearly stand aside."

He paused for effect. "Ladies and gentlemen, I hereby announce my candidacy for president of the United States of America."

The press corps, professionally committed to journalistic neutrality, momentarily remained in frozen silence, with a handful of ever-so-brief subdued smiles and frowns, betraying one's code. It was NBC who was the quickest to recover. "Mr. Vice President, sir, do you expect, under the circumstances, to be anointed as the lone and unchallenged presidential candidate representing the Democratic Party?"

Johnson smiled and panned his audience, "For my own selfish reasons, I wish that I could answer the question with a resounding *yes*. However, in reality, the American public deserves the normal democratic process to play itself out; regardless of the compressed campaign schedule we've been unavoidably handed."

CBS jumped in, "Sir, have you chosen a running mate, or could you at least give us a preview of your short-list?"

Johnson grinned and shook his head, "I can share this with you; as I speak, I'm no further than twenty-four hours ahead of this storm than the American public as they view this news conference." He raised his hands in a halting manner, "The answer to you question is no and no." He chuckled, "First, I have to get over the shock of this; then, second, catch my breath."

The *Boston Globe* tossed an obvious barb at the vice president over his well known adversary. "Sir, what about Bobby Kennedy; surely he'll be on your short list."

Johnson hid his irritation, "At this point, all options are on the table."

* * *

Mrs. Lincoln spoke into the intercom. "Sir, Bobby is on the line."

He put his feet on the desk and leaned back in his chair. "Hey, Bobby, good morning."

"How's Jack this morning?"

"Just fine and you?"

Bobby laughed and the president continued. "Well, do you think you'll make Lyndon's VP short-list?"

He laughed again, "I'm afraid I'm hoping beyond hope."

Jack laughed, "If the tables were turned, would he make your short-list."

"You did say *short*, didn't you?" Laughter.

"Now, now, Bobby." Laughter

"Seriously, Jack, in all fairness the bad blood between us is mutual."

Jack adds, "We both know that he did fire the first shot."

"Yeah, the day you appointed me as your Attorney General."

"Very true . . . . And, your announcement?"

"That's actually why I called. As we speak, my office is making arrangements for an early evening press conference."

"Good, I'll stay tuned."

* * *

"Excuse me sir, Lady Bird is on the line."

The vice president smiled as he picked up the phone. "What a pleasant surprise."

She got right to the point. "Did you hear the news?"

He leaned forward in his chair. "What news?"

With a note of sarcasm, "Little Bobby Kennedy is calling for a press conference for this evening."

He tossed his gold pen down on his desk. "That little bastard . . . . he can't even wait for my dust trail to settle."

She started to speak and was cut off, "Sorry, gotta go, my campaign manager is on the other line."

* * *

Mary got word of Bobby's news conference from her car radio, after having gone to lunch with her sister, Toni. She parked herself in front of her television with a fresh cup of coffee at the start of the six o'clock news. Like his brother, his conference was journalist free, held within his own Attorney General office.

"Good evening. At the top of the hour we'll take you live to Attorney General Robert Kennedy's news conference."

Bobby sat behind his expansive clutter-free desk in the Kennedy mold; looking very presidential. "My fellow Americans, over the past two days we've had our president announce that he was unable to run for a second term, and his vice president announce his run for the presidency." He paused for effect, "With little time remaining in the current Democratic campaign period, I hereby announce my candidacy for the president of the United States."

He took a sip of water, "Although I will hold an open press conference by week's end, I can clearly state that my presidential policies will mirror that of our current administration. In addition, I will, throughout the course of my campaign, announce a handful of signature policies."

He gave a Kennedy smile, "I'm sure most of you are asking yourselves, who will share my ticket? Well, we've developed a very short list and have been working like men possessed on the vetting process. I hope to make an announcement within a couple of days."

"Although at this point the Democratic presidential race is open for additional candidates, I would like to wish my current opposition all the best in his campaign efforts."

* * *

Vice president Lyndon Johnson flicked off his office television, as he grumbled to his top aide. "His announcement should come as no surprise . . . . the little north-eastern prick."

He slammed his open palm on his desk and laughed. "I wonder what tricky Dicky Nixon thinks . . . . a bigger prick by far."

CHAPTER 14

The following morning's news focused on two political stories; one, the GOP was making political divide-and-conquer hay with Bobby's announcement to run for the presidency immediately following LBJ's announcement to do the same, exposing, in their opinion, the clear divide and rift within the Democratic Party. The second story was that the earliest of polls indicated a near ten-percent margin favoring RFK over LBJ . . . . without either candidate having spoken from a *stump*.

Although LBJ was without hard evidence of JFK's roll in Bobby's clearly well-oiled and choreographed candidacy, it brought tension into their working relationship that would last throughout the remainder of their shared-term.

The very moment that RFK announced his candidacy, his campaign manager pulled out all stops in the final vetting for Bobby's running mate. Having worked beneath the radar prior to announcing his candidacy, they did manage to narrow down the vetting to a very short list, establishing a strategic advantage over LBJ who was still trying to gain traction.

*　　*　　*

As the RFK team made arrangements for a mid-morning press conference, their VP candidate was being secretly flown, via private jet, from a small rural airport to Washington, DC.

When informed that RFK's news conference was to be held in the White House press corps room, LBJ was furious. "The little prick is deliberately trumping my earlier position-of-power as the sitting vice president . . . . as the fucking *mere* sitting Attorney General."

*　　*　　*

Again, the press corps room was abuzz in speculation, with the consensus all but unanimous amongst the press; RFK was to announce his running mate.

White House press secretary Pierre Salinger entered and brought the usual hush to the room as he got right down to business. "Ladies and gentlemen, I bring you the United States Attorney General, Mr. Robert Kennedy."

The press corps was mildly surprised when RFK entered the room alone and stepped directly to the podium. "Ladies and gentlemen, good morning." He paused as the corps murmured a collective response. "I want to thank all of you for your attendance." He paused and panned the room. "With America facing a compressed Democratic presidential campaign, we can all expect to see things unfold accordingly."

"Having said that, I'm here today to announce and introduce my running mate . . . . the one that I have personally chosen to share my ticket."

He paused to build anticipation, "The gentleman I've chosen is a leader within the progressive party of the great state of Texas." He paused to let the first clue sink in. As he continued, he motioned his right arm toward the door behind him. "Ladies and gentlemen, welcome the next vice president of the United States, the prominent senator from Texas, Mr. Ralph Yarborough."

With that, the White House entrance door to the press room opened and the senator stepped through the door into an awaiting bear hug from Bobby. Yarborough was a striking, well-fit man of sixty, who had the countenance of the WW II Lieutenant Colonel of his youth. He had a warm smile and possessed disarming charm.

The selection of Yarborough was well thought out; he was the very likable alter ego to LBJ within the Texas political community. Whereas Johnson had a history of turning into a strong-arm bully at the drop of a hat, Yarborough was the eternal man of charm and grace, ever willing to extend a warm firm hand across the political aisle. He was often quoted, "Let's put the jam on the lower shelf so we little people can reach it." He was a true champion for the blue-collar working middle class.

* * *

Realizing that he had all but been neutralized by the Yarborough announcement, Johnson kicked his office trash can and ranted to his campaign manager. "Always the clever little prick; the bastard knows exactly what he's doing." He opened his office bar and poured himself a way-to-early generous Cutty and rocks."

Overtime, it had become a clear general opinion that JFK had chosen Johnson in order to secure the Texas vote, even though he despised the man; Bobby had chosen the same tact, except, unlike JFK and LBJ, Bobby and Ralph had a mutual friendly relationship, politically and socially.

Johnson seethed with frustration; here he was barely out of the starting blocks and was about to be lapped by the sitting hero president's popular younger brother. Early polls clearly indicated that Democrats, and the lion share of Independents, wanted to establish a Kennedy legacy, with several leading Democrats already quietly calling, from behind the scenes, for Johnson to bow out of the race.

Not to mention, the GOP was also grumbling, behind the scenes, of the 'unfair advantage'.

CHAPTER 15

By the time Easter rolled around LBJ found his presidential hopes hanging by a mere thread, with RFK flirting with a near fifteen point lead. With the compressed election cycle, some DNC leaders were calling for Johnson to withdraw from the race.

As the Nixon camp continued with their divide-and-conquer strategy, RFK changed the focus of the discussion to that of Vietnam, which served to neutralize the GOP strategy. It also allowed him to stake a claim of having a more opposing position to Nixon on Vietnam while maintaining a positive exit philosophy. This appealed to the masses of young voters, as well as the parents of draftees serving in Vietnam.

Behind the scenes, a more serious problem crept into the White House, in that the president was all but back in his wheelchair . . . . full-time.

Coincidentally, as Jack's time in the wheelchair increased, Jackie spent more and more time away from the White House, more often than not, taking Carolyn and John with her. The flip side of the situation found Mary spending more time with Jack, both in his private quarters and throughout the White House, tending to Jack.

In Jackie's absence, Mary wheeled the president in his chair throughout the course of the day, always remaining quietly within reach except when conversations dealt with security level subjects. The more Jack resisted help from the nurses and personal aides during Jackie's absence, the more tongues within the White House staff and beltway wagged.

Chapter 16

By mid-summer solstice, LBJ's party support and financial resources all but dried up; that, plus trailing by nearly fifteen points in a consensus pole, he was forced to withdraw from the presidential race.

Out of party loyalty, certainly not love, LBJ came out publicly in support of the RFK-Yarborough ticket. Subsequently, Bobby became the sole focus of GOP campaign tactics.

Although the unspoken rule within the 60's era of the journalism profession was to remain silent about dalliances among DC politicians, especially within the White House, the news profession was none the less charged with reporting the actual news. With LBJ out of the race, Bobby's steady five point lead over Nixon suddenly grew to that of near ten points.

With Nixon well-known for his dirty tricks, his campaign surrogates began to ever-so-softly, and covertly, question the moral authority of the Kennedy clan males. The Nixon surrogate team cleverly infiltrated the beltway journalism circuit, undermining their unwritten, and seldom spoken, code of silence regarding the most personal moralistic failures by the powers-that-be. Before long, beltway journalist, in the name of competitive survival, began to demonstrate clear signs of rag journalism in their daily ink.

By summer's end, journalist, and subsequently the public, began to question the name and position of a naturally attractive blond whose presence was becoming more and more visual over time.

The Nixon tongue wagging surrogates had stirred up enough controversy that the Kennedy clan, less the president, gathered at their Hyannis Port stronghold to develop a united front strategy regarding the clan's philandering male reputation.

At the end of the day, the clan decided on a three-pronged strategy. First, through the Kenney family PR firm, as well as through Bobby's campaign advisors, all focus and attention, regardless of the intensity launched by the Nixon surrogates, would be on Bobby, his wife Ethel, and their eight children. The second prong of the strategy was, through Bobby, to strongly encourage Jackie to stay at home, in the White House, and be as visible as possible through the November seventh election . . . . a mere twelve weeks off. The third prong of the strategy, through Jackie, would be to encourage Mary to all but eliminate her visibility in and around the White House. For the occasional multi-guest dinner party, Mary, along with her sister Toni, would not be seated at her customary table with the president.

The clan would immediately implement focus on Bobby's solid marriage and large close-knit family, utilizing existing film footage stored and catalogued with the clan's PR firm. With the existing film footage in play, they would immediately begin *production* on as many *candid, impromptu* RFK family photo shoots as possible, in addition to arranging a *"60 Minutes"* feature of Bobby's brood.

With Jackie and the children on vacation, the second prong of the clan-plan would have to be delayed a week to ten days. Jackie, her children, along with her her sister were guests aboard the private yacht of a billionaire Greek shipping tycoon Aristotle Onassis.

Two days before Jackie's return home, Mary had spent her entire usual week day tending to Jack's every need, with the White House limo picking her up from her Georgetown home at seven thirty in the morning. However, unlike other mornings, Jack insisted she pack an overnight bag for a dinner for two within his private living quarters. As Mary showered and was in the course of dressing for dinner, Bobby called to report the outcome of the family meeting. Jack nursed a dry gin martini and patiently listened to his younger brother before commenting.

"Bobby, I can assure you that Jackie and I will do the best we can to smile and put on a façade of being the happy first couple."

"Great, Jack, I . . . ."

"Hold it, Bobby, hear me out." He leaned forward and placed his hand on Bobby's shoulder. "*However*, in all honesty, Bobby, I must tell you that Mary is *not* going away."

"But Jack . . . ."

"Bobby, I said hear me out." He paused to take a breath. "Although I'll do my best to keep Mary below the radar, and perhaps dress her as a hospital orderly; I will *not* permit her to go away."

Silence, as Bobby was now leery and hesitant. "Bobby . . . . between you and me, what I'm being forced to say is that I *can* get through my eventual premature life-ending medical dilemma *without* Jackie, but *not* without Mary."

Bobby broke a long silence in a sober subdued tone, "Holy shit, Jack . . . . what the hell can I say or do?"

Jack responded in like tone, "Nothing, Bobby . . . . *nothing.*"

CHAPTER 17

While in Greece, Jack alerted Jackie, in the briefest of ways, that the campaign was to focus on Bobby and his family as a diversion from the negative reputation involving Kennedy men. She simply chuckled, "No way in hell can Nixon find a counter-diversion for eight children."

Their first night back together, over dinner in their private quarters, Jack waited for Jackie to bring up the subject of the clan-plan. It was halfway through dinner, and well into a second generous glass of wine, that she broached the subject.

"Tell me more about the so called clan-plan."

Jack shifted in his wheel chair knowing that he had merely given a superficial account of the plan to Jackie while she was in Greece. He hesitated as the staff waiter poured wine, before raising his glass toward Jackie. "To the plan." He chuckled as Jackie snickered while he continued. "Although I gave you a one-liner of the plan while you sunbathed in Greece, it represented only one part of a three pronged attack."

The first lady rolled her eyes and Jack continued. "The other two prongs of the plan are you and Mary."

Jackie's wine glass froze just short of her lips. She withdrew the glass as her senses heightened. "Me . . . . and Mary?" She chuckled and spoke cynically, "Sounds like a bad news, good news situation."

Jack smiled warmly, "Before I speak of the plan, keep in mind the election is only twelve weeks off."

Jackie laughed, "I'm willing to bet that is the only good news."

Jack placed his wine on the table, "My family decided it would be best if you stayed home and at my side as much as possible through November seventh."

Jackie rolled her eyes and took a sip of wine. "Pure and simple . . . . I'm grounded."

"If you say so . . . . for twelve short weeks."

Sarcastically, "I'm to be confined to my room?"

"Please Jackie." He shifted in his wheel chair. "They want you visibly at my side as much as possible."

"Oh God, Jack . . . . please, I'll take my room."

More silence, broken by Jackie, "I'm sure that's a good segue into the third prong . . . . as *the clan* calls them."

"Now then, Mary?"

"Ah yes, my dear friend Mary."

"She *is* your old dear friend, Jackie."

Jackie went into a thousand-yard stare. "Yeah . . . . but . . . . never mind."

Silence as the dust settled, "Mary's part is quite easy; they simply want her to duck below the radar."

Silence, over their dinners gone cold, "Let's see if I understand; while I'm grounded at your side, Mary is essentially set free."

"That depends on what you mean by set free."

Jackie chuckled at the simplicity, "Set free, as in gone from the White House."

Jackie becomes stern, "Listen Jack." She leaned forward in her chair and placed her forearms on the edge of the dinner table. "As an unwritten marital pre-nup agreement, I've turned a blind-eye on your philandering more times than I can begin to recall, rationalizing that your playmates were no more than prostitutes working for free . . . . making them, of course, mere sluts."

"Jackie, I . . . ."

She raised her hands in a halting fashion, "Hear me out, Jack, please." She sat more erect. "I need to get this off my chest . . . . or should I say my back." Another pause, "It's bad enough that my earliest recollection as an adolescent was overhearing the hushed conversations about my father . . . . good ol' Black Jack Bouvier . . . . being a womanizer of the highest degree. More often than not, my mother would simply say, 'boys will be boys'." She raised her hands again, "Jack . . . ." She dabbed her eyes with her linen napkin. "It's become very clear to me over time that Mary is *not* simply a friend turned plaything. Trust me Jack, a wife knows what she sees . . . . Mary, although I love her to death as a friend, has got to go. In all the years, Jack, this is the *only* women that I ever said 'had to go'."

Long silence.

"Jackie . . . . at this point in my life . . . ." He took a deep exasperating breath, ". . . . all I can do is be honest with us both." He spoke with finality. "I *can not* let Mary go."

His statement hung in the air in deafening silence for what seemed like a long time.

Jackie suddenly dabbed her lips with her napkin and stood. She spoke as if it were a chore. "If you'll excuse me, I need to be alone."

As she slowly closed the door behind her, it seemed as if the fun, sun, laughter, and *love* in Greece were such a long time ago.

CHAPTER 18

By Labor Day, with the presidential election nine weeks off, the president's sexual prowess had clearly fallen victim to debilitative creepage. Jackie, realizing that she had been a long-term enabler in the growing love between Mary and her husband, found herself having reached a strange-like level of acceptance and forgiveness. As painful as it remained, she managed to find a level of paradoxical peace in seeing how good Mary and Jack were for one another. As a result of the painful reality, Jackie began making behind the scene plans to return to Greece immediately following the election. She felt liberated and entitled to a ten day dose of Aegean Sea sun before facing the Christmas holiday madness, celebrated within grim north-eastern snow storms. She had come to accept the reality of having conceded to her unwritten marriage pre-nuptial agreement, to turn her head on Jack's philandering addiction. She knew that her marriage had been doomed to failure. She rationalized that *it is what it is* . . . . and not the end of the world.

The first prong of the clan-plan, to focus on Bobby and his brood of eight, was working so well that the Nixon dirty tricks surrogates soon became overwhelmed and frustrated by the family of ten. With Jackie being highly visible at 'home' with Jack, and Mary hidden well below the radar, the wagging tongues all but ceased, save the White House staff and those within the belt-way closest to the administration. Consequently, by summer's end Bobby had increased his lead over Nixon to eleven points.

Behind the scenes, the first-marriage was moving in a steady negative direction, with Jackie and Jack having secretly agreed, strictly between them, to a separation. Jackie had moved into one of the guest bedrooms within the White House presidential living quarters. Other than that, their lives appeared normal. Of course, secrets, by default, are meant to be shared, even within the highest office of the land; Jack shared the separation secret with Mary as part of an intimate conversation.

216

With the election a mere eight weeks off, and Bobby all but locked in as the clear winner, talk shifted to what Jack would do after leaving office in his debilitating condition. Some within the media were hinting that Bobby would appoint his brother to an ambassadorship. However, if the media was fully aware of the current state of the president's debilitation, they would never have entertained the idea.

Behind the scenes, Bobby had been having private conversations with his brother regarding his post-presidential fit within his upcoming administration. They decided that Jack would do best serving as unofficial traveling ambassador, and, of course, as his behind the scenes advisor. His job, so to speak, would be to spread goodwill amongst friends of the U.S. and otherwise.

The unaddressed question was who would be the ex-president's traveling mate, for Bobby was still not privy to Jack and Jackie's separation. Jackie had kept the secret from Bobby's wife Ethel, as did Jack from his own brother.

CHAPTER 19

With the presidential election a mere four weeks off, and with Bobby maintaining a nine plus point lead, his campaign folks decided to make one final stump swing throughout the west-coast, with his final stop being Los Angeles.

The first day of fall was un-seasonally hot in Southern California, with the evening turning pleasantly warm, with a light balmy Pacific on-shore breeze. The sky was clear, with a bright three-quarter moon. A full crowd of shirt-sleeve RFK supporters gathered in the Embassy Room of the Ambassador Hotel located in the posh mid Wilshire District.

As Bobby was ushered though the crowd that spilled through the lobby and out and beyond the hotel's expansive entrance, there was the usual small number of boisterous, placard carrying opposition present. Bobby's eye caught one sign, "No Nepotism", which prompted him to feign a gasp and put both hands on his chest.

At the time, the government provided Secret Service protection for incumbent presidents, but not for presidential candidates. Kennedy's only security was provided by former FBI agent William Berry, and two unofficial body guards, Olympic Decathlon gold medalist Rafer Johnson, and professional football player Rosey Grier.

In spite of his brother's near fatal assassination, Bobby welcomed contact with the public, and often people would manage to touch him in their excitement.

When finished speaking, Kennedy had planned to walk through the ballroom in route to a gathering of supporters elsewhere in the hotel. However, travel deadlines forced him to forgo the second group. As he finished speaking, he moved to cross the ballroom when William Berry stopped him, "No, there's been a change, we're going this way." Campaign aide Fred Dutton and Berry cleared the way for Kennedy to go to his left through double swinging doors into a wide kitchen corridor. However, hemmed in by the crowd, he was forced to follow maître d'hôtel Karl Uecker through the back exit.

Uecker took Kennedy by the right wrist, frequently releasing it as Kennedy shook hands with those he encountered. They headed down a passageway that narrowed by an ice machine against the right wall and a steam table to the left. Kennedy turned to his left and shook hands with busboy Juan Romero, just as a small stature man with dull black hair and two days growth of heavy black beard stepped down from a low tray-stacker beside the ice machine, rushed past Uecker and repeatedly fired a handgun at Kennedy.

As Kennedy fell to the floor, Bill Barry saw the shooter holding a small caliber handgun and hit him twice in the face while Raefer Johnson and Rosey Grier grabbed the assassin, as he continued to fire his weapon randomly. With innocent lives at stake Rosey, a massive NFL lineman, snapped the shooter's neck causing him to fall dead to the floor like a rag doll.

As Raefer and Rosey shifted to crowd control, Barry knelt on the floor and placed his folded jacket beneath Kennedy's head. Identifying the weapon that lay on the floor adjacent to the Senator, as a .22 caliber, he hoped the degree of the wounds would be minor. With the senator transitioning into shock, Barry disturbed Bobby as little as possible in order to access the extent of the damage. He quickly determined the wounds to be minor. Losing all sense of time, Barry was unable to gage if the paramedics arrived quickly, or otherwise. By the time they put Bobby on an I V the sense of he being in shock waned and he began to speak in a slow and confused manor. Upon close examination the paramedics verifier three non life threatening wounds made by solid point bullets. The scariest of the three was a two and a half to three inch long crease, to the surface of Bobby's skull, which ran from his left temple in an upward and back direction slightly above the ear. If the bullet's impact would have been two to three degrees more direct, the senator would have been killed. The second wound went through the left tricep, with the third wound having ripped through the fleshy, web-like area between the base of his thumb and the base of his index finger of his right hand. The second two wounds were clearly of the self-defense nature, as the senator instinctively tried to shield his face and eyes.

Programmed for middle of the night crises, the President was calm as his aide handed him the phone at three AM. "Sorry Mr. President, it's California calling about Bobby."

It was the odd phrase, 'calling about Bobby', that did send a jolt of adrenalin into Jack's system. "This is the president, what's the problem?"

He bolted upright in spite of his handicap, "Oh my God, no . . . . how is he?"

He was given a detailed report on the three wounds. "And you say one to two days in the hospital and he's free to hit the campaign trail again; that's good news . . . . praise God." He responded further, "Of course, within reason . . . . sure, of course."

He was then given the details of the assassination attempt and the fate of the middle-eastern appearing shooter, and that he was without any form of identification. "Thank you very much, and keep me informed. Also, have Bobby call me just as soon as he's able."

The president hung up the phone and pushed the intercom button. "I'm up for the day. I'll have my newspapers and breakfast right after I bathe." He pulled himself into his wheel chair and wheeled down the hall to Jackie's bedroom.

Jack gently awoke Jackie and shared with her the latest Kennedy family tragedy. She sobbed, "When . . . . will . . . all the . . . madness . . . end?" He worked his way from the wheelchair to sitting on the edge of her bed, took her in his arms and consoled her. When she calmed, he worked his way back into the wheelchair and negotiated his way toward the door as she called, "I'm up for the day, and will be having breakfast with you, as soon as I call Ethyl and shower."

As the president wheeled through Jackie's door, she added, "I swear, Jack, our country is turning into a banana republic."

CHAPTER 20

With the dust having settled on Bobby's failed assassination, and his injuries being of the flesh wound level, the opposition wasted no time in making political hay. Nixon went on record while stumping that the last thing the American people needed was another "hit-list" president.

Bobby responded quickly, appearing on live television bandaged and gauzed, looking like a victim of war. "If doing the right thing for the American people is a threat to my life, then so be it." With that, the Nixon play backfired to the point of setting the stage for a possible landslide election.

On November 7th, the early east-coast exit polls signaled the makings of a lopsided race that experts claimed had a negative impact of west-coast poll turn out, to the point that victory was boldly claimed by the Kennedy clan before the sun set over the Pacific.

Jack and Jackie watched Bobby's acceptance speech on television within their White House presidential quarters; Jack in his wheel chair and Jackie steeling glances, as she busily packed for her morning departure to Greece. Jackie half jokingly comments, "Well, your Kennedy clan has its legacy."

Mary's eyes welled in tears as she watched Bobby's acceptance speech from home alone. Still frazzled by the near loss of Jack's younger brother, she spoke aloud to the four walls. "Thank you Lord . . . . thank you."

Mary switched off the television and began to pack for an extended stay with Jack.

CHAPTER 21

While Jackie was airborne to Greece, a White House limo picked up Mary from her Georgetown home, which was down the street and around the corner from her sister Tony and her husband Ben Bradlee.

A Secret Service agent announced Mary's arrival through an intercom, and the door to the Presidential private quarters electronically clicked open. Being pre-announced Mary stepped through the door with her suitcase in tow. The president immediately wheeled himself into the foyer, and greeted Mary with a warm hug as he half stood from his wheelchair.

"Mary, Mary, I'm so glad to see you," They embraced. "You just filled a void in my heart."

He sat down to relieve the strain in his back as Mary kneeled on the posh carpet and warmly wrapped her arms around Jack kissing him repeatedly as she spoke. "Oh Jack .... Jack .... Jack .... alone at last."

She was pleased to feel the strength in his arms. "Oh Mary, It has been too long."

She held him at arms length, brushed his hair back with her hand as she looked him in the eyes. "Jack, I love you so much."

He half chuckled, "Even in my current state."

She moved to a partial position on his lap and placed her right arm around his neck. "Jack, listen to me honey." She pecked him on the lips, "It's your current state that made me realize how much I love you .... y .... o .... u .... period."

Choked up, he buried his head in her neck for several moments before speaking. "You know, Mary, all these years, and, yes, all those women, and the bottom line in my life has come down to the woman ...." He chuckled, "... I mean young girl I was smitten by years ago at a high school dance."

She giggled like a young girl, "Yes, I remember, my date was Billy Attwood."

Still in each others arms, Jack laughed, "Yeah, my current Ambassador to West Africa."

Mary kissed him on the lips and held him tightly. "Yes, and as I recall, he was not too pleased with you that evening."

"Yeah, I kept cutting in on him on the dance floor."

"Yes, and I was loving every minute of it." She giggled, "You were sooooo handsome . . . . Mr. President."

"And you, Mary, were the prettiest girl at the dance . . . . without question."

"Oh, Jack, you're so kind."

"No ma'am, I'm not, you stood out like a shiny new penny . . . . clearly head and shoulders above every young lady present."

*   *   *

Greek shipping magnate, Aristotle Onassis, smiled to himself as he reshuffled his business calendar in order to share the entire following day, and hopefully evening, with Jackie Kennedy aboard his private yacht. He was more excited than during her previous visit, because of what his highly paid intelligence revealed to him about the First Couples troubled marriage.

With Jack and Bobby in the midst of a presidential transition, Jackie in Greece, and Mary Pinchot more and more visible within the White House, Aristo saw the planets coming quickly into alignment. Ari chuckled as he thought of Mary as his good as a secret personal alley. What more could he ask of her; with Jackie out of town Mary was steadily seen with the president, by the White House staff and a handful of journalist covering the president; she was either sitting beside him, standing behind him in his wheelchair, or wheeling him about the White House throughout the course of his day.

At first the questions were more whisper-like rumors, but recently they were being openly raised by credible journalists. Ari grinned. If his plans came to fruition, those questions would soon be coming from the public.

During the week leading up to Thanksgiving, tenacious European paparazzi struck *rag-sheet* gold with his discovery of Jackie's secret whereabouts. The news broke in the United States with a five-by-seven front page photo of Jackie, taken through a telephoto lens, on the deck of a massive private yacht anchored well offshore of the Greek island of Mykonos. Jackie was shown sunning her lithe, bikini clad body, lying along side Aristotle Onassis in a brief European style bathing suit. The two wore stylish sunglasses, and smiled with beverage in hand.

With the presidential election over and the RFK team in transition, all the GOP was left to do was grumble at the growing scandalous focus on Jackie and Mary.

With Jack transitioning out of office, and he and Jackie in the midst of a secret, unofficial marriage separation, all he had to do was smile and say that he was well aware of where Jackie was vacationing and who she was with. He further explained to the reporters that the paparazzi photo cleverly failed to capture the handful of people on the yacht's bow, below deck, and water skiing beyond the blind side of the luxury craft. When Jack was pressed about Mary's seemingly continuous presence at the White House, he simply smiled and said that she was an old college friend of his and Jackie, and that she was helping Jack as much as she was helping Jackie.

Jack raised a glass of red wine toward Mary, across from him at the dinner table in the White House private quarters. "Here's to us, Mary."

Mary winked, "Yes, Jack, to us."

Silence.

Mary smiled, "With Jackie due back tomorrow night, and the holidays upon us, tonight could very well be our last White House sleepover."

Jack shook his head while staring down at the table. "Oh, God, Mary . . . . you may be right." Pause, "And after I leave the White House, our situation will become a geographic challenge."

"Yes, we've been spoiled with you here and me a stones throw away in Georgetown."

Jack slowly shook his head, "Well, with Jackie's post White House plans being somewhat elusive at this point, you and I are left unknowing."

While Mary searched for words dealing with Jack's ever debilitating health dilemma, Jack must have read her mind. "As we speak, every known place of my post president residency, or I should say temporary residency, is being structurally made . . . ." He paused before spitting out the words, ". . . . handicap friendly."

Mary reached across the table and softly placed her hand in his. "Jack, trust me, we'll manage." She squeezed his hand, "Our lives may be more intermittent and less convenient, but we *will* manage."

Silence.

She squeezed his hand again, "Whatever the case, Jack, you are, without question, well worth it." She smiled warmly, "I love you, Jacko."

The soon to be private citizen shifted in his wheel chair. "Me to you, Mary, Mary."

Silence.

"Mary, I know it's too early for bed, but could we just lie together for a while?"

"You bet Jack, you bet." She chuckled as she stood, "Play spoons, now . . . ."

They both burst into laughter.

CHAPTER 22

On the one year anniversary of his failed assassination, Jack, clothed in pajamas, bathrobe, and slippers, sat in his wheelchair behind his Oval Office desk, preparing for a series of meetings scheduled for the following day. He grabbed his personal-line phone mid second ring, "Jack here."

She chucked, "Jackie here."

"Hey, I was informed that your plane landed, welcome back. Where are you calling from?"

"I'm three quarters of an hour from the White House."

"Great; you in the mood for a nightcap?"

"I'd love one."

"Me too, see yah."

Jackie spoke while Jack was in the process of hanging-up. "Jack . . . . Jack?"

"Yeah, I'm here."

Her voice took on a steely tone, "We need to talk, Jack."

His heart sunk, "Yeah . . . . sure . . . . of course."

With that, the line went dead."

* * *

With sons Mark and Quentin due home for Thanksgiving weekend, Mary hummed a cheery tune while putting away the Turkey and trimmings when the phone rang. She noticed the street light came on as she grabbed the phone.

"Pinchot residence."

"Mary, it's jack."

Jokingly, "Are you calling from the red or the black phone?"

Pause.

Chuckle, "I guess it's a matter of perspective."

Pause.

"Oh, oh, Jackie's back."

His voice turned sober. "And she initiated a long talk."

Mary, slowly sat down at the kitchen table, "And?"

"After Bobby is sworn in, she's openly filing for a legal separation."

Jack broke a long silence, "Enter Onassis."

Mary shifted in her seat, "The paparazzi photo."

"Yeah, she said the photo was what it was . . . . it was just the two of them with a skeleton crew making themselves invisible."

"Which would be easy to do on such a massive yacht."

"Yes."

"Was there any mention of the word divorce?"

"No . . . . nor did she use the term trial separation."

Long pause, "Jack, I'm truly sorry."

"Mary, I know that comes from the heart, and I appreciate that."

Pause, "What now, Jack?"

The president took a long exasperating breath, "Mary, with this, along with my debilitating health . . . . you are truly my only hope." He dropped his voice, "Having said that, I've got to go."

The line went dead, and Mary placed her face in her hands and wept.

CHAPTER 23

During a White House new administration transitional lull between Thanksgiving and Christmas, Mary answered her phone as she poured her first cup of coffee, while viewing the fresh dusting of snow through the kitchen window.

"Pinchot residence."

JFK's personal secretary, Evelyn Lincoln, spoke in a near whisper, "Mary, it's me, Evelyn."

Mary chuckled and whispered back. "Is everything all right?"

"Have you seen this morning's Washington Post?"

"No, but I was about to retrieve it from the front porch."

"I hope . . . . I think you'll enjoy the front page story of the Local section."

Before Mary could respond, "Oh, I see that Jackie's on wheel chair duty this morning." Chuckle, "In spite of her smile, she seems a thousand miles a way."

Wanting to give Jackie the benefit of the doubt, she ignored the comment.

"Thanks for the heads-up; I'll grab my newspaper post-haste."

Evelyn dropped her voice lower yet, "Gotta go, see yah."

Mary stirred her coffee and took a generous draw before retrieving her Washington Post. Paper in hand, she sat in her favorite living room chair. Before opening the paper, she switched on the television to the local news station. She took another draw of coffee and removed the elastic band from the newspaper. She unfolded the Local section of the paper and was taken aback by the three-by-five picture of her guiding the president to, or from, behind his Oval Office desk. The full half-page article, continued on page three, was titled "The First Angel of Mercy".

As she read the article, she found it to be a bit of a paradox in that while it referred to Mary as a "mystery women", the journalist went on to disclose a surprising level of personal information about her. A stranger reading the article discovered Mary and Jack to be friends since Mary's early days at prep school, and that her ex-husband was employed by the CIA. The reader further discovered that she had been a frequent guest, of the first-couple, at the White House, Jack's sailboat, and the Kennedy family compound at Hyannis Port. The reader found Mary to be a journalist, poet, author, painter, and one time fashion model. The athletic reader would be pleased with Mary's athletic prowess in tennis, basketball, and aggressively competitive in all things sport.

Mary winced, and set her coffee down, as she read about the tragic loss of her beloved son Michael. With that, she broke for a coffee refill and Kleenex.

When Mary resumed reading the article, she was proud to read of her family's accomplishments and contributions to society, over four generations, in particular her uncle Gifford Pinchot having been a two-term governor of Pennsylvania and having served as a cabinet member in the Teddy Roosevelt administration.

The journalist ended the article by restating what a dedicated 'angel of mercy' she was to the president, as well as to the first lady.

Mary finished the article with a sigh of relief, and a long draw from her coffee mug. She was relieved that the article did not so much as hint of the White House love triangle that would, in time, be public knowledge.

As timing would have it, her phone rang, "Hello, may I please speak with the angle of mercy/"

"Oh, Jack." They laughed, "Yes, dear, I've seen the article."

Jack added, "A very nice one at that."

"Yes it is . . . . and not a single barb."

"Don't hold your breath, trust me, they are on their way."

"Well, they had better hurry with Bobby's inauguration being ten days off."

"Don't worry, ex presidents and the opposition are forever."

CHAPTER 24

Mother Nature truly blessed the Washington DC region on inauguration day 1965. The air was still and a brisk thirty-nine degrees. The Sky was cloudless, egg shell blue, and crystal clear. President elect Robert Fitzgerald Kennedy, showing no visible sign of his assassination wounds, stood poised in front of the Bible held by Chief Justice of the United States, Earl Warren. His wife, Ethyl, clearly proud, stood to Bobby's right holding their newborn baby, Maxwell, with the remaining eight children, Kathleen, Joseph, Robert Jr., David, Courtney, Michael, Kerry, and Christopher, standing in a single row at right angles to their parents and facing the audience. Next to the children, in his wheel chair, was outgoing president, John Fitzgerald Kennedy, with Jackie at his side, and Mary standing directly behind Jack with her hands free of the wheel chair.

Although Mary had deliberately dressed-down for the historic occasion, as a matter of respect for Jackie and Ethyl, the nation's eyes were still drawn to Mary's simple, wholesome beauty.

The *Associated Press* had grabbed hold of the *Angel of Mercy* article from the *Washington Post* making Mary a near household name across America. Aware of that, the TV commentators took the opportunity to give Mary more than her share of air time, starting what would soon become a national obsession.

With the growing interest in Mary, and the broad public interest in JFK's post-presidency plans, Jack was the featured guest on Sunday morning Meet the Press the week following the inauguration.

The program staff and panel members were surprised when their ex-president showed up nearly an hour early, quietly and without fanfare, pushed in his wheelchair by a very young male aide, flanked on both sides by a Secret Service agent.

The show began with JFK talking about the smooth and seamless transition with Bobby's administration, in regard to foreign policy in general, with the emphasis on nuclear disarmament and ending the Vietnam War between late '66 and early '67. After much back and forth about foreign and domestic issues, the panel clearly relaxed and moved on to Jack's post-presidential plans.

"Well, the reason Bobby has made no mention of the role I'll play within his administration is because I will not be acting at any official staff capacity. The role we have agreed on is that of one of the president's several unofficial, non-staff advisors."

The panel discussed that role for several minutes before Jack continued. "Additionally, I'll act in the envious position of vacationing ambassador."

The panel chuckled as one member commented, "Vacationing ambassador, isn't that a fair description of all ambassadors stationed in trouble-free locations .... like Paris, Rome, London, etc.?"

Jack smiled and added, "Honolulu." The panel laughed and Jack continued, "While traveling I'll be working as an author .... of my memoirs, as well as a fictional novel that I'm keeping under wraps for a while."

The panel immediately tossed out topics hoping to open up the president.

"Your war experiences?"

"Your failed assassination?"

"A murder in the White House?"

A more daring panel member, offered, "An Angel of Mercy?"

The panel was surprised when their ex-president reacted openly and without hesitation.

"Ah, yes, Mary Pinchot, Jackie and my very dear friend." He smiled, "She is without question a true angel." Again, he smiled, "She has been an immeasurable .... immense .... help to Jackie and me."

The panel was relaxed further by the president's openness with the subject of Mary.

"Tell us, Mr. President, how far back does your friendship with Mary go?"

Jack chuckled as he looked back in time, "Well, as far back as I can remember in my early childhood, the Pinchot name was a household word in my family .... for social and political reasons. However, I did not personally meet Mary until a Choate private boarding school dance in 1935. I had graduated from Choate a year earlier and was a freshman at Yale. At the time of the dance, Mary was a sixteen year-old freshman at Choate." He chuckled, and then sighed, "I'm sure you, as a panel, as well as the viewing audience, will get a kick out of Mary and my initial meeting .... talk about fate and destiny." He shifted in his wheelchair and seemed to glow at the recollection. "At the dance, where Mary and I met, she was the date of none other than Bill Attwood. Of course, Bill grew up and became my ambassador to South Africa."

"And your date, Mr. President?"

He laughed, "Actually, I was stag; I came with a buddy of mine from Yale."

"And, Mr. President, did you dance?"

"Indeed I did; it's as vivid as yesterday. I danced often . . . ." He laughed, ". . . . all with Mary. You know, after all these years, ol' Billy, that's Attwood, is still bugged with me for monopolizing his date."

A panelist shrugged his shoulders, "But why Mary, I'm sure the dance was loaded with pretty girls?"

"Ah . . . ." He smiled as he reflected, ". . . . but you had to be there. Mary was, by far, the prettiest girl at the dance . . . . without question."

"Let's get back to your travel; what are your near future travel plans?"

"My . . . . or I should say our first trip is being scheduled as we speak, for the entire month of May."

"Including?"

"Italy, including the Vatican, France, Germany, and England . . . . not necessarily in that order."

"And your entourage?"

"Jackie, of course, and the kids on a part time basis, along with a pair of aides, an administrative assistant, a press agent, a physician, and a couple of Secret Service agents."

Silence.

"And Mary?"

Without hesitation or blinking, "Jackie and I have invited her to cherry pick a week of personal interest, but she has yet to get back with our travel people." He chuckled, almost to himself, "Knowing Mary, her decision will be based on sun and the outdoors."

"Mr. President, in your position, so to speak, as a non-staff traveling ambassador, can you give us a flavor of your itinerary and whom you will be meeting with along the way?"

"You're correct in that I will be non-staff, not acting in any official capacity. Therefore, I will not be *meeting* with people, I'll be *visiting*."

"And the people are kings, queens, presidents, the Pope . . . . and?"

"An array of ambassadors, including our own."

"Of course the first lady will be at your side during the visit."

"Yes, of course." He laughed, "If the truth be known, they are all more interested in Jackie, than they are in me."

They all laughed, with one married panel member adding, "I know the feeling." More laughter.

"Mr. President, I hate to be the one to bring it up, but all of America is very concerned about your health."

Again, the president did not hesitate, "Yes, and the people have every right to know." He shifted in his wheelchair, as Mary sat spellbound in front of her television in Georgetown. "Well, as you all know, my condition is debilitating, and my condition, barring any unforeseen problems, can be projected and tracked in a near linier fashion. Having said that, I will remain active, starting with my traveling, for a year to eighteen months."

Pause.

"And beyond then, Sir?"

"Well, it becomes more of a stay at home situation, then . . . ." His voice trailed off. He cut off a question before resuming, "One thing for certain, I continue to praise God for any and all time he's given me beyond that day in Dallas."

CHAPTER 25

Ironically, it was the morning following JFK's appearance on *Meet the Press* that Jackie met secretly with her attorneys and filed for a secret, yet formal, marriage separation. Although, she and Jack had agreed ahead of time to keep the separation a secret until after the initial round of their post-presidency travels, Jackie's plans to be a part of the travels remained firm.

Meanwhile, the GOP, still licking their wounds over their landslide defeat, wasted no time reacting to JFK's traveling entourage. They demanded answers, with the threat of an investigation, as to who was paying for the "vacationing global rock-star tour" of Jack and his friends. They went so far as to ask for a daily printed accounting of each and every travel expense. Expecting such political gamesmanship from their seriously wounded counterpart, the new administration and JFK were prepared ahead of time to respond, in kind, to the GOP through the printed media. The front page, below the fold, article in the *Washington Post* read, in part:

> "*A spokesman for the Robert F. Kennedy administration has no comment on the financial aspect of the travels of the former president, first lady and minimal staff, for, aside from the Secret Service, none of the traveling party are members of the current administration, or any other government payroll. The entire cost of the subject travels is being covered by the Kennedy Foundation as well as by a non political group of donors formally registered as "The Friends of JFK".*" The article went on to say, "*However, due to the very nature of the ex-president's travels, the White House will have privy to a detailed itinerary, as well as a daily report of each day's travels and events.*"

The GOP quickly retorted through the printed media, "This new administration has yet to clear the runway, and they are already entertaining a cover-up."

Over breakfast at the Kennedy family Hyannis Port compound, clearly irked, Jackie folded and tossed a section of the *New York Times* on the floor near her feet and reached for her coffee with a frown. "Jack, I want you to know how irritated I've become over you, Mary, and the press."

Being legally separated, Jack feigns interest, "And how's that, Jackie?"

Sensing his lip service, she rolled her eyes, "Well, since you left office, it's as if the news media, as well as the public, are only interested in their ex-president and his *Angel of Mercy*." She spoke with sarcasm as she bracketed *Angel of Mercy* with her fingers.

Jack shifted in his wheel chair, slowly folded his newspaper, and took a long draw from his coffee. "Well, Jackie, trust me, it will only get worse."

Her face signaled disgust as she shifted in her chair, turned ninety-degrees away from Jack, and pulled her bathrobe closed around her chest as Jack continued. "Get over as well as used to it, Jackie, the unstoppable public wheels are in motion; smelling blood, they're slowly moving in an ever shrinking circle." He took a sip of coffee and continued, as Jackie began to slowly and silently drum the fingers of her right hand on the stark white linen table cloth. "And, a secret within the beltway, such as our separation, whether one is in or out of office is, at best, described," He bracketed with his fingers, "a slow leak in a dam that is destined to collapse under the strain of its own secrecy."

Frustrated by the unexpected cold dose of reality, Jackie turned in her chair and faced Jack. "Oh, Jack, stop it!"

He shrugged his shoulders and picked up his newspaper. Jackie's thoughts turned to that of Ari.

CHAPTER 26

Americans increasingly clamored for information related to their patriotic national wounded warrior. Therefore, they were excited with the detailed itinerary of JFK's imminent diplomatic tour, published nationally through the media,.

The six week itinerary clearly indicated that Mary would join the travel group the last two weeks of the trip. Looking at the itinerary one would assume that Jackie was on board throughout the trip, while, in fact, she was leaving the group three days after Mary was to join the party.

The first diplomatic stop was London, where Queen Elizabeth greeted the international hero with a royal dinner party of forty-eight, representing the lion share of who-is-who in the London vicinity.

The English were doubly saddened as the party departed for Ireland, realizing in their hearts that it would be the last time that JFK would grace London with his presence. Further, they were enviously saddened by the thought of having to share that bit of history with their *friends* to the north.

The following day, the group headed by motor caravan the 120 miles south-west from Dublin to the location of his family roots in county Wexford, the small village of Dunganstown. Jack had visited the village in June 1963; sadly, during the visit he was in his prime and so full of promise, and was being viewed through the prism of immortality by a full crowd, comprised primarily of the entire village populous.

With Jack returning under his current internationally known debilitating state of health, the overwhelming crowd of admirers reflected the unspoken understanding of that being his final visit.

There was not a dry Irish eye as their native son, by roots, spoke from a temporary dais set up in the town square, flanked on both sides by small obelisk war memorial honoring local heroes; to his left WWI, and to his right WWII. Jack's speech was broadcast on radio, as well as loud speaker throughout the massive crowd that spread throughout the small village and into surrounding farmlands.

The local crowds, as well as in every Irish pub within Ireland and throughout the world, roared as mauve thick cream-capped Guinness raised in cheer as the ex-president of the United States capped his speech in a heavy Irish brogue, "*Is Éireannach mé*" . . . . I am Irish.

The entire travel group relaxed, as they crossed the English Channel. Not only had the English and Irish made them feel loved and welcomed, they foreshadowed how sensitive and well prepared every hosting country would be in comfortably and seamlessly making provisions to dealing with their most honored guest, who was sadly confined to a wheel chair.

The Germans handled their honored guests in kind, aside from an expected paradoxical blend of stiff-friendship. Unlike during his famous July '83 speech in Berlin, with the infamous wall as a backdrop, JFK deliberately failed to repeat his famous speech closing, "*Ich bin ein Berliner*" . . . . I am a Berliner. Much of the German press focused and speculated on the meaning of the omission, especially after proudly claiming to be Irish a few days earlier.

No sooner had they checked into the French hotel, Jack received a call on his direct line. "Hi, Jacko, it's Mare."

Jack glowed with joy, "Oh, Mare, it's so great to hear from you."

Jackie rolled her eyes, stood and dropped the current edition of *Vogue* in her chair, walked to the window and crossed her arms as she heard one side of the conversation.

"You're in Paris, surprise, surprise."

Mary laughed, "I had a change in plans and decided to join the party a few days early."

Jackie shook her head while continuing to stare out the window as Jack replied. "A woman always has a right to change her mind . . . ." He laughed, ". . . . especially if her name is Mary."

Mary chuckled, "Especially when she's contraire as well."

Jack, clearly delighted, draws another head shake from Jackie. "Right again, Mare." Pause, "So where are you?"

"I'm here in the hotel . . . . room 620 . . . . in the cheap seats." Soft chuckle, "I did not tell the front desk that I was with your group."

"Of course, you did, Mary, that's who you are." Laughing, "I'll call the desk and fix that."

"No, Jack, please,' Laughter, "I feel right at home . . . . seriously."

Pause, "OK . . . . you're priceless, Mare."

She laughed, "Yes, I know . . . . as in cheap seats."

Again, he laughed, "Anyway, we're having happy hour in our presidential suite in an hour; can you be ready?"

"Oh, Jacko, you know me, all I need to do is drag a rake through my hair."

He thought of the extreme contrast between Jackie and Mare. "They could certainly never color you pretentious, Mare."

Again, Jackie shook her head.

"OK, Mare, I'll send a Secret Service agent to escort you . . . . in one hour."

Jokingly, "Roger that."

Jackie turned from the window, "Oh how silly puppy love can be."

Jack calmly replies, as he turned his wheel chair toward his bedroom. "So you find the *real deal* painful to the ear, do you?

With their marriage, arranged by Jack's controlling, politically motivated father, sticking in her craw, Jackie lashes back. "So you'll know, Jack, I've made arrangements to swing through Greece for ten days on my way home next week."

Without blinking or looking back, Jack replied as he rolls into his room. "Yes, I was informed as soon as you booked your flight."

She bit her tongue in anger as he stopped his chair and began to close the door. "It's time for you to accept the fact, as I have in your case, Jackie, that Mary and I are as much of a number as you and Aristotle." He deliberately referred to the Greek by his formal name.

CHAPTER 27

Happy hour in the hotel's Presidential Suit was nearing full-steam as Franz Mignion, op-ed journalist for Paris' *LeMonde* newspaper and regular contributor to the *International Herald Tribune*, chatted with a Kennedy aide, and US ambassador to France. Franz's ever roving journalistic eye observed, from across the room, a secret service agent respond to an apparent knock at the suite door, along with a message in his wired ear. The newspaperman's eyes widened, as he immediately recognized the Associated Press' much acclaimed US Presidential *Angel of Mercy* enter the room, followed by a the second secret service agent. Through his peripheral vision Franz noticed the former First Lady excuse herself from a pair of ambassadors and step toward *angel* Mary Pinchot.

Jackie warmly greeted her old friend, "Mary, it's so good to see you; we're all so pleased that you managed to join our little group earlier than planned."

"Jackie, it's good to see you as well. It was a schedule change beyond my control that enabled me to join you earlier."

Both ladies treasured their long friendship, in spite of their personally known, but not spoken, cross-involvement.

They accepted proffered glasses of champagne and touched glasses as Mary continued. "My new schedule now gives us what . . . . five to six days together?"

Jackie raised her glass, "Sounds close enough." She smiled as she wondered just how much Mary knew, or was privy to. If the truth be known, Mary was current in all the details of Jack and Jackie's private lives. She was well aware of Jackie's plan to spend several days aboard Onassis' massive private luxury yacht sailing the Aegean Sea with her children, her sister, Princess Lee Radziwell, her husband, Polish prince *Stanisław Albrecht Radziwiłł*, and their children. Mary also knew that Aristotle was scheduled to be present, collectively, five of the ten days at sea. Aside from Mary, the only people privy to such detail was the Secret Service, Jack, and the Presidential travel team, who were sworn to secrecy, Lee, her husband, and, of course, Aristotle. And for those who really knew Aristotle, his secrecy was proportional to his own personal devious interest.

Mary suddenly had to steady her champagne glass as her legs, from behind, received unexpected hugs from squealing Carolyn and John, John. "Auntie Mary, Auntie Mary."

She managed to set her champagne on the hors d'oeuvres table, and turned to greet her favorites with hugs and kisses. "Wow, what a pleasant surprise . . . . my two favorite angels."

They resumed squealing and grabbed hold of the legs from the front.

Franz turned from that scene and resumed looking across the room at the president, whose entire demeanor had been uplifted sine Mary entered the room. However, it was what happened after Jackie left the room to usher her kids to bed, and Mary was finally able to work her way across the room to finally greet the recent most powerful man on the planet. Franz observed the two of them lock eyes and immediately emit joy and happiness. Mary approached Jack with open arms and stepped into Jacks awaiting arms and embraced one another in warm mutually responsive embrace. They smiled as they spoke into one another's ear. Totally uninhibited, the president pulled Mary onto his lap as he shifted in his wheel chair.

The attention of the room suddenly shifted toward Jack and Mary. Jack beamed and spoke to the gathering, as Mary stood up from Jack's lap. "For those who don't know her, I would like to introduce my personal *angel of mercy*, Mary Pinchot, who has joined our group for the balance of our travels." He waited for the applause to die, "Mary is a long-time very personal friend of both me and Jackie."

Mary blushed, and accepted a fresh glass of champagne. "It's so nice to be a part of this evening's happy hour, as well as an honored member of this wonderful traveling group." She smiled as she panned the room, "During the course of the evening, I will make a point to meet and chat with each and every one of you." She raised her glass, "In the mean time, enjoy."

With that, Mary turned, bent down and pecked Jack on the lips and whispered in his ear as she squeezed his hand. "I love you, Jacko." He squeezed her hand and whispered, "Me too you, I'm so glad you joined the group earlier than planned." As she turned and walked forward, Jack discreetly patted her on the behind. At that point, Franz slowly worked his way through the crowd, patiently waiting for an opening to introduce himself to Mary.

After an ambassador and a chatty French socialite, Franz saw his opening. He extended his hand and spoke English in a polished French accent. "Mary Pinchot," correctly pronouncing Pinchot with a silent T, "what an absolute pleasure; my name is Franz Mignion." Her handshake was firm, "I'm a journalist with Paris' *LeMonde* newspaper and regular contributor to the International Herald Tribune."

Mary smiled, released his hand and replied in French . . . . through the remainder of the conversation. "I was a journalist my first few years out of university."

There was an instant connection through the language. "And, how were you trained in the French language . . . . at University?"

She smiled, "Actually, with my French roots, I was raised with the language." She took a sip of champagne and chuckled, "Of course, back home it's English first, as it should be. However, I think it's sad when immigrants fail to pass on their native tongue." Take me as an example; I'm a fourth generation American, and my children also speak fluent French."

He nodded his head in approval as he raised his glass, "And, as an added bonus, I think we can both agree French is the most beautiful of all languages."

She raised her glass in agreement.

"Mary, I couldn't help but notice how well received you were when you entered the room."

His eyes said, *"And?"*

"You know, Mary, as a journalist, I can say that your *Angel of Mercy* title solidly precedes you."

Uncomfortable with flattery, even when well intended, "Yes, thanks to *Associated Press* . . . . although it started with the *Washington Post*."

Sensing her discomfort he proceeds with caution. "Mary, I hate to appear as imposing, however, we are ships passing in the night."

They smiled, and she touched his forearm in a comforting gesture, "Under such fleeting circumstance, I promises not to bite."

He relaxed, "Mary, I would be honored and privileged if you would agree to a quick, say fifteen minutes, camera interview before you leave Paris."

He was surprised when she did not hesitate or blink, "Sure, Franz, how about tomorrow morning . . . . early?"

Taken aback, "Ahhh . . . . how about nine?"

She winked, "The day is half gone by nine . . . . how about seven-thirty?"

Franz smiled and extended his hand, "We're going to get along just fine."

He was further surprised when she shunned his hand and gave him a warm hug, "Of course we will; I went straight from university into journalism."

He laughed, "As in being cut . . . ."

She completed his thought, ' . . . . from the same clothe."

Mary signaled the end of their conversation by switching seamlessly back to English, as she spotted Jackie re-entering the room. "Sorry, Franz, I've got to go; Jackie and I have some catching up to do."

"Sure, Mary, I'll call you from the lobby tomorrow morning."

She winked, "Seven-thirty. Nice meeting you Franz."

As she crossed the room and met Jackie, Franz thought about how taken he was by Mary, prompting him to accept a fresh glass of champagne and mumble beneath his breath. "*Smart, friendly, unpretentious, charming . . . . and oh so beautiful.*" He took a long draw of champagne, "*I can truly see the attraction . . . . Mr. President.*"

* * *

At eight the following morning, Franz bid farewell to Mary following her interview, and walked away from his film crew with a spring in his step. He mumbled to himself as he moved toward the hotel cafe, "Wow, there is far more to Mary this morning than there was last evening . . . . what a remarkable woman."

Knowing that the travel group had an eight-thirty breakfast coordination meeting, he selected a table in the café giving him a clear shot at the conference room door and part of the hallway, where the traveling group was scheduled to hold the meeting.

Well into his second cup of coffee, Franz heard muffled commotion in the hallway adjacent to the café. Within moments, he recognized the Secret Service agent leading the traveling group. Immediately behind the agent was the presidential aide, in charge of the group. Following the aide was the president with Mary pushing him in his wheelchair. Behind Mary was the travel group followed by the second secret service agent. The group entered the conference room with the secret service agent closing the door and assuming his guard position.

Conspicuously absent from the group, was Jackie.

Franz's journalistic instincts told him that it was clearly time for him to dig further.

Chapter 28

With the French fanfare behind them, save for their departure for Italy, the travel group arrived at their Paris hotel late in their final evening, retreated directly to their rooms, and all but collapsed.

With Jack and Jackie having been catered to throughout the long day of nonstop goodwill activities, they had enough fuel in their tanks for a nightcap over televised news. The pair of English language stations had excellent condensed coverage of their day's activities, with the primary focus being on the two of them. However, as the coverage progressed, the more Mary appeared in the coverage, with the commentator finally speaking to who the striking blond in the group was, before segueing into the private film interview with Mary, conducted by Franz earlier that very day . . . . all in flawless French.

As with Mary, Jackie Bouvier was also of French roots and raised in the language, whereas Jack, knew enough French to get the gist of a conversation. Halfway through the interview, it was Jackie who angrily broke the silence.

"For Christ sake, Jack, Mary's been with us one lousy day and she's already become the focal point."

Jack, with a flick of his wrist, dismissed Jackie, while not breaking his focus on the television nor his snifter of brandy. "She's simply a fresh face in the group; she'll soon be yesterday's news."

Unappeased, she gulped the last of her brandy and stood, "Yeah, by then I'll have left the group and she'll regain her position."

Irritated, "It's called loosing your place at the table, Jackie . . . . get over it."

With fresh brandy, she changes course, "And, of course, even you, Jack, could not help but notice that the staff and the rest of the group have been falling all over Mary at every turn."

Jack chuckled, "No, as a matter of fact, I did *not* notice"

Jackie retreated to her room in a huff, with brandy in hand, "Oh, Jack .... please."

The Italian government was forced to take back seat, with the group's first two days being spent in Rome. The first day's agenda stirred excitement throughout the group, for they *all* had an audience with Pope Paul VI. This would be Jack and Jackie's second Papal audience; the first as president, within days of Pope Paul VI having taken office, in June of 1963.

As the group entered the Vatican proper, Jackie, for show, took control of Jack's wheelchair from Mary. Although Mary very graciously stepped clear of the chair, much of the group's demeanor clearly expressed resentment.

As they entered the room where Popes have been giving private audiences for well over a century, the atmosphere immediately turned as hushed and hallowed as that of a cathedral sanctuary.

Jackie immediately noticed that unlike their earlier presidential Papal visit, there were two chairs set apart for her and Jack in a prominent front row position, as opposed to being close together. The balance of the group was in two relatively short rows set back from her and Jack's chairs.

A distinguished looking Papal aide stepped forward and escorted Jack and Jackie to the front row seats, placing Jack, in his wheelchair, to the right hand side of the left front row seat. The aide then seated her in the chair to Jack's left.

To Jackie's dismay and hidden anger, the Papal aide then ushered Mary forward to the second front row chair spaced within four feet to Jack's right. While a Papal cameraman filmed the *entire* visit, an edited copy for the news media, and a raw copy of the film earmarked for the Vatican Library, Jackie maintained her poise and dignity .... under fire.

The Papal aide moved to the left of the gold gilded thrown-like chair reserved for the Pope, and spoke in a hushed reverent tone. "Mr. President, First lady, Mary, and all honored guests, please stand and silently welcome Pope Paul the VI."

Out of respect, Jack, with Jackie's aid, struggled to his feet.

Mary was not *formally* raised as a Christian, although her Catholic roots were traceable to the French Huguenot era. With a self exposure to Christianity, her core beliefs were in alignment with the Nicene Creed. She strongly felt that Biblical reference to "His church" encompassed the "Communion of Saints", comprised of all the saved both living and dead. Therefore, she found the countless Saints canonized by the Catholic Church to be no more than a Catholic hall of fame. She considered herself a saved Christian, therefore she was a saint.

Although she respected the authoritative position of the Pope in the Roman Emperor Constantine the Great's established catholic (universal) church, she stood on the side of history regarding Papal lineage. Records indicate that the first head (Bishop of Rome) of Christianity was *arguably* Peter, whereas the first Pope of the catholic church, established by Roman Emperor Constantine, was Pope Miltiades, who was in the middle of his three year reign as Bishop of Rome, with the word *pope* never mentioned in the Bible. Emperor Constantine established the position of Pope, which is now one in the same with Bishop of Rome. Mary felt that she was in audience with the 232nd Pope, not the 263rd Pope. Of course, this was typically Mary.

Although Jackie's hidden anger was silently directed at the President for Mary's seating position of prominence, it was actually the Pope himself who was responsible. He had been strongly influenced by the *Associated Press* article on Mary as an *Angel of Mercy.*

Whereas Jack and Jackie had the honor of a previous audience with Pope Paul VI eleven days after the Pope's inauguration, this would be Mary's first face-to-face with His Holiness.

As the group stood, Mary took a deep breath and relaxed as the pope slowly entered the room. The Pope stepped in front of his chair and addressed the group, starting with the former President.

"Good morning."

The group responded in unison as previously instructed.

Mary was in complete awe, as the Pope spoke to Jack.

"Mr. President, I'm deeply honored to have you, the recipient of my countless personal prayers, standing before me today; you, sir, are a living example of Divine intervention."

Unlike Mary, the President was born and raised a Catholic, he blindly believed the Pope to be the Vicar of Christ, and that of a continuous succession of Popes. Therefore, regardless of him having been the most powerful man on planet earth for a period of four years, he too was in awe being in his presence.

Beginning to feel a bit shaky on his feet, Jack reverently bowed his head before addressing the Pope. "Your Holiness," He paused. "It is I who am honored by your presence as well as by your divine help, through your personal prayer, in my miraculous recovery." He paused to carefully measure his words, "Your Holiness, I humbly and willingly accept my subsequent current condition as the will of God." He slowly bowed his head and continued, *"Thy will be done on earth as it is in heaven."*

The Pope spread his hands in a blessing gesture, "Amen."

The Pope stepped laterally in front of Jackie. "Welcome to you as well, Jackie, you have been an example to the world by your strength, courage, and dignity though faith throughout your husband's tragic ordeal." He smiled warmly, "May God continue to touch and bless you."

With hands folded in steeple-like tradition, Jackie bowed reverently. "Thank you, Your Holiness." She paused and smiled softly, "The Lord has truly blessed Jack, me, our family, and all of America; and He continues to do so through Jack's debilitating condition."

The Pope continued to his left and faced Mary with a warm smile. "Mary . . . . what a beautiful name, indeed . . . . with an appropriate title of *Angle of Mercy*." He gave a near silent chuckle, "Yes, I do read the lay press; specifically, the *Associated Press* article about you, as the President's," he motioned toward Jack, *"Angel of Mercy."* He smiled and gestured toward the first couple, "What a tremendous help you have been to your President and First Lady." Again, he smiled. "I applaud you." Suddenly he was clearly speaking to the entire group. "As Christ speaks to us in Mathew 25:40, *"As much as you have done unto one of the least of My brethren, you have done unto Me."*

Dumbstruck, Mary was without words.

"Bless you, Mary."

"Th . . . thank you, Your Holiness."

Jackie seethed inside, and smiled toward the Vatican camera, as the Pope stepped toward the balance of the group.

*   *   *

No sooner did their hotel room door close behind them, Jackie released her pent up anger rooted in pure jealousy.

"Ok, Jack, whose idea was it to have the Pope, through Mary, overshadow me . . . . and you, for that matter?"

Jack was as successful at choking back his joy as Jackie could be with her anger.

"Trust me, Jackie, it was all His Holiness' doing; it was not me, and I know for a fact it wasn't our group coordinator."

Wanting no part of reason or fact, Jackie upped the ante. "You know, Jack, as smoothly as Mary has pushed me aside and overshadowed me; it's a good thing I'm leaving town."

Jack choked off a grin, "Leaving town is a good way to stop what you feel is going on . . . . in your own mind, I might add."

Jackie froze, straddling her bedroom's threshold. "All I can say, Jacko, is brace yourself for my return from Greece."

CHAPTER 29

Mary was enjoying a fresh self brewed cup of coffee while reading the hotel complimentary copy of *The International Herald Tribune,* when the phone broke the stark silence of her room.

"Hello."

"Mornin', Mare, did I wake you/"

She laughed, "I'll take that as a rhetorical question."

Jack laughed, "Touché, Mare." More laughter, "Yeah, I know, I know, you're a daybreak riser, like me."

'Yeah, I've already showered, ingested two cups of room brewed coffee, and all but devoured *Herald Tribune.*"

"I didn't hear you mention breakfast."

Coyly, "I was praying for an offer."

Jack laughed, "It must be yesterday's audience with His Holiness, because your prayers have been answered, young lady."

Mary chuckled, "You mean I'm having breakfast with the Pope."

More laughter, "No, but will *His Loliness* work for you . . . . as in, an over-the-hill Irishman?

"My favorite . . . . how did you know?"

They wind down, "So, Mare, when can you come to my suite for breakfast?"

"Give me five minutes."

"Five minutes . . . . are you sure that you're not a man."

"On a serious note . . . . I'm far better than most men."

"That you are, Mary, that you are . . . . see you in five."

The secret service agent smiled and nodded as Mary approached the door of Jack's suite, "Good morning, Mary, the president is expecting you."

He knocked and cracked the door open, "Mary is here, Mr. President."

She stepped across the threshold to see Jack walking slow, proud and erect to greet her in the suite's spacious entryway, where they embraced warmly.

"Oh, Jack, it's been too long since having you all to myself."

"Yes, I agree," With arms still tightly around Mary, he leaned back just far enough to make eye contact. "But the time spans will soon shorten."

Mary looks quizzically, and replies in a hush. "Shorten?"

"Let's talk about it over coffee; breakfast is on the way."

Mary spoke and poured coffee as Jack settled into his wheelchair. "I take it that Jackie got off for Greece alright this morning?"

"Yes, for security reasons, and to avoid the press, she left just before daybreak, from the hotel receiving dock."

Silence over coffee.

"Mare, so you'll know . . . . she dropped a bomb in anger last night, as she was going to bed."

With her coffee cup stalled between table and lips, "Bomb . . . . in anger?"

"Yeah . . . . let's start with the anger."

The secret service knocked softly on the door, "Breakfast is here, Mr. President."

"OK, bring it in, please."

Jack grinned sheepishly, "I hope you don't mind; I took the liberty to order for you." He turned to the agent, "Thank you, Peter."

As the door closed, Mary winked, "As if you don't know my breakfast likes by now."

'Sadly, Mary, I know more about the real you than I do Jackie."

Mary pondered the statement as Jack continued. "Now then, the Jackie's anger that I mentioned."

Mary stepped to his side of the table and served him. "Thanks, love." He patted her on the behind as she turned toward her side of the table.

She winked and sat down as Jack continued, "Jackie's anger is frustration and jealousy rooted."

They took their first bite of breakfast.

"How's that?"

"She's frustrated that her public stature, both actual and perceived, as well as within our group, has diminished."

Jack took a sip of coffee, as Mary forked a small piece of sausage, "There are two things in play; one, the post-office let down, when it's all about the new First Lady . . . . as in Jackie who?"

Mary peered over the rim of her coffee cup, "OK, fair enough, that's a given." She took a sip of coffee, "However, one that I don't personally understand."

Jack spoke respectfully, "I know how you feel, Mary, however, the difference in the two of you is secure verses insecure." He raised his hand in a silencing gesture, "In all fairness, Mare, there is no comparison between you and Jackie."

Agreeing, but wanting his viewpoint, "How's that?"

"While you are totally secure and comfortable in your skin, Jackie is totally insecure, with a low sense of self esteem . . . . totally different from how she appears." He picked up his orange juice, "She is always searching for validation . . . . a deep need to be shored up."

"You said that there are two things feeding her anger."

"Jackie is jealous, ... and it appears to be growing on a daily basis."

Mary placed her empty cup in its saucer, "Jealous . . . . of who or what?"

"Of you, Mare."

Mildly taken aback, "Of course . . . . you and me."

"Yes, as a couple, but that's just the tip of the iceberg."

"Then what's below the water line?"

"As I said . . . . you, Mare . . . . she is jealous of you."

He raised his hand, "Hear me out." Pause, "Jackie is jealous of who you are as a person . . . . open, unpretentious, and totally comfortable in you skin." Jack shifted in his wheelchair, "You see, she is not and will not be those things, because of her insecurity. Jackie sees how you disarm people and how they are, in turn, open to you." He halted Mary again, "I'm almost done," He smiled, "Mary the moment you joined our group in Paris you, unknowingly, began to displace Jackie by your mere presence. Mary, it's so natural for you, you cannot see it. The moment people meet you, they are taken by you, with no conscious effort on your part." He reached across the table for Mary's hand. "Just as I was taken by you years ago at a high school dance . . . ."

* * *

With unheard of preferential luggage and passenger handling at Athens airport, Jackie and the children were quickly ushered by a dark windowed stretch limo, to an awaiting private helicopter owned by Aristotle's maritime giant, Olympic Shipping.

No sooner had they settled into the posh aircraft, as the lone passengers, she was served champagne and caviar with crust less plain Blinis with Crème Fraiche. The children, of course, were overjoyed with their cookies and ice cream. Within little over an hour the English speaking Greek co-pilot announced, "We are approaching Aristotle Onasis' privately owned island of Scorpios. In keeping with landing procedure, we will circle the island.

Aristotle had turned the fifty square mile barren, unoccupied island into internationally coveted private resort. Jackie, Caroline, and John were the last of the party to arrive. Her excitement heightened as Ari's 325 foot luxury yacht, *"Christina-O"* came into view. Her party waived as they had gathered in the sprawling manicured landscaping that edged both the dock and heliport.

The furthest things from Jackie's mind were Italy, Jack, and Mary . . . .

CHAPTER 30

The chartered jet touched down at Reagan International, signaling the end of the thirty-five day "JFK and Friend Goodwill Tour". The end of Jackie's Greek vacation had placed her home three days earlier.

As they taxied toward the private terminal, Jack squeezed Mary's hand as he leaned over and kissed her on the lips. "Well, Mare, being back is classic good-news-bad-news: Good news being that we're back in the USA; the bad news being that our group will disband and all but go their own ways."

She chuckled, "True, Jack, however, I'm available most any tine, so don't hesitate to call."

He squeezed her hand as she stood in the aisle of the plane. "There you go; I feel better already."

She leaned over and kissed him on the lips; since Jackie left the group for Greece, they had concealed nothing from the group, only from the public."

They hugged on the tarmac, "Thanks again, Jack, for arranging a limo home for me."

"You bet, Mare."

He patted her on the behind, turned away in his wheel chair, and spoke over his shoulder as she stepped toward her awaiting limo. "I'll call you in the AM, Mare." An aide appeared out of nowhere and took control of his wheelchair.

By car, he and Jackie's Wexford country estate was a good hour's drive, whereas by chopper, a mere ten minute flight.

With Jackie being a horse person, Jack had bought the raw land and built their home primarily to her specifications. They had taken occupancy of their new home in the spring of 1963.

The sun was dropping below the D.C. skyline as the chopper lifted off. Jack felt a sudden rush of excitement over being minutes away from hugs and kisses from Caroline and John. His joy was dashed as he thought of the negativity that was sure to come from Jackie.

As the chopper set down on the estate's landing pad, Jack beamed as he saw the children scamper from the house in the cool evening dusk. Within moments the three were giggling and entwined as one, while Jackie stood by, along with a medical aide.

With the children tucked away for the evening, Jack and Jackie settled down for a light dinner with wine. After discussing what had occurred on the tour after her departure, Jack switched subjects.

"Tell me, how was Greece?"

Jackie's entire demeanor changed as she shifted in her chair. "Jack . . . . this is . . . the most painful thing I've had to say." She leaned forward on the white linen table cloth, "Jack, I . . . ah . . . ."

Jack completed the sentence for her, ". . . . want a divorce."

Jackie was taken aback, "How did . . . ."

Calmly, "Let's cut to the chase, Jackie. Call it what you want, but it's simply pay back time."

Jackie started to speak.

"Hear me out, Jackie, please." He shifted in his wheelchair and remained calm and measured. "I have no right to complain, for it's been a long time coming; one that I deserve, without question. Let's call it what it is, it's payback for my incessant womanizing." He calmly cut her off again, "Even though you agreed, as part of the marriage arrangement by my father, to accept the male Kennedy character flaw, you had no idea how painful that it would become."

Silence.

"Well said, Jack, but please don't put it all on you, for even though I'm the one asking for the divorce, I am clearly not without fault."

"Jackie, it's tough enough being married to the President of the United States, without having to deal with my reckless, inconsiderate behavior." He again stopped her from speaking, "Then, to top things off," He motioned to himself in a wheelchair, "You'd be left with a man in a wheelchair who is on a collision course with premature death."

Somber silence.

Jackie took a deep exasperating breath and spoke in kind. "Jack, when I first became involved with Ari . . . . Aristotle . . . . I felt terribly guilty because of two things; the children, and your condition. However, at this point in time, my only concern is the impact of our divorce on our children."

It was Jackie's turn to not be interrupted, "Jack, my feeling toward you has transformed from one of guilt, to that of concern. The more I saw the interaction between you and Mary, following your assassination attempt, the more my feeling of guilt diminished." She again kept Jack from speaking, "Jack, Mary is, without question, a natural caregiver." Jackie leaned forward and smiled warmly, "Jack, there is no hiding it, you and Mary are clearly in love, and are clearly meant for one another." She chuckled softly, "Of course, all of that, on my part, was preceded with extreme jealousy and anger . . . . at, and of, Mary."

Pause.

"Jackie, you couldn't be more right, and yes, Mary and I are very much in love. You see, Jackie, the more disabled I become, the more Mary loves me, Jackie . . . . she's simply incredible."

"I couldn't possibly be more happy for you both."

Silence, as Jack smiled and thought to himself.

"And, you and Aristotle?"

"We, as a couple, are the driving force behind my request for a divorce."

"In all honestly, Jackie, I was expecting an announcement, not a request."

She slowly shook her head in a somber manner, "Jack, Jack . . . . in all due respect, with your condition, I could only make a request . . . . which is what it is."

Looking her squarely in her tear welled eyes, "For what it's worth, Jackie, that means a lot to me." He half smiled, "The truth shall set us free."

They raised their glasses in unison, with Jackie coming quickly back down to earth. "Now then, Jack, we need to talk about Carolyn and John."

CHAPTER 31

As the sun broke the horizon, Mary started the washing machine, doing a light load from her travel laundry, before pouring her first cup of coffee. She was retrieving the *Washington Post* from her flower lined front walk, when the phone hastened her back to the kitchen.

"Hello, the Pinchot residence."

In sober monotone, "Mare . . . . Jack."

She sat down and reached for her coffee, "Oh, oh."

A deep breath followed by a pause, "Oh, oh, is right; last night over dinner Jackie dropped the other shoe."

"Again . . . oh, oh."

"Yeah . . . . you can forget announcing our formal separation; she's going straight to announcing a divorce."

She set her coffee down, and put her hand on her chest, "Oh, Jack, I'm so sorry; even though it was just a matter of time, it surely doesn't ease the pain." She shifted in her ccahir. "I personally know how terrible it feels; it stands next to the death of a loved one."

Long pause by the former president, "You know, Mary, the hell with us adults; it's the children, as innocent bystanders, that always feel the brunt of a divorce."

"You're right, Jack, and by the time they become adults, and are able to, perhaps, understand, the psychological damage is often times beyond repair."

Long silence.

"What now, Jack?"

Deep breath, "Well, I hope, Mare . . . . please . . . . that it's now you and me."

"Jack, I love you dearly, and I always will . . . . only say the word and I will never leave your side."

With sudden life, "The word is yes, Mare, a resounding yes."

"Jack . . . . I could not possibly be happier."

"Me too, Mare."

He sighed. "You know, Mary, life is funny . . . . how it takes unexpected twists and turns . . . . and at the end of the day, it's fate that seems to rule the day . . . . God, of course, is who were dealing with."

"You're right . . . . just look at my life."

Silence.

"Mary?"

"Yes, Jack."

"I think at this point you're entitled to know something so intimate, that nobody knows, including Jackie, other than my psychiatrist."

Apprehensive, "Yeah . . . . sure, Jack."

"Well, I've been seeing this renowned psychiatrist since right after taking office, in an attempt to stay better focused and clear headed. As all shrinks do, he started with my family relationships: mother, father, siblings, including the pecking, or birth, order of each of us. You know the drill."

"Sadly, I do."

"There is so much more to the sessions that I'll go over with you later in detail. However, for now, I'll just cover what is germane to me and you . . . . me more than you."

He took a deep exasperating breath, "Over a period of several months this doctor probed into my sexual behavior and the various women in my life . . . . as far back as *birth*." He took a deep breat. "Late into these discussions, the subject of our relationship came up . . . . not by name, mind you, for there were no names."

Mary chuckled, "As if he couldn't guess, in my case."

"You're right, Mary, because by the time the subject of you came into the dialogue, chatter within the beltway was such that it made it easy for the shrink." He hesitated. "I'll get to an abbreviated bottom line, and save the drawn out details for later."

"Ok."

"So, then, Mary, brace yourself for the bottom line of the meaning of *women* in my life." Even though on the phone, he bracketed the word *women* with his fingers.

"I'm braced, Jack."

"My internationally renowned and respected psychiatrist concluded, after nearly a year's discussion, that I have *never* . . . . his emphasis was on the word *never* . . . . loved a women in my entire life . . . . sadly, he said, that includes my *own mother*."

Mary silently held her breath as Jack continued, "Of course, my shrink added, except for the women currently in your life, which he is absolutely convinced, and I agree, I've loved since I was nineteen and she was sixteen."

Mary leapt to her feet and began to parade aimlessly around her kitchen and dinning room with her hand on her forehead. "Oh my God . . . . oh my God . . . . Jack, it's us . . . . it's us . . . . at the school dance."

"Yes, Mare . . . . we've been validated by one of the world's best . . . ."

CHAPTER 32

Later that same week, in the study of their Wexford estate, Jackie and Jack's lawyers snapped their attaché cases shut. As they stood to leave, Jackie's lawyer spoke kindly.

"I think it's fare to say that I'm speaking for me, as well as my counterpart, when I thank you both for being so well prepared, and amiable, in dealing with this matter."

Jack added, "Well, it's one thing to fall out of love, but falling out of civilized friendship is too sad for words."

Jackie place her hand on his shoulder, "Even more so when children are involved."

The four shook hand and exchanged niceties, with the presidential aide showing them to the front door, closing the study door behind him. With the positive air remaining in the room, Jack spoke in kind as he wheeled himself to the bar. "Well, Jackie, the sun is below the yardarm somewhere to the east, what do you say to a glass of sherry."

"Please, Jack," She chuckled, "and be *quick*."

"Well, I sure in the hell can't be *nimble*."

They both laughed, as Jack poured. He handed her a sherry. "Adding to what your lawyer said, the key factor in our settlement equation, of course, is the clearly delineated litigious rules of our individual family trusts."

Jackie sat in a comfortable, cushioned, armed chair, and Jack wheeled near the front of her. They savored a sip of sherry before Jackie spoke. "Jack, now that it's official, I want you to know that Ari is pushing for a public announcement."

Jack, living in reality and acceptance, somewhat surprised Jackie, "To be honest with you, now that I am, in reality, merely a *John Q citizen*, with an asterisk adjacent to my name, I'm able to respect your decisions from here on out, regarding this matter."

Although happy and comfortable with his response, she chose not to tell him that Ari was also pushing to announce that they had been secretly engaged . . . . which Jack, himself, was not aware of. What Jackie didn't know was, depending on how willing Jack was to acquiesce to Ari's wishes, he was in the process of laying his own, behind the scenes, media leak campaign to align with his own personal wishes.

Adding to the mix, which Jack, Jackie and Ari were all unaware of, was a secret parallel media campaign in the works. Paris journalist Franz Mignione, with *Le Monde*, had launched his own investigation, utilizing personal and professional contacts within France, Greece, and the United States.

* * *

As fate, or luck, depending on what side of an issue one sets, Jack and Jackie shook the globe with the announcement of their mutually consented divorce, while at the same time, the French press released an expose of Jackie and Onasis. The good news was that the article was in French which delayed its appearance in the US press by one day. Still, the US public was rocked by the news of the former first couple's divorce announcement.

As the Americans tried to deal with the shock of the Kennedy divorce, Jackie received a call during the French expose language time delay period.

"Hello, Jackie speaking."

Skipping the usual niceties, Onasis gets right to the point, "Brace yourself, Jackie, the French are coming."

"The . . . ." He cut her off.

"Yeah, Mary's buddy, the French journalist Franz Migneont."

"To be fair, he's not Mary's buddy, but, go on."

"Anyway, the Frenchman's tabloid style piece, with paparazzi photos, about you and me, was published in this morning's *Le Monde*, all in French." He grunted. "So, sweetie, brace yourself because tomorrow, your time, the English version of the article will spread like wild-fire across America."

Angry, "And, just how damaging is it?"

He chuckled, "Well, no matter what, I'll be the bad guy by virtue of what I'll ultimately do . . . . take America's princess away from her adoring fans." He cleared his throat, "In answer to your question; it's equally about us both. However, when you consider that Europeans could care less, it all really falls on you."

"Crap . . . . it looks like a long recovery."

"Thanks to your friend."

"Please, stop it, Ari," She paused to gather her wits, "Trust me, Ari, Mary has none of this in her character."

Silence.

"Ok, ok . . . . it's *lucky* for Mary that I trust your instincts."

"Whatever that means . . . . thanks."

More silence.

"You know, Jackie, this story really paves the way for us to announce our engagement."

She stood and dropped her voice as she turned toward the closed door, "Shh, I don't know where you are, but keep it down, the walls have ears."

He chuckled, "Don't worry, hon, it's our secret until you decide otherwise . . . . I promise."

Within a minute of hanging up her private line, there was a soft knock at her door.

"It's Jack, do you have a minute?"

Half irritated, "Can it wait."

"Depends on whether you want to read a bootlegged news article now, or wait until the morning paper."

Instinctively, she knew. "Ok."

She opened the door and, still having an occasional mental lapse, looked straight forward before looking down at Jack in his wheelchair."

"Please, come in." She stepped aside, "What's up?"

"My aide just pulled this off the wire . . . . from the *Associated Press*."

"I just got off the phone with Ari; is it the article by Franz Mignione?"

"Yes, it is."

"So best we get right down to damage control."

CHAPTER 33

The previous day's divorce announcement by the former First Couple, sent a shock wave around the globe, with the US at the epicenter.

As Americans tried to wrap their arms around the historic enormity of the *first divorce*, they were hit by an aftershock, a mere twenty-four hours later, of near equal proportions.

Franz Mignione's French language, tabloid style article was grabbed by the *Associated Press*, translated into English, and made front page of every major US newspaper, including the *International Herald Tribune*.

For the American people, the article took the amiable, and mutually agreed to divorce and turned it on its head. It was bad enough for Jackie to be perceived as the bad guy in the divorce, but a strong undercurrent was suddenly developing in favor of Jack, as well as Mary.

Jackie and Ari's behind the scenes effort in damage control seemed to be in vain; Jackie wept as she saw years of positive image building efforts seemingly go down the drain.

"Jack, I realize that I all but brought this upon myself, but that doesn't help ease the pain."

Feeling her pain, "Jackie, for what it's worth, I, along with Mary, will do everything in our power to try and right your ship." He cut her off, "Keep in mind that it will take time." He held his hand in a halting gesture, "Mary and I truly feel that we're all in this together . . . . including Aristotle. Trust me, Jackie, Mary is one of your biggest allies"

Jackie, half calmed down, to a deep breath. "So you'll know, I so much as told Ari that when he tried to implicate Mary in Franz's article."

"That's a given. Neither you or I think that Mary has a mean spirited gene in her body."

The day following the now infamous Franz article, Jack and Mary were contacted by the news media, inquiring if they were up to giving a pre-taped television interview on the following morning. The presidential aide said that he would get back to them as quickly as possible.

The former first couple agreed the need for them to set the record straight, or at least give a favorable spin, as quickly as possible. To avoid the potential dynamics of awkward, and consequently ineffective, back and fourth triad style interview, they both agreed that Jack alone would represent them as a couple . . . even if one in separation. They agreed that Jack was the more charming of the two, and certainly more weathered in the full spectrum of interviews. They agreed to a time, a day later than what was requested. The aide simply told CBS that Jackie would not be available for an interview until the following week, at the earliest; Jackie agreed to pull a disappearing act for the day.

Jack's interview with NBC took place two days later in Jack's Wexford estate Library.

NBC journalist and news anchor, John Chancellor, rang the front door bell, as the film crew began to unload their van. Through the door he heard, "I'll get it." And, within a moment, John was stunned when the former President of the United States opened the front door in his wheelchair.

Jack extended his hand upward, "Good morning, John, please do come in."

John was also shocked when told, the previous day, that the president did not need to pre-approve the list of questions, nor did he place any restrictions on the content of the interview. He told the NBC officials that he was fully prepared, and comfortable, in adlibbing or winging it.

Taken aback by Jack's greeting, as well as by his weakening grip, John paused just long enough at the threshold to bring a smile to Jack's face. "I finally found a job I can handle, John." They laughed and Jack added, "Whoa . . . . but don't ask the opposition for an opinion."

He smiled warmly., "Sir . . . . Mr. President, it's nice meeting you again."

"Likewise, John; it's been awhile."

"Yes sir, since before . . ." His voice trailed off.

"Yes, before Dallas." He smiled and swung his wheelchair aside, "Please, come in and make yourself comfortable."

John stepped into the spacious entryway, "Thank you, sir."

"Please, John, do call me Jack."

"Yes, sir . . . . ah, Jack."

They laughed, and John added, "Except during the interview."

"Yeah, sure, of course."

"We've got juice, coffee, sweat rolls, and fresh cut fruit, on its way for the whole gang."

"Sounds good."

John noticed through his peripheral vision that a male aid or servant appeared, seemingly from nowhere, to greet the camera crew.

Jack led John into his spacious library, "What you'll notice right off the bat is that I am no longer in any kind of a hurry."

"I'm sure that's a welcome change."

"You have *no* idea, John."

They, and the camera crew, exchanged niceties, and had breakfast as they casually set up. The crew was surprised when it was Jack who suggested that personal photos be shot with he and each individual member of the crew. Jack also gave them each a copy of his PR photo, personally inscribed and autographed. Later, the crew members would rave to their families of how kind and personally engaging the former president was to them all.

With the makeup applied, and the stage set, John proffered Jack a bullet list of questions. "Well, sir . . . . Jack, we're ready, but you might want to run through this list of questions before we start."

Jack politely turned the list face down on the table, "Thanks for the consideration, John, but as I said earlier, I'm more than comfortable just winging it." He smiled. "It'll flow nicer, and appear less scripted."

"Jack . . . . you're a rare exception these days."

Silently, Jack struggled from his wheelchair into a comfortable arm chair. They sat opposite from one another at a small round walnut table, containing clear half filled glasses of water and matching blue, NBC logoed, coffee mugs. For camera ease, their chairs were turned slightly away from the table.

The producer queried, "Are you two ready?"

They looked at one another and nodded.

"Ok, here we go." Pause, "Silence! Three, two, one."

Solo on the screen, "John Chancellor here, of NBC, I'm honored to be with the former President of the United States, John Fitzgerald Kennedy, in the library of his Wexford estate." With that, the camera panned back to include JFK.

They moved seamlessly through the introduction niceties, the president's health status, and skimmed through the highlights of his *Goodwill Tour* before moving into the point of the interview.

"Mr. President, on behalf of the American public, I offer my personal condolences on the recent announcement of your and Jackie's divorce."

"Thank you, John, we appreciate that."

"You're welcome, on behalf of all America." He hesitated. "On one hand, it's a situation that has hit every family tree in America; on the other hand, it hits all of America when it involves our First Family."

"Well said, John, the situation does not discriminate."

"True, sir."

Jack swallowed and placed his coffee mug on the table. "And, with that thought in mind, we're here to try and clear up the *he said, she said, they said* comments that are a part of all divorces." He shifted in his chair, "As the former First Couple, we sincerely feel that Americans have a right to know the facts first hand, as opposed to what's being said and printed by every imaginable source . . . . both domestically and abroad."

"We appreciate your candor, sir." John picked up his coffee mug, "Having said that, sir, I would appreciate it if you would take the lead, and I'll ask questions along the way."

Jack nodded, "Well, John, as we know, divorce does not just happen overnight, they are a culmination of a slow simmer over a period of years, often decades. So, what becomes a focal point to an outsider looking in, is the proverbial spark that ignites what has been smoldering beneath the surface, which, of course, is invisible to the public."

As Jack paused for a sip of coffee, John comments, "We can all agree and identify with that, sir."

The president nodded, "Yes, and another point that needs to be made is the degree of guilt." He smiled. "Very seldom is only one person at fault; due to the long simmering, both parties are at fault, or to blame, which is nearly always skewed by personal points of view."

"Sadly, sir, we've all been there, either first hand or as innocent bystanders . . . . so to speak."

"And, of course, one of the main reasons for us being here today." He shifted in his seat. "Now then, I'll attempt to get down to where the rubber meets the road." He paused for effect. "In our marriage, I sadly have to admit that for years, it's been solely my fault." . . . . "As if being the wife of any politician, especially that of the president, is not stressful and lonely enough, I shamefully added to the mix by years of reckless, irresponsible, inconsiderate philandering." He bowed and shook his head in shame, "Yes . . . . let it be known, that I was a womanizer." He paused to let it sink in, "Although I'm now being open and honest with you, and the balance of America, I'm full of shame and guilt, with which I've been dealing with professionally for quite some time."

He and Jackie agreed ahead of time that he would make no mention of, or allude to, the seemingly womanizing trait within the male Kennedy gene pool.

Jack paused for a sip of coffee, "You, John, along with all of America are probably asking: why is he coming forth with all of this shocking news; it's not only news to all of America, but most of those within the so-called Beltway?"

* * *

Mary moved to the edge of her seat as she spoke at her television, in the comfort of her Georgetown home. "Yes, Jack, yes . . . . confession is good for the soul. Put it all out there for the American public, so they can have a clearer vision of what has really gone on." She dabbed her eyes with Kleenex, "The public's beating up on Jackie has got to stop . . . . God bless her."

*   *   *

John took the opening, "In all honesty, Mr. President, as a member of the news media, I am amongst the masses that were, until moments ago, literally in the dark." John shifted in his seat, "And it does beg the question, *why.*"

"Good question . . . . by all Americans . . . . with a simple straight forward answer." He paused for effect and looked straight into the camera. "The American public, especially the news media, needs to switch their focus, and subsequent blame, from Jackie and place it squarely on me."

"I must say, sir, you're not only being extremely open and honest, but also very noble and admirable."

"That comes natural and easy when one realizes Jackie's and my relationship. You see, I still love Jackie as a friend, and as the wonderful mother to our children." He paused. "People must understand that by me wishing Jackie all the best carries over to her and my entire family. Post-marriage relationships, for entire families, are forever doomed with a *win-loose* attitude."

John nods his head, "I'm sure that our viewers have sadly found that to be true."

"A win-win philosophy also has a profound positive effect on the couple's entire network of friends."

With a wry smile, the ex-president continues, "And, I strongly suggest to all viewers, that arbitration be their first choice, and do not agree to attorneys unless they are aboard with your win-win philosophy."

"Good advice."

The president's demeanor signaled that he was through with the subject.

"Well, sir, I think that we've carried that as far as need be. Now then . . . ." The interview continued with indirectly related issues.

*   *   *

Jackie gave a big sigh of relief, "Thank you, Jack, thank you for your courageous honesty . . . . *not* that I'm as pure as the driven snow."

Chapter 34

The John Chancellor's interview with the former president was effective in that the perceived blame of the divorce on Jackie all but ceased. However, the worldwide speculation and interest in Jackie and Onasis became prominent within the respected news media and, of course, the usual rag sheets.

With Aristotle's resources anonymously fanning the flames with rumors of his and Jackie's secret engagement, the critical refrain had become: 'so soon after the divorce?'.

Jackie's absence from the Wexford country estate became increasingly more frequent; between visiting friends in Florida, California, Canada, and the Caribbean, as well as her sister in Europe, she found time for the occasional sneak-away rendezvous with Aristotle. Half the time the children were left behind in Wexford, where they had nanny care, school tutoring, and their father. Of course, Caroline and John were overjoyed when *Aunt Mary* was the occasional house guest.

Within a week following Jack's interview, Jackie had taken off to Florida, prompting Jack to call Mary.

"Hello, you've reached . . . ."

"Yes, I know, the Pinchot residence."

Excitedly, "Oh, Jacko, I was just thinking about you."

"Call it ESP." They laughed, "Hey, Jackie's in Florida for a few days, so I'm calling to make a proposal."

Feigned gasp, "Over the phone?"

He laughed, "No, not that kind."

"Oh, darn, and here I thought it was to be my lucky day."

"No, but it's without question a step closer to *our* lucky day."

The laughter trailed off, "With Jackie scheduled to be gone, off and on, over the next several weeks, I'm proposing that we convert one of the Wexford guest rooms into your *home away from home.*"

Taken aback, "Jack . . . . ah, I'm both . . . . honored and flattered." . . . .
"Tell me more."

"It's pretty straight forward, Mare; while Jackie is phasing out, you'll be phasing in."

"I can't begin to tell you how happy I am."

"Mary . . . . listen carefully; by phasing in, I mean, in the long run, *permanently*."

Mary searched for words as Jack continued, "You see, Mare, I really was not playing with words when I initially said that I called to make a *proposal*."

Mary felt faint, "Oh, Jack, I'm . . . . so overwhelmed, all I can say is *yes*."

"Thank you, Mary, now I'm the one who is honored. And I could not possibly be happier."

"Me too, Jacko."

Chuckle, "Keep in mind that this informality will eventually become a full blown, formal proposal."

"You're one surprise after another this morning."

"Ok . . . . one final surprise; Jackie is on board with all of this."

Gasp, "Oh . . . . my . . . . God."

"After all of these years, I finally have my *Jolie Blon* . . . ."

She laughed, "I'm now truly Franco-American . . . . I went from Parisian French, to the honor of American Cajun French."

*   *   *

Moving in part-time with the ex-President of the United States was not as simple as waltzing in with an overnight bag with a half dozen changes of clothes. In all fairness, and at his insistence, Jack provided Mary an unlimited expense account for a wardrobe that ran the political and social gamut. At the end of the day, her part time bedroom's spacious walk-in closet was left without spare space.

Adding to the clothing mix was the fact that Mary preferred to dress as the artist that she was, and was known to have to borrow a formal dress from a friend in order to attend a formal White House social event. Therefore, her need covered the full spectrum of non-creative or imaginative left brain, to the casual, sometime flamboyant, right brain wardrobe.

Jack was in love with the casual right brain Mary, who could turn on a dime to her left brain and debate complex issues with men of power and influence.

Her bathroom was easy, simply duplicate everything she had in her Georgetown bathroom. Her makeup needs were for eyebrows, eyelashes, lipstick, and hair care, which amounted to shampoo and dragging a brush through a head of natural blond waves. If an occasion was formal, she might powder her face, other than that, makeup was at a minimum and from the corner drug store.

*　*　*

Mary's move-in went smoothly, and she immediately took temporary residency upon Jackie leaving for a period of three or more days, save for the days that her son's were home during school holidays. However, when the boys were home for the summer, she and Jack, together, would pick and chose which days she would spend at Wexford.

*　*　*

It was late in the third month of Mary's part-time living arrangement that Jack called her at her Georgetown home. Mary had learned to pause a few moments before speaking when answering her phone in case it was Jack.

"Hi, Mare."

Hey, Jack, to what do I owe this pleasure."

He chuckled, "In all honesty, that would be Jackie."

"Oh . . . . and, how is that."

"As you know, she's leaving in two days for a ten-day trip to Greece."

"Yes?"

"Well, she informed me this morning that on her second day in Greece, she and Aristotle are calling for a press conference to announce their engagement, with the wedding scheduled for eight weeks later."

Gasp, "Oh my God, Jack; how are you with that?"

A deep exasperating breath, "You know, Mare, when I've already accepted the fact, what difference does a date mean . . . . anyway."

"You're right there, Jack . . . . I'm glad that you see it that way."

"On a brighter note, I also see it as enabling us to begin to make concrete plans on our life together."

Struggling, "I'm sorry, Jack . . . . I can't . . . . help it . . . . I'm going to cry."

"You go right ahead, Mare, after all you've been through, you deserve a big cry. In fact, go ahead, and hold nothing back. When you're through purging your emotions and feel like talking, call me back."

Between sobs, "Yes . . . . please." More sobs, "I . . . . love you . . . . Jack."

"Me too you, Mare."

CHAPTER 35

In spite of several weeks of speculation and rumors, the much anticipated news bulletin announcing the engagement of Jacqueline Lee Bouvier and Aristotle Socrates Onasis still sent shock waves throughout planet earth.

Adding frustration on top of shock, was the brevity of the official Bouvier family betrothal announcement. The bride's mother announced the historic event through a family spokesman:

"Mrs. Hugh D. Auchincloss' daughter, Mrs. John F. Kennedy, is planning to marry Mr. Aristotle Onasis."

End of statement . . . . full stop.

Waiting for more news to break; some were shocked because they viewed her as turning her back on Jack in his debilitating hour-of-need; while others were bemused at the twenty-three years difference in age; still, some saw her as a gold digger; and some were concerned about the well being of the globe-hopping children.

With Jackie having had a drunken, womanizing, distant father, in John *Black Jack* Bouvier, the professional, and self educated, psychiatrists of the world saw the much older Onasis as the father that Jackie never had. While finally, the romantics of the world saw the engagement as, quite simply, two people in love. If the truth be known, Jackie's conscious and subconscious motivations were probably all of the above. Whereas, the motivation of Onasis was the fact that he was known to always get what he wanted, and he could now lay claim to the most internationally recognizable and famous trophy wife.

Jack, when questioned, in any manor of ways, simply wished Jackie and Aristotle all the best, and assured the world that the children, who were paramount in both he and Jackie's minds, would be just fine.

As human nature would have it, the further Jackie moved toward Aristotle, the closer Mary became to Jack, and the public, to the point where it soon became *all about Mary*.

As a result, Mary suddenly found herself hounded by the press, talk show hosts, and anyone who was anybody within the DC Beltway, to the point where Jack provided her with her own combination personal aide and press secretary, all at Jack's expense.

She and Jack agreed on a pact, in that although they may be *seen* together, they would not *appear* together. As a result, the very few interviews that she agreed to, she always appeared solo, even though nearly all that requested an interview asked that it include both she and the former president.

Although there was ample evidence for the press to assume that they had been lovers long before Dallas, Mary skillfully talked around the issue, leaving the interviewer with her and Jack's official position; that they were near life-long friends, letting time and patience determine the outcome of their relationship.

Being the lady that Jackie was, she reserved her comment to that she, Jack, and Mary were old, old friends, and that Mary and Jack could speak for themselves.

CHAPTER 36

With the focus having shifted from Jackie, the American public could not seen to get enough of Mary . . . . in a very positive, yet very frustrating, way. It was clearly beginning to wear quite thin on Mary, as well as Jack. Then one Saturday morning out of the public blue, and fashionably too soon, the *New York Times* headlines screamed, *"Jackie and Onasis to Wed"*.

Jack and Mary received the official news from Jack's aide and medic, who had traveled with them to a private villa on a perch above Italy's famed picturesque Portofino. With Italy in a time zone six hours earlier than New York, Jack and Mary received the news while brunching on their balcony with a breathtaking view; while the *New York Times* was still one hour shy of the early morning edition press time.

Having been made privy to the wedding plans by Jackie, Jack smiled and raised his champagne glass. "Well, Mare, this all but clears the way for us to move on with our lives."

Mary winked as her champagne glass touched his, "Yes, and I get more excited as their wedding day nears."

Jack refreshed their champagne as an ocean breeze wafted through Portofino and across their balcony. "I as well, Mare, and six weeks will come and go before we know it."

Silence, broken by Mary's deep sigh, "And, with us not attending the wedding . . . . I should say not invited . . . . we are under absolutely no pressure." She rolled her eyes. "So, we can simply sit back and relax." She chuckled, "And, enjoy the media frenzy."

"Oh . . . . I can well imagine."

"On a more serious note, Jack, how are things moving with the Vatican?"

He grinned and rolled his eyes, "Well, seeing that I monetarily greased the Papal skids, I'll have my weeding annulment document in hand a few days following Jackie's weeding."

269

"Are you sure that I'm not in need of an annulment, Jack?"

"Yes, I'm sure; my Bishop said that seeing that you were married at home by a preacher, not within a Catholic Church, the Vatican does not recognize your wedding." He interrupted Mary, "We, therefore, can be married in a Catholic church . . . . by a Priest."

"Great, and . . . ."

He anticipated her question, "And our big day will come right on the heels of the Greek extravaganza."

"Oh, Jack, I can't believe . . . . it's been so long since my high school dance."

Jack reached across the table and took her hand. "I know . . . . I know."

She sighed. "I'm open, Jack, I'll leave the timing totally up to you."

He released her hand, leaned back, and raised his champagne glass, "Done."

CHAPTER 37

To ease the post-wedding domestic transition, primarily for the sake of her children, Jackie began, weeks before the wedding, to set up households on Onasis' private island of Skorpios, as well as within his exquisite, and spacious Paris apartment.

Jack and Mary also took advantage of the transition by limiting their vacations to that of Eastern Europe, in order to spend as much time with Caroline and John in helping them ease into their new life style. Looking beyond Jackie's wedding, they thought it wise to lease a flat of their own in Paris, within close proximity to where the children would call home. Because of Jack's deteriorating health, he insisted on focusing on only a one-year lease. Of course, France's weak *handicap access* laws narrowed their rental options.

With the wedding one week away, Jack and Mary retreated for a three week stay in one of their favorite Italian coastal cities of Positano. Two weeks prior to that, unbeknownst to one another, they were both planning a surprise for one another. Jack had purchased, and had awaiting for her in Positano, a portable traveling oil painting kit, that contained a half dozen blank canvases, oils, brushes, spatulas, and palette. Whereas, Mary had contacted a sail boat agent in Positano in search of a sail boat to rent that met the same specifications as Jack's own 25' Wianno Senior named *Victura*. She was thrilled when the agent managed to find and rent a craft that met her requirements that included the owner-skipper services to assist Jack as much as necessary.

As a separate activity, they set out to collaborate in creating something common for one another, utilizing Mary's artistic skills. They decided to design a split pendent, his-and-hers, necklace. The stark difference between the two pendants was his was done in silver, hers in gold. The design would be a Jade inlay of an astrological, or zodiac, wheel. Jack's silver half would, of course, be Mary's birth sign of Libra, with a Sapphire stone inlayed next to her astrological sign, with *Jack Loves Mary* inscribed on the plain silver back of the broken pendent. Of course, Mary's half of the pendent would contain Jack's birth sign Gemini, with an inlayed stone of Agate, with *Mary Loves Jack* engraved on the gold back. In keeping with the split, or broken, charm design, the jagged break would be a perfect fit to one another.

The two went about designing the split love pendant with all the enthusiasm and excitement of a pair of teenagers in love. They collaborated on several sketches before coming to a design that delighted them both. Mary's final colored detailed drawing was a work of art in itself, leaving nothing to the imagination of the craftsman.

With the Greek wedding one week away, Jack and Mary arrived in Positano and settled into their spacious, lofty, cliff side apartment with a breathtaking view of the ancient romantic harbor, the Amalfi coast, and the shimmering emerald hued Tyrrhenian Sea.

As the aide showed them through their new temporary housing, they were in awe of the view that was hard to imagine as being better that that of Portofino. Mary was even more stunned when the aide opened the door of the spare room and she discover an art studio.

She gasped, and put her hand on her breasts. "What the . . . ."

Jack cut her off, "Surprise, surprise . . . . I know you'll put it to good use."

Thrilled, she stooped down to wheelchair level and threw her arms around the former president. "Oh . . . Jack . . . yes, yes . . . . almost immediately." She stood and dabbed tears from her eyes.

"I have a very simple rule, Mare . . . . if you're happy, I'm happy."

She bent and kissed him on the lips, "Well, then, Jack . . . . you couldn't be happier."

"I am, Mary, I am." Prowdly. "I can hardly wait to see your first work."

"I already know what it'll be."

Incredulously, "So soon . . . . already? And, what might that be?"

She smiled and took on a mischievous look. "I can't tell you until later this week."

"Ahhhh . . . . and the plot thickens."

Shortly before lunch, Mary carefully checked the time before pulling a pair a newly purchased quality binoculars from her travel bag and held them out toward Jack. "Here you go, honey, seeing that you're such a sailing fan I thought these would be of use on the balcony."

Jack beamed, "Gosh, Mare, thank you very much . . . . they're a brilliant gift." He examined them, "12 x 50 . . . . perfect for the task." Saisfied. "Very, very nice, thank you, hon."

Thrilled with his reaction, she wheeled him toward the balcony. "Let's giv'm a try."

He laughed, "Aye, mate."

"You've got lots of time, champagne brunch on the balcony won't be served for nearly an hour."

Jack removed the lens covers, and began to adjust the thumb wheel as he panned the beautiful boat filled harbor. "Gosh, Mare, I can read the names of the boats . . . . and some registration numbers."

At that point, Mary stood behind Jack and waved her arms in the air, as she focused on a predetermined location in the harbor, about 200 meters away. At the same moment a man standing in an anchored sailboat returned Mary's wave in kind . . . . right on queue.

Excitedly, "There, Jack," She pointed, "Look, there's a man waving at us."

He joked as he swung the binoculars to his right, "Yeah, sure, Mare . . . . he's waving at us."

He stopped his pan, "There he is, I've got him." He chuckled, "Shall I reach out and shake his hand?"

Still positioned behind the wheelchair, she began to pump her fist up and down.

"What's he doing now, Jack?"

"He's just waving . . . . no, he's now pointing down with both hands . . . . at, I would guess, the boat."

"Why is that?"

"Hell, I don't . . . . wait a sec, hold on . . . . oh . . . my . . . God, Mare"

She giggles to herself and she stepped from behind his wheel chair to his right side. "What is it, Jack?"

In excitement, he shifted in his chair, "I'll be damned . . . . it's a twin to my own twenty-five foot Wianno Senior . . . the *Victura*."

Mary laughed as she gave the all clear sign to the gentleman in *Jack's* boat. "Surprise, surprise, Jacko."

Jack turned in his chair, "What the . . . ."

"Jack, the twin to your boat, *Victura*, is ours for the entire three weeks."

He took her hand as he looked up at her smiling face. "Oh . . . . Mary, Mary . . . . you never cease to amaze me . . . . *and* please me." He wiped a tear from his cheek. "I'm lost for words."

Mary stooped down and hugged him. "When you're happy, I'm happy." He pulled her onto his lap as they both laughed.

As they wound down, Mary spoke with her head on his shoulder. "The man in the boat that was waving and pointing is the owner and skipper; he comes with the boat."

As Mary stood, Jack playfully pats her on the behind, "Thank you Lord . . . . for the skipper, for I was momentarily panicked with You sticking me with Mary, Mary as my inept deck hand."

Feigning indignation "Well, I may be unskilled at sailing . . . . but, I've never been accused of being inept . . . . at anything."

As they wound down, Jack refocused on the boat, "I can hardly wait to meet the skipper."

Mary smiled, "Well, Jacko, you won't have to wait long, he's on his way up as we speak; he's having brunch with us."

"Great, Mary . . . . there you go again."

"Sailors, a pair . . . . keep a kicker and draw two."

"And you, Mary, are definitely the *kicker*."

They laughed as the cook began to set the brunch table for three.

"Mare, I can hardly wait to ask him about his boat; if it's not one of mine, it's a hell of a duplicate . . . . European genes."

Minutes later, with the table set and the food ready to serve, and wine to pour, the aide announced their guest's arrival, and ushered him onto the balcony before disappearing into the apartment.

Mary immediately stepped to their guest with her hand extended. "Ricardo, I'm Mary Pinchot; it's so nice to finally meet you face-to-face."

"Finally, Mary, what a pleasure."

She turned toward Jack, in his wheelchair, "And this is my boyfriend who is your fellow sailor, Jack."

Ricardo momentarily froze, for he recognized the face; however, because of the setting and Jack's condition, his mind went blank as he failed to make a connection. Jack read his face as he took his extended hand. "Nice to meet you, Ricardo, and I'll make it easy for you." He chuckled, "I'm the *infamous* JFK."

He gasped, "Oh, my God . . . . you're not Mr. Pinchot." Almost overwhelmed, "Holy Mother of God . . . . you're the ex-president of the United States."

Jack laughed, "But let's keep things in perspective, Ricardo . . . . for the next three weeks; I'm just a deck hand on your beautiful boat . . . . so, please do call me Jack."

Ricardo laughed, looked at Jack, then Mary, and laughed, "I can't believe it . . . . my new deck hand called Jack." Again he laughed, "With one hell of a resume', I might add."

Mary added, "But a lousy sailor, no doubt . . . . so be tough on him, Recardo, I understand he's a slow learner."

The chemistry within the trio was truly divine intervention.

Ricardo suddenly turned back to Mary in a start. "And of course, Mary, you are Jack's *angel of mercy*."

Ricardo anticipated Jack's reaction, "Yes, Mr . . . . ah, Jack, I do read newspapers after I've dropped anchor."

Again they laughed, as brunch was announced.

The three casually eased into their brunch and Sangria, while exchanging niceties. It was Jack who finally turned toward the sea. "And the name of our craft, Ricardo?"

The handsome, middle aged, Italian smiled, *"Ruboto"*.

Mary chuckled and raised her glass, "To the *thief* or *robber*." Their wine glasses touched above mid-table as she continued with a flare, "And tell me, will we fly the *Jolly Roger*, or the *il tricolore*?"

Ricardo, loving it, "Like I said earlier, I'm essentially your servant, so I'm open to your call."

Jack dramatically closed one eye, "Argh, mateee, it'll be *il tricolore* by day, and *Jolly Roger* under the cover of darkness."

Laughter all around.

Ricardo turned serious, "I cannot begin to tell you how honored and comfortable I am with the opportunity to serve you both."

Jack responded in kind, "Ricardo, we feel so fortunate to have been blessed with a skipper such as you. We are looking forward to the entire three weeks." He raised his glass of Sangria, "Starting with tomorrow morning, if possible."

With wine glass raised, "Thank you for the vote of confidence . . . . *alla salute*."

Mary raised her glass, *cin cin*."

They drank, "Now then, as far as sailing tomorrow, just name the time."

Jack nodded, "We've already discussed it; how about eight o'clock?"

"You're on."

With the aid of Jack's binoculars, Ricardo pointed out the dock with handicap boarding.

CHAPTER 38

Finally the day of the Greek wedding arrived, one week following Jack and Mary's arrival for their three week stay in Positano, Italy.

Throughout their first week, Jack and Mary had spent a great deal of time sailing the Tyrrhenian Sea, enjoying each other's company as well as that of the warm gracious friendship of Captain Ricardo. At times they would drop the sails and lazily drift, when unable to anchor, with the three of them enjoying a leisurely basket lunch over Chianti. Mary made it a point to take several photos for memories, with one particular posed shot for yet another surprise.

With sea scented air and sun on their faces, it was Jack who looked at his watch and yelled above the sound of wind and fluttering sails. "Ricardo, we need to drop the sails and drift for a bit."

Within moments they were drifting in peaceful silence on calm seas. Again, Jack looked at his watch, "It's time we propose a toast to the new bride and groom; crack open some champagne, Ricardo, while Mary gets the glasses."

Mary and Ricardo had agreed that morning before setting sail that they would not mention Jackie's wedding as the time neared. Mary joyfully responded as she stepped below deck. "Aye, aye . . . . Co-Captain."

Jack laughed, "Just don't call me Lyndon."

Jack and Mary were surprised when Ricardo retorted, "And don't refer to your first mate as Lady Bird." His comment was punctuated by the pop of a champagne cork, with laughter all around.

As Ricardo poured the bubbly, Jack spoke in a sober tone. "Ricardo, in case you didn't know, my ex-wife is marrying Aristotle Onassis today."

"Yes sir, I did know . . . . it's all over the news."

Jack nodded, "Now a toast." He glanced at his watch, "As I speak, Jackie is getting married on Aristotle's private Greek island, Skorpios." He nodded in the direction of Greece, "Located just over the Italian *boot*, off the north-east coast of Greece." They all held their full glasses in that direction as Jack continued. "Let it be known, Ricardo, that Mary and I sincerely wish Jackie all the love and happiness she hopes for, and deserves." He cleared his throat and yelled into the warm sea breeze, "To Jackie and Ari, we wish you all the best."

With the sea movement, air, and sound, seeming suspended, the three touched glasses and drank.

* * *

Jackie looked stunning in her lace-covered beige dress, by Italian Couturier Valentino, as the relatively small group anticipated the initial cords from the organ within the small private Greek Orthodox chapel. As to be expected, there were no Kennedy family members invited, nor would have they attended. Unbeknownst to the Kennedy clan, Ted Kennedy had negotiated a prenuptial agreement for Jackie just days before the wedding. Representing Jackie's family were her mother and stepfather, Hugh Auchincloss, and, of course, Jackie's children Carolyn and John.

Invited but not present, for a good reason, was Jackie's younger sister, Carolyn Lee Bouvier Canfield Radziwill, to whom she was very close. Her sister had a long standing affair with Onassis before he had met Jackie; she was bitterly disappointed by him marrying her older sister Jackie.

The balance of the guests were a small number of Onassis' closest friends and business associates.

The ceremony itself was a very abbreviated Greek Orthodox wedding, where immediately prior to the bride and groom being pronounced as husband and wife, the priest lead them, hand in hand, three times around the alter in keeping with Greek tradition, symbolizing that God would transform them into a triune relationship.

Immediately following the wedding, a full-on Greek reception was held on the Onassis 325 foot royal yacht, *Christina O.*

The moment that Jackie said *I do,* she forever lost her right to U.S. Secret Service protection granted to a First Lady . . . . married or divorced.

* * *

After their respectful champagne break and toasts to the newlyweds, Jack and Mary had Ricardo set sail for port, whereupon they called it a day.

Chapter 39

As much as Jack and Mary thoroughly enjoyed Potafino and Positano Italy, they were glad to be home in Jack's Wexford country estate; and, yes, Mary was now calling it home. She decided to keep her home in Georgetown until her sons graduated from college and rooted elsewhere.

The first week back home, Jack received word through his aide that the Roman Catholic Church had granted him a marriage annulment . . . . *paid in full*. He wheeled himself to the breakfast table with a big Cheshire cat grin.

Mary poured him a cup of coffee and sat down with a grin of her own. "Well, are you going to share whatever it is with me or has your face frozen in time?

Jack chuckled and pumped his fist, "Yes . . . . yes!"

"Yes what, Jack . . . . you're killing me."

He placed his arms in the air in a sign of victory, "The Vatican has issued me a formal marriage annulment."

He turned his right arm into a high five which Mary responded to with a pop. "Yes . . . . yes!"

Jack settled down and calmly reached for his coffee, "Which means . . . . my dear Mary, Mary . . . . we can start making our own wedding plans." He raised his hand in a halting gesture, "That is if you're still willing to marry this old wreck."

She stepped around the table and sat in his lap. "Your not old, nor are you a wreck; you are, in fact, the love of my life." She planted a good kiss on his lips. "And, yes, I'm still honored to marry the boy I met at my high school dance." She laughed, "Even without the approval of Bill Attwood."

"Oh god . . . . I can hardly wait to tell ol' Billy . . . . he'll for sure be green with envy."

They both laughed, as Mary returned to her chair.

"As far as plans go, Jack, I'm open to whatever you suggest."

"You know, Mare, I've had enough pomp and circumstance to last a lifetime . . ."

She interrupted with a wink, with coffee cup in hand, "Go ahead Jack, I like where you're taking me."

"I'm glad, but not all that surprised, that you feel that way." He chuckled. "Because I'm thinking the lowest end of the wedding spectrum . . . . with zero brouhaha."

"Great, now that we're on the same end of the scale, give me some detail."

"For openers, I'm thinking Acapulco, Mexico."

"Ole!"

They laugh while raising their coffee cups.

"Now then . . . . the guest list." He gave the famous Kennedy smile, "I'm afraid we'll leave millions of people on the *bubble*, because I'm thinking my aide and Secret Service Agent."

Silence.

"And?"

"And that's it." He interrupted Mary, "Now, being a strong proponent of democracy, I do want your input."

Mary smiled, "What about my vote?"

"Of course, of course."

"That's easy." and gave a thumbs up. "Perfect." She shrugged her shoulders with a silly grin. "And the press?"

He chuckled, "The who?"

"Great . . . . we're definitely in sync, Jacko."

Jack added, "And of course, the Aide and Secret Service are sworn to secrecy."

"And, the Priest?"

"You mean, the Bishop."

She rolled her eyes, "Wow, rank has its privileges."

"Ahhh, yes . . . . the best *silence* money can buy."

Long pause.

"Seriously, Jack, how silent do you think our marriage will be?"

Jack shifted in his wheelchair, "Excellent question, Mare. We forewarned the Bishop that a personal paper trail was created leading to his very generous payoff . . . . like I said, he's bought and paid for." He winked. "Further, the Bishop has agreed to not turn in our paperwork to the Mexican government until the week following our departure from Mexico."

"I see."

"Now then, the weak link in the system is name recognition from our documentation. The Bishop assured us that he will buy off a relative, who is a government official, to walk our paper through the system to minimize the opportunities for name recognition."

Mary nodded her head and Jack continued.

"However, I'd be foolish to think that the word would not eventually leak out into our own government bureaucracy and or journalism corp."

Mary smiled, "Of course, our primary intension being to avoid an international news extravaganza . . . ."

Jack completed her thought, ". . . . and to let things very slowly percolate through the system."

Mary continued, "Serving notice that we intend to be as private as all possible . . . . as a married couple." She reached across the table and gave the ex-president of the United States, the most powerful man in the universe, a proletariat high-five.

Lots of laughter.

"Jack, honey, I couldn't be happier." She stepped around the table and sat in Jack's lap, and gave him a warm embrace.

"Do you realize, Mare, that this is the first time in my life that I feel both free and whole."

She grinned and pecked him on the lips, "So much for all the hype over fame and fortune."

More laughter.

"What kind of timing are we talking about, Jack?"

"No more than a month from now."

"Well, it's good that I start my Catholic conversion instruction tomorrow."

He grinned, "It makes it nice that our Pastor agreed to give you personal instructions right here at the house."

"Which means?"

"I'm thinking the middle of next month; if that's ok with you, I'll get the travel folks started right away."

She kissed him on the lips, "All I can say is wonderful."

He kissed her back, "Me too, Mary, Mary . . . . my future bride."

Long pause as she cradled her face into his neck, exposed above his flannel bathrobe collar.

"And let's not forget your Baptism."

"That's right . . . . when and where?"

"I was thinking the morning of our wedding."

She hugged him, "Oh, Jack, it all seems like a wonderful dream . . . ."

CHAPTER 40

As European interest in the Greek wedding steadily declined to the point of withering on the vine, Jackie's global public profile followed in kind. That, along with her new husband being extremely disliked throughout Europe, Jackie felt her own public persona lessoning at a near exponential rate. At her new home away from home, she despondently found herself viewed as just another of Europe's steady stream of ex first ladies.

Jackie soon found that spending time on Ari's private island was just that, lonely and isolated, while time in his posh Paris penthouse was being lost in the masses of strangers, with her umbilical cord between Europe and the States quickly becoming frayed and weakened.

All the while, Jack and Mary's happiness seemed to be growing without end. Jackie's sources painted Jack as the celebrity that he always was, and Mary's stature growing both by osmosis and her own personality and aura.

The time had come for Jack and Mary's departure for Acapulco. With Mary having successfully completed her private Catholicism conversion course, she and Jack viewed their trip to Mexico as clearly being life changing of the highest order.

Although their wedding could not be of a lower profile, they agreed that their attire would reflect all the dignity of marriage. Jack decided to wear a charcoal grey suite that he had worn only once before, at Bobby's inauguration ceremony. Mary purchased an off the rack dress from Sax Fifth Avenue. The beige, lace covered dress was surprisingly similar to that of Jackie's high dollar custom made dress by exclusive Italian couturier Valentino.

The evening before their departure for Acapulco, Mary excitedly called out to Jack from her Wexford art studio. "Jack, honey, when you get a chance, would you come to my studio?"

Since arriving home from Positano, Mary had politely declared her studio as off limits to Jack, therefore he responded post haste. "I'm on my way, Mare."

Playfully, Jack stopped his wheelchair just shy of the studio threshold. "Well, Mare, are you going to release me from your off limits orders?"

"She thought the setting was perfect, and laughed. "No, no . . . close and cover your eyes . . . . and keep them closed, Mr. ex-President of the United States."

He laughed with his hands covering his eyes. "It shows how far I've slipped from grace, when I'm following orders from a right-brained, female, hippy artist."

She giggled as she took control of his wheelchair. "You've got that right . . . . Mr. big shot."

"Ex big shot."

"It's your call."

Hands still covering his eyes as she wheeled him into the room. "Coming from a Frenchwomen, shouldn't the 'T' be silent on big shot . . . . Miss Pinchot."

"Have it your way, ex Mr. *big sho*."

She maneuvered Jack to within a respectable distance before an easeled canvas. "Ok, Jacko, open your eyes."

He was too stunned to speak for several seconds, "Oh . . . . my . . . . God." He gasped, "Mary, Mary, Mary . . . . I cannot believe my eyes." He pulled her onto his lap. "I all but forgot about the picture you had Ricardo take of us on the boat" He kissed her several times on the lips. "Oh, Mary . . . . you are simply too damned good to me and for me."

There they were, the two of them in rich oil colors . . . . looking exactly like the snapshot. They were sitting on the stern of Ricardo's sail boat, Jack's arm around Mary, with beautiful blue water between them and the classic coastal view of Positano.

"Did you notice what's around our necks?"

He turned back to the painting and leaned closer to the canvas. ""Yes, yes . . . . now I see." He kissed her warmly on the lips. "We're wearing our split-pendants."

"Yes . . . . a full ten days before they were presented to us by the craftsman."

"You can't see any clear detail of the pendants, but there is absolutely no doubt what we're wearing."

Back down to earth, Jack continued to study the painting. "Mare . . . . you did such a wonderful, realistic job; and here you're noted for your abstract work."

"Good point, Jack." She reached for his hand, "That's because I just got so caught up in that whole Washington Color School movement." She squeezed Jack's hand. "Actually, I can paint anything I set my mind to."

Jack made a sweeping hand motion the width of the painting. "That you can, Mary, Mary, that you can."

"Jack, honey, I'm thrilled to death that you like it."

"Mare, I can't put it into words how much I *do* love it."

She did a playful pirouetted between Jack and the painting. "As soon as we return . . . . as one . . . . we'll have it mounted, framed and hung."

"For all to see."

Playfully, "There's one more surprise in the painting, Jack." She giggled, "See if you can spot it."

"Ok, Mare, you're on."

He slowly examined the details of the boat, the sea, the Positano coast line and cliff dwellings, then to him and Mary. "Hmmm . . . . I don't know Mare . . . . I think you've got me . . ." Then suddenly, "There!" He proudly pointed just shy of the drying oils.

She squealed with joy, "You found it, Jack . . . . you found it."

"Again, Mary, for all to see . . . . long after we're gone . . . . our wedding bands."

She sat back in his lap and hugged him warmly, with Jack whispering into her ear. "Again, Mary, you make me so, so, so happy." She could not see his eyes well up as he continued in her ear. "Mary, you're something I've been longing for my entire life . . . . and now I have it."

She looked at him and giggled, as they began to dab the tears from one another's eyes, and continued to hug one another in long silence before Jack spoke. "Of course, by the time we unveil this to the world, they will have discovered our marriage."

She sighed, "Amen, Jack, Amen."

CHAPTER 41

In spite of Jack having debilitated to the point that Mary had to depend on his aide or Secret Service Agent to assist him in and out of his wheelchair, off they went to Acapulco for a two-week get away.

Although the Acapulco quarters envied those of Portifino and Positano, Italy, they did offer that of absolute privacy, for the villa was only accessible by its private boat dock or helicopter landing pad.

Late in their stay, the big day arrived for two life changing events, that of Mary's Baptism and her marriage to Jack. The full immersion Baptism was scheduled for sunrise at the shores edge. While full immersion was not the Catholic *standard*, Mary said if it was good enough for Christ, at the hands of John the Baptist, it was a must for her. Of course that was Mary, which was all out or nothing. The wedding and Mass were planned for early evening, timed to culminate at sunset, set on the spacious balcony with a stunning view of the Pacific Ocean.

With the first sign of dawn, the intimate Baptism procession led by the elderly Bishop Jose de Pilar Quezada Valdes, followed by Jack and Mary hand in hand with the Presidential Aide in control of the wheelchair, then by the Secret Service Agent. They moved from the villa, through the dew covered, flower scented garden, and down the adobe brick pathway to the water's edge.

Although the day was forecasted for a high in the low eighties, the morning was comfortably cool. The sun had yet to break the ten-thousand foot Sierra Madre' del Sur mountain range at the procession's back. Although by choice, it was too bad the world could not be a party to such a glorious site. Mary looked stunningly angelic with her blond hair, fair complexion, wearing a stark white ankle length smock, with subtle traces of thick woven gold thread and topical white lace. Beneath the smock she wore a simple short sleeve white blouse, and white calf length slacks, with simple white sandals.

Jack wore a tropical white short sleeve shirt, with the same woven gold thread effect as Mary's smock, with white slacks and shoes. He and Mary, of course, wore their split-pendent necklaces beneath their clothing, with Mary displaying a small, plain, gold Crucifix on a fine gold chain.

Much to the chagrin of the Bishop, Mary carried a white leather covered King James Version of the Holy Bible, as opposed to a Catholic version containing the Apocrypha; seven additional Old Testament books considered to be un-inspired, according to internationally recognized and respected Bible authorities.

A long narrow mat ran from the shore's edge into the calm water of the villa's remote private beach on Bahia De Acapulco. Jack's wheelchair stopped just short of the mat, with the break set. The Bishop, preferring the Catholic tradition of pouring a few ounces of Holy Water on the recipient's forehead, reluctantly stepped into the chilly water, stopping as he reached waist level depth; he then turned to face the small party on shore.

On cue, Mary bent at the waste and kissed Jack, released his hand, handed him her Bible, before slowly following the mat into the water stopping adjacent to the Bishop, before turning to face Jack with a radiant smile.

The Bishop spoke in a heavy Spanish accent which carried across the surface of the still waters as the light, absent of the sun, gradually increased.

"Mary Pinchot, do you reject Satin?"

Hands folded and gazing upwards toward the heavens, "I do."

"Do you accept Jesus Christ as your personal Lord and Savior?"

Eyes closed tightly, "*Yes*, I do."

The Bishop produced a small bottle of Holy Oil, and anointed Mary's forehead, lips and breast in the sign of a cross, speaking Latin in a faint whisper.

The Bishop then, in a smooth slow motion, placed his one hand behind Mary's head and his other hand on her breast bone as he spoke with passion, using Mary's patron Saint Michael's name, in honor of her late son, for the first time.

"Mary *Michael* Pinchot, I Baptize thee in the name of the Father, and of the Son, and of the Holy Spirit." As if sealing the deal, the Bishop repeated the sign of the cross in Latin. "In nomine Patri, et Fillii, et Spiritos Sancti, Amen."

Mary, in anticipation, squeezed her nose as the Bishop smoothly, and completely, submersed her head three times beneath the water, in symbol of the Holy Trinity.

Mary smiled and appeared radiant as she folded her hands and gazed into the heavens, as the sun broke the crest of the mountain she was facing.

"Thank you Lord, *thank you.*"

At the same moment, with eyes welled over, the former President of the United States raised his arms as he too faced the heavens.

"Thank you Lord, for we are now both saved, and will, in time, be rejoined in eternity."

As Mary sloshed ashore as a saved Christian, Jack welcomed her with opened arms.

"Here you go, Mare . . . ." Laughing, ". . . . right here in my lap."

They embraced as he continued in her ear, "Oh, Mare, just when I thought it impossible to love you more."

"Oh, Jack, it feels so fresh being saved."

"Yes Mary, Mary, yes . . . . we are both now fully saved." He hugged her tight, "So you'll know, while you were getting ready this morning, the Bishop heard my Confession . . . . for the first time since I can't remember when."

Playfully, she gasped and covered her mouth. "Oh, oh . . . . the Bishop's ears have got to be damaged for life."

Jack whispered in her ear, "It's a good news bad news scenario. Bad, in that I dumped on him *big time;* and good news in that he is sworn to secrecy, by the Vatican, under the pain of *eternal* damnation."

They high-fived one another as they laughed aloud.

The well paid Bishop slowly sloshed ashore, half gasping for air. "Jack, Mary, do you mind if I go straight to the villa and get out of these wet clothes."

Jack chuckled, "Sure, Bishop, make yourself at home," He turned toward his aide and Secret Service agent, "You guys go ahead, Mary and I want to hold back and savor the moment alone." He turned to the Bishop with a wink, "Great job, Bishop, thank you so much."

The Bishop winked back, speaking in silent volume to one another. "We'll be up shortly, for the champagne brunch begins shortly."

Again, the Bishop winked with a devilish smile, "Of course, I'll get into the champagne post-haste."

CHAPTER 42

Following Mary's sunrise Baptism and brunch, where spirits were high and champagne flowed, Jack and Mary honored the age old Mexican tradition of a siesta. They awoke refresh and with ample time to ready themselves for their sunset wedding.

The aroma of a full-on traditional Mexican post-wedding dinner wafted throughout the sprawling, three story villa. As the bride ushered the groom's wheelchair from the elevator, leading to their private quarters, they were greeted with excitement by the Bishop, Presidential Aide, and Secret Service Agent.

Mary looked stunning in her simple beige, lace enhanced dress, matching heels, with a delicate white orchid affixed near her left shoulder. Just above the dress neck line appeared the same small gold crucifix worn during her Baptism. Of course, hidden beneath their clothing, again, Jack and Mary wore their split pendent necklaces.

Jack looked great, alongside Mary, in a grey flannel suite; worn once before at Bobby's presidential inauguration.

The stage was set on the spacious balcony with its breath taking sprawling view of Bahia De Acapulco, opening out into the shimmering, blue, Pacific Ocean.

There were two large sprays of flowers, one at each end of the balcony. Center stage was an Alter, covered with a starched, pure white, gold thread laced linen cloth, upon which sat two golden candelabras holding fresh white candles with gold crowns. Between the candles sat a large, red leather covered Mass Bible opened to the Mass liturgy and setting on a slanted oak book saddle. The pair of water / wine Communion preparatory crystal carafes were split, one at each end of the alter; for, as luck, or fate, would have it the aide and agent were both products of Catholic parochial schools, and were trained, veteran Alter Boys.

The Alter Boys wore traditional white, short bell sleeved, starched pull-over smocks, while the Bishop wore full customary Cathedral Mass attire.

As with the morning Baptism, Jack and Mary set the start of their wedding ceremony by the position of the sun, timing the culmination of their wedding service at sunset.

The full ceremony would include the Holy Sacrifice of a Mass, followed by the wedding ceremony itself.

In great spirits, Jack spoke in kind, "So what do you say we take time before the ceremony for a few champagne toasts." He playfully glanced toward the sun, "Which means it's time to pour."

No sooner did he speak, the aide popped a cork as the agent produced glasses all around.

Mary stood from Jack's lap, offering her yet to be filled glass. "The sun has definitely fallen below the yard arm."

They all raised their glasses with the aide offering, "To the bride and groom; may they have life-long happiness together."

They all drank to several toasts, to the point where their pumps were well primed, as the Bishop looked at his watch. "Well, are you two *youngsters* ready?"

They raised their glasses, the Bishop adding with a mischievous grin. "I hereby give dispensation and permission for us all to receive Holy Communion in the spirit in which we consumed abundant champagne."

Jack playfully raised his empty glass, "I'll drink to that . . . . ahhh . . . . best we wait until after the service."

They all laughed and raised their empty glasses, "We'll drink to that as well."

The Bishop wound down and spoke with reverence, "The time has come to join you two in the Holy Sacrament of Marriage."

Mary took Jack's hand and they both attempted to speak, with Mary smiling warmly at Jack, "Go ahead, honey; I can read your mind . . . . so speak for us both."

Jack's eyes were locked onto Mary's, "I want you all to know that this is the happiest day of *our* lives."

The Bishop, again, spoke with reverence, "Let's take our set position on the balcony."

The Bishop stood between the altar and the balcony railing, with his back to the sea, facing the bride and groom, while the altar boys sat in chairs at each end of the alter, also facing the bride and groom.

Jack and Mary sat six feet in front of the altar, facing the falling sun on a dynamic orange-gold horizon, Jack in his wheelchair and Mary in a comfortable arm chair. They took each other's hand as the Bishop began the Mass, making a slow sweeping sign of the cross with his right arm."

"In nomine Patri, et Fillii, et Spiritos Sancti, Amen."

With the altar boys, Mary and Jack speaking along with the Bishop in Latin as they, too, made their personal sign of the cross.

The Catholic Holy Sacrifice of the Mass consists of three main parts; the Offertory, the Consecration, and the Communion, with scriptural readings and homily coming between the opening prayers and the Offertory.

The Bishop's opening prayers were actual read in Latin from the Mass Liturgy, with the congregation of four giving their response in Latin. The Bishop then spoke a handful of prayers in English to which the congregation responded, *Amen*.

He nodded toward the Presidential Aide, Alter Boy. "Now we'll have the first reading; with all of today's readings personally selected by Jack and Mary."

The Aide stood from his chair and opened his personal Bible.

"The first reading is from the Book of Tobit, 8:4b-8."

He looked at Mary and Jack, "This reading is often subtitled: *Allow us to live together to a happy old age.*"

> *On their wedding night Tobiah arose from bed and said to his wife,*
>
> *"Sister, get up. Let us pray and beg our Lord to have mercy on us and to grant us deliverance."*
>
> *Sarah got up, and they started to pray and beg that deliverance might be theirs. They began with these words:*
>
> *"Blessed are you, O God of our fathers; praised be your name forever and ever. Let the heavens and all your creation praise you forever. You made Adam and you gave him his wife Eve to be his help and support; and from these two the human race descended.*
>
> *You said, 'It is not good for the man to be alone; let us make him a partner like himself.'*
>
> *Now, Lord, you know that I take this wife of mine not because of lust, but for a noble purpose. Call down your mercy on me and on her, and allow us to live together to a happy old age."*
>
> *They said together, "Amen, amen."*

The Aide concluded before sitting down. "This is the word of the Lord."
The congregation, along with the Aide spoke aloud as one.
"Thanks be to God."
With that the Bishop stood and nodded toward the Secret Service Agent.
"We'll now have the second reading."
The Agent stood from his chair and opened his personal Bible.
He paused, "The second reading is from the first Letter of Saint Paul to the Corinthians 12:31-13:8a."
He looked at Mary and Jack, "This reading is often subtitled: *If I do not have love, I gain nothing.*"

Brothers and sisters:

Strive eagerly for the greatest spiritual gifts. But I shall show you a still more excellent way. If I speak in human and angelic tongues but do not have love, I am a resounding gong or a clashing cymbal. And if I have the gift of prophecy and comprehend all mysteries and all knowledge; if I have all faith so as to move mountains, but do not have love, I am nothing.

If I give away everything I own, and if I hand my body over so that I may boast but do not have love, I gain nothing. Love is patient, love is kind. It is not jealous, is not pompous, it is not inflated, it is not rude, it does not seek its own interests, it is not quick-tempered, it does not brood over injury, it does not rejoice over wrongdoing but rejoices with the truth. It bears all things, believes all things, hopes all things, and endures all things.

Love never fails.

The Agent concluded before sitting down. "This is the word of the Lord."
The congregation, along with the Agent spoke aloud as one.
"Thanks be to God."
With that the Bishop stood, "I will now do the third reading."
"The third reading is from the holy Gospel according to John 15:12-16
He looked at Mary and Jack, "This reading is often subtitled: *This is my Commandment: love one another.*"

Jesus said to his disciples:

"This is my commandment: love one another as I love you.

No one has greater love than this, to lay down one's life for one's friends. You are my friends if you do what I command you. I no longer call you slaves, because a slave does not know what his master is doing. I have called you friends, because I have told you everything I have heard from my Father. It was not you who chose me, but I who chose you and appointed you to go and bear fruit that will remain, so that whatever you ask the Father in my name he may give you."

He looked up from the Bible, "This is the word of the Lord."

The congregation along with the Secret Service Agent spoke aloud as one. "Thanks be to God."

With that, the Bishop proceeded with the Consecration of bread and wine; the Altar Boys stood, turned toward the Bishop before picking up their carafes; one with water, the other with wine.

The Bishop picked up his personal gold, bejeweled chalice, turned and extended the chalice toward the Altar Boy to his right. The Altar Boy poured a couple of ounces of wine from his carafe into the gold chalice.

The Bishop turned and faced forward, raising the chalice in the air and whispered a prayer in Latin, transforming the wine into the blood of Christ. With the chalice still raised he spoke aloud.

"Take this and drink of it, for this is My blood, the blood of the new and everlasting Covenant."

He then drank the transformed wine from the chalice before turning to the Altar Boy to his right, who poured water into the now empty chalice. He rolled the water around the chalice before drinking it; he then wiped the chalice dry with a small, pure white, linen towel.

The Bishop reached beneath the alter and produced a small gold ornate box, which was a portable Sacristy containing a single three inch diameter pure white host, or wafer, of enliven bread. He held the host between the thumb and forefinger of both hand, raising it in the air as he had done with the chalice.

Again, he whispered a prayer in Latin, converting, through *transsubstantiatio*, the host to that of the body and blood of Christ. He then spoke aloud, "Take this and eat from it, for this is My body and blood of the new and everlasting covenant."

The congregation responded aloud along with the Bishop, "Oh Lord, I am not worthy to receive you, but only say the word and I shall be healed."

At that point the Bishop lowered the host and broke it into five pieced, placing them in the chalice before slowly genuflecting.

The bishop carefully removed a single piece of the broken host from the chalice, in order to receive Communion, pausing the host just short of his mouth. "This is the body of Christ, Amen" With that he placed the host on his tongue and bowed his head in silent personal prayer as he swallowed the consecrated host.

With that, he picked up the chalice and slowly moved to the front of the altar, and stood before the bride and groom who had their hands reverently folded. As if her wedding was not enough for any bride, this was to be Mary's First Holy Communion as well. As her eyes welled over in tears, Mary responded to the Bishop who removed a piece of the host from the chalice and offered it to her.

"Mary, this is the body of Christ."

She responded, "Amen.", before extending her tongue, as a tear rolled down her right cheek. As Jack looking on with a smile, the Bishop placed the host on her tongue, stepped in front of Jack and offered him a piece of the host, "Jack, this is the body of Christ."

Jack responded, "Amen", then immediately reached over and took Mary's hand as they bowed their heads in personal prayed as they swallowed the host.

The Bishop administered communion to the Altar Boys before resuming his position behind the Altar, wiped the chalice clean, closed the Bible, and opened his arms to the congregation, "The Mass has ended, go in peace."

He then stepped to the front of the altar and faced the bride and groom, with the Altar Boys moving to his left and right side; he paused with a smiled.

"We are gathered here this evening to join Jack and Mary in the Holy Sacrament of Marriage".

He paused, "Please turn to face one another."

The bishop, again, paused and smiled. "Jack and Mary, have you come here freely and without reservation to give yourselves to one another in marriage?"

They answered as one, "Yes, we have."

"Will you honor each other as man and wife for the rest of your lives?"

"Yes, we shall."

The Bishop turned toward the groom, "Jack, do you take Mary to be your wife? Do you promise to be true to her in good times and in bad, in sickness and in health, to love her and honor her all the days of your life?"

Jack nodded. "Yes, I do."

"Mary, do you take Jack to be your husband? Do you promise to be true to him in good times and in bad, in sickness and in health, to love him and honor him all the days of your life?"

Mary nodded, with eyes welled over. "Yes, I do."

On queue, the presidential Aide produced the rings on a small white satin pillow, extended the pillow to the Bishop who paused to bless the rings, making a Sign of the Cross motion above rings as he spoke in Latin.

"In nomine Patri, et Fillii, et Spiritos Sancti, Amen."

He picked up each ring and held them between his thumb and forefinger of both hands.

"A circle is the symbol of wholeness, perfection, and unity. Like circles, these rings have no beginning and no end. They are tokens of the growing relationship that Mary and Jack have come here to celebrate and confirm."

He placed the matching plain gold bands back on the pillow, paused and nodded to Jack, who, in turn picked up the smaller of the rings and smiled at Mary.

He placed the ring on her finger, "Mary, take this ring as a sign of my love and fidelity."

On queue, Mary picked up the ring, smiled radiantly at Jack, and placed the ring on the finger of his now frail hand, "Jack, take this ring as a sign of my love and fidelity."

The Bishop smiled before declaring aloud, "What God has joined, men must not divide"

He spread his arms, "I now pronounce you man and wife" With his right hand in motion, "In nomine Patri, et Fillii, et Spiritos Sancti, Amen."

As the sun began to sink below the orange-red Pacific Ocean horizon, the Bishop smiled as he nodded toward Jack.

"You may now kiss the bride."

Mary sat in Jack's lap, wrapped her arms around him and kissed him warmly several times before burying her face in his neck and wept.

CHAPTER 43

In spite of having insisted that there were to be no wedding gifts from the participants, the Presidential Aide and the Secret Service Agent collaborated with the Bishop to arrange for a day of sailing, utilizing a boat and skipper of one of the wealthy local businessman and member of Acapulco's Lady of Soledad Cathedral. This was arranged, with the approval of Jack and Mary, the afternoon they arrived in Acapulco in order to not interfere with other plans.

The morning following their wedding, Jack and Mary awoke excited as children with a day at Disneyland before them. Since Mary's sailing gift to Jack while vacationing in Positano, Italy, sailing had become their favorite outdoor activity. As Mary had come to love sailing, the love for the sea, sailing in particular, was in Jack's blood; his prime reason for enlisting in the Navy during WW II.

Boarding and de-boarding the sailing craft made for an awkward, if not humbling, start and finish to their adventure. Although the villa had its own private dock, the keel draft of the donated craft was such that it could not utilize the dock. The *Levanto* (hot southeasterly wind) was a good five feet longer than Jack's personal twenty-six foot Wianno Senior sailboat *Victura*. This meant that Jack had to be assisted onto a motor craft, and then transferred onto the sailing craft, and, of course, in reverse. Jack and Mary were so upbeat and excited, neither one of them blinked or uttered a negative tone during the process. Their mood was: By god, this was the day following the best day of their lives and their last day of vacation in Acapulco.

No sooner had they boarded, the owner appeared from the galley to greet them; a tall, slim, early sixties appearing man, with grey hair, unusually broad shoulders, and a disarming smile. Anxious to meet the one-time president, he eagerly offered his hand.

"Sir, I'm the proud owner of this craft, my name is Enrique Enriquez, call me Hank."

Jack smiled as he removed his sunglasses for eye contact, "The name's Jack Kennedy." He scanned the boat, "And, proud you should be, Captain, she's a fine looking vessel."

"Thank you, sir."

Jack winked, "Call me Jack, Hank."

Assuming the Bishop honored his word, he turned toward Mary, "And this is my *fiancé* Mary Pinchot."

The skipper smiled and half bowed as he took her hand. "A pleasure to meet you, Mary."

As if on queue, the crew of two appeared. "Jack and Mary, this will be your skipper for the day, Hank Ontovaros."

Jack shook his hand with a smile, "It's a pleasure .... ah ... *Hanks* a pair, keep a kicker and draw two."

Laughter all around.

"And this is your all around deck hand, Lupe Gonzalez." While Ontovaros was built like a lineman, Gonzalez gave the appearance of a scat back.

"The pleasure is mine, Lupe .... and all of you, please do call me Jack."

The Captain chuckled, "As long as I can call my boat *Navy-One* for the day."

As they laughed, a bottle of champagne and glasses appeared, as the captain announced, "I've got to dash off for a day of business, but not until we start the day with a little bubbly."

Cheers all around.

Following a few glasses of champagne, the boat owner de-boarded into a motorized skiff and sped toward Acapulco's main harbor. The skipper wasted no time in weighing anchor and within minutes Mary and Jack were happily seated aft, holding hands with the balmy sea air in their face.

Jack squeezed Mary's hand, "You know, Mare, it doesn't get any better than this."

She pecked him on the cheek, "Right you are, Jacko."

Silence, before Jack gave Mary a soft elbow, "Except, of course, in the hereafter, Mare."

She squeezed his hand and placed her head on his shoulder, "And we're now assured of where we'll spend our hereafter."

Jack sighed for affect, "And to think .... me with a new and perfect body."

She snuggled closer, "Then you'll have a choice of any women you want."

He squeezed her hand, "You'll still be my one and only."

CHAPTER 44

Mary zipped up the last of the suitcases and nodded to the aide, "They're all yours."

"Great, the boat's here, we're on our way." He placed the suitcases on a dolly, "Your chopper will be here shortly." He paused at the door, "By the time we transfer from boat to limo and drive to the airport, you'll be on your way."

"Thanks, we'll see you at the airport."

With Jack now a private citizen, his travel itinerary remained top secret, Jack had personally waived Secret Service coverage for the short flight to General Juan N. Alvarez International Airport, with Secret Service coverage to resume upon his landing. Also, the private chopper charter was scheduled to pick up American's Mr. and Mrs. Joseph H. Bouchard of Green Bay, Wisconsin . . . . not a former President of the United States

Mary turned to Jack as the aide left the bedroom. "What do you say we have coffee on the balcony while waiting for the helicopter?"

She paused at the bedroom threshold, as she wheeled Jack toward the elevator. "Say goodbye to our honeymoon suite." She kissed Jack on the cheek. "I hope we'll see it again."

"Oh, I'm sorry, Mare, I forgot to tell you.' He squeezed her hand, "The owner's agreed to reserve the place for our first anniversary." He chuckled, "Although I couldn't tell him that we were married."

Mary cheered, as she wheeled Jack to the elevator. "Hurray for our side!" She pushed the button. "I'm already looking forward to it, Jacko."

Jack hid his concern about his failing health, "Me too, Mary, Mary, me too."

With the morning sun still behind the villa, Jack stirred his coffee, as he looked out onto blue Acapulco Bay dotted with sail boats with pure white, wind filled sails. "Mary, I can't possibly put into words how happy I am with you in my life, especially now as my wife."

She placed her hand in his, "Oh, Jack, me too." Silence, "With finite lives, you wonder why it takes so long to find happiness?"

"If ever, for some, Mare."

"Very true Jack." She slid her chair closer and placed her head on his shoulder. "All I can say is, praise God."

"Amen, Mary, amen."

Long silence, with a balmy breeze across the balcony, was broken with the faint sound of an approaching helicopter.

Jack spoke in a mocking voice, "De plain, de plain."

They laughed like children as Mary stood and took control of the wheel chair.

"I'm really anxious to see Carolyn, Jon, Quentin, and Mark."

"Me too, Jack; with their stays overlapping by four days, we'll have one great big family dinner."

Long pause in route to the helicopter, "You know, Mare, today, between Acapulco and home, we need to have a serious discussion on when to reveal the marriage to our families."

"I agree, it would be unconscionable to have them find out through the media."

The helicopter flight to General Juan N. Alvarez International Airport was just under fifty miles by air. The flight path would take a short passage over one end of Bahia Del Acapulco, across the Peninsula de Las Playas, then south along the mouth of the Bahia Del Acapulco, they would then skirt Bahia De Puerto Marquez, before taking a short pass along the Pacific coastline before a button hook pattern onshore into the coastal airport.

The limo carrying the Presidential Aide, Secret Service Agent, and their baggage would be on their last leg to the airport and on watch for the chopper in flight.

The pilot and co-pilot carefully lifted the former president, strapped in his wheelchair, up into the helicopter and mechanically clasped and secured the wheelchair into place, with a device custom designed for wheelchairs and bolted to the floor. With Mary belted into her conventional seat across the aisle from Jack, the pilot and co-pilot assumed their positions, restarted the engine, gave and received a thumbs up from Jack and Mary.

The chopper slowly lifted straight up about ten feet above the pad turning clockwise until facing south-west onto Bahia Del Acapulco, at that point the chopper quickly moved simultaneously upward and forward out to sea. After reaching a mile off shore and having obtained an elevation of

1500 feet, the aircraft banked to the south and continued to climb upward. Amid the noise within the chopper, Jack and Mary merely smiled at one another as they held hands across the narrow aisle.

As the aircraft banked due south and began its short parallel run along the Pacific coastline, a loud backfire shook the entire aircraft. Jack and Mary glanced upward toward the engine, and, in spite of being veteran fliers, gave each other a nervous smile and attempted to re-settle.

Within less than a minute from the initial backfire, there came an equally as violet backfire followed by a pause, then a loud cough from the overhead rotary engine. Jack and Mary tensed and tightened their grip on one another's hand, as they locked fear-filled eyes. As the engine backfired yet again, a shrill pulsating alarm echoed within the small cabin.

Jack and Mary glanced out the window and saw nothing but blue sea and a coastline with little definition. The pilot yelling into his helmet-mounted mike pulled their attention away from the sea, "Mayday, mayday".

At that same moment the Presidential Aide and Secret Service Agent, just short of the airport in their limo, had visual contact with the chopper when its engine belched three time delayed clouds of black smoke. The closed limo prompted the Secret Service Agent to lower his window and yell to the driver to cut the radio. At that point there was another cough and backfire with a belch of much heavier black smoke.

"Holy shit," He yelled at the Aide, "Get on the horn."

No sooner had the Agent yelled, the helicopter engine stopped, bringing eerie silence to the skies.

The chopper seemed to pause and momentarily defy gravity before beginning to silently gyro downward toward the Pacific, a half mile below. As the engine stopped, the pilot yelled over the multiple wailing alarms, in Spanish, into his headset that his aircraft was going into the drink, along with critical positioning data for would be rescuers. At the same time, the co-pilot turned toward Jack and Mary, yelling instructions in broken English.

"Man your life vests were headed into the drink."

With Jack, his U.S. Naval courage-under-fire training, in spite of all the lapsed years, immediately kicked into gear. While with Mary, Mother Nature switched everything into slow motion to aid her, along with her fear-nothing genetic trait.

Jack yelled, "Stay calm and brace yourself for impact, before we make our move."

No sooner had Jack spit out the words, the chopper impacted into the *solid* Pacific salt water with a jarring blow, causing severe damage to the belly of the craft and structural framing in general. The damage from the impact silenced the alarms, and the whooshing sound of the gyroing blades, while amplifying the yelling of orders from the front of the craft.

"We've got two to three minutes to abandon the craft. I'll release the lock on your door and it will automatically blow open." The door lock made loud mechanical sounds to three failed attempts to release the door. Again, in broken English "The door jammed on impact; you'll have to crawl through the front cab."

At that point Mary had released her seat belt, stood ankle deep in sea water, and reached for two May-West hanging on the wall. Although her heart sunk with the news from the front cab, Mary felt confident that between the flotation from the life vest, assistance from the crew, and her own physical strength and athleticism, they would successfully remove Jack from the sinking craft.

Knee deep in water Mary slipped the May-West over Jack's head, "Ok, honey, release your seat belt while I secure your vest."

With water having reached the seat of his wheelchair, Jack struggled in vain to release his seat belt. "What's wrong, Jack?"

"The impact with the water bent the vertical frame inward, pinching my seat belt buckle against the metal frame of the wheelchair . . . . I simply cannot break the buckle free, and without a knife to cut the belt, we're out of luck, Mare."

"Nonsense, honey, we'll simply release the chair itself from the floor clasp."

"Great idea, Mare."

At that point water was at Jack's waste, and at Mary's hip, as Jacked reached for the release on the floor wheelchair clasp, with water lapping at his chin. "Mare, I don't know if it's my lack of strength or what, but I cannot release the clasp."

With the water relentlessly rising, "Let me try, Jack." As Mary reached for the clasp release, her face was in and out of water. "I can't release it either." She studied the mechanical assembly with her hands, "Oh, crap, Jack, the entire chair-clasp assembly was bent on impact and rendered inoperable."

The pilot yelled from outside the helicopter, "Hurry up, hurry up, save yourselves."

Jack did not blink as the water reached his solar plexus, "Mary, please, save yourself, my days are clearly limited."

The co-pilot tried his luck, yelling from outside the ill fated craft, "Hurry, please, hurry, save yourselves . . . . at least yourself, Mrs. Bouchard."

As Mary locked eyes with Jack, a sudden blanket of peace and tranquility enveloped the tragic inevitability of the situation.

"Oh Jack, don't even think that." As she had done countless times since Jack's confinement to a wheelchair, Mary calmly sat in his lap. "Jack, honey,

I cannot lose one more person that I love." Her smile was comforting, "Especially if that person is *you* . . . ." She winked, with her trademark sly grin. ". . . . Jacko."

As the water neared Jack's shoulders, and Mary's breasts, Mary, in one smooth deliberate motion, unbuckled her dress belt, looped it through Jack's inoperable seat belt, cinched it tight and re-buckled her belt . . . . and they became one.

In calm resignation, a peace suddenly consumed their very being. As they hugged each other tight, Mary whispered in Jack's ear, as water lapped at their neck lines. "There now, honey, you're going nowhere without me . . . . including to the other side."

Again, the pilot yelled, "Hurry, time is up . . . . are you two ok?"

Mary yelled, "We're just fine . . . . trust us."

In total calm, to the background sound of gurgling sea water and the hissing sound of rising water upon hot metal, "I love you dearly, Jackie boy."

"Me to you, Mary, Mary."

As the water inched passed their lips and touched their noses, their hug intensified as they spoke their final words through muffled, yet audible, bubbles.

"On the other side, Mary . . . ."

She smiled as sea water stung their open eyes,

"Momentarily Jack . . . . mo . . . men . . . tar . . . ."

The chopper paused momentarily in its decent, listed slightly in the direction of the United States, as if in a final salute for the former President of the United States, before disappearing beneath the sea.

It was an eerie final form of payback for Jack, having survived his PT-109 ordeal at sea . . . .

PART III

CHAPTER 1

Within moments of the chopper's May Day, a rescue effort was launched by the Mexican State of Guerrero air search and rescue team, operating out of General Juan N. Alvarez International Airport. In spite of the quick response, the President's chartered helicopter slipped beneath surface of the Pacific as the rescue chopper cleared the coastline.

Within those same moments, the President's phone rang within the White House Oval Room, with his secretary, Evelyn Lincoln, announcing through the phone intercom.

"Excuse me, Mr. President, you have a call from Mexico, there seems to be a family emergency."

Words to the effect of *Russia, nuclear, or Hanoi*, would have drawn a calm, steely reaction from the single most powerful man on planet Earth; however, the word *family* drew the typical startled lay reaction as Bobby grabbed the phone from its cradle.

"What . . . ah . . . . hello, POTUS speaking. What is it?"

"Mr. President, this is Secret Service agent Mike Majors calling from Acapulco, Mexico's international airport, in regard to your brother Jack'"

With his brother's extensive travel schedule, Bobby draws a momentary blank.

"Yes, what's the problem?"

"Sir, moments ago we received a May Day from the pilot of your brother's helicopter off the coast of Mexico . . . . questionably within Mexican waters."

Hurried, yet calm. "And?"

"Sir," he paused, "The chopper pilot said that they had experienced engine failure and were starting an emergency gyro decent . . . . at that point we lost all verbal contact. However, we do have a clear signal from the craft's emergency transponder and, as we speak, a rescue craft is clearing the runway."

Bobby glanced at Vice-President, Ralph Yarborough, as he quietly slipped into the Oval Office with a queried look upon his face, as Bobby responded to the Secret Service agent.

""The rescue plane's ETA?"

"Less than two minutes, I'll get back with . . . ."

"No, I'll hold."

"Yes sir, Mr. President."

Bobby took a deep breath as he covered the receiver with his free hand. "Jack's helicopter went down in the Pacific, off of Mexico."

Ralph gasped as he sat down across the expansive desk from the President.

"Oh, my God . . . . he's with Mary?"

"They're inseparable."

As Bobby leafed through his Kennedy Clan calendar, Ralph queried, "Where were they heading."

"Let's see . . . . yeah, they were heading home from an Acapulco vacation." He closed the date book, "No doubt the chopper was taking them to the airport."

The agent came back on line. "Sir, the rescue helicopter is circling over the down site as we speak." Respectfully. "I'm sorry, sir, their reporting that the only visible survivors are the pilot and co-pilot in May Wests."

Bobby groaned into the phone, "Oh, dear God, no . . . . no . . . . not Jack." Bobby stood, half bent over in pain." He struggled with the words, "Which means . . . my brother . . . . and Mary . . . went down with the craft."

The agent struggled as well, "I'm afraid so, sir."

Zombie-like, Bobby sat down behind the same desk that his brother had used throughout his presidency. With an elbow on the desk and face in his hand, he choked back a reply.

"Mike . . . . ah . . . . make yourself available, while I get my family . . . and others . . . involved."

"Yes, sir."

"Oh . . . . and, Mike . . . . keep this under rap as long as humanly possible."

"Will do, sir; the fact that the charter was booked under a pair of alias names will help some."

"Great . . . . try to play that out as long as you can."

"Yes, sir . . . and, sir, I'm so sorry . . . . that it happened on my watch."

"Mike, as Commander and Chief, I order you to not beat yourself up over this . . . . let's just move forward."

"Yes, sir."

"Of course, Mike, I don't have to tell you to brace yourself, because all hell is about to break loose, and the scene will by swarming with competing government teams . . . . as well as Kennedy clan team."

CHAPTER 2

"Teddy, it's Bobby"

Sensing the tone.

"What's up, brother?"

"Bad news . . . . brace yourself."

"Oh no, here we go again."

"That's right; I just received word that Jack's helicopter went down off the coast of Acapulco. The search and rescue folks said that Jack and Mary went to the bottom with the craft."

"Oh, dear God, no . . . . no . . . what the hell have us Kennedys done?"

Staying focused on the crises, Bobby cut off his younger brother. "The fact that the chopper was chartered under a pair of aliases, buys us time to seize family control of the situation."

As if cold water had been thrown on his face, Ted immediately falls in line. "What's the plan?"

"At this point, the only people who know that it was actually Jack and Mary on board are, you and me, Ralph, who was in my office when I received the call, my secretary, and of course, Jack's Secret Service Agent, and his personal Aide, who are both in Mexico on, or I should say behind, the scene." He paused, "And, of course, they are all sworn to secrecy."

"Sadly . . . . we are off to a good start."

"No listen, Teddy, we Kennedys will have our time to mourn, but for now we need to stay very focused during the front end of the crises."

"We're on the same page, Bobby, don't worry."

"Ted, what I want you to do immediately, is to contact the family's Mr. Fix It and the two of you head to the crash scene . . . . and I mean immediately."

"Got it, Bobby." He dropped his voice, "We'll be on the family plane and in the air post haste."

"Good, I'll give you the necessary time cushion to be adequately ahead of all the forces that I'm going to release."

"What about our folks currently on site?"

""For the time being, I've got them in communication lock-down. In the mean time, I'll call them and let then know that you're on the way, and that I'll release the full barrage of hounds when I'm comfortable. Also, I'll tell them to keep their thumbs on the pulse of what's happening on their end, without exposing ourselves, until we're certain of being first on the scene in the U.S. line."

"Good, I'm on my way, and I'll keep you in the loop."

"Likewise, little brother." Pause, "And Teddy . . . I'm sorry for acting so presidential, but I'm serious in that us Kennedys will have our time to mourn."

"Your right, Bobby . . . . we always do."

CHAPTER 3

No sooner had the president hung up from giving Ted his marching orders, he excused Ralph, his vice-president, in order that he make personal calls to the family. His first call was to his wife, Ethyl, who sobbed uncontrollably for several minutes before agreeing to immediately call Jackie in Paris. The next half dozen calls were to family hierarchy.

With family calls, where he had to show strength, out of the way, the president retreated to his private Oval Office rest room where he locked the door and wept. When finished, he rinsed his face in cold water, and took a half dozen deep breaths before returning to his older brother's business . . . . behind Jack's old desk

With Ted and the family aide well enroute to Acapulco, Bobby did, in fact, release the hounds . . . . in spades.

In pre-planned rapid fire succession, the President of the United States contacted and gave orders to the Secret Service, the FBI, the CIA, the American Ambassador to Mexico, and issued a carefully worded press release, all within an hour. Within a matter of minutes from issuing the press release, the news of the fate of the global hero had super charged the airwaves and news wires throughout the world.

By the time Teddy arrived in Acapulco, the slo-mo, ma ana, recovery operation had accelerated to the global crises level that it had suddenly become. The local journalists were already revising their initial news reports of a pair of *Juana and Jose Doe Americanos'* to that of the *'former President of the United States, John Fitzgerald Kennedy, along with his internationally revered Angel of Mercy, Mary Pinchot'*.

The Mexican authorities had set the stage for the U.S. recovery team. Through the aid of the radio signal transmitted from the downed helicopter's emergency transponder, they pinpointed the location of the craft and set an anchored buoy marking its location.

Acapulco marine biologist, Dr. Alexandero Padilla, described the helicopter's position as resting on the Inner Continental Shelf, at 330 feet below the surface of the Pacific. He went on to say that the craft rested on terrigenous sediment derived from the erosion of the continents; the majority being relict sediment deposited during the ice age. He further declared the sub-sea location as a marine environ friendly to a rescue operation.

CHAPTER 4

As the sun sat on the ill fated craft's location marker buoy, the private jet carrying Ted and the Kennedy family aide touched down. By then, Jack's presidential aide and secret service agent had stepped forward as the breaking news bulletin had re-identified the victims of the downed helicopter as the former President of the United States, JFK, and his *personal caregiver*, Mary Pinchot. Being the first and only US representatives present, they did managed to commandeer a small empty office building located between the western edge of airport and the Pacific waterfront.

Shortly before midnight, Ted got wind of the Mexican government's struggle to obtain a sea going vessel with a heavy duty crane. With that, he placed a call to Bobby, who was still awake and proactive to the cause.

"Bobby, Teddy here."

"How can I help you?"

We need immediate access to a ship or sea-barge with a crane capable of hoisting Jack's helicopter from off the Continental Shelf."

Having spoken to Teddy several times since his arrival, Bobby did not linger on line.

"Consider it done, brother."

Bobby's quick results trumped the faltering effort of Mexico President Gustavo Diaz Ordaz, who ended up publicly humbled and embarrassed. The humble pie was even less palatable when the source of the rescue vessel became public.

The US State Department commandeered a 210 foot by 60 foot sea barge with deck mounted 210 short ton capacity crane with 85 foot pick reach from the Mexican government oil company PEMEX, Petróleos Mexicanos. The barge was in use on a PEMEX-Exxon joint venture project located 100 miles north-east of the crash site, off the coastal region of Ixtapa

/ Zihuatanejo. With the aid of a three quarter moon, the barge was in route with the aid of two sea-tugboats, with a midmorning ETA.

No sooner had the sun broke the horizon, the crash scene marker buoy seemingly became an international magnet. Circling the site was a half dozen new helicopter, four of which were leased by American and European news agencies. As they circled, they shot footage of a large privately owned yacht loaned to the Kennedys. Also, there was a 140 commercial craft commandeered by the US government from an American based corporation's Acapulco operation. The second craft contained FBI, CIA, State Department, and a trio of deep sea divers and there associated equipment, and several crates of various high tech equipment to aide in the recovery effort.

As the overhead craft heard radio news of the barge crane in route, they peeled off and raced toward the barge reported to be twenty-five to thirty miles north-east of the buoyed site, in hopes of gaining exclusive news cover advantage over one another. All that, while, of course, the world sat glued to their black and white televisions.

With the time difference, Bobby and First Lady Ethyl watched the news coverage over lunch within their White House presidential quarters.

"I still can't believe it, Bobby; Jack survives his PT-105 ordeal, and a major assassination attempt, and now he goes while on a pleasure trip to Acapulco."

"You're right . . . . death does not discriminate . . . . As in the loss of our sweet Mary, an innocent victim by loving association."

"Sadly, Bobby, it is comforting to know that Jack was not alone, and that he was with the one he truly loved . . . . in it's own way, it's truly romantic."

Bobby's demeanor changed as he shifted in his seat.

Ethyl noticing the change, "Is there something I should know?"

"Well, I guess you have the right . . . ."

"You guess?"

"Actually, you do have the right." He shifted in his seat and picked up his coffee. "It's about Mary . . . . actually, Jack *and* Mary."

"So . . . what's the secret?"

"Ethyl, it's not so much a secret as I haven't got around to telling you."

"Seeing that as the President you are sort of busy, I'll give you that."

They both laugh and raise their coffee cups.

"Anyway, my clan met over how to handle *our* latest tragedy. Well one of the decisions involved Mary." Struggling for words "While we all love her to death . . . . oh, God, where's my speech writer . . . . and agree that she was the best thing that could have possibly happened to Jack, what is paramount for the Kennedy family and for Jack's image and legacy."

"So?"

"We've instructed our family PR agent to downplay Jack and Mary's relationship, which, if left on its own, could possibly be damaging to Jack or the family image."

"Knowing all too well she had zero say in such matters, Ethyl lets out an exasperating sigh. "All I ask is that you go easy on Mary . . . . may she rest in peace."

CHAPTER 5

It was mid afternoon when the crane barge arrived at the marker buoy, with the balance of the day spent positioning the barge over the site with the crane's pick distance relative to the wreckage being a critical factor. Positioning was one thing, anchoring the four corners of the barge in the proper location was another issue. For the time being, they were blessed with a calm Pacific.

By the time the barge was set, and the necessary rescue related material and equipment transferred to the barge deck and properly set up and positioned, the mid-fall seasonal sun was quickly dropping toward the horizon. They used the fading daylight to launch a small remote controlled camera submarine, with flood lamp, in order to examine the wreckage laying position and extent of structural impact damage to the body of the aircraft, in order to plan the rescue itself. Of course, before attaching the lift cables, the deceased would be removed from within the craft. However, setting darkness and particulates within the water itself prohibited making visual verification that the deceased were, in fact, on board the fallen craft. Until verified otherwise, they were going with the verbal report from the pilot and co-pilot who were in close proximity of the craft as it disappeared beneath the surface.

Well after sunset, a behind the scene diplomatic skirmish ebbed and flowed between Mexico's President Diaz, who had been embarrassingly trumped by the U.S. over the crane-barge situation, and the U.S. diplomat. President Diaz was insisting that his government take full control of the remains of the crash victims, up through and including an autopsy and cause of death ruling, including loading the victims onto a U.S. aircraft where they would sign over care-custody-control to the U.S. The sole reason being that the aircraft went down in Mexican waters . . . . by a mere quarter of a mile.

Sadly, what broke the stalemate was a personal emotional plea from Bobby, on behalf of his older brother Jack and his entire clan. Some say that was Diaz's plan all along, as a payback for his public helping of humble pie. However, internationally, the situation diminished Diaz's already weakened stature.

As the sun broke the ten-thousand foot peak of Sierra Madré del Sur mountain range, the ever expanding rescue flotilla took on a life of its own, below the circling news helicopters.

While most of the Acapulco tourists were enjoying an elaborate hotel breakfast buffet, the U.S. Navy divers entered the water in full deep-dive gear rated well beyond their decent goal of 320 feet.

Although the dive critical support equipment was properly located on the deck of the barge, the audio-visual communication had dual input and feedback capability, one to the barge located dive operators, with the second to the Navy vessel, containing the Secret Service, CIA, FBI, Teddy, and the Kennedy clan PR agent. All conversations and visual imaging would be recorded aboard the naval vessel, where the same non-recorded data on the barge would be considered and rated as mere hear-say for time and memoriam.

As the divers reported back to the surface, from an approximate half-point, that "all was going well", Jackie Onassis's private jet, containing she, John and Carolyn, touched down at New Jersey's Newark Liberty International Airport. As she and the children transferred to an awaiting limo, unencumbered and free of unwanted eyes, Jackie's face was sober, drawn and ashen, as she moved unsteady on her feet, while the children had the appearance of being sleepy and bewildered as they clutched their mother's hand and their favorite blankets.

The dive captain's voice was one of relief as he reported, "We have reached the fallen craft, and although there is visual damage to the craft's lower frame, it is positioned for what appears as a trouble-free lift . . . . We are now approaching one of the craft's damage free windows."

Long pause, as those aboard the naval vessel hovered around the visual screen, whose image was on the fuzzy side. Teddy mumbled, as he impatiently drummed his fingers on the viewing table. "Comon' . . . . comon'."

Within moments the dive captain reported, "We have made visual contact . . . . they are together in the craft . . . . I'm now positioning the camera." Within a half dozen heart beats, those in the viewing room gasped in unison before the room went dead silent. There, on the screen, they could she Jack and Mary, appearing as huddled together in death. They could see the back of Mary's head, which blocked Jack's face, with her blond naturally wavy hair moving-floating-waving at the whim of the Pacific.

Out of respect, the viewing room remained silent for what seemed a long period, with Teddy breaking the silence with an agonizing groan, "Oh, no . . . . my beloved brother Jack . . . . and Mary . . . . his true *Angel of mercy* . . . ."

CHAPTER 6

The divers called for the twin recovery basket, which had been lowered with, and just above, the divers, to be extended to the ocean bed. While one diver managed the basket, the other set to open the passenger door of the chopper.

"Oh crap . . . . the door is jammed shut from impact."

The barge deck captain added, "That very well may be the reason for the entrapment."

The diver pulled a five-foot long pry-bar from the large wire-web tool basket, as his partner positioned the rescue basket in a workable position.

He reported his intention to the barge, "We'll attempt to force the jammed door open with a large pry bar."

He groaned into his helmet mike with each push against the bar. "No luck . . . . the two of us will give it a try." After a half-dozen gut wrenching grunts, "Here we go . . . it barely started to move."

The two divers repositioned themselves and their foot placement, "Here we go again."

The group hovering around the video screen aboard the naval vessel feigned the moves of the divers against the pry bar.

A half dozen more collective surges against the bar finally paid positive dividends, as the jammed door suddenly broke free, launching the divers forward against the shell of the downed craft, as the top-side observers breathed a collective sigh of relief.

Breathing heavy, "We've just begun . . . . we now have to tug the door open as it drags against the ocean floor."

Careful not to raise a cloud of ocean floor sediment, one diver slowly shoveled and scraped away thick and heavy bottom sediment in the estimated shape of the door swing path. The top-side spectators gave silent approval as the two divers slowly tugged the chopper door open ninety-degrees. Teddy breathed a sigh of relief, "Good job, guys."

As one diver began to carefully enter the craft, his partner repositioned the dual rescue basket near the open door. The top-side folks, again, held their breath as they saw Jack and Mary slowly fill their viewing screen. The lead diver raised the communications to a personal level. "Mr. Kennedy?"

The Kennedy PR man gave a soft elbow to Teddy, who was like a deer frozen in headlights. "Ah .... yes ... it's Ted Kennedy; what is it."

"Sir, I want you to know first-hand that no matter how things appear from your end, we will pay the utmost respect to your Brother Jack and Mary as we go about their extraction."

"Yes, sir, I realize, and appreciate that very much."

"We'll start with Mary."

With three clear attempts to lift Mary, the diver reported, "That's strange ...."

Teddy interrupts, "How's that?"

"The two seemed to be *joined together as one.*"

"Again, how's that?"

As the diver pulled his knife from its sheave, "They're simply strapped together, sir." Pause, "I'm cutting the strap now."

Teddy's voice trailed off, "Strapped .... what the ...."

As his knife easily cut through Mary's designer belt, Mary slowly rolled away from Jack .... exposing their faces to the camera.

Teddy groaned, breaking the eerie silence, "Oh .... no .... Jack .... Mary ...." Gasping., "Please, sir, ... close their eyes."

Both Mary and Jack nearly looked straight into the divers head camera .... eyes wide open, with a clear trace of peace forever etched upon their faces.

The diver reverently closed their eyes before gently taking Mary into his arms.

He laid Mary, on her back, into the awaiting rescue basket; her arms slowly fell aside in an open position, as if to say, "Here I am Lord, take me .... I am yours."

The second-in-command diver positioned Mary's arms across her breast, and covered her with a bright yellow canvas, before strapping her into the basket.

Ted unashamedly wept, as the process was repeated for his beloved brother, He buried his face in his hands as the bright yellow canvas covered his face.

CHAPTER 7

With the extraction in progress, Air Force One left the runway outside the nation's capital, with the deceased ex-president's brother, Robert F. Kennedy, staff, and press corps aboard. At the same time preparations were in progress for a full State-Military funeral as the nation and international friends mourned the former President of the United States, WW II military war hero, and heroic assassination attempt survivor.

At the same time Mary's family, primarily her sister Tony, would act on behalf of the Pinchot family, while Mary's ex-husband Cord did the same, as it applied specifically to her sons Quentin and Mark. Tony and Cord agreed that they would not get involved with Mexico, and would depend on the government to take responsibility up until Air Force One landed in the states, whereupon they would assume care custody and control of their beloved Mary.

News of the successful extraction, with a lift to top side in progress, spread quickly throughout the rescue flotilla, the numerous surrounding lookie-loo private pleasure crafts, and hovering news helicopters.

The dive captain was the first to break the calm Pacific surface, followed by the twin rescue basket, and immediately after by the second diver. Stark against the blue water were the bright yellow tarps, covering Jack and Mary, for the entire world to view on black and white television.

The dual basket was raised and lowered onto the deck of the naval vessel, where it was immediately covered by a large potable tent-like housing. The tent was vacated and declared off limits by the ship captain, to all accept for a naval Medical Examiner and his female assistant. Two Seaman quickly placed a large stainless steel table and a roller cabinet, containing unseen equipment, inside the tent.

The examiners entered the tent wearing surgical masks and latex gloves . . . . all of which was televised and reported. In the privacy of the tent, they removed the yellow tarps from the victims. The female assistant was the first to comment.

"How can tragic victims look so at peace . . . . with a hint of a smile on both of their faces."

The senior Medical Examiner did not acknowledge, "The Presidents drawn face is clear evidence of his failing health."

They placed a double layer of large towels on the table before lifting the former President from the basket onto the towels.

The assistant echoed her superior, "You're right, he is surprisingly light."

Most of the sea water had drained off and through the wire baskets, leaving their clothes damp. Towels would further leach moisture, as they patted down the front clothing, all before placing Jack into a standard zipper body bag in preparation to transport them ashore for further handling.

They repeated the process for Mary, as she lay on the table next to Jack, who had been bagged, with the zipper closed to his sternum. With Mary, they zipped her bag fully closed. The examiners then turned their attention back to Jack, with the female carefully combing his hair as she best remembered from countless television viewings. She then rolled a towel and placed it around his neck, crossed it over his chest, giving the appearance of white heavy ascot.

The tent was then cleared out, leaving only the table containing the bagged remains, with Jack's face exposed.

The Chief Medical Examiner notified the ship Captain that all was set for Jack's youngest brother, Teddy.

Within moments, Ted and the Kennedy PR man walked arm in arm across the spacious metal deck, with Ted's face ashen and drawn, while unsteady on his feet . . . . in full view of the world.

They paused outside the tent entrance, while Ted took a deep breath of fresh salt air, mumbling, "Give me a minute alone with Jack." With the flotilla knowing what was taking place, all one could hear aboard the naval vassal, was the agonizing sobs of a brother over a brother . . . .

CHAPTER 8

Robert Kennedy's personal aide advised him that Air Force One was on its final, Pacific required, approach into Acapulco's General Juan N. Alvarez International Airport, and that within moments the crash rescue site could be clearly viewed from his in-flight office window.

News of the U.S Presidential aircraft's final approach spread like wildfire throughout the Acapulco region. People, natives and tourists, could be seen from every imaginable prominent point or structure, with camera and or binoculars in hand.

Security around the airport, and designated Air Force One landing destination, was extremely high, with crowd security and control testing the local authorities, U.S. Secret Service, and the well over 200 U.S. troops flown in on special duty.

The temporary reception area, filled with dignitaries, press, and local people of influence, was abuzz with anticipation.

The U.S. military full color guard stood at their designated post.

Bobby's heart sank as the rescue crane-barge, and ever shrinking flotilla, came into view. As if waiting for his fly over, the crane, with his brother's ill-fated craft in its grasp, swung the damaged chopper over and above the barge before lowering it to rest on the barge deck. Within a moment, the barge dropped from site, leaving forever a snap-shot in Bobby's mind.

He sighed, as he turned from the window to his desk, raking his hand through his thick hair. "Dear God . . . . please have mercy on his soul." With that, he laid his head on his forearms and wept.

As Air Force One came to rest, Bobby stepped into his private restroom, rinsed his face with cold water, combed his hair, slipped on his tie and suit jacket, took a deep breath, and glanced in the mirror, "Time to be presidential, that's why they elected you."

With the stairs deployed, red carpet in place, Bobby, stepped into the public view, and smiled as the military band struck up, "Hail to the Chief". The band and the cheering crowd allowed Bobby to speak aloud to himself before descending the stairs. "They're playing our tune, Jack."

His heart warmed as he was greeted at the base of the stair by his lone surviving brother, Teddy, along with long time Kennedy family friend and public relations manager. As the band played on, they hugged one another before continuing a short distance on the red carpet to a portable, shade covered, dais. They mounted the dais to be greeted by the President of Mexico, Gustavo Diaz Ordaz, the U.S. Ambassador, and a handful of local political dignitaries.

Bobby stepped to the microphone, and smiled as he panned the audience. "As President of the United States, I wish that I was here under happier circumstances." With most of the Mexican population being Catholic, he continued. "However, as Christians we are gathered here as a result of an act of God's divine will. As mere mortals, our vision is laser beam narrow compared to that of our Creator. So it's through faith that we have trust and acceptance in His will, and, therefore do not pick and choose what we accept. As we are so clearly told in the Our Father prayer: *Thy kingdom come thy will be done on earth as it is in Heaven . . .*"

He paused for effect. "However, we must be mindful that it was God's will that spared my beloved brother Jack's life during his World War II PT-109 tragedy, and again during his assassination attempt, both of which collectively blessed us with over thirty additional years of his love, friendship, and service."

He cleared his throat, and excused himself. "This time, however, was different, and within a blink of an eye Jack was embraced by his Lord and Savior with: *You have run the race, you have fought the fight, and you have kept the faith; well done, Jack, My good and faithful servant.*"

He paused. "We are also here to receive and honor the worldly remains of Mary Pinchot, Jack's old friend and dedicated care giver . . . . and *Angel of Mercy.*"

"I would like to thank the Mexican government and its entire people for your support and kindness throughout this painful ordeal, as well as all of those who played a part in the rescue effort. I thank you from the bottom of my heart, and you will remain in my thoughts and prayers."

He folded his hands and bowed his head, "May Jack and Mary rest in peace." The crowd answered, "Amen."

With that he turned and shook hands with President Ordaz, and the U.S Ambassador. As he stepped from the dais, the band began the Chopin Funeral March, and within a half dozen cords, two white funeral hearses appeared, moving at a walking pace. The lead hearse containing Jack stopped at the foot of the much broader stairway onto Air Force One, while the second hearse continued to the rear of the plane, stopping at the base of the loading conveyer. From a distance and angular viewpoint from the dais, one could partially see Mary's white casket with gold handles as it was loaded onto the conveyer by mortuary employees. As she disappeared into the planes hold, the conveyer ramp-door immediately closed.

At that moment, with Bobby, Teddy, and family friend standing at the foot of the stairs, six military officer pallbearers stepped forward. As the rear door of the hearse opened, the band stopped playing. As they began to off load Jack's casket, the band began "Hail to the Chief." They slowly carried Jacks flag draped casket up the stairs and into the plane that he so loved. As the casket disappeared into the plane the door was immediately closed.

With that, Bobby, Teddy, and friend mounted the front stairway. Bobby paused at the entrance, waved to the cheering crowd and stepped into the plane. The door immediately closed, and the portable stairway was rolled away. The plane's tow tractor towed the plane to a runway approach ramp. The plane engines were started, the pilot gave the tow tractor driver a thumbs-up, and the plane was set free. The plane rolled to the head of the runway, paused for a signal from the tower, and roared down and up off the runway to a distant cheering crowd.

As the Air Force One passengers were given permission to walk about the plane, Bob and Ted disappeared into the spacious Presidential Office where Jack's flag draped casket lay in state. With the office door locked they both draped their arms and upper bodies on the casket and openly wept.

All the while Mary was alone in the plane's hold.

Bob, Ted, and the family PR man, James Hickey, paused, as their dinner was placed before them in the Presidential private office. James continued as Ted freshened up the wine glasses, while James reached in his jacket packet and pulled out a folded manila envelope.

He held the envelope aloft, "This contains the personal belongs worn by Jack and Mary, and it appears that we may need to put some hush money to work."

Bob and Ted looked perplexed, as James dumped the jewelry in the center of the table. "The necklaces are harmless love split-pendants; the problem lies with the matching, engraved wedding bands."

CHAPTER 9

Out of patriotic respect, the Pinchot family agreed to delay Mary's New Jersey funeral until after Jack's drawn out national state funeral.

The line on Capitol Hill leading to the Rotunda where jack lay in state was three miles long by six in the morning. An estimated 250,000 mourners had solemnly filed past the casket by closing at nine the following morning.

Robert, Ted and Jacqueline arrived thirty minutes after closing and knelt in silent prayer until the body bearers arrived to remove the casket. The uniformed bearers wearing white gloves, dampened to improve their grip, carried the casket out of the Rotunda, down the outdoor stairs, and placed in ceremonially onto the horse drawn caisson

The cortege left the Capital Hill Rotunda and slowly made its way to the White House, where a walking procession would file in and continue to Saint Matthew Catholic Church.

As the cortege and caisson arrived at the White House, five-year-old John Kennedy Jr., standing near his mother Jacqueline, salutes his father's casket as Carolyn stares blankly with a stone and ashen face. Robert and Ted Kennedy take their place directly behind the caisson, while Jackie and her sister Caroline Lee Auchincloss fell in behind the brothers.

Throughout the three quarter mile walk behind the caisson to St. Matthew's Cathedral, the muffled rumble of drums set up a heartbreaking echo.

The caisson arrived at Saint Matthews, and those in the procession were immediately ushered to their seats. Jackie felt further reduction in stature as she, her children, and sister were placed in the fourth Kennedy family pew . . . . wondering what might have been. She felt guilty for the death of her two best friends

Also seated were John Maguire, Ed Drewitch, George "Barney" Ross and Gerald Zinser, all PT-109 crew members whom Kennedy had helped save in August 1943.

The solemn Catholic High Mass, with an amazing choir and organ, was so very sad, with half of those present crying throughout the service. Cardinal Richard Cushing's eulogy was, of course, very touching, and while saying Mass in Latin, he suddenly broke into English: "May the angels, dear Jack, lead you into paradise. May the martyrs receive you at your coming."

The Mass ended and the flag draped coffin was placed back upon the caisson. The band played Hail to the Chief, and Jackie whispered to her son, who raised his right hand in a salute.

The funeral motorcade left St. Matthew's for Arlington National Cemetery; with Americans standing eight to 10 feet deep along a seven-mile funeral route to get a look at a flag-draped caisson go by is one of the most moving sights one could imagine.

The silence of the crowd was deafening, save for the sound of people sobbing. The procession moved at a somber pace. There was nobody trying to run out into the street or alongside. People had tears streaming down their faces. It was just a bare, cold solemn atmosphere . . . . bleak and wintry.

Air Force One is circling between Andrews Air Force Base and Washington, awaiting a signal to begin its run for the Arlington National Cemetery flyby.

Black Jack, the riderless horse, pranced nervously behind the caisson, as its charge worried that the horse might bolt from his grip.

At two o'clock, the procession arrived at Arlington Cemetery. As U.S. and foreign officials and Kennedy family members gather around the gravesite, the Marine Band played The Star-Spangled Banner, followed by the Air Force bagpipes with Mist-Covered Mountain. The coffin is raised from the caisson and carried to the grave.

Fifty jet fighters, flying in a V formation with the last plane missing to symbolize the fallen leader, roar over the cemetery, and then Air Force One dips its wings over the grave.

One official later stated: "Suddenly, seeing this flight of fighters come across, just screaming jets, with one plane missing from the formation—that was heart-wrenching. Then, Air Force One came across the same way.

"I never saw a plane that size, fly so low in my life. And it came over, and dipped its wings, before it took off and gained altitude."

The Irish cadets executed a silent drill. Cardinal Cushing conducted the commitment. A 21-gun salute and three volleys of rifle fire echo across the cemetery

Taps is played, echoing across Arlington, leaving not a dry eye

The crowd stood in chill and silence, as the casket team folded the flag that had been draped over the coffin and handed it to Bobby. The Marines played Eternal Father. Cushing blessed the torch for the eternal flame.

———

Bobby lit the eternal flame, signaling the end of the service

When the crowd finally fell away, the press was asked to leave out of respect. When they begrudgingly dispersed, the lowering device slowly lowered the casket into the awaiting concrete vault.

At the White House, Bob and Ted tirelessly received heads of state and other dignitaries who attended the funeral

As the White House became eerily silent, and after several belts of Irish Whiskey, Bob and Ted called for a driver to make another visit to Arlington cemetery.

As the clocks struck midnight, the brothers laid a single Irish Rose on Jacks grave and poured the balance of their Irish Whiskey on hes freshly sodden grave.

In the quiet privacy of the limo, Ted broke the silence with a trace of a whiskey induced slur. "You know Bobby, even though the clan voted unanimous to James' proposal to erase the paper trail of Jack and Mary's marriage . . . . I feel bad for Mary; by all rights she should, as we speak, occupy the burial vault next to her husband . . . . or brother."

Silence.

With eye contact. "You know Teddy, we can't let feelings . . . . good or bad . . . . stand in the way of Kennedy image and legacy." He dropped his voice as he looked away. "Besides, what the Pinchots don't know, won't hurt them."

"I guess you're right, Bobby . . . . even if it sounds a bit cliché."

Teddy broke a long silence, as the White House came into view. "I assume that the necklaces, wedding rings, and oil painting will be secretly stashed in the usual place."

"Correct . . . . according to James."

CHAPTER 10

Milford, Pennsylvania, Cemetery is located a mile, as the crow flies, from the Pinchot family sprawling estate, Gray Towers. The estate, along with 102 acres had been donated to the federal government during the Kennedy administration, September 24, 1973; ironically, both Jack and Mary were present during the signing-over ceremony . . . . a mere twenty-eight days away from *Dallas*.

The four car funeral caravan, including two black limousines, drove, at a crawl, the half mile from The Church of the Good Shepherd to the cemetery. At high noon, the raw, late fall day was deathly still, gray, and with a very light drizzle . . . . a couple of degrees short of snow flurries. The small town was quiet and vacant.

Mary's only sibling, Tony, sat in the first limo with her husband Ben Bradlee, along with their two pre-teenage children.

Tony spoke in low monotone as she held Ben's hand and stared ahead through the rear window of the black hearse at her sister's white, flower spray covered casket.

"I keep thinking of all the good times we shared over the years at Gray Towers . . . . from childhood through adulthood." She turned to Ben, "Who would have ever thought . . . ." Her voice trailed off as she shivered, pressed closer to Ben, and placed her head on his shoulder.

Ben, twenty-four-seven editor of the Washington Post, was thinking of the Post's exclusive coverage, and hoping that his reporter-photographer, who had just covered the funeral, was waiting at the cemetery for the procession.

"You're right, Tony, who would have ever thought that Mary would die with a former President of the United States."

"And much more, Ben . . . . and *much* more."

Grieving in the second car were Mary's ex-husband, Cord Meyer, and their two sons, Quentin, at twenty, and Mark, at seventeen. Quentin, still harboring anger over his parent's divorce, mumbled icily while staring straight ahead. "And to think that you and Mom could have prevented this entire ordeal."

Cord, ever the top CIA Operative, responded in kind. "Spoken out of immature ignorance . . . . as usual,"

Mark remained silent as he focused on his loving mother and brother Michael, who would soon have the long awaited company of his mother.

The third car, filled with loud rock and roll, were the four children from Tony's previous marriage, the eldest, the eighteen year old driver, Andrew Pittman. The youngest sibling, twelve year-old Tamara Pittman, spoke above Chubby Checker.

"Out of respect for Aunt Mary, could you turn the radio down . . . . or, better yet, *off*."

With sarcasm, "This is just the way Aunt Mary would like it."

Third eldest, niece, Rosamond, chimed in as she popped her gun, "Yeah . . . Aunt Mary was definitely cool."

Alone in the second black limo, Jackie wept yet again . . . . for her second best friend. Wanting to avoid exposing Caroline and Jon to more trauma, with the loss of their beloved *Auntie* Mary, she decided it best to attend the service alone. She shivered as the procession stopped at the burial site.

A canvas weather shield protected the open grave, the pile of displaced earth, along with thirteen chairs. Immediately adjacent to the open grave stood a weather worn vertical gravestone: *Michael Pinchot Meyer, October 6, 1947 ~ December 18, 1956.* The stone silently proclaimed, 'Here I am Mommy, I've been waiting for you'.

The preacher stood solo at the head of the open grave, clutching his Bible to his cold chest.

If one was searching, as was Ben Bradlee, one could spot the reporter-photographer from the *Washington Post* . . . . peering from around the mausoleum of Gifford Pinchot, two time Pennsylvania Governor, and member of Teddy Roosevelt's cabinet; as the founder, and head, of the U.S Forestry Service . . . . and Mary's Uncle.

The hearse door opened and Cord, Ben, Quinten, and Mark stepped forward, with grim faces, and slowly carried Mary's light remains a hundred feet up a slight incline, to the burial site, located in cluster a of bare skeletal towering Elm trees.

As the Lutheran minister began the service, ironically the light drizzle turned to ice crystals as each harbored their own thoughts:

Cord: *Irony*
Quentin: *The love for his Mother, and anger toward his Father*
Mark: *The love for his Mother, and envy of Michael*
Ben: *The Washington Post's exclusive report*
Jackie: *What could have been . . . at her own hand, and the absolute disastrous marriage she had entered into . . . . as an alternative to the here and now.*
Tony: *The undying love of her much admired, ever protective big sister.*

Tony did not hear a *spiritual* word said during the heart of the service as she, almost smugly, with a wry smile, thought of the secret she and Mary shared . . . . only as loving sisters can.

The head of the handful of those outside the Pinchot family that harbored the secret had forewarned her, *for her own good*, to never utter a word to anyone . . . . even in death.

Tony returned to the here and now as the Minister closed with: "May Mary rest in peace."

Tony and all present answered "Amen"

Le fin, ć est tout
An deireadh, c̓rioch
The end

PART IV

THE PASSING(S)

In keeping with the genre(s) and objective of this literary endeavor, Part I ended short of the actual deaths of the two lead characters, whereas their deaths were fictionalized in Parts II and III; clearly it would be unconscionable to close without setting the record straight about the actual passing of JFK and Mary . . . therefore, Part IV.

JFK

Unlike the death of Mary Pinchot-Meyer, the details of the assassination of John Fitzgerald Kennedy, the 35th president of the United States, are well known by all Americans as well as by many foreigners of all nations. Because of this, and not out of disrespect to the reader, details of the assassination are kept to a minimum.

On November 21, 1963, President Kennedy flew to Texas to give several political speeches. The following day, Friday, as his open limousine drove slowly past cheering crowds in Dallas, shots rang out. Kennedy was seriously wounded and died a short time later. Within a few hours of the shooting, police arrested Lee Harvey Oswald and charged him with the murder. On November 24, another man, Jack Ruby, shot and killed Oswald, thus silencing the only person who could have offered more information about this tragic event. The Warren Commission was organized to investigate the assassination and to clarify the many questions which remained. Sadly, the Warren report created more questions and doubt than it provided concrete answers.[337]

MARY

On Monday, October 12, 1964, the sky above Washington DC was clear and blue, the verdant foliage stubbornly staved off the effects of fall with an abbreviated streak of Indian summer. The imposing dome of the Capital and the crisp white Washington Monument faced one another across the Mall in a landscape of lush green and marble, central within the *city of magnificent distance.*[338] However, beyond the edges of the postcard-like view of the great District, at ground level Washington, laid a paradoxical sprawl of poverty. Entire sections of the crime, rat, tuberculosis infested hidden city were crumbling beneath decades of poverty. Blacks represented the majority within the shameful stealth city of decay, many living in slum houses erected for black refugees of the Civil War—some, appallingly, without plumbing, electricity, or phones.[339]

The White House, in all of its historic glory and architectural splendor, remained a symbol of the tragic assassination of John F. Kennedy less than a year earlier.

One mile, as the eagle flies, from the White House lay old colonial Georgetown, linked to DC by two bridges spanning the deep chasm route of Rock Creek. Civility ruled in the city delineated by clean narrow cobblestone tree-lined streets edged with red used brick sidewalks, fronted with renovated and pseudo restored late 1800 circa two story stone and brick houses. The sidewalks were vacant, save for the occasional black domestic servant scurrying to her work quarters, or an elegant white woman visiting friends. Generally, the sight of men in daylight was a rarity, for these important international figure residents merely slept there, while they all but lived their jobs across the bridges in D.C.

In an above garage studio behind the ivy covered red brick Georgetown home owned by Washington Post journalist Ben Bradlee, a woman was painting. She had short blond hair, striking blue observing eyes that missed little, and full sensuous lips that were quick to smile. Mary was two days short of turning forty-four and, even under the worst of conditions, passed for being a full ten years younger. Divorced, and her two teenage sons at school in Connecticut and New Hampshire, she was alone and free to choose her companions—most of which were vivid and artistic.[340]

Although she had entertained British theater director Peter Brook the previous evening,[341] it was there, inside her studio, where she felt most alive. The shelves were lined with paint and an assortment of art supplies placed between a collection of small personal items of special meanings, fall leaves, odd shaped stones, and late season roses from the garden. Various sizes of brightly colored paintings and blank canvases leaned against all available wall space. She glanced out the window above the sun blanketed rear garden and, for future artistic purposes, registered the intense blue of the cloud free sky. It was clearly an ideal day for walking.

Just short of noon, she propped up before a fan to dry the canvas that she had spent the morning covering with pale blues and grays in a style named after the Washington Color School, of which she was a charter member. Satisfied, she slipped into a pair of tan pedal-pusher slacks, a powder blue mink and lamb's wool sweater, and paint spattered canvas sneakers. She donned her Ray-Bans and set off for her daily walk along the Chesapeake and Ohio Canal towpath. Upbeat from her morning's progress, she left the little studio in the alleyway off N Street and strolled down the cobble stoned hill toward the Potomac River, passing trim brick houses with red and gray doors with ornate brass mail slots and door knockers.[342]

While crossing M Street, a long black sedan with official plates slowed as the rear window rolled down. One of the capital's most prominent women, Polly Wisner, wife of Frank Wisner, head of the CIA's worldwide covert operations. Polly, on her way to London where her husband was stationed, waved and bid her friend goodbye in a refined accent of a movie star, "Good-bye, Maahry." She would be the last friend to see the artist, author, and journalist alive.[343]

Soon she was on the canal towpath far below street level, and passed below the old brownstone trolley garage, now used by the CIA as a training site for third-world police forces.[344] Continuing along the towpath, distancing her from town and civilization, she encountered someone near a cottonwood tree. Two men working on a disabled automobile on the street high above the path heard her scream her last words, "Someone help me!" [345] Before the mechanics could cross the busy street, look over the stone ledge and into the woods, two shots rang out. As if by a trained shooter, the first shot was to the back of the head that would have eventually killed her. She clung to the Cottonwood tree before losing consciousness and falling to the ground. The killer then placed the muzzle of his weapon between her shoulder blades and fired a second shot that missed the spine and tore through her aorta and cut off the blood flow to her heart, turning everything black in one final breath. The killer disappeared into the thick sprawling woods, leaving her body to the police . . . and speculation through the ages.[346]

THE FUNERAL

The massive gray stone National Cathedral is located at the highest point on Wisconsin Avenue, overlooking Georgetown. Construction of *America's cathedral* took a century, and parts of it remained unfinished on this day. Two hundred mourners gathered inside the cathedral's Bethlehem Chapel to pay their final respects to Mary Eno Pinchot-Meyer on what would have been her birthday, October 14, 1964. It fell to her brother-in-law, Ben Bradlee, to make and coordinate the funeral arrangements. The heavy scent of white lilies and chrysanthemums filled the air of the crowded chapel. With the coffin draped in the flag, many of the deceased artist's closest friends felt that journalist, Bradlee, had overdone it, given Mary's penchant for simplicity. However, the setting was apropos to many of the mourners who were accustomed to pomp.[347]

Most attending the service that day were members of Washington's higher echelon, insiders of the social scene of the Kennedy administration, accustomed to exclusive clubs, White House invitations, and privates jets. The men were of the nation's most influential politicians, lawyers, diplomats, journalists, spies, and fixers. Their women were conversant in the latest political gossip, were witty, and wielded power in their cocktail party and dinner lists. Their government salaries were made redundant by family money. Many were tight-knit residents of Georgetown.[348]

The brutal murder of Mary stunned the little community. She was well-liked and a respected member of the social group formed around the Kennedy administration and the cold warriors. Her ex-husband, Cord Meyer, was one of the highest officers in the CIA, and her brother-in-law, Ben Bradlee, was Washington's highest profile journalist.[349] Prior to Mary's demise, she was a member of *the* tight social circle and subsequently had become a fixture at the White House . . . and JFK's lover up until his ill-fated departure to Dallas. Additionally, she was the only one of Jack's lovers, who he fondly and openly referred to as *Mary-Mary*, which Jackie ever insisted he "get rid of". Her intuition told her that Mary was more than one of his usual playthings; Jack and Mary were clearly soul-mates. These facts formed the central mystery and cold irony surrounding her untimely death.

With the mourners seated, Episcopal bishop, Paul Moore, slowly approached the altar. The bishop was a family friend who had known Mary, her ex-husband Cord, and Ben Bradlee since the 1930s. He spoke of Mary's "friendship, honesty, sensitivity, and beauty that flowed into the lives of all present." He then called for forgiveness, "We cannot know why such a terrible, ugly, irrational thing should have happened." He paused, "We can only sense it was some way bound-up with sin and sickness of the entire world . . . somewhere perhaps in a pattern invisible to anybody else except God Himself." He then asked for prayers for "that demented soul" who caused the "senseless tragedy"[350], and went so far as to imply that the heinous act was the act of poverty and injustice . . . as if the killer were the real victim. This caused much hushed murmuring within the chapel. A minority did believe the police theory that Mary was the unlikely victim of a random assault by a twenty-five-year-old black day laborer, named Ray Crump Jr., who was arrested not far from the scene. However, a wide majority within the chapel were concerned with Mary being a sometimes reckless woman with access to the highest levels of the American government. Ironically, there were several US government spies mourning within the chapel that very day.[351]

It had been less than a year since the assassination of President Kennedy. The Warren Commission's report had been released just two weeks prior to Mary's murder. The report concluded that Lee Harvey Oswald had acted alone in the shooting of the president. Most Americans did not question its conclusion—at least not yet. However, the murder of the president's lover coming so soon after the assassination was disquieting, especially within the Georgetown community. Many found it strange the way the police and newspapers rushed to judgment about who had *assassinated* Mary.[352]

Cord Meyer wept inconsolably throughout the ceremony, as his and Mary's teenage sons, Mark and Quentin, sat still and quiet like deer caught in headlights. Until that day, many in Georgetown had not realized how much he still loved the woman who had divorced him seven years earlier. Cord Meyer was comforted in his pew by a CIA colleague and warm personal friend, Richard Helms, who would eventually head the CIA. The two went back more than a decade in the CIA and had weathered many storms together. Cord was a tall handsome man whose glass eye, which replaced the one destroyed by shrapnel from a Japanese grenade, always stared straight ahead. Instead of a life he had envisioned full of success and public acclaim, he was buried deep within the secret bureaucracy of the CIA. He was currently a top CIA cold war operative overseeing a network of CIA front groups. Cord was known around Georgetown and D.C. as a confrontational man who sometimes drank too much; his passionate need to win every disagreement had become legendary.[353]

The fact that Mary's death concerned the CIA bigwigs is noted within an FBI memo written by William C. Sullivan, J. Edgar Hoover's number-two man, to reschedule a meeting between CIA director John McCone and Helms and other FBI officials, from 10/14 (the day of the funeral) to the following day. In the memo, Helms explained that he and Angleton had been very much involved with matters pertaining to the death of Mrs. Mary Pinchot-Meyer.[354] Years later, Helms claimed that he could not recall exactly what the matters were that pertained to Mary's death other than attending the funeral.[355]

The "Angleton" referred to in the memo was James Jesus Angleton, Cord's closest friend and fellow Yale graduate, second only to Hoover as the nation's greatest collector of personal secrets. Angleton had been personally close to Mary as well. He occupied the post of CIA counterintelligence chief. Half Mexican, and half Anglo-Saxon, Angleton was stooped and cadaverous, with fingers stained yellow from years of smoking. He had a reputation for paranoia, and never opened the blinds or the curtains in his office. He was rarely seen, but his pronouncements were taken seriously. Some referred to him as "the CIA's answer to the Delphic Oracle."[356]

In his fight against Communism, Angleton made it his business to stay on top of the private affairs of those residents of Georgetown with lives so intimately connected to national security that they seemed obvious tempting targets for a Communist looking to recruit a traitor. He had already gained possession of Mary's diary, letters, and papers that revealed the story of her most personal life. Ben Bradlee had personally handed Angleton the information in an act of national security . . . and family embarrassment. Later Angleton would boast of having bugged Mary's phone and bedroom; [357] he hypocritically served as an usher at Mary's service.[358]

The pews were sprinkled with CIA spies and operatives involved in many things the American public would be made aware of years later. They were intimately involved in the CIA's attempt to assassinate Castro, and other foreign leaders. Rafael Trujillo of the Dominican Republic was one such victim . . . killed with American supplied weapons. They were responsible for the CIA's mind-control drug experimentation on unwitting civilians. They were covertly influencing the politics of countries from Italy to Iran, and much of Latin America. Cord had recently organized student protests and phony labor strikes in the Dominican Republic and

Brazil to thwart Communism. Angleton knew that the CIA was illegally opening mail of American citizens to aid the battle against Communism; he would later defiantly tell congressional investigators that he was personally overseeing the operation.[359]

Many journalists filled the pews as well, most always knew more than they could print, chief amongst them was Mary's brother-in-law, Ben Bradlee. He was of a prominent banking family, was Harvard educated, and spoke fluent French, but concealed his pedigree behind a streetwise front honed as a war hardened military officer. His controlled savvy and street persona enabled him to fit right in with the Hollywood Rat Pack style favored by the late president. On first meeting Bradlee, one male acquaintance thought that *Newsweek's* Washington bureau chief was a bookie.[360]

Bradlee was married to Mary's younger sister Tony, her second marriage. Together they were raising six children in the large brick Georgetown house where Mary resided in the back house and above garage studio. As one of Georgetown's golden couples, they had frequently dined alone with Jack and Jackie, in the White House. Like Mary, Tony was also blond, blue eyed, and beautiful, but taller and more angular. She was a stunning dresser and more restrained and formal than her older sister. At the service, Tony sat next to her mother, Ruth Pickering-Pinchot, a New Yorker, and former journalist herself, who would become increasingly reclusive following the death of her eldest daughter.[361]

Many of the mourners were artists who knew Mary as an artist, and through gallery openings and cultural events. One of Mary's former lovers, Kenneth Noland, traveled down from New York for the service. His affair with Mary coincided with one of the more productive periods of his career. It was at the funeral that he met Cord Meyer for the first time, who he would later recall as being on the *spooky side*. Alice Denney, the assistant director of the Washington Gallery of Modern Art, was in attendance; she had exhibited Mary's work in the past. She was horrified by the murder, with the presence of all of the intelligence agents only adding to the sinister undertone for her; she had never seen this side of Mary's world.[362]

William Walton, a former war correspondent, and artist, who had been a close friend of Ernest Hemingway, was present. He had served as Mary's *walker* on several occasions, escorting her to intimate evenings in the White House on the pretext that she was his date. Also present was portrait painter, Marian Cannon Schlesinger, wife of Arthur Schlesinger, who had played tennis with Mary at the White House.[363]

A tight-knit group of women in the chapel were Vassar graduates who had spent their college years in the early forties with Mary on the Poughkeepsie, New York, campus. They were confident, elegant and refined by lives formed by old money. Most were married in kind, were mothers, and considered Mary's independence, and somewhat Bohemian lifestyle, as a source of light and vitality. They sat together in a daze and found it hard to believe their vibrant friend was dead.[364]

Anne Chamberlain, an impish journalist for *Time* magazine, was one of Mary's best friends. She had covered Jackie as the future first-lady waited, pregnant, in Hyannis Port for Jack to win the Democratic nomination in 1960. Chamberlain, born Anne Nevin, was divorced and, like Mary, was adventurous. She had spent one full vacation from Vassar driving solo across the Andes in Peru before living in Paris. [365]

Unable to attend the service were two of Mary's closest of friends, James and Anne Truitt; they had recently moved to Tokyo, as he accepted the position of Japan bureau chief for *Newsweek*. Anne was, like Mary, an artist and a mother. Mary trusted the Truitts so much that she had confided in them about her intimate relationship with President Kennedy. James came from a prominent Maryland family, and was well known for his intelligence, eccentricity, social graces, heavy drinking, and being close personal friends of both Cord Meyer and Angleton. Unlike Mary, Anne was a graduate of Bryn Mawr. [366]

The night following Mary's death, Anne placed a phone call from Tokyo to Georgetown that ignited a chain of events that would shroud Mary's life and death in mystery for decades. As they sat at home in shocked silence, Ben and Tony Bradlee received the call. Anne told Tony, it was a matter of urgency that they find Mary's diary before the police got to it and her private life became a matter of public record. Anne then repeated the phone message to CIA counterintelligence chief James Angleton. Although neither party knew all of the details of her relationship with the late president, they knew enough of her lifestyle to agree with Anne Truitt. Mary's papers must not end up in the wrong hands. A frantic search began. [367]

Mary Meyer's murder and the national security community took on an atmosphere of the unknown that permeated her life as the wife of Cord Meyer. At the time of her death, the CIA was engaged in an intense covert intelligence war spread from Washington to the back alleys of Saigon. There was an enormous paranoia rooted secrecy issue that pervaded the intelligence community. There were spies everywhere in DC and Georgetown; spies for France, Germany, Israel, England, and Russia.[368] The spies often plied their trade over three-martini lunches in plain view of anyone who cared to watch. The casual observer might even notice a manila envelope being passed beneath the dining table between a foreign diplomat and an American State Department official or an American intelligence agent. The FBI and CIA went so far as to plant bugs beneath and around restaurant dining tables in an attempt to snag a traitor or foreign spy. Some waiters and busboys were known to be federal agents. Real life was truly stranger than fiction within cold war Washington.[369]

Highly ambitious, competitive, and power hungry men have always been attracted to Washington. The bulk of the cold-war warriors, having served as officers in WW II, evolved into brash, atomic-era like machismo men hungry for both action and power. They emulated the popular Rat Pack lifestyle, and adorned themselves with numbers of women. If a wife did not find this attractive, they were very unhappy women. Men simply overshadowed their women, and felt far too important to involve their wives in what they were doing. There was no room for partners in it, the women were isolated and reduced to mere social decorations. Socially, the gatherings were polarized with men talking work, while the wives were left to talk about children and school . . . the wives were just wives. [370]

Mary was a mysterious woman in life, and in life her real personality lay just beneath the surface. Like the lives of her female friends, hers was domestic and private. She and her friends were understandably affected by the condescending attitude and treatment by their men. During the Kennedy era, women remained in the background, with the prevailing notion that they were present for male amusement. Although they were very educated, refined women, they never asked to share power with their husband in any public way, they simply remained willing mothers of the baby-boom. After dinners, in time-honored tradition, women retreated to a room separate from the men. [371]

In male centered Washington, women had their own code of ethics. One thing was they were skillful flirts, for men were the only way to economic and political power. With a powerful man at their sleeve, certain women became leaders, with her whims and behavior copied as high school girls in a clique. However, a nonconforming individual would occasionally appear; one of them was Mary Pinchot-Meyer. Her manner and charm were natural and forthcoming, but there was a reserve to her as well. She allowed but a few to gain entry to her inner self. Mary, in one word, was complicated. She wanted personal freedom and authority at a time when society rejected such qualities in a woman. She was attracted to glamour and drama, yet radiated warmth and simplicity. Being in smoke filled rooms with powerful men and vivid conversation quickened her blood and her sense of belonging. She had a special effect on men, one stating that she reminded him of a cat walking on a rooftop in moonlight.[372] She was polished and cool, and paid attention to men, making them feel interesting and special. Mary had become a White House insider at a time when being a member of the Kennedy clique was the ultimate of a Washington woman's achievement. [373]

The tragedy of Mary's death was amplified by its timing. Born into luxury, and with unquestionable beauty, she was well educated and she appeared to have led, at least on the surface, a very charmed life. But she had endured family suicide, marriage to a difficult wounded World War II veteran, the tragic accidental death of her son Michael, and then a divorce. Through it all, Mary had retained the energy and vitality her friends loved and admired. In her final years, she had made inroads into carving out a niche for herself as a rare creature for her time . . . that of an independent woman. Mary was killed in the prime of her life.[374]

It was a combination of her personality and her access to Kennedy and other powerful men that made her the figure of power and mystery after her death. One insightful journalist referred to Mary as the Lady Ottoline Morrell of Camelot, referring to the famed British incurable romantic who was friend and patron to many artistic people. Others claimed that Mary was a force for peace during the most frightening years of the Cold War. However, it was in death that Mary left the private world she shared with the closest of her female friends and became part of a legend. [375]

THE ARREST

Two mechanics tending to a disabled Nash Rambler on Canal Road, high above the towpath, were the only ones to hear Mary's final plea, "Somebody help me!"[376] Moments later, they heard a gunshot. One of the mechanics stepped into the street toward the wall that separated the road from a view of the towpath below; in route, a second shot was fired. By the time he threaded his way through traffic, reached the wall and peered down to the towpath below, he saw a small black man, wearing a tan jacket and dark baseball hat, scurry from the prone body of a woman that lay on the towpath approximately 120 feet in a line of sight from where the mechanic stood. The *apparent* assailant immediately disappeared into the thick woods adjacent to the towpath. [377]

Looking at Mary's body coiled motionless in a fetal position, it was clear to the auto mechanic that something terrible had just occurred. He quickly drove to the ESSO station, near Key Bridge, less than a minute away, and called the police. As he exited the phone booth, a squad car pulled into the station. Police estimates claim that within four minutes of the police arrival to the crime scene (approximately fifteen to twenty minutes from the shooting), all *conventional* exits from the towpath were sealed, with the only *apparent* means of escape being to swim the river and climb the dangerously steep cliff to Canal Road.[378]

More than a dozen uniformed officers from the Seventh Precinct participated in a foot search of the sprawling heavily wooded area. Within forty-five minutes of the shooting, the head of a black male was spotted as it momentarily poked out of the thicket located a mile east of the crime scene. Thirty minutes later, an hour and a quarter from the shooting, a lone officer stumbled across the *alleged* shooter about three-hundred feet east of where Mary lay. A small black man, soaking wet, dressed in a white T-shirt and black pants stepped from the undergrowth into a clearing within twenty-five

343

feet of an officer. As the officer approached, the man made no attempt to flee. The suspect produced a valid driver's license identifying himself as Raymond Crump, Jr., age twenty-five and a resident of Washington, D.C. When asked, he claimed to have fallen in the water while fishing. As the officer and Crump approached the crime scene,[379] the auto mechanic, who phoned the police, excitedly pointed at Crump and claimed he was the man he had spotted earlier running from Mary's prone body into the woods . . . even though the alleged shooter was no longer wearing a hat or jacket. Crump was immediately patted down but no weapon was found, he was then handcuffed and placed under arrest.[380]

Later that afternoon, police recovered a light tan zippered jacket floating in the river within a thousand feet of the murder scene; in a pocket was a pack of Pall Mall cigarettes, Crump's brand. The following day, the police fished a dark baseball cap from the river near the crime scene. The jacket and hat were identified by Crump's wife as belonging to her husband[381]. A fishing pole was found in the closet of Crump's home the evening of the murder.[382]

At the police station, as well as later at his arraignment, Crump repeated his fishing story, adding that he had heard shots that were close enough to him that he squatted, soaking wet, close to the ground in fear of being hit.[383]

Crump was held in jail without bond as authorities tried to identify the dead woman. She was beautiful and there was something about her, even in death, that suggested money and importance. The auto mechanic that called the police, and later identified Crump as the assailant, said that she even looked beautiful with a bullet in her head.[384]

As Crump was being booked, interrogated, and jailed, the police scrambled to identify the murder victim. The only personal effect on the body was a tube of lipstick in her pocket. She carried no identification, however, there was a faint cleaners mark "Meyer" on the inside of her expensive soft leather gloves. The police spent short of eight hours phoning every Meyer listed in the D.C. white pages before they finally identified her relationship to *Newsweek's* Washington bureau chief Ben Bradlee. That night, insisting his wife Tony remain at home, Bradlee undertook the grim task of identifying his sister-in-law's body at the morgue.[385]

THE ACCUSED

Ray Crump Jr. was born February 25, 1939, in the small cotton farming hamlet of Norwood, North Carolina. All of the black Crumps in the Norwood area were descended from slaves owned by the white Crump family. The black and white Crumps had been living for nearly two centuries in the Norwood region at the time of Ray's birth. The current and future of the black Crumps living in the Norwood region at the time of Ray's birth was grim at best.[386] When Ray was ten, the advent of advanced farming technology coupled with residue from the Great Depression forced his family to join the great black northern exodus to Washington, D.C., Philadelphia, New Jersey, and New York. The Crump family arrived in Washington and settled into the city of Southwest, the smallest and poorest of the capital city's four sections.

By the time Ray Crump was twenty-one, he had attained his full adult height of five feet six inches. He was a small man, with a head that seemed disproportionably large, his poor eyes did not match, had a clear learning disability, and did not graduate from high school. He suffered from severe headaches thought to be caused by a beating he received during a 1962 attempted robbery on him. His drinking problem surfaced as a teenager, and he was jailed more than once for public intoxication. He was known to be a violent drunk, and had a record of physical abuse against his wife. There is no record of a toxicology test being taken during his arrest.[387]

Ray worked as a day-laborer, more occasional than not. On the day of Mary's murder, he was supposed to be doing menial construction work, gained by standing in a worker selection line in a vacant lot on the northwest side of town at daybreak; there was no record or witness of him having been in the line on the morning of the murder.[388]

THE TRIAL

Martha Crump's biggest fear was that her son, Ray, would be yet another racial victim of a judicial system controlled by white society . . . even more so if left to the hands of a public defender. She, therefore, pleaded with the pastor of her Second Baptist Church for help. In turn, the day following Mary's funeral, the pastor and Martha Crump visited black attorney Dovey Roundtree.[389]

Dovey, nee Johnson, Roundtree was both perfect for and up to the task, for she had experienced and witnessed first-hand a lifetime of racial injustice; starting as a child growing up in Charlotte, North Carolina, up through her years within the D.C. judicial system. She told Ray's anguished mother and the pastor that their fears were well-founded. They related that the D.C. black community felt that even if Ray was innocent, he was a dead duck.[390]

Dovey had, in fact, been following the headlines of Mary's murder. In accepting the case, she considered it a clear omen that Martin Luther King had been awarded the Nobel Peace Prize on the very day of Mary's funeral.[391]

The day she agreed to represent the defense, the case was already moving at a fast pace. The prosecution had already dispensed with a preliminary hearing, a fact that Dovey would object to and appeal. A trial date of less than a month away had been set. Dovey immediately got a continuance.[392]

At the time of Dovey's initial meeting with Crump, he had been locked up for four days in the D.C. jail, an old stone building some compared to a dungeon. He was being held in solitary confinement. She was struck by his small stature and utter sense of dejection. He just kept crying and crying, she recalled. She found him extremely uncommunicative and apathetic, which made it difficult to plan a defense. She found him a little man, completely terrified. She was startled that he could not remember why he was there.[393]

Martha Crump was sure that her son would be killed by the white guards or inmates, and she called Dovey on a daily basis with pleas to get her son out of the building.[394]

One of Dovey's first moves was to try to get Crump ruled insane and unfit to stand trial. Ray was moved from his cell to the local mental hospital where psychiatrists examined him. After six days of examination and interviews, the accused was pronounced fit to stand trial. Undeterred, and with the trial several months away, Dovey was not about to let her client be railroaded into a death sentence or life in prison verdict . . . his only two options if found guilty. Dovey put up a gallant pretrial fight using every legal trick and maneuver in the book. She set forth motions to suppress evidence, and was denied. She formally objected to Ray being indicted without a preliminary hearing, the government won on the basis that the grand jury had found cause to indict him. She objected to the prosecution's request to take a sample of hair from Crump's head; that too was denied.[395]

Crump's trial pitted the old white establishment against the black discriminated underclass, at a time when few whites wanted such a fight. In this fight, the white elite was represented by the victim. In addition, the white police force and a white prosecutor's office were under the control of Attorney General Robert Kennedy. The U.S. Attorney for D.C. was David Acheson, son of former Secretary of State Dean Acheson. David had been a personal friend of Mary Meyer, and had attended Yale with Cord. The judge assigned to preside over the case was Judge Howard Corcoran. His law clerk for the trial was a young lawyer fresh out of law school named Robert Bennett, who would later represent President Bill Clinton in a sexual harassment lawsuit. In spite of the array of prosecution firepower, the prosecutor himself, Alfred Hantman, could very well be a stroke of luck for the defense. Although a twenty-five year veteran of the D.C. criminal court system, Hantman lacked creativity and was uninspiring in his court room style. What he lacked is what Roundtree had to her very bone marrow . . . charm. Furthermore, Hantman was not privy to the social connection that linked the victim, the U. S. Attorney, and the C.I.A. [396]

Roundtree was not privy to those connections either. No matter how hard she tried to know Mary, she came up empty handed. It was as if Mary existed only on the towpath the day of her murder.[397] She had learned that Mary was divorced, lived alone, was the mother of two teenage boys who were away at boarding school, and that her ex-husband was responsible for their education. She remained clueless as to what Cord did for a living, other than being a civil servant. Roundtree thought if Mary had a promiscuous lifestyle, there was the possibility of a jilted lover or even an angry ex-husband being the killer.[398] However, Judge Corcoran, in pretrial admonishments, refused to allow either side to mention the private lives, or families, of the defendant or the victim.[399]

On July 20, 1965, the trial began. The jury pool, of sixty men and women, selected from the voter registration rolls, were a cross-section of D.C., mostly black, over forty, and mostly government employees. What they saw the opening day was a study in human contrast. While the prosecutor, Hantman, looked grim, and every bit the air force officer he had once been, the defense, Dovey Roundtree, was far younger than Hantman, soft featured, neat graying hair, and wore a pastel colored dress to offset the darkness of the business at hand. Crump sat quietly at the defense table, head bowed, wearing a new suit that his mother's church congregation had bought him for the trial. [400]

Journalists packed the courtroom, amongst them was a young man named Sam Donaldson of future television fame. Dovey took note of the high class white people in the crowd, the men mostly wearing well tailored grey suites.[401]

By the end of the first day, a jury had been selected, eight women and four men—two of them were white—with an average age older than forty.[402] Most were housewives or federal employees. The jury foreman was a black male and worked for the Job Corps of Economic Opportunity. Both Roundtree and Hantman thought they had a fair jury.[403]

On the second day of the trial, Hantman delivered his opening statement pacing back and forth in front of the jury box. In cold military fashion, he checked off a minute-by-minute account of Mary's final walk on the towpath, her death struggle, her final screams, the gunshots, the man seen standing over the body, the finding of Crump's jacket and hat, and the discovery of Crump-soaking wet. He detailed the closing of all *known* exits from the towpath, the expediency of the police arrival, search, and discovery of the accused. In closing, Hantman promised to bring in a map of the towpath area proving that, with the exists sealed, there was no escape from the crime scene except by swimming the Potomac River or climbing the all but vertical cliff up to the roadway where the mechanic witnessed the scene. He even went so far as to suggest that he would bring in the very tree that Mary clung to in her final attempt to remain upright before receiving the second bullet between her shoulder blades.[404]

Hantman was so confident that it was an open-and-shut case he closed by stating that there would be no weapon or any blood that tied the defendant to the victim. Although an extensive search of the towpath area and dredging of the river took place two full days following the murder, the weapon was never found. They had even gone so far as to drain the canal by closing an upstream lock—all to no avail.[405]

As first witness for the prosicution, Hantman called Ben Bradlee, Washington Bureau chief for *Newsweek* and future *Washington Post* editor who would one day collaborate with Woodward, Bernstein, and *deep-throat* of Watergate fame. Bradlee established that he was the victim's brother-in-law, in that he was married to Mary's younger sister, Antoinette, and that he had officially identified that the dead woman had indeed been Mary Eno Pinchot-Meyer. Hantman asked Bradlee, under oath, if he had gained entry to the studio behind his house that was occupied by Mary. After answering to the affirmative, he asked him if he had recovered any personal documents and writings in his search of the studio. Strangely, he mentions a few letters and miscellaneous documents but never made mention of having, in fact, found Mary's most personal diary. It has never been made clear as to whether Hantman knew of the diary and had been instructed to stay clear of it, or if Bradlee had intentionally committed perjury. Hantman then asked if Bradlee had any other information germane to his sister-in-law's death. The journalist answered in the negative and was excused.[406]

The medical examiner was the second to testify. The two shots were both fired at point-blank range, proven by what the examiner referred to as 'dark haloes' on the skin around both entry wounds—including the one beneath the layer of a sweater and blouse.[407] The first shot had come from someone holding the gun to the back and side of the head, and the bullet traversed the base of the skull, lodging at the other side. The medical examiner stated that a person with that kind of wound could possibly move up to twenty-five feet before losing consciousness. He said that explained the blood on her gloves, for during that period she instinctively brought her hands up to her temples. The second shot went between her shoulder blades, missed the spine and severed the artery carrying blood to the heart.[408]

Next, the prosecutor presented the government's first piece of evidence, a fifty-five foot map of the towpath area designed by a Park Service employee. The mapmaker testified that there were only five ways out of the towpath within miles from the murder scene. The mapmaker proved to be a disastrous witness for the prosecution when Roundtree raised a series of objections, the strongest questioning being his and his map's integrity. She had him add the word '*known*' to the number of exits from the towpath,[409] for every young boy in the neighborhood of the towpath knew of several 'favorite' and 'secret' exits. At that point, the mapmaker lost his temper and demolished the map's credibility. The mapmaker cooled down, and admitted that he could only speak to the official records kept within his office. The jury members familiar with the area later stated that there are multiple non-charted exits that a killer could have used for an escape and not be noticed.[410]

The second day of the trial, the government's star witness took the stand; he was the twenty-four year old mechanic who had witnessed a black man standing over Mary's body from a street high above and away from the murder scene. The mechanic, an ex-military MP, said that he was attending to a Rambler automobile that had broken down on Canal Road which paralleled the towpath located below. He testified that he heard the victim scream, followed momentarily by two shots separated by three to five seconds. After hearing the second shot, he turned from the Rambler, crossed the street and peered over a stone wall and down at the towpath where he observed a black man standing over a prone motionless woman laying in a fetal position on the towpath. He estimated the distance to be one fifty to two hundred feet from his position on the cliff to that of the victim. When questioned, the mechanic stated that the black man standing over the body was wearing a dark baseball cap and tan jacket. He estimated his size at five foot eight and weighing one hundred eighty-five pounds. He further stated that the accused appeared to have nothing in his open hands.[411]

Fortunately for Crump, the mechanic had overestimated the weight and the height of the perpetrator—by two inches and forty-five pounds. Cross-examining the mechanic, Roundtree pounded home the discrepancies. After the trial, he complained that the police had failed to back up his identification by further detailed investigation. He further said, with disappointment, that "It was me against Crump."[412]

The city police officers had little to add to the mechanic's testimony, other than that they had responded as promptly as humanly possible to the crime scene, and immediately sealed off all exits from the towpath. Roundtree gently ridiculed their testimony, asking if the police had stopwatches on the towpath that day to verify that they had arrived at the scene precisely four minutes after the murder. She further corrected their statement mentioning *five exits* from the towpath to that of five *known exits*.[413]

The police testified about the conflicting reasons he had given for being on the towpath on the day of the crime in his condition, soaking wet, with minor bleeding from his right hand, with his pants torn and half unzipped. He had told one officer that he cut his hand on some rocks while trying to retrieve his fishing pole from the water. He told another officer that he had cut his hand on a fishing hook. He told a third officer that he had fallen into the river while walking away from his fishing site, and yet another officer that he had fallen into the river while asleep.[414] Neither pole nor fishing equipment were found at the scene, although what he claimed as a second pole and tackle box was discovered by police in his home closet. The police also stated that Crump's wife had identified the dark baseball cap and tan jacket fished out of the river as belonging to her husband. She further stated that her husband had left the house early in the morning on the day of the crime, with the understanding he was going to work as a day laborer—wearing the dark hat and tan jacket, with no fishing equipment in his possession.[415]

The prosecution presented its theory about Crump's movements after the crime. They alleged that he had run west through the woods for about a mile, dropping his cap then his jacket in the river. He then poked his head out of the woods, just long enough to spot an officer, before running back in an easterly direction to and then five-hundred feet beyond the body. Finally, he got wet trying to swim around an open culvert before literally running into the arresting officer. However, the moment of the murder remained invisible as Hantman was unable to re-create it. The jury, and all viewing the trial, were left wondering about what had transpired during the time frame of the crime itself.[416]

When the weekend recess arrived, Hantman was beginning to feel a little queasy. Somehow, Dovey Roundtree had managed to subvert his case—and she had yet to make her opening statement. His witnesses and evidence were not holding up to her cross-examination. Further, she had managed to expose his temper with her constant objections. At one point, while questioning one of his witnesses, she forcefully interjected, "Don't testify, council." When he angrily rebutted, "Your honor, please, I'm either going to present my case or sit down and allow the defense to put on the Government's case." The judge strongly admonished him for his outburst and ordered Hantman's angry outburst stricken from the records.[417]

The second week of the trial began with testimony from the FBI, who had conducted lab tests on the bullets, Mary's clothing, Crump's clothing and hair. Roundtree injected doubt into the testimony of nearly all the witnesses. A firearms expert testified that because Crump had been in the river prior to being tested for having fired a weapon, he could have washed off the nitrates from his clothing and hands. Roundtree elicited from the witness that when hands were tested for gunpowder in the lab, they were often washed with soap and water after the initial test and then tested a second time, as opposed to canal water without soap. She stated that common testing procedure proved that her client had not fired a weapon.[418]

Another FBI agent testified that Crump's hair matched that which was found inside the dark baseball cap, in twenty-one of twenty-two characteristics. Results such as that were said to be proof positive that the hair in the cap indeed belonged to Crump. Roundtree had been studying the science of hair testing and brought in a dozen supporting text books and stacked them conspicuously on the defense table. She quizzed the FBI expert in the witness chair about the literature, most of which he admitted that he had not read nor was familiar with. She went on to state that the sheer number of books and conflicting opinions on the science pointed to the absurdity of the so-called science. She further got him to admit that he had never studied hair analysis at any accredited university, and that he was not familiar with many of the experts she cited.[419]

The biggest defeat for Hantman came late in the trial when he tried to keep an earlier promise to the jury that he would bring in the bloodstained tree trunk to which Mary clung in her final moments. The defense thought it would be inflammatory to do so. The tree led to an open and heated debate between Hantman and Roundtree. The debate ended abruptly when the judge injected incredulously, "What has the tree got to do with it, and how big is the tree?" As Hantman went into a long-winded description of the tree, and that it had contained Mary's blood, and how it related to her struggle that was central to the defense, the judge again interrupted angrily, "You're making a mountain out of a molehill and I hereby rule the tree evidence inflammatory, and not allowed." The judge further told Hantman, in the privacy of his chambers, that just because he had a lot of material, it doesn't mean he should put it all forward as evidence. He said that in his opinion, the government was hurting its case.[420]

As the prosecution was about to rest, Roundtree had yet to give her opening statement; she had cross-examined witnesses and made as many objections as reasonable. Hantman was left with no idea what the defense was up to. The courthouse rumors were rampant that the entire case would hinge on Crump's testimony; Hantman was literally chomping at the bit to get at Crump. However, Hantman was in for a surprise.[421]

Dovey Roundtree sat in the shade of her back porch on a hot, muggy July Saturday afternoon, enjoying ice tea with a yellow legal pad in her lap. She was massaging her opening and closing arguments while pondering whether or not to place Crump on the witness stand. While she leaned in favor of placing him on the stand, her colleagues were strongly opposed. They argued that, from where they had been sitting, away from the defense table, Hantman's twenty-seven witnesses and nearly fifty pieces of evidence had not proved the case. With the wrong physical measurements given in testimony, the government's failure to place Crump at the crime scene, let alone place the unfound weapon in his hands. Why, they asked Dovey, give Hantman a chance to shred Crump in front of the jury?[422]

On Monday, while Dovey rode the elevator up to the courtroom, the black female elevator operator made the case for not putting Crump on the stand. The short, graying, middle-aged, black, 'invisible' lift operator told Dovey that moments earlier, within her elevator, the white prosecution team had been joking about how they couldn't wait for her to put Crump on the stand. The image of the white men chortling about her strategy, oblivious of the elevator operator, made it a done deal; she would share with no one, that Crump would *not* take the stand the following day.[423]

Tuesday morning Roundtree stepped into the courtroom, bright and cheery, in a dress bought especially for the occasion. Appearing as a breath of fresh air, all eyes seemed to focus on her cool attire of a pink and white pinstriped seersucker dress and thin white belt, with white pumps, white earrings, and a necklace of round white buttons.[424] Dovey made her opening statement short and simple. She pointed out that the first part of her argument had been made for her, in that the government had been unable to prove Crump guilty in the first half of the trial. "There are a number of things which, at the proper time, we shall pull out from the great quantity of evidence and show to you in substantiation of our contention that you may not find from this evidence that Raymond Crump Jr. was the person who fired the gun on that fatal afternoon causing the death of Mrs. Mary Pinchot-Meyer," Roundtree said, preparing the jury for her final argument.[425] The second part of her defense was what she referred to as "Exhibit A", setting before them in the person of Ray Crump Jr. She turned and looked directly at the jury, "I want each and every one of you to look at Mr. Crump and weigh him beside the evidence that you have had before you these long and tedious days of the trial."[426]

She went on to tell the jury that, "Evidence of good character may be sufficient alone to raise a reasonable doubt, and having raised a reasonable doubt in your minds, then you may not convict Mr. Crump as charged of murder in the first degree." She presented three character witnesses, all friends of Ray Crump's mother from the Second Baptist Church. Their testimony lasted twenty minutes, in which they said that they knew Ray from church and that he was peaceful, orderly, and non-violent. Hantman cross-examined the witnesses trying to prove that they barely knew Crump. All three witnesses remained steadfast. In a total of thirty some minutes, Roundtree rested her case. A dumbfounded Hantman approached the bench, "If your honor please, I am caught completely flat-footed at this moment because I never anticipated in my wildest dream that counsel would rest her case."[427] The judge simply called the court to recess to allow the government to prepare for jury instructions.

One journalist mumbled while exiting the courtroom, "The tortoise has just overtaken the hare." [428]

Two court reporters had watched the entire trial and were stunned by what had just occurred. They knew more than the jury was allowed to hear about Crump's evasive, multiple, conflicting reasons for being on the towpath, as well as his movements within the critical window of time. Further, they were all but convinced that Hantman had blown the trial. He had failed in dealing with the discrepancies in Crump's height, and the fact that he had been wearing elevator style shoes when apprehended. As reporters, they were committed to impartiality, however, they were all but convinced that a guilty man was about to be set free. After much consternation, they decided to talk to Hantman, who in turn went to the judge. After hearing him out, the judge simply asked, "Why haven't you argued this?"[429]

In her closing argument, Roundtree made the estimated size of her client as her focal point. Additionally, she pointed out that if there had been a body-to-body struggle, as the prosecution claimed, there would have surely been blue fibers from her mink and lamb's wool sweater discovered on Crump's clothing, as well as fibers clinging to the much touted tree. She also planted a seed with the jury regarding the murder weapon. She theorized that the FBI had failed in their search for the weapon because it had been carried out of the towpath area, by the real killer, via one of the several uncharted exits. She made the point that it was possible to do so within the critical window of time—especially if it were a well planned and executed murder. She clearly demonstrated how the prosecution had done the rest for her, on behalf of the accused. She concluded, "Ladies and gentlemen of the jury, I leave this little man in your hands." She paused long enough to slowly scan the eyes of each and every juror. "And I say to you, fairly and truly, if you can find he is five feet and eight inches tall, that he weighs 185 pounds, irrespective of what he wore that day—if you can find—I cannot from this evidence—and I say you must have substantial and reasonable doubt in your minds, and until the government proved its case beyond such doubt, then you must bring a verdict of not guilty."[430]

The following day, Hantman tried to recoup. Earlier in the trial, when he submitted the shoes as evidence, he failed to point out the raised heels. During his closing argument, he placed the shoes in front of the jury on the lectern. "Look closely at these shoes, there is at least two inches of heel." He began to pace, "Do we quibble about two and a half inches of height when the defendant was wearing shoes with heels as you see here?"[431]

Despite the sense that he had been outfoxed by the defense, Hantman still thought he stood a good chance of a conviction. His closing argument had been flat and logical compared to that of Roundtree's, but he trusted that logical minds would prevail.[432]

The following morning, Judge Corcoran gave the jury its instructions. He explained that Crump, by law, was not required to take the stand and that the fact that he hadn't was not to be taken as an admission of guilt. He defined "reasonable doubt". The government, he said, was not required to prove guilt to mathematical or scientific certainty. Reasonable doubt would cause a reasonable person to hesitate or pause in the graver and more important transactions of life. Further, he instructed them about the elements of first degree murder, with which Raymond Crump was charged, which included malice and premeditation. First degree murder was punishable by death, by the electric chair, or life in prison without the possibility of parole, Corcoran said, and the jury would have to choose between the two. If the government did not prove Crump to be guilty of first degree murder, the jury might still convict him of second degree murder, which required malice without premeditation.[433]

At three that afternoon the jury went into deliberation. At ten that evening the foreman sent a message to the judge that eight members of the jury had reached a verdict and four have not; did he consider this jury to be deadlocked? The judge replied that he did not, and that because of the lateness of the hour, he ordered the jurors to retire for the night.[434]

Late the following morning, the jury announced that, after a total of eleven hours, they had reached a verdict. As the jury filed into the courtroom, just before noon, Hantman noticed that two elderly white women jurors were weeping—a bad sign for him, he felt. Whereas Roundtree noticed that the jurors looked at her, always a good sign. The conventional wisdom was that if the jury was going to convict, they would not look at the defense, and visa versa.[435]

Crump seemed unsteady on his feet, as his mother, just out of reach, appeared both frail and frightened. Cicely Angleton felt anxious and breathed shallow from the back of the courtroom. As the verdict was handed to the judge, time seemed to stand silently still. He asked the jury to please stand. He cleared his voice and paused, seemingly for effect. "Members of the jury, we have your verdict which states that you find the defendant Raymond Crump Junior not guilty, and this is your verdict, so say you each and all?" The jurors indicated their affirmation.[436]

Crump swayed forward as if to faint but was saved by the hug and embrace from Dovey Roundtree. She then turned to take congratulations from her law partners. Martha Crump and all of her friends from the Second Baptist Church jumped to their feet and began to sing praises to their Lord before Hantman cast one furtive glance at Roundtree; he refused to congratulate her, as he turned his back and walked away. Years later, Dovey would say that he never spoke to her again. However, the judge remained impassive. "Raymond Crump, you are a free man."[437]

Crump, frozen like a deer in headlights, didn't move until Dovey took him by the arm and led him from the courtroom, past reporters and flash bulbs, to a jubilant throng of well-wishers from his mother's church.[438]

Reporters waited for the jury foreman as he exited the jurors' lounge. What had swayed the jury?, they clamored. "There were many missing links." He shook his head. "We just could not place the man at the scene of the crime."[439]

POST TRIAL

It became a bitter pill to swallow for Al Hantman that he had lost his most important case. Before the trial he had not been aware of Mary's social connections, nor was he aware of the controversial diary or her being a mistress to the president of the United States. Years later, he would claim that if he had been privy to all of that information, it wouldn't have made a bit of difference to him because he was convinced, at least in his own mind, that they had their man. "It all hung in the presentation of the case and the summation at the end," Hantman said. "I'm not a preacher and my argument didn't go over well. But if you base it on logic and to what conclusion reasonable minds might come, there was a fair argument that Crump was the one." After the trial, Mary's brother-in-law, Ben Bradlee, called Hantman for his assessment of what went wrong. "I told him it's a flip of the coin. You could describe it as jury nullification. If the jury were true to its oath, it would follow the law and the only way it could come out would be with a verdict of guilty. But if they don't like personality or race, they go off and do whatever they want. And there was a guy that just walked."[440]

With Ray Crump acquitted, he is considered innocent in the eyes of the law. As a result, the case was officially considered closed and, after a procedural period of twenty-five years, the police disposed all of the evidence. Therefore, it is impossible to apply current scientific technology to try to solve the murder now. Whatever happened on the towpath, it is certain that Mary did not go easily. "She was fearless," said her friend, Kary Fisher. "She would have fought back."[441] One thing remains all but certain, and that is that the murder weapon walked out of the towpath area along with the killer.

Over time, Roundtree scoffed at Hantman's conclusion, simply writing it off to the painful reality of defeat. She further contended that if Ray

Crump was such a timid little man, if he had been guilty, he would have confessed everything on the spot as soon as the police apprehended him. Worrying about his safety, she had put her client on a bus back to his relatives in North Carolina, where he remained for a month before returning to Washington. Over the years, Crump led a life of mostly petty crime that Roundtree claimed was due to the trauma of months spent in jail charged with a heinous crime he didn't commit, in addition to his mental instability coupled with extreme poverty. For all Ben Bradlee knew, as a DC journalist, Crump spent the remainder of his life outside the city limits,[442] for his crimes never reached the white part of town, let alone the *Washington Post*. However, the sense of civic peace that had prevailed within Georgetown was gone. Homes had to be protected by locks and security guards.[443]

Dovey Roundtree's case notes from the Crump trial went to the Columbia University Law School, where they were used to teach law students the ideal way to defend a circumstantial-evidence case. She would later lecture there on the subject.

A week following Mary's murder, a white cross appeared on the towpath where Mary laid in the fetal position mortally wounded. Also, in white spray paint, someone scrawled on the face of Key Bridge, spanning the towpath and Rock Creek, the words "Mauvais Coup, Mary". The phrase is a French idiom that translates as, "Bad luck, Mary"—Pinchot being French, with a silent T. [444]

Cord Meyer remarried in 1966. Soon thereafter, he was exposed by the press for being the brains behind the CIA's infiltration into American college student political organizations, and his career seemed to stall. He was bypassed for promotion to the head of the covert action department, and in 1973 he was shifted to London where he served as station chief. At the end of the London assignment, he resigned from the CIA and began to write newspaper columns, with a hard right edge, in partner with his old friend, Charles Bartlett. His reputation for argumentativeness never abated. In the seventies, he was diagnosed with cancer and continued to live in Mary's Thirty-Fourth Street Georgetown townhouse. He passed away March 13, 2001 and, as a First Lieutenant Marine, and recipient of a Purple Heart and Bronze Star, was buried with full military honors in Arlington National Cemetery. His twin brother Quentin was killed five decades earlier on Okinawa. [445]

The following statement was released by the Director of the CIA, George Tenet, on behalf of Cord Meyer:

I am greatly saddened by the death of Cord Meyer, a passionate defender of freedom around the world. During a remarkable intelligence career spanning more than a quarter of a century, Cord defined the concept, doctrine, and implementation of covert action on behalf of the security and interests of our nation. At the height of the Cold War, he played an instrumental role in America's effort to counter Soviet influence. His leadership, innovation, and creativity inspired his colleagues and helped shape the Agency's history.

After retiring from the Agency in 1977, Cord's passion and his profound knowledge of world affairs was reflected in his thoughtful columns on a wide range of issues.

It was with great pride that CIA honored Cord Meyer as one of its Trailblazers when the Agency celebrated its 50th anniversary in 1997.

I want to express my deepest condolences to the Meyer family on behalf of all the men and women of the Intelligence Community.[446]

Mary and Cord's sons, Mark and Quentin, graduated from Yale, and both gradually turned toward religion. Mark became a missionary for the Seventh Day Adventist Church in China before returning to Washington, where he translated Chinese documents for the Government. Quentin also lives in Washington. Through 1997, neither son has ever married.[447]

For over a decade following the murder, Georgetown spoke in a whisper about Mary Meyer and her rumored diary, with her affair with JFK known for certain by only a privileged few. Cocktail party gossip was as far as the whispers about Mary carried, until an early 1976 *National Enquirer* front page splash, "Former *Washington Post* V.P. Reveals 2-Year JFK White House Romance." The article included prominent photos taken within the White House private quarters, including Mary, looking young and gorgeous, and JFK casually dressed with a broad smile, along with Ben and Tony Bradlee, and Angleton sporting a sly smile, and James Pruitt wearing a black turtleneck and rolling a *cigarette*. The story's biggest bombshell was Truitt's claim that Mary and JFK had smoked marijuana several times together in the White House. The story further revealed that Kennedy had hidden one of Mary's undergarments in the Presidential safe. Truitt further claimed that Mary truly loved Kennedy, but realized their romance could not elevate beyond an illicit affair.[448]

To report the story, the tabloid sent reporters down to San Miguel de Allende, Mexico, to interview Truitt. The tabloid also contacted Tony Bradlee and Angleton, and tried to talk to Ben Bradlee. Bradlee was furious when a reporter showed up at his *Washington Post* office; he erupted into a shouting rage and had the reporter thrown out of the building.[449] With all that Truitt and Bradlee had gone through together over time, socially and professionally, Bradlee was hit hard by Truitt's betrayal.[450]

No one knows what motivated Truitt to sell Mary's story. Some journalists believed he wanted to embarrass Bradlee in the wake of his best-seller, "Conversations With Kennedy". Truitt resented Bradlee getting credit as a champion of the First Amendment for exposing the sordid side of Nixon in his Watergate coverage, after having all but overlooked Kennedy's hypocrisies. When Truitt heard of Bradlee's plans to publish a Kennedy book, he wrote and demanded to know if he planned to expose Kennedy's affair with his sister-in-law. For at the time, the *Post* was running editorials demanding that the White House reveal all in the Watergate matter. Bradlee mentioned Mary five times in his book, never divulging a hint of her true relationship with the president. Truitt clearly did not betray Mary for the money for he was paid a mere one thousand dollars for his story in 1976. Coincidentally, the *National Enquirer* did not run the article until after the revelation of Judith Campbell Exner's affair with Kennedy was made public.[451]

Mary's friends were angered by the *Enquirer* article and disappointed that it had been at the hands of one of their husbands. Their efforts to counter the article came in the form of unsourced comments in venues such as *Time Magazine*. While not denying the sex, they spun it in a ladylike context, as opposed to the sordidness of the *Enquirer*. "She was not the kind of person to get into a dalliance. This was not some tawdry affair."[452]

Mary's younger sister, Tony Bradlee, responded to the *Enquirer* story by matter-of-factly confirming the romance, downplaying it to fling as opposed to an affair. She added the caveat, "Neither the contents of my sister's very personal diary nor her relationship with JFK have been made public before." She told a journalist, "It was nothing to be ashamed of. Jackie suspected it for a long time before finding out it was, in fact, true."[453]

In 1981, James Truitt committed suicide at his home in Mexico. His widow, Evelyn, remained there and knitted her own set of conspiracy theories. She did claim, however, that her husband's highly personal papers, along with a copy of Mary's diary, were secretly removed from her husband's safe by the CIA. She suspected that Angleton, the CIA keeper of secrets, was behind the looting of the safe.[454]

After the widespread revelation of Mary's affair with Kennedy, her unsolved murder took on new depth and meaning. Exposure of the affair came during the 1976 election year in the midst of post-Watergate atmosphere of deep distrust of everything government, especially the CIA and FBI. The CIA was being investigated on Capitol Hill, with the daily revelation of its assassination plots, poison pills, testing of psychoactive drugs such as LSD, and domestic mail opening, all done when Mary was alive and closest to the center of power.[455]

The first public person to attempt to decode the mysterious reality of Mary's life and death was her old friend, Timothy Leary, in 1976. Although a fading icon of the psychodelic era, he was still the caricature of a danger to society as branded by G. Gordon Liddy and the US Government. While serving time for drug charges, Leary read the tabloid news, with glee, of Mary's affair with the president, and especially their shared marijuana joints. Was it possible that the president himself had turned on with LSD? The fondest hope of the acid movement may have come true without Leary knowing. Could there be a hallucinogenic link in the Kennedy assassination? From the first news of Mary's murder, he was convinced that there had been a cover-up, and that things were not as they seemed. When he first read of Mary's death in 1964, Leary learned for the first time that the beautiful woman he knew as Mary Pinchot had been married to Cord Meyer. Coincidentally, Leary knew Cord from the days when both were members of the American Veterans Committee. He recalled loathing young Cord for his efficient campaign to wipe out the left-wing element within the organization. He knew from mutual acquaintances that Cord was now in the CIA, conducting even vaster secret campaigns. With everything that the CIA touched turning into a hall of mirrors, Mary's death was in that labyrinth, and he decided to investigate and expose it.[456]

Upon his release from prison, Leary launched his own private investigation which eventually led nowhere; he was advised by his attorney that nobody wanted the incident investigated, that it was too dangerous to pursue. However, that did not stop Leary from writing a follow-up article in the magazine *Rebel*. The 1983 article detailed the activities of a mysterious blond from Washington including speculation about her death. Leary hinted, but never stated outright, that Mary had dropped acid with the president. He had no proof aside from his supplying Mary, and "her male friend in a very powerful position", LSD during the period of her affair with the president. He submitted that the only proof that might have existed was within Mary's diary that was "taken care of by the CIA."[457]

With the highly subversive image of LSD by the American public at the time of Mary's death, it stands to reason that the CIA would be highly interested in a woman's diary that documented her and the president's use of the drug. Former CIA director, Richard Helms, believed that Angleton confiscated the diary to ensure that the president would not be embarrassed posthumously.[458]

Leary's scores of followers seized the Mary Pinchot-Meyer story and made it their own. They embellished the story to the point that Mary became a feminist drug icon trying to sow world peace through the intelligent use of psychedelics, before being struck down in a hit authorized by the enemies of peace and drug use. In 1992, journalist Nancy Druid penned an article for the magazine *Mondo 2000* headlined "America's First Psychedelic President". The article imagined that Mary and JFK had done drugs together in the White House, and that Mary had been a part of a cell of Washington women who actively plotted to turn-on the president and other powerful men. The article further claimed that Mary was in partnership with Lisa Howard and Dorothy Kilgallen—two women who also died of mysterious causes after the president's assassination. Mary "became the person most dreaded by intelligence agencies—labeled the runaway wife," Druid wrote. Howard's death appeared to be an accidental drug overdose or, perhaps, a suicide. Dorothy Killgallen's death in 1965—shortly after she had a private interview with Jack Ruby, the man who shot Lee Harvey Oswald—is mysterious. Just days before her death, attributed to a lethal combination of alcohol and barbiturates, she had boasted, "In five more days, I'm going to bust this case wide open."[459] Leary and his followers regarded Mary as a martyr in the battle to bring hallucinogenic peace and wholeness to the world.

Adding fuel to the growing legend of Mary's death being tied to Kennedy's assassination, was Robert Morrow, a writer and CIA contractor. In two of his earlier books he claimed involvement in having acquired Mannlicher rifles to kill Kennedy. He further claimed that he had provided sophisticated communication devices to three hit teams that killed Kennedy. According to Morrow, the assassination was a collaborative effort between the mob and intelligence agencies. In yet another book, published in 1992, he injected Mary into his conspiracy theory. He claimed that Marshall Diggs, deputy comptroller of the treasury under FDR, called and requested an urgent meeting with Morrow two weeks before Mary's murder. Morrow wrote that Diggs told him that a prominent lady in Washington knew far too much about the *Company*, its Cuban operations, and more specifically, the President's assassination. Diggs also told him that Mary had told a close friend of his that she positively knew that Agency-affiliated Cuban exiles and the Mafia were responsible for Kennedy's assassination. Diggs also told him that CIA official, Tracy Barnes, was concerned about Mary, and that the Cuban exile leader, Robert Kohly, ought to be informed. When informed, Kohly supposedly replied, "Tell Diggs I'll take care of the matter." The following week, Mary Pinchot-Meyer was dead.[460]

The problem with Morrow's story is that everyone involved in the discussions he described is dead. Further, there are no written or taped records *to be found* of his alleged discussions, therefore, the House Select Committee on Assassinations *determined* Morrow to be an unreliable source.[461]

With the advent of the internet, the legend continued to grow. In one internet theory, Mary was a pawn in the CIA's mind control experiments, and JFK the ultimate project guinea pig. Another internet theory claimed that Timothy Leary himself was in the CIA, and that Mary Pinchot-Meyer served as some kind of courier or connection between Leary and the agency. Other theories linked her murder to every suspicious or tragic national event between 1963 and 1974, beginning with Phil Graham's suicide and ending with Watergate.[462]

It's clear that the CIA had an interest in Mary. Photographers and journalists attempting to cover Mary's murder were kept from the crime scene on the far side of the canal for an unusually long period of time. One AP photographer recalls having to take pictures utilizing a telephoto lens, and even then found it difficult because of the extraordinary number of plainclothesmen swarming the scene and impeding his coverage. The 'suits' were in addition to multiple uniformed police, sport coated detectives, and lab jacketed crime scene investigators and photographers, and, of course, reps from the coroners office.[463]

There is no doubt that the mere presence of Jim Angleton in Mary's life only served to fuel the conspiracy theories about her. Angleton's involvement in the Kennedy assassination and investigation remains a mystery and the subject of legitimate inquiry. With the millions of pages of classified documents generated by the assassination, his role remains a mystery. Angleton kept his thumb on the writing of the Warren Commission report, bringing a sigh of relief from the CIA when the report was formally issued. The incompleteness of the report allowed the CIA to escape the opening of the agency's Pandora's Box of embarrassing facts about assassination plots and Mafia ties, and later served to raise further suspicions about the president's assassination. Also omitted from the report was the fact that the CIA had kept track of Lee Harvey Oswald for a long period of time, including their having photographed Oswald in Mexico City a year before the assassination. The report also failed to mention the numerous ties between the CIA, the Kennedy administration, and the Mafia assassination attempts on Castro. The report so intensively focused on Oswald that Kennedy biographer, William Manchester, suggested it be subtitled, "The Life of Lee Harvey Oswald."[464]

The CIA conducted its own investigation; the man in control was Mary Pinchot-Meyer's friend and her ex-husband's closest confidant, James Jesus

Angleton. Angleton had apparently manipulated the Warren Commission through former CIA director, Allen Dulles. In early 1964, Angleton had debriefed Russian defector Yuri Nosenko, who he believed had been sent by Moscow to trick the Americans. Nosenko defected right after Kennedy's assassination and informed the CIA that the KGB knew of Oswald before the murder but had nothing to do with the assassination. Through Dulles, Angleton influenced the commission's report, ensuring that it was sufficiently skewed in that the CIA had 'proven' Nosenko to be a liar . . . the CIA was not about to be duped.[465]

In a July 1964 CIA memo, reference was made in how to best handle the Nosenko situation without having a negative effect on the Commission report. It concluded that Angleton was the most suitable person to work through Dulles directly on the matter.[466] Dulles and Angleton successfully steered the Commission away from the ties between the CIA and the Mafia, the Kennedy brothers' involvement in those ties and the CIA plots to assassinate Castro using American hoodlums. The final report made no mention of those activities, and it took more than a decade before they were officially admitted by the agency.[467]

As the great collector of secrets, Angleton was in an ideal position to manipulate the flow and content of information from the CIA regarding the Kennedy assassination in the post-assassination years. He strongly speculated that a conspiracy was behind the assassination when he stated, "A mansion has many rooms and there were many things going on . . . I am not privy to who struck John."[468] Typically, Angleton never explained that remark. History is left to ponder whether he was simply indulging his taste for metaphor or implying knowledge of a conspiracy.[469]

The fact that the Warren Commission report was released just before Mary's murder is deemed very significant in the legend of her death. Conspiracy theorists are convinced that she knew something, but something that was at odds with the Commission's report. They further see endless links and coincidences between her killing and Kennedy's. Both occurred in broad daylight, almost at high-noon. Both were killed by two bullets, hit style, to the head and upper torso. Both of the men arrested were physically short misfits from mean circumstances, and both were without worth or influence of whom little was understood and, therefore, much could be suggested. As the theorists believed that Oswald was set up, they believe that Crump was lured to the towpath, and that the mechanic who witnessed a black man in a tan jacket and dark baseball cap standing over Mary's body, was lured to the spot to make an identification that would protect the real killer.[470] All details related to the stalled Nash automobile, that the mechanics were called to lend assistance, remain unanswered . . . it simply disappeared from the scene.

The theories are many and varied, but they all contain one common element . . . the desire to identify some order to the randomness of Mary's murder. Full of suspicion about the secret activities of the U.S. government, they instinctively turn to the all-powerful CIA. They are firmly convinced that the CIA designed a murder in broad daylight to silence a woman they regarded as the leading female figure in the movement for world peace through psychedelics, as well as the leading lady in JFK's secret life.[471]

Those in a position to put such stories to rest, have not. To this day, a protective silence around Mary remains. Even though Ben Bradlee strongly endorsed the people's right to know philosophy of the 1960's, the rules changed when the subject of the story was his sister-in-law. Bradlee, the First Amendment champion of the Watergate investigation, felt that Mary's diary did not belong in the careless hands of the police, the contents were far too personal, and it was justifiably *disposed* of by the CIA.[472]

Other Georgetown journalists also felt too close to the people involved to talk about it, let alone write about it. Charles Bartlett said nervously, "Oh, I just can't. Too many of my friends are a part of that one." Further, Kay Evans, wife of Rowland Evans and close friend of Mary's, was a journalist in her own right and another Vassar girl. She told friends that she could not imagine a book written about Mary "without all the sex."[473]

James Angleton could have answered many questions. However, throughout his entire adult life, he cultivated an aura of mystery. He truly amused himself playing cat-and-mouse and rope-a-dope with journalists. He took mischievous pleasure in parceling out bits of facts and opinions that could not be confirmed, simply feeding grist to the conspiracy mill. He told one writer that Mary had written in her diary that she and JFK had used LSD together, after which they made love. During another interview with a lone journalist, he implied that Mary was a woman who influenced policy with her pacifist beliefs.[474] He also claimed that a number of men and women had read the diary, not just him and the Bradlees.[475]

Angleton continued to alternately lie about destroying the diary, but remained steadfast about the truth of the affair. In all fairness to Angleton, he became the unofficial godfather to the Meyer children, and somewhat of a surrogate older brother to Cord. He watched over the Meyer boys, minding their money and meeting with school authorities in times of trouble. He died of lung cancer in 1986, with his final words, according to his wife Cicely, being, "'I've made so many mistakes."[476]

The sad perception from within the White House that they were always right on matters of foreign policy held fast during the Vietnam War, and generated youth upheaval during the 1960's that tore Georgetown CIA families apart. While the cold war fathers were hawks, their children were dead against the war. The explosive tempers of self-righteous, never erring fathers became the personal Tet Offensive of their offspring. The shocking behavior of the government was not too close to home . . . it was home. One CIA family was thrown out of a Georgetown restaurant during a heated conversation about Vietnam, which ended with a son telling his WW II veteran father that he planned to avoid military service. The same heated revolt played out within the Meyer household, although Quentin did serve in Vietnam. Cord visited his sons in their prep schools, and political arguments would erupt that continued after his departure, via the mail, with Cord still arguing his point. He was a typical CIA cold warrior who would *not* give an inch when national policy principles were at risk; they would *never* admit to having mistakenly embraced a wrong ideal or policy.[477]

Mary's vibrant life cut short was a simmering subject within a Georgetown younger generation of distrust of both government and family heads. Many grew up convinced that the CIA had something to do with the murder. To them, Mary was an icon, a rebel who posed a threat to national security. Quentin remained haunted by his mother's unsolved murder. During that period, he called Timothy Leary in the middle of the night and identified himself as Quinton Meyer before asking, "What happened to my mother?" Leary had no answer.[478]

There is little to no resemblance between the Georgetown of the Kennedy era and that of today. In the new Washington, there remains little humor, zest for life, with the art of conversation all but lost. The WWII veteran cold war warriors of yesteryear are today's draft dodging chicken hawks that had more important things to do, or took shelter in the Air National Guard rather than defend their country. Their wives are more likely to be lawyers or career civil servants like their husbands, as opposed to artists, writers, or stay-at-home moms.[479]

Right before her death, Mary finished a painting she named *Half Life*. It belongs to the National Museum of American Art in D.C., a gift from her sons. With Mary considered a minor artist, the painting is kept in a stowage space, and can be viewed by appointment only. The balance of Mary's paintings, along with those created by her Georgetown set, remains obscure, hanging in family homes, printed in self-published books, and shared between the closest of their friends. To this day, most of her Georgetown friends continue to paint, sculpt, and write. Over time, most have turned inward and toward the philosophical, mystical, and religion. Ben and Tony Bradlee, along with the Truitts, visited a Methodist minister and part-time spiritual "reader", named Ted Swager, in an attempt to link with Mary in death. Swager had been well publicized in articles written in the *New York Times*, and Truitt was working on a follow-up cover story for *Newsweek*. Swager eventually left the ministry to devote full-time efforts traveling around the country doing readings. Truitt later thanked him for his contact with Mary, "The most amazing part came with you suddenly exclaiming, "Mary, Mary, Mary, etc." Truitt further wrote, "What emerged about Mary was remarkable".[480] Truitt later told journalists that during the session, Mary described her grave in Milford and spoke of the Kennedy brothers being there with her.[481]

With the common thread of secrecy woven tightly through the lives of Georgetown wives of CIA cold warrior husbands, coupled with the mysterious death of one of their own, the occult and mysticism proved as natural attractions. Tony and Mary's aunt Cornelia Pinchot regularly consulted with psychic, Jeane Dixon, in Cornelia's home. Eventually, Anne Truitt held weekly spiritual meetings called *sat sang* sessions in her home. *Sat sang* subscribed to an *ersatz* Buddhism involving reincarnation, in that they were all on the way to becoming "perfect masters". Anne Truitt came to believe she had a special spiritual connection with Alexander the Great, and often spoke of Mary as if she were still around.[482]

The women of Mary's Georgetown group really never conquered their fears; they remained permanently haunted by the imagined and real deeds of their cold warrior husbands. Like their men, these women had given the best part of their lives to the cold war. On top of being raised to believe that sphere of Washington was reserved for men, they were kept totally in the dark by their husbands about their secret war. Further, the cold war secrets remain a personal matter to these women, and they guard their past carefully. They were always fearful of the countless investigations that took place over time of what new coup or illegal domestic or foreign plot that might reveal the name of their loved ones. And so it was, and still is, with their friend Mary, whose life and death remains an indelible blot of doubt and sorrow on their minds. They remain wary of the possibility of an awful revelation about her sex life and her murder. The elderly Georgetown women remain bound by their knowledge, not of conspiracy, but of their late friend's female freedom, her total lack of fear, her acceptance into the inner circle of men, her sexual expression, and her reckless pursuit of experience through her senses—all long before a liberation movement. Cicely Angleton summed it up when she referred to Mary as a "beautiful mysterious woman, but not at all representative of her generation." [483]

Unlike Mary, the vast majority of the women of her generation were unable to shift from their post debutante world into the liberating environment of the 1960s. At the time of her death, Mary Pinchot-Meyer had moved boldly beyond old school female philosophy to become well immersed in psychedelia and the holistic worldview. She died before assassinations, racial strife, resistance to war, and youthful and sexual rebellion spun *old* Georgetown off its axis into a chaotic future. For men, the natural path to a solution was to appropriate more power to stave off change. The women retreated into the mystics, writing, and painting as an escape, as opposed to social change, confrontation, and reality. As these women enter the winter of their lives, hindsight, tempered by three decades of social evolution, enables them to recognize that Mary Pinchot-Meyer's attempts to venture well beyond the long standing social positions "were not really so shameful". And they would like to believe that her very fearlessness and assurance she possessed, ultimately led to the circumstances of her death.[484] But, then again, perhaps . . . .

What a difference she could have made to the fabric of Americana, and what an impact she could have made in the lives of her sons and family had she been allowed to live and not caught in the evil "jaws" of the CIA, and the mind-sets of that era. To think they had, and still have, the power to murder anyone they chose is chilling.

FOOTNOTES

FOREWORD

1. Nina Burleigh, *"A Very Private Woman"*, Bantam, 1999, pages 1-7

PART I

CHAPTER 1

2. Peter Collier and David Horowitz, *"The Kennedys: An American Drama"*, Encounter Books, 2nd edition 10-2001
3. Amos R. E. Pinchot, *"History of the Progressive Party 1912-1916"*, edited with biography foreword by Helene Maxwell Hooker, New York University Press, 1958, page10
4. Nina Burleigh, *"A Very Private Woman"*, Bantam, 1999, page 33-34
5. William Gaston, author (Burleigh) interview, 1996
6. Nina Burleigh, *"A Very Private Woman"*, Bantam, 1999, page 54-55
7. Francis Kilpatrick Field, author (Nina Burleigh) interview, 1996
8. Brearley Yearbook, 1938
9. William Attwood. *"The Reds and the Blacks: A Personal Adventure"*, Harper & Row, 1967, 133
10. Nina Burleigh, *"A Very Private Woman"*, Bantam, 1999, page 57
11. Brearley Yearbook, 1938
12. Nina Burleigh, *"A Very Private Woman"*, Bantam, 1999, page 58
13. Carol Severance, curator Grey Towers Historic Landmark
14. Nina Burleigh, *"A Very Private Woman"*, Bantam, 1999, page 58
15. *"Park Avenue Social Review"*, November 1938
16. Nina Burleigh, *"A Very Private Woman"*, Bantam, 1999, page 58
17. Barbara Blagden Sisson, author (Burleigh) interview, 1996

18. *"Life"*, November 14, 1938, cover story on Brenda Duff Frazier
19. David Middleton, author (Burleigh) interview, 1996
20. Nina Burleigh, *"A Very Private Woman"*, Bantam, 1999, page 60-62
21. Mary McCarthy, *"The Vassar Girls"*, from *"On The Contrary: Articles Of Belief"*, 1946-61, Curtis Publishing Co., 1961, pages 195-97
22. Mary Truesdale, author (Burleigh) interview

CHAPTER 2

23. Elaine Showalter, ed., *These Modern Women: Autobiographical Essays from the Twenties* (New York: Feminist Press, 1989), page 126. Peter Janney, "Mary's Mosaic", Skyhorse Publishing, 2012, Pages 146-47
24. Ruth Pinchot, *"A Deflated Rebel"*, from *These Modern Women: Autobiographical Essays from the Twenties*, edited with an introduction by Elaine Showalter, Feminist Press, 1978, page 60.
25. Amos R. E. Pinchot Papers, Family Correspondence, 1863-1941, Container 5, May 29 1935, Amos to William Eno.
26. Nina Burleigh, *"A Very Private Women"*, Bantam, 1999, page 45
27. Nina Burleigh, *"A Very Private Women"*, Bantam, 1999, page 43
28. Nina Burleigh, *"A Very Private Women"*, Bantam, 1999, page 33
29. Carol Severance
30. Nina Burleigh, *"A Very Private Women"*, Bantam, 1999, page 33
31. *"These Modern Women"*, pages 125-26
32. *"These Modern Women"*, pages 125-26
33. Confidential source of Nina Burleigh, *"A Very Private Women"*, Bantam, 1999, page 31
34. Nina Burleigh, *"A Very Private Women"*, Bantam, 1999, page 35-37
35. Amos R. E. Pinchot, *"History of the Progressive Party 1912-1916"*, edited and with biographical foreword by Helen Maxwell Hooker, New York University Press, 1958, page 13 (referred to hereafter as Hooker).
36. Hooker, page 12.
37. Nina Burleigh, *"A Very Private Women"*, Bantam, 1999, page 48
38. *The WPA Guide to New York City: The Federal Writers' Project Guide to 1930s New York, prepared by the Federal Writers' Project of Works Progress Administration,* with an introduction by William Whyte, New Press 1992.
39. Nina Burleigh, *"A Very Private Women"*, Bantam, 1999, page 49
40. Gifford Pinchot Papers, Container 314, Nov. 9, 1931, Amos to Gifford.
41. Gifford Pinchot Papers, Container 369, April 10, 1933, Amos to Gifford.

42. Robert S. McElvaine, *"The Great Depression"*, Times Books, 1984, pages 204-5.
43. Ibid., page 79
44. Amos R. E. Pinchot Papers, General Correspondence, Container 59.
45. Nina Burleigh, *"A Very Private Women"*, Bantam, 1999, page 51-52
46. Amos R. E. Pinchot Papers, Family Correspondence, 1863-1941, Container 5, Dec. 12, 1938, Amos to William Eno.
47. Amos R. E. Pinchot Papers, Family Correspondence, 1863-1941, Container 5, Dec. 12, 1938, William Eno to Amos
48. *New York Times,* April 26, 1937.
49. Nina Burleigh, *"A Very Private Women"*, Bantam, 1999, page 53
50. Amos R. E. Pinchot Papers, Family Correspondence, 1863-1941, Container 5, July 1, 1941, Amos to William Eno
51. David Middleton, author (Burleigh) interview, 1996

CHAPTER 3

52. Nina Burleigh, *"A Very Private Women"*, Bantam, 1999, pages 54-55
53. Francis Kilpatrick Field, Interview by Nina Burleigh, 1996.
54. Brearley Yearbook, 1938.
55. William Attwood, *The Reds and the Blacks: a Personal Adventure,* Harper & Row, 1967, page 133.
56. Choate School letter to Leo Damore, October 5, 1992. The letter documents William Attwood's date as Mary Pinchot for Winter Festivites Weekend, February 1936, and the fact that John F. Kennedy (Class of 1935) was in attendance. Peter Janney, "Mary's Mosaic", Skyhorse Publishing, 2012, Page 151.
57. William Attwood diary entry, February 21, 1936. Peter Janney, "Mary's Mosaic", Skyhorse Publishing, 2012, page 151.
58. Ibid
59. Nina Burleigh, *"A Very Private Women"*, Bantam, 1999, page 58
60. Carol Severence.
61. Nina Burleigh, *"A Very Private Women"*, Bantam, 1999, page 58
62. Barbara Blagden Sisson, Interview by Nina Burleigh, 1996.
63. *Life,* Nov. 14, 1938, cover story on Brenda Duff Frazier.
64. David Middleton
65. *Life,* Nov. 14. 1938
66. *Park Avenue Social Review,* Nov. 1938
67. Mary Pinchot, "Requiem," *New York Times,* January 25, 1940, page 15. Peter Janney, "Mary's Mosaic", Skyhorse Publishing, 2012, pages 154-55.

68. *Life*, Dec. 6, 1963, page 133.
69. Nina Burleigh, *"A Very Private Women"*, Bantam, 1999, page 60-61
70. Nina Burleigh, *"A Very Private Women"*, Bantam, 1999, page 63
71. Mary McCarthy, "The Vassar Girl," from *On the Contrary*: Articles of Belief, 1946-1961, Curtis Publishing Co., 1961, pages 195-97.
72. Nina Burleigh, *"A Very Private Women"*, Bantam, 1999, page 64
73. Mary Truesdale, interview by author Nina Burleigh, 1996.
74. Frances Prindle Taft, interview by author Nina Burleigh, 1996
75. Unnamed source.
76. Nina Burleigh, *"A Very Private Women"*, Bantam, 1999, page 65
77. Mary McCarthy, pages 202-3
78. Mary Truesdale
79. Frances Field
80. "Futility," *Vassar Review and Little Magazine*, April 1941, pages 5-6, 21
81. Wayne Koestenbaum, *Jackie Under My Skin: Interpreting an Icon*, Plume, 1996, pg 193.
82. Nina Burleigh, *"A Very Private Women"*, Bantam, 1999, page 68
83. Amos R. E. Pinchot Papers, Family Correspondence, Container 5, Sept 30, 1941, Amos to Gifford
84. Gifford Pinchot Papers, Container 369, Nov. 17, 1939, Amos to Gifford.
85. Nina Burleigh, *"A Very Private Women"*, Bantam, 1999, page 69
86. Amos R. E. Pinchot Papers, Family Correspondence, Container 5, Sept 30, 1941, Amos to son Gifford
87. Nina Burleigh, *"A Very Private Women"*, Bantam, 1999, page 70-72
88. Barbara Gair Scheiber, interview by author Nina Burleigh, 1996

CHAPTER 4

89. Nina Burleigh, *"A Very Private Women"*, Bantam, 1999, pages 81-82.
90. Cornelia Bryce Pinchot Papers, Library of Congress, Manuscript Division, Box 410, May2, 1945, Ruth to Cornelia.
91. Cord Meyers Papers, Container 5, journal entries, Dec. 20-27, 1961.
92. Cord Meyers Papers, Container 5, journal entries, July 6, 1958.
93. Nina Burleigh, *"A Very Private Women"*, Bantam, 1999, page 81-86.
94. Croswell Bowen, "Young Man in Quest of Peace," *PM Magazine*, June 1947, page M6.
95. Ibid, page M7.
96. David Challinor, interview by author Nina Burleigh, 1996.

97. Hamilton, *JFK,* page 703. Peter Janney, "Mary's Mosaic", Skyhorse Publishing, 2012, Pages 173-74

98. Ibid, pages 690-91, Peter Janney, "Mary's Mosaic", Skyhorse Publishing, 2012, Page 174

99. Mary Goodhue, Interview by Nina Burleigh, 1996.

100. Bishop Paul Moore, Interview by Nina Burleigh, 1996.

101. Nina Burleigh, *"A Very Private Women",* Bantam, 1999, page 90-91.

102. Harris Wofford, *Of Kennedys and Kings: Making sense of the Sixties,* Farrar, Straus, Giroux, 1980, page 29.

103. Description of the genesis of Kennedy's dislike for Cord Meyer can be found in Ben Bradlee's book *Conversations with Kennedy* (Pocket Books, 1976), page 35, in which he says Kennedy never forgot Cord's refusal to be interviewed and decided to "get even." There is also some discussion about the uneasy relations between the two men in Cord Meyer's own journal entries, in which he chalks it up to Kennedy's class inferiority. The animosity and the anecdote about the interview were confirmed to the author by Kennedy aide Dave powers through Myer Feldman.

104. "Young Men Who Care," *Glamour,* July, 1947 pages 27-29. Peter Janney, "Mary's Mosaic", Skyhorse Publishing, 2012, Page 177

105. Cord Meyer, "On the Beaches, *Atlantic Monthly,* page 39.

106. *PM Magazine,* June 1947, page M9

107. Nina Burleigh, *"A Very Private Women",* Bantam, 1999, page 94-98

108. "Steps to Peace": The Cord Meyer, Jr.," *Mademoiselle,* Sept. 1948, page 198.

109. *Glamour,* July 1947, page 27.

110. Cord Meyer Papers, Container 5, journal entry, Nov. 12, 1945.

111. Nina Burleigh, *"A Very Private Women",* Bantam, 1999, page 100-104

112. Cord Meyer Papers, Container I, correspondence 1950-51 between Cord and Dean Acheson, Averell Harriman, McGeorge Bundy, and Arthur Schlesinger. These letters give a good indication of Cord's early connections to the men who would eventually figure prominently in Kennedy's administration.

113. Robin Winks, *Cloak and Gown,* William Morrow, 1987, page 440.

114. Meyer, pages 64-5.

115. Nina Burleigh, *"A Very Private Women",* Bantam, 1999, page 106.

116. Freeman Dyson, "The Race Is Over", *New York Review of Books,* Mar 6, 1997, page 4.

117. Martin Walker, *The Cold War: A History,* Henry Holt, 1994, page 37.

118. Walker, page 58.

119. Lois Gordon and Alan Gordon, *The Columbian Chronicles of American Life*, 1910-1992, Columbia University Press, 1995, page 408.
120. Cord Meyer Papers, Container 5, journal entry, March 18, 1950.
121. Confidential source to Nina Burleigh, *"A Very Private Women"*, Bantam, 1999, page 108
122. Cord Meyer Papers, Container 5, journal entry, May 24, 1951.
123. Cord Meyer Papers, Container 5, journal entry, June 8, 1951. Peter Janney, "Mary's Mosaic", Skyhorse Publishing, 2012, Page 179-80
124. Nina Burleigh, *"A Very Private Women"*, Bantam, 1999, page 109

CHAPTER 5

125. Jane Barnes, Author Nina Burleigh interview, 1996.
126. CIA files obtained through The Freedom of Information Act by Nina Burleigh, *"A Very Private Women"*, Bantam, 1999, page 111.
127. *Counterspy*, April 1981, page 17. The article describes the effects of CIA labor infiltration in Japan and the Philippines.
128. Sallie Pisani, *The CIA and the Marshall Plan*, University of Kansas Press, 1991, page 143.
129. Peter Coleman, *The Liberal Conspiracy: The Congress for Cultural Freedom and the Struggle for the Mind of Post-war Europe*, Free Press, 1989, pages 46-8.
130. G.W. Domhoff, *The Higher Circle*, Random House, 1970, pages262-3.
131. Tom Mangold, *Cold Warrior James Jesus Angleton: The CIA's Master Spy Hunter*, Simon & Schuster, 1991, page 55.
132. Meyer, pages 70-1.
133. Nina Burleigh, *"A Very Private Women"*, Bantam, 1999, page 115-116.
134. Constance Green, *The Secret City: A history of Race Relations in the Nation's Capital*, Princeton University Press, 1967, page 314.
135. Evan Thomas, *The Very Best Men: Four: Who Dared: The Early Years of the CIA*, Simon & Schuster, 1995, page 106.
136. Nina Burleigh, *"A Very Private Women"*, Bantam, 1999, page 118-120.
137. Confidential source to author Nina Burleigh.
138. Nina Burleigh, *"A Very Private Women"*, Bantam, 1999, page 122.
139. Peter Janney, author Nina Burleigh interview, 1996.
140. Polly Wisner Fritchey
141. Eleanor Lanahan, author Nina Burleigh interview, 1996.
142. Joan Bross, author Nina Burleigh interview, 1997.
143. Peter Janney
144. John Gittinger, author Nina Burleigh interview, 1996.
145. John Gittinger

146. Mangold, page 51
147. Tim Weiner, "The Spy Agency's Many Mean Ways to Loosen Cold-War Tongues," *New York Times*, Feb. 9, 1997, page E7.
148. Cord Meyer Papers, Container 5, journal entry, Oct. 9, 1961.
149. David Middleton
150. Anne Truitt, *Turn: The Journal of an Artist*, Penguin Books, 1986, page 35.
151. Ben Summerford, author Nina Burleigh interview, 1996.
152. Nina Burleigh, *"A Very Private Women"*, Bantam, 1999, page 130-134.
153. Cord Meyer Papers, Container 5, journal entry, summer 1965.
154. Unnamed source, per author Nina Burleigh.
155. Confidential source, to author Nina Burleigh.
156. Nina Burleigh, *"A Very Private Women"*, Bantam, 1999, page 137-138.
157. Cord Meyer Papers, Container 5, journal entry, Oct. 18, 1956.
158. Ben Bradlee, *A Good Life: Newspapering and Other Adventures*, Simon & Schuster, 1995, page 159.
159. Cord Meyer Papers, Container 5, journal entry, Feb. 27, 1955.
160. C. David Heymann, *A Woman Named Jackie*, Lyle Stuart, 1989, page 85. The Bouvier sisters' scrapbook, called *One Special Summer*, was eventually published in 1974.
161. Thomas C. Reeves, *A Question of Character: A Life of John F. Kennedy*, Prima Publishing, 1992, page 115.
162. Cord Meyer Papers, Container 5, journal entry, Oct. 18, 1956.
163. Nina Burleigh, *"A Very Private Women"*, Bantam, 1999, page 139.
164. Cord Meyer Papers, Container 5, journal entry, Oct. 18, 1956.
165. Thomas Reeves, pages 137-38.
166. Cord Meyer Papers, Container 5, journal entry, Oct. 18, 1956.
167. Nina Burleigh, *"A Very Private Women"*, Bantam, 1999, page 142-144.
168. Thomas C. Reeves, page 139.
169. Peter Janney.
170. Confidential source to author Nina Burleigh.
171. Nina Burleigh, *"A Very Private Women"*, Bantam, 1999, page 145-146.

CHAPTER 6

172. Nina Burleigh, *"A Very Private Women"*, Bantam, 1999, page 147-148.
173. James Truitt told reporters for *Times* magazine the psychoanalyst was named Dr. Eden
174. Kenneth Noland, interviews by author Nina Burleigh, 1996-97.
175. Alice Denney, interviews by author Nina Burleigh, 1996.
176. Nina Burleigh, *"A Very Private Women"*, Bantam, 1999, page 149-150.

177. Cord Meyer Papers, Container 5, journal entry, Jan. 14, 1957.
178. Cord Meyer Papers, Container 5, journal entry, Sept. 3, 1957.
179. Washoe County Court document No. 175609, *Mary P. Meyer vs. Cord Meyer, Jr.*
180. Cord Meyer Papers, Container 1, letters from Pittman to Meyer, Apr. 11, 1957.
181. Washoe County Court document No. 175609.
182. Marie Ridder.
183. Confidential source to author Nina Burleigh.
184. Nina Burleigh, *"A Very Private Women"*, Bantam, 1999, page 151.
185. Cord Meyer Papers, Container 5, journal entry, May 26, 1963.
186. Calvin Tomkins, *Off the Wall: Robert Rauschenberg and the Art World of Our Times*, Doubleday, 1980, page 33.
187. Calvin Tomkins, page 46.
188. Ed Kelly, interview by author Nina Burleigh.
189. Nina Burleigh, *"A Very Private Women"*, Bantam, 1999, page 156-158.
190. Lynn Noland, interview by author Nina Burleigh, 1997.
191. Nina Burleigh, *"A Very Private Women"*, Bantam, 1999, page 160.
192. Helen Husted-Chavchavadze, interview by author Nina Burleigh, 1996.
193. Kenneth Noland
194. Nina Burleigh, *"A Very Private Women"*, Bantam, 1999, page 161.
195. Alice Denney.
196. Elizabeth Eisenstein, interview by author Nina Burleigh, 1996.
197. Otakar "Kary" Fischer, interview by author Nina Burleigh, 1997.
198. Sam Gilliam, interview by author Nina Burleigh, 1996.
199. Jenny Greenberg, interview by author Nina Burleigh, 1996.
200. Kenneth Noland
201. Jenny Greenberg.
202. Elizabeth Eisenstein.
203. Kenneth Noland
204. Anne Truitt, *Turn: The Journal of an Artist*, Penguin Books, 1986, page 150.
205. Truitt, *Turn*, page 164.
206. Nina Burleigh, *"A Very Private Women"*, Bantam, 1999, pages 168-169.
207. Unnamed source.
208. Nina Burleigh, *"A Very Private Women"*, Bantam, 1999, page 169.
209. Truitt, *Daybook*, page 165.
210. Timothy Leary, *Flashbacks: A Personal and Cultural History of an Era*, G. P. Putman's Sons, 1983, page 130.
211. Robert Greenfield, interview by Peter Janney, "Mary's Mosaic", Skyhorse Publishing, 2012, Page 222.

212. Nina Burleigh, *"A Very Private Women"*, Bantam, 1999, page 194. Burleigh's interview with White House counsel Myer Feldman provides the most specific, thorough documentation of how closely President Kennedy relied on the counsel of Mary Pinchot. Peter Janney, "Mary's Mosaic", Skyhorse Publishing, 2012, Page 218.

213. *42. Sally Bedell Smith, "Grace and Power: The private world of the Kennedy White House,"* New York: Random House, 2004, page 255. Peter Janney, *"Mary's Mosaic"*, Skyhorse Publishing, 2012, Page 218.

214. Timothy Leary, *Flashbacks: A Personal and Cultural History of an Era*, G. P. Putman's Sons, 1983, pages 128-129.

215. Ibid., page 155.

216. Ibid., page 178.

217. Timothy Leary, interview by author Nina Burleigh, 1996.

218. Cornelia Reis, interviews by author Nina Burleigh, 1996-97.

219. Nina Burleigh, *"A Very Private Women"*, Bantam, 1999, page 171-172.

220. John Marks Documents, National Security Archive, Washington, DC, Box I.

221. Marks, page 62.

222. John Gittinger.

223. Marks provides a well-documented description of the CIA's LSD tests, pages 57-133.

224. Marks, page 130.

225. Martin A. Lee and Bruce Shlain, Acid *Dreams: The CIA, LSD and the Sixties Rebellion*, Grove Weidenfeld, 1985, page 93

226. Nina Burleigh, *"A Very Private Women"*, Bantam, 1999, pages 173-174.

227. Unnamed source.

228. Kary Fischer.

229. Nina Burleigh, *"A Very Private Women"*, Bantam, 1999, page 175

230. Unnamed source.

231. Kenneth Noland

232. David Middleton

233. Eleanor McPeck

234. Nina Burleigh, *"A Very Private Women"*, Bantam, 1999, page 177

235. Kary Fischer.

236. Marian Cannon Schlesinger

237. Barbara Gamarikian, interview by author Nina Burleigh, 1996.

238. Confidential source

239. Angleton's presence in the Meyer son's lives in evidenced in various letters between Cord and his sons over the years. In one 1969 letter about money Cord told Quentin that "Jim and I are going to turn it over to you to squander as you please."

240. Nina Burleigh, *"A Very Private Women"*, Bantam, 1999, page 180
241. Thomas Reeves, page 242, on Pam Turnure
242. Nina Burleigh, *"A Very Private Women"*, Bantam, 1999, page 180
243. Confidential source interview by Peter Janney, *"Mary's Mosaic"*, Skyhorse Publishing, 2012, Page 207.

CHAPTER 7

244. Nina Burleigh, *"A Very Private Women"*, Bantam, 1999, page 183.
245. Alice Denney, Eleanor McPeck
246. Eleanor McPeck
247. Alice Denney, Eleanor McPeck
248. Nina Burleigh, *"A Very Private Women"*, Bantam, 1999, page 183.
249. Norman Mailer, "Superman Comes to the Supermarket," *Esquire*, November 1960.
250. Gerald Clarke, *"Capote: A Biography"*, London: Cardinal, 1989, page 271. Peter Janney, "Mary's Mosaic", Skyhorse Publishing, 2012, page 98
251. Nigel Hamilton, JFK: Reckless Youth (New York: Random House, 1992), pages 690-91. Peter Janney, "Mary's Mosaic", Skyhorse Publishing, 2012, page 209
252. Peter Janney, "Mary's Mosaic", Skyhorse Publishing, 2012, page 209
253. Peter Janney, "Mary's Mosaic", Skyhorse Publishing, 2012, page 209
254. Peter Janney, "Mary's Mosaic", Skyhorse Publishing, 2012, page 213
255. Goodwin, Fitzgeralds and the Kennedys, pages 837-38. Peter Janney, "Mary's Mosaic", Skyhorse Publishing, 2012, page 227.
256. Nina Burleigh, *"A Very Private Women"*, Bantam, 1999, page 184.
257. Richard Reeves, *"President Kennedy: Profile of Power"*, Simon & Schuster, 1993, page 58
258. Michael Beschloss, *The Crises Years: Kennedy and Khrushchev, 1960-63*, HarperCollins, 1991, pages 26-27.
259. Richard Reeves, page 33
260. Thomas, pages 228-29
261. Ibid., pages 142-48.
262. Ibid., page 150.
263. Bradlee, A Good Life, page 232. Peter Janney, "Mary's Mosaic", Skyhorse Publishing, 2012, page 228.
264. Richard Reeves, page 175.
265. The Secret service required everyone entering the White House gates to be signed in, with the time and the person they were intending to see also recorded. When a visitor was going to see the president, the gate log indicated it by "Evelyn Lincoln," "Mansion," Residence,"

or "President." The handwritten logs, organized chronologically by month and year, are available for public inspection at the John F. Kennedy Library at Columbia Point, Boston. The gate logs are probably only a partial record of Mary Pinchot-Meyer's visits. They indicate Mary's name, sometimes misspelled, fifteen times, usually entering around 7:30 P.M. Other nights, she may have been inside but was escorted by one of Kennedy's aides. On those occasions, she and others are indicated in the gate logs with notations that read "David Powers plus one," or "Bill Thompson plus one," or "Bill Walton plus one." For purposes of these notes, cites referring to these logs will read: Secret Service Gate Logs, date, JFKL.

266. Mary's name also appears on guests list preserved at the JFK Library in the White House Social Files, which are indexed by guest name. Full guest lists and menus for each event are preserved in those files. For purposes of these notes, cites referring to those documents will read: White House Social Files, JFKL.
267. Jean Friendly, interview by author Nina Burleigh, 1995.
268. Nina Burleigh, *A Very Private Women*, Bantam, 1999, page 188-89.
269. Tony Summers, *Goddesses: The Secret Life of Marilyn Monroe*, G. K. Hall, 1986, page 202.
270. Richard Reeves, page 313
271. Nina Burleigh, *A Very Private Women*, Bantam, 1999, page 191-92.
272. Bradlee, *Conversations With Kennedy*, page 27.
273. William Attwood, The Reds and the Blacks: A Personal Adventure, Harper & Row, 1967, page 133.
274. C. David Heymann, *A Woman Named Jackie*, Lyle Stuart, 1989, page 227. Confirmed to author Nina Burleigh by Kenneth Noland.
275. Evelyn Lincoln letter.
276. *San Francisco Chronicle*, Feb. 23, 1976, page 1.
277. Ron Rosenbaum and Phillip Nobile, "*The curious Aftermath of JFK's Best and Brightest Affair*" New Times, July 9, 1976, page 25. Peter Janney, "Mary's Mosaic", Skyhorse Publishing, 2012, page 144.
278. Ibid Page 33, and page 144
279. Peter Janney, "Mary's Mosaic", Skyhorse Publishing, 2012, pages 144-45.
280. Helen Husted.
281. Nina Burleigh, *A Very Private Women*, Bantam, 1999, page 193.
282. Jay Gourley, interview by author Nina Burleigh, 1997.
283. Myer Feldman
284. Davis Powers, in response to written questions from author Nina Burleigh, 1996.

285. Pamela Turnure, oral history.
286. Nina Burleigh, *"A Very Private Women"*, Bantam, 1999, page 196.
287. Thomas Reeves, page 322.
288. Nina Burleigh, *"A Very Private Women"*, Bantam, 1999, pages 197-99.
289. Bradlee, *Conversations with Kennedy*, page 159.
290. Laura Bergquist, oral history, JFK Library.
291. Mary Ridder.
292. Helen Husted.
293. Confidential source to author Nina Burleigh
294. Nina Burleigh, *"A Very Private Women"*, Bantam, 1999, pages 200-202.
295. Helen Husted.
296. Nina Burleigh, *"A Very Private Women"*, Bantam, 1999, page 202.
297. Kary Fischer.
298. Nina Burleigh, *"A Very Private Women"*, Bantam, 1999, page 203.
299. Nina Burleigh, *"A Very Private Women"*, Bantam, 1999, page 207.
300. Secret Service Gate Log, January 22, 1962, JFKL.
301. Bradlee, *Conversations with Kennedy*, page 49.
302. Pamala Turnure, oral history.
303. Kary Fischer, recalling Mary Meyer's description of events, confirmed to author Nina Burleigh what James Truitt told the Washington Post and National Enquirer regarding the routine that was followed when Mary spent private time with the president.
304. Secret Service Gate Logs, JFKL, and White House telephone logs, JFKL. The phone logs are handwritten memos tat were jotted down whenever the president received a call. The logs also indicate whether he took the call or not. They are all filed chronologically at the JKF Library.
305. Mary Feldman.
306. Secret Service Gate Logs, March 15, 1962, JFKL.
307. Secret Service Gate Logs, March 16, 1962, JFKL.
308. Winzola McLendon, "President's Mother to Be His Hostess," *Washington Post*, July 16, 1962, page A12.
309. "BPW Head Blasts Kennedy for Bypassing Women in Cabinet," *Washington Post*, July 16, 1962.
310. *San Francisco Chronicle*, Feb. 23, 1976, page 1.
311. Ibid.
312. White House telephone logs, July 17, 1962, JFKL.
313. Heymann, page 375.
314. Secret Service Gate Logs, July 30, 1962, JFKL
315. Donald H. Wolfe, *The Last Days of Marilyn Monroe*, (New York: William Morrow, 1998), pages 461-62; Donald H. Wolfe, interview

by author Peter Janney, June 2, 2005. Wolfe's account was meticulously researched and substantiated by several different sources. Peter Janney, "Mary's Mosaic", Skyhorse Publishing, 2012, page 231.

316. Donald H. Wolfe, *The Last Days of Marilyn Monroe*, page 462. Peter Janney, "Mary's Mosaic", Skyhorse Publishing, 2012, page 231.

317. Bryan Bender, *"A Dark Corner of Camelot,"* *Boston Globe*, January 23, 2011. Peter Janney, "Mary's Mosaic", Skyhorse Publishing, 2012, page 231.

318. Secret Service Gate Logs and White House phone logs, August 6, 1962, JFKL.

319. Nina Burleigh, *"A Very Private Women"*, Bantam, 1999, page 214

320. Secret Service Gate Logs, October 1, 1962, JFKL.

321. *Washington Post*, October 1, 1962, page A7.

322. Nina Burleigh, *"A Very Private Women"*, Bantam, 1999, page 215

323. White House Social Files, JFKL.

324. White House Social Files, JFKL.

325. Nina Burleigh, *"A Very Private Women"*, Bantam, 1999, page 215

326. Peter Janney, "Mary's Mosaic", Skyhorse Publishing, 2012, page 238.

327. Anatoly Dobrynin, *In Confidence: Moscow's Ambassador to America's Six Cold War Presidents*, Times Books, 1995, page 85.

328. White House Social Files, JFKL.

329. Katharine Graham, *Personal Histor*, Knopf, 1997, page 136.

330. Clair Clark.

331. Secret Service Gate Logs, June, July, August 1963, JFKL.

332. Ralph G, Martin, *Seeds of Destruction: Joe Kennedy and His Sons* (New York: G. P. Putnam's Sons, 1995) page 372. Peter Janney, "Mary's Mosaic", Skyhorse Publishing, 2012, page 252.

333. Peter Janney, "Mary's Mosaic", Skyhorse Publishing, 2012, page 252.

334. White House Social Files. Mrs. Kennedy's correspondence is preserved in the social files.

335. Grey Towers National Historic Landmark, archived videotape.

336. Nina Burleigh, *"A Very Private Women"*, Bantam, 1999, page 219.

337. Hugh Sidey.

PART IV

338. JFK official website

339. Nina Burleigh, *A Very Private Woman*, Bantam, 1999, page 9

340. Ibid, page 10

341. Ibid, page 10

342. Nina Burleigh 1997 interview of Otakar "Kary" Fischer.

343. Nina Burleigh, *A Very Private Woman*, Bantam, 1999, page 11
344. Nina Burleigh 1996 interview of Polly Wisner Fritchey.
345. Nina Burleigh 1996 interviews of Washington journalist Charlie Peters, and retired CIA officer Samuel Halpern. The CIA refused to confirm or deny any use of the garage.
346. United States District Court for the District of Columbia, *United States of America v. Ray Crump Jr.*, transcript, volume I, page 290.
347. Nina Burleigh, *A Very Private Woman*, Bantam, 1999, page 12
348. Ibid, page 12
349. Ibid, page 13
350. Ibid, page 15
351. "Bishop at Meyer Rites Asks Prayer for Killer," *Washington Evening Star*, Oct. 15, 1964, page B2.
352. Nina Burleigh, *A Very Private Woman*, Bantam, 1999, page 16
353. Nina Burleigh 1996 interview of Eleanor M. McPeck.
354. Nina Burleigh, *A Very Private Woman*, Bantam, 1999, page 17
355. The document was obtained through the Freedom of Information Act. William C. Sullivan was operationally in charge of all FBI criminal, intelligence, and espionage investigations. He has thirty years of service with the FBI between 1941 and 1971. He died in a hunting accident just before his book critical of the FBI was published. The Soviet press agency, TASS, claimed the death was suspicious, bur U.S. government ruled it accidental.
356. Nina Burleigh, *A Very Private Woman*, Bantam, 1999, page 17
357. Tom Mangold, *Cold Warrior: James Jesus Angleton: The CIA's Master Spy Hunter*, Simon & Schuster, 1991, pages 53-5.
358. Nina Burleigh 1997 interview of Joan Bross.
359. Nina Burleigh, *A Very Private Woman*, Bantam, 1999, page 18
360. Ibid, page 19
361. Howard Bray, *The Pillars of the Post*, W. W. Norton, 1980, page 67.
362. Nina Burleigh, *A Very Private Woman*, Bantam, 1999, page 20
363. Ibid, page 21
364. Ibid, page 21
365. Nina Burleigh 1996 interview of Mary Truesdale.
366. Nina Burleigh, *A Very Private Woman*, Bantam, 1999, page 22
367. Ibid, page 23
368. Ibid, page 24
369. Nina Burleigh 1996 interview of Myer Feldman.
370. Nina Burleigh, *A Very Private Woman*, Bantam, 1999, page 24
371. Nina Burleigh 1996 interview of June Dutton.
372. Nina Burleigh, *A Very Private Woman*, Bantam, 1999, page 26

373. Philip Nobile and Ron Rosenbaum, "The Mysterious Murder of JFK's Mistress," *New Times*, Oct., 1997, page 25.
374. Nina Burleigh, *A Very Private Woman*, Bantam, 1999, page 27
375. Ibid, page 27
376. Ibid, page 27
377. *United States of America v. Ray Crump Jr.*, U.S. District Court for the District of Columbia, Criminal Case No. 930-64, transcript, testimony of Henry Wiggins.
378. Nina Burleigh, *A Very Private Woman*, Bantam, 1999, page 232
379. Ibid, pages 232/3
380. *United States of America v. Ray Crump Jr.*, U.S. District Court for the District of Columbia, Criminal Case No. 930-64, transcript, testimony of Roderick Sylvis.
381. Nina Burleigh, *A Very Private Woman*, Bantam, 1999, pages 233/4
382. "Women Painter Shot and Killed on Canal Towpath in Capital," *New York Times*, Oct., 14, 1964.
383. Nina Burleigh, *A Very Private Woman*, Bantam, 1999, page 234
384. "Mary P. Meyer Believed Victim of Robbery Attempt," *Washington Post*, Oct., 13, 1964.
385. Philip Nobile and Ron Rosenbaum, "The Mysterious Murder of JFK's Mistress," *New Times*, Oct., 14, 1964, page 24.
386. Nina Burleigh, *A Very Private Woman*, Bantam, 1999, page 235
387. Stanley County Registrar of Deeds, Birth Records, 1939.
388. Nina Burleigh, *A Very Private Woman*, Bantam, 1999, page 242
389. *United States of America v. Ray Crump Jr.*, U.S. District Court for the District of Columbia, Criminal Case No. 930-64, transcript, opening statement of the Government. Confirmed by Dovey Roundtree to author Nina Burleigh.
390. Nina Burleigh, *A Very Private Woman*, Bantam, 1999, page 254
391. Ibid, page 255
392. Ibid, page 255
393. Ibid, page 255
394. Nina Burleigh 1996 interview of Dovey Roundtree.
395. Nina Burleigh, *A Very Private Woman*, Bantam, 1999, page 256
396. Ibid, page 257
397. Ibid, page 259
398. Nina Burleigh 1996 interview of Dovey Roundtree.
399. Ibid
400. Nina Burleigh, *A Very Private Woman*, Bantam, 1999, page 259
401. Ibid, page 260
402. Nina Burleigh 1996 interview of Dovey Roundtree.

403. This is Hantman's recollection of the jury. The court did not record the racial makeup of juries at that time. Bob Bennett also recalled the jury as predominately black.
404. Nina Burleigh, *A Very Private Woman*, Bantam, 1999, page 161
405. *United States of America v. Ray Crump Jr.*, pages 2-17.
406. Nina Burleigh, *A Very Private Woman*, Bantam, 1999, page 262
407. *United States of America v. Ray Crump Jr.*, pages 45-7.
408. Ibid, pages 70-9.
409. Nina Burleigh, *A Very Private Woman*, Bantam, 1999, pages 262/3
410. *United States of America v. Ray Crump Jr.*, page 124.
411. Nina Burleigh, *A Very Private Woman*, Bantam, 1999, page 263
412. Ibid, pages 264/5
413. Nina Burleigh 1996 interview of Dovey Roundtree.
414. Nina Burleigh, *A Very Private Woman*, Bantam, 1999, page 265
415. Police testimony at the trial revealed conflicting stories.
416. Nina Burleigh, *A Very Private Woman*, Bantam, 1999, page 265
417. Ibid, page 266
418. Ibid, page 267
419. Ibid, page 267
420. *United States of America v. Ray Crump Jr.*, page 803.
421. Ibid, page 693.
422. Nina Burleigh, *A Very Private Woman*, Bantam, 1999, page 269
423. Ibid, page 269
424. Nina Burleigh 1996 interview of Dovey Roundtree.
425. Ibid
426. *United States of America v. Ray Crump Jr.*, page 881.
427. Nina Burleigh, *A Very Private Woman*, Bantam, 1999, page 270
428. *United States of America v. Ray Crump Jr.*, page 893.
429. Nina Burleigh, *A Very Private Woman*, Bantam, 1999, page 270
430. Nina Burleigh 1997 interview of Roberta Hornig.
431. *United States of America v. Ray Crump Jr.*, page 944.
432. Ibid, page 948.
433. Nina Burleigh, *A Very Private Woman*, Bantam, 1999, page 272
434. Ibid, page 272
435. *United States of America v. Ray Crump Jr.*, page 993.
436. Al Hantman and Dovey Roundtree.
437. Nina Burleigh, *A Very Private Woman*, Bantam, 1999, page 273
438. *United States of America v. Ray Crump Jr.*, page 995.
439. Nina Burleigh, *A Very Private Woman*, Bantam, 1999, page 274
440. *Washington Evening Star*, July 30, 1965, page A1, "CrumpAcquitted in Towpath Slaying of D.C. Socialite".

441. Al Hantman.
442. Ben Bradlee, *A Good Life: Newspapering and Other Adventures*, Simon & Schuster, 1995, page 270.
443. Nina Burleigh, *A Very Private Woman*, Bantam, 1999, page 277
444. Ibid, page 277
445. Ibid, page 282
446. *New York Times*, contemporary press report, March 15, 2001.
447. C.I.A. press release, March 14, 2001
448. Nina Burleigh, *A Very Private Woman*, Bantam, 1999, page 285
449. Ibid, page 288
450. Jay Gourly.
451. Nina Burleigh, *A Very Private Woman*, Bantam, 1999, page 286
452. Ibid, page 287
453. *Time* magazine, March 8, 1976, page 42.
454. Jay Gourly.
455. Evelyn Patterson Truitt, letter to Nina Burleigh, August 2, 1996.
456. Nina Burleigh, *A Very Private Woman*, Bantam, 1999, page 289
457. Ibid, page 290
458. Nina Burleigh 1996 interview of Timothy Leary. Shortly before his death, Leary continued to express the belief that Mary Pinchot-Meyer might have dropped acid with Kennedy but he admitted he had no proof. In his last days his continuing interest in Mary Meyer was evidence by a well-thumbed copy of Cord Meyer's book near his bedroom, filled with marginal notes.
459. Richard Helms.
460. *Ramparts* cited Killgallon's death as one reason to reopen the Kennedy assassination investigation in 1966.
461. Robert D. Morrow, *First Hand Knowledge: How I Participated in the CIA-MAFIA Murder of President Kennedy*, Spi Books, 1994, pages 277-80.
462. Nina Burleigh 1996 interview of Gaeton Fonzi. Fonzi, one of the House Select Committee investigators, interviewed Robert D. Morrow and found he knew a lot about counterfeit-money schemes to fund the Cubans, but in the area of the JFK assassination "he was a bullshitter. He was concocting a lot."
463. Nina Burleigh, *A Very Private Woman*, Bantam, 1999, page 293
464. Arthur Ellis was interviewed for *People* magazine in 1976.
465. Nina Burleigh, *A Very Private Woman*, Bantam, 1999, pages 294/5
466. Ibid, page 295
467. National Archives, JFK Collection, RG 233, Memo from CIA Deputy Director for Plans, re discussions with Dulles.

468. Nina Burleigh, *A Very Private Woman*, Bantam, 1999, page 295
469. *New York Times*, December 25, 1974, page A25.
470. Nina Burleigh, *A Very Private Woman*, Bantam, 1999, page 296
471. Ibid, page 297
472. Ibid, page 297
473. Ibid, page 298
474. Ibid, page 298
475. Philip Nobile.
476. Nina Burleigh, *A Very Private Woman*, Bantam, 1999, pages 298/9
477. Tom Mangold, *Cold Warrior: James Jesus Angleton: The CIA's Master Spy Hunter*. Simon & Schuster, 1991, page 353.
478. Nina Burleigh, *A Very Private Woman*, Bantam, 1999, page 302
479. Timothy Leary.
480. Nina Burleigh, *A Very Private Woman*, Bantam, 1999, pages 302/3
481. Nina Burleigh 1997interview of Ted Swager.
482. Nina Burleigh, *A Very Private Woman*, Bantam, 1999, page 304
483. Nina Burleigh interview of unnamed source.
484. Nina Burleigh, *A Very Private Woman*, Bantam, 1999, page 306
485. Ibid, page 307

INDEX

A

About the Author

www.michaelpinchot.com

"Michael Pinchot draws from an extensive career in the global engineering-construction field, a lust for intrigue, a patriotic distrust of government and journalistic agendas, and a hyperactive imagination. He and his wife, Diana, reside in Orange County, California."

Author
Michael Pinchot
Paying homage to Hemingway

Moments before the author's 5th run with the bulls in Pamplona, Spain, during the annual week-long San Ferim Festival

---

Other Published Works By Author

"PANAMANIAN TUNDRA", the *only* Trans Alaska Pipeline novel of *global* proportions

"TRUTH TO POWER: The Pope Has No Clothes", a Scriptural litmus test of selected Roman Catholic Church dogma and doctrine

IN PROGRESS

"PATTAYA M.I.A.", A Vietnam deserter, has lived a secret life for over thirty years as a beach-front bar owner, with a Thai wife, stepdaughter, and son . . . . until all hell breaks loose.

"THE MOORGATE WELL CLUB", The private, below street level club, adjacent the Moorgate London Underground station (a mere weapon's throw from Jack The Ripper's hunting grounds), proves as a great cover for an American ex-pat serial killer on assignment in London with his American based engineering company.

RECOMMENDED READING

"A VERY PRIVATE WOMEN", by Nina Burleigh

"MARY'S MOSAIC", by Peter Janney (best friends with Mary's son Michael at the time of Michael's tragic death).

Printed in Great Britain
by Amazon.co.uk, Ltd.,
Marston Gate.